I0887789

Reshaping the Video Game Landscape With AI and GenAI

João Paulo Pereira Sousa
https://orcid.org/0000-0002-9005-084X
CeDRI, SusTEC, Instituto Politécnico de Bragança, Portugal

Rogério Junior Correia Tavares
CeDRI, SusTEC, Instituto Politécnico de Bragança, Portugal

IGI Global
Scientific Publishing
Publishing Tomorrow's Research Today

Vice President of Editorial | Melissa Wagner
Director of Acquisitions | Mikaela Felty
Director of Book Development | Jocelynn Hessler
Production Manager | Mike Brehm
Cover Design | Jose Rosado

Published in the United States of America by
IGI Global Scientific Publishing
701 East Chocolate Avenue
Hershey, PA, 17033, USA
Tel: 717-533-8845 | Fax: 717-533-7115
Website: https://www.igi-global.com E-mail: cust@igi-global.com

Copyright © 2026 by IGI Global Scientific Publishing. All rights reserved. No part of this publication may be reproduced, stored or distributed in any form or by any means, electronic or mechanical, including photocopying, without written permission from the publisher. Use of this publication to train generative artificial intelligence (AI) technologies is expressly prohibited. The publisher reserves all rights to license its use for generative AI training and machine learning model development.

Product or company names used in this set are for identification purposes only. Inclusion of the names of the products or companies does not indicate a claim of ownership by IGI Global Scientific Publishing of the trademark or registered trademark.

Library of Congress Cataloging-in-Publication Data

Names: Sousa, João Paulo, Adjunct Professor editor | Tavares, Rogerio Junior Correia, 1967- editor
Title: Reshaping the video game landscape with AI and GenAI / edited by João Paulo Sousa, Rogerio Tavares.
Description: Hershey, PA : IGI Global Scientific Publishing, [2026] | Includes bibliographical references and index. | Summary: "This book provides a comprehensive exploration of current and emerging innovative uses of AI and Generative AI in video games. It aims to present theoretical perspectives, practical case studies, and discussions on the challenges and opportunities these technologies bring to game development and the gaming experience"-- Provided by publisher.
Identifiers: LCCN 2025029115 (print) | LCCN 2025029116 (ebook) | ISBN 9798337346373 hardcover | ISBN 9798337346380 paperback | ISBN 9798337346397 ebook
Subjects: LCSH: Video games--Programming | Video games industry--Technological innovations | Artificial intelligence--Engineering applications
Classification: LCC QA76.76.V54 R47 2026 (print) | LCC QA76.76.V54 (ebook)
LC record available at https://lccn.loc.gov/2025029115
LC ebook record available at https://lccn.loc.gov/2025029116

British Cataloguing in Publication Data
A Cataloguing in Publication record for this book is available from the British Library.

All work contributed to this book is new, previously-unpublished material.
The views expressed in this book are those of the authors, but not necessarily of the publisher.
This book contains information sourced from authentic and highly regarded references, with reasonable efforts made to ensure the reliability of the data and information presented. The authors, editors, and publisher believe the information in this book to be accurate and true as of the date of publication. Every effort has been made to trace and credit the copyright holders of all materials included. However, the authors, editors, and publisher cannot assume responsibility for the validity of all materials or the consequences of their use. Should any copyright material be found unacknowledged, please inform the publisher so that corrections may be made in future reprints.

Table of Contents

Preface xiv

Chapter 1
Adaptive Learning With AI in Virtual and Augmented Reality Education 1
Usharani Bhimavarapu, Department of Computer Science and Engineering, Koneru Lakshmaiah Education Foundation, Vaddeswaram, India

Chapter 2
AI for Dynamic Game Balancing and Optimization: Machine Learning for Understanding Player Behavior 25
Kaushalya Thopate, Vishwakarma Institute of Technology, India
Tanvi Pokale, Vishwakarma Institute of Technology, India

Chapter 3
AI-Assisted Game Mechanics Optimization for Multiplayer Environments 63
Usharani Bhimavarapu, Department of Computer Science and Engineering, Koneru Lakshmaiah Education Foundation, Vaddeswaram, India

Chapter 4
Co-Creating Narratives: Ludonarrative Agency and Generative AI in Digital Games 87
Cátia Ferreira, CECC, Universidade Católica Portuguesa, Portugal

Chapter 5
From Technical Feasibility to Industry Reality: Implementing LLM-Driven Dialogue Systems in Video Games 123
Juan Rodríguez Suárez, University of La Laguna, Spain
Jesús Miguel Torres Jorge, Universidad de La Laguna, Spain
José Demetrio Piñero Vera, Universidad de La Laguna, Spain

Chapter 6
From Trackers to AI: Generative Music in Contemporary Game Design 179
Jörg Burbach, IU Internationale Hochschule, Germany

Chapter 7
Innovative Procedural Content Generation (PCG) Using Generative AI: A New Paradigm in Game Design 205
Monika Kumari, Poornima University, Jaipur, India
Sheena Tahira Khan, Poornima University, Jaipur, India
Kapil Gulati, Poornima University, Jaipur, India
Prarthana Sharma, Poornima University, Jaipur, India
Nikhil Kumar Goyal, Poornima University, Jaipur, India
Mohammed Firdos Alam Sheikh, Poornima University, Jaipur, India

Chapter 8
Procedural Generation and Adaptive Gameplay: The Role of AI and Generative AI in Contemporary Game Development.. 233
Aparajita Biswal, Parul Institute of Engineering & Technology, Parul University, Vadodara, India
Kush Bhushanwar, Parul Institute of Engineering & Technology, Parul University, Vadodara, India
Parag Gurdharbhai Paija, B.H. Gardi College of Engineering and Technology, India
Khyati Zalawadia, Parul Institute of Engineering & Technology, Parul University, Vadodara, India
Prangya Parimita Pradhan, Centurion University of Technology and Management, India
Syed Ibad Ali, Parul Institute of Engineering and Technology, Parul University, Vadodara, India

Chapter 9
The Evolution of Artificial Intelligence in Shaping the Future of Interactive Entertainment 259
Mohamed Elgazar, Faculty of Engineering, Mansoura National University, Egypt
Mohamed Elafifi, Faculty of Engineering, Mansoura National University, Egypt
Majed Elshenawy, Faculty of Engineering, Mansoura National University, Egypt
Mohamed Ebrahim, Faculty of Engineering, Mansoura National University, Egypt
Mohamed Setate, Mansoura National University, Egypt
Mohamed Fayed, Mansoura National University, Egypt
Mohamed Ramadan, Faculty of Engineering, Mansoura National University, Egypt
Abdelrahman Mansour, Faculty of Engineering, Mansoura National University, Egypt
Sarah M. Ayyad, Computers and Control Systems Department, Faculty of Engineering, Mansoura University, Egypt

Chapter 10
The Future of AI and Generative AI in Virtual Worlds and the Metaverse: Transforming Gaming Experiences 311
Ayush Shekhar, Marwadi University, India
T. Premavathi, Marwadi University, India
Damodharan Palaniappan, Marwadi University, India

Chapter 11
The Role of AI in Preserving and Remastering Classic Games 325
P. Selvakumar, Department of Science and Humanities, Nehru Institute of Technology, Coimbatore, India
S. Poorani, Kongu Engineering College, India
Vinod Waiker, Datta Meghe Institute of Management Studies, India
Satheesh Kumar D., Hindusthan College of Engineering and Technology, India
Pallavi Jaggi, Chandigarh School of Business, Chandigarh Group of Colleges, Jhanjeri, India
Mohit Sharma, Maharshi Dayanand University, Rohtak, India
Manjunath T. C., Rajarajeswari College of Engineering, India

Compilation of References 351

About the Contributors 389

Index 397

Detailed Table of Contents

Preface xiv

Chapter 1
Adaptive Learning With AI in Virtual and Augmented Reality Education 1
Usharani Bhimavarapu, Department of Computer Science and Engineering, Koneru Lakshmaiah Education Foundation, Vaddeswaram, India

Artificial Intelligence (AI) is the driving force behind Immersive Technologies like Virtual Reality (VR), Augmented Reality (AR), Mixed Reality (MR), and Extended Reality (XR) now. Combined with these technologies, AI provides immersive dynamic worlds with the potential for greater realism, interactivity, and personalization. AI provides predictive modeling and simulation-like behavior in VR and real-time object recognition, contextual overlay, and gesture commands in AR. MR is enhanced with AI-synchronized physical and virtual content so that realities can be merged together in a smooth manner to facilitate training and operational uptake. AI integrates them into essential XR and functions through multimodal data sets, enhances personalization, and enhances decision-making in health care, education, retail, and manufacturing. Bi-stacked GRU and later more advanced models build all such technologies into sequential data stream processing, prediction of user intent, and adaptive response enablement. Added to the fusion of AI with immersive technology, they bring forth a new generation of intelligent, user-focused, forward-thinking experience bursting beyond entertainment into actual practical real-world applications.

Chapter 2
AI for Dynamic Game Balancing and Optimization: Machine Learning for Understanding Player Behavior 25
Kaushalya Thopate, Vishwakarma Institute of Technology, India
Tanvi Pokale, Vishwakarma Institute of Technology, India

In this chapter we discuss the inclusion of Artificial Intelligence (AI) in dynamic game balancing and player behavior modeling, particularly how the use of machine learning can improve personalization, challenge, adaptivity, and overall player engagement. It analyses on-line the strategies such as supervised learning, clustering, reinforcement learning, or time-series analysis which have been known for reducing response time to the real-world player actions. Procedural content generation and recommender systems is introduced as means to provide and adapt custom game-play experience. The chapter also discusses important ethical issues such as the prevention against manipulative design (dark patterns), fairness in multiplayer systems, and the need for transparency in the decisions made by AI. Case studies in AAA and indie games examine the use of AI in design and the even newer industry infrastructure on which it relies, while VP AI at Unity, Danny Lange, reflects on how AI is changing the gaming industry and how things might continue to evolve into the future. Finally, faced with future challenges including real-time inference and VR/AR integration, this chapter presents a roadmap for these intelligent, ethical and adaptive game systems.

Chapter 3
AI-Assisted Game Mechanics Optimization for Multiplayer Environments 63
Usharani Bhimavarapu, Department of Computer Science and Engineering, Koneru Lakshmaiah Education Foundation, Vaddeswaram, India

Dynamic game balancing needs to be performed in order to sustain the interest, challenge, and enjoyment of players in contemporary computer games. The static balancing techniques have failed to ascertain variations across various skill levels of players and thus will result in frustration or boredom. The article explores the application of artificial intelligence (AI) algorithms for dynamic game balancing and optimisation for real-time tuning of game parameters. Gameplay data, such as interactions between a single player, groups of enemies, stage manager, and world objects across a set of test levels, are gathered and preprocessed for computation. Remora Optimization-based features are chosen to restrict computational complexity without undermining important gameplay dynamics. Bi-Stacked Long Short-Term Memory (LSTM) network is employed to learn player and enemy movement short- and long-term trends in order to facilitate predictive and adaptive compensation. The system continues to balance in real time, optimizes assets even further, and applies enemy activity for ultimate balance and availability. AI balancing tests identify higher play engagement, dynamically calibrated challenge, and reduced jankiness, defining the path of smart game creation. The research holds the promise of uniting state-of-the-art AI models with mass market games with the ability to produce adaptive, optimized, and player-level experiences.

Chapter 4
Co-Creating Narratives: Ludonarrative Agency and Generative AI in Digital Games 87
Cátia Ferreira, CECC, Universidade Católica Portuguesa, Portugal

This chapter explores how narrative agency, authorship, and co-creative practices in digital games are being transformed by generative AI systems, with an emphasis on AI Dungeon. It views storytelling in GenAI environments as a type of procedural co-authorship—distributed, negotiated, and frequently unpredictable—drawing on theories from narrative studies, game design, and AI ethics. The chapter identifies important dynamics like narrative drift, editorial intervention, and ludonarrative friction by qualitatively analyzing twenty structured gameplay sessions. It suggests that participants are continuously negotiating meaning and coherence with algorithmic systems in their roles as authors, editors, and curators. For academics, designers, and teachers attempting to understand the emerging field of interactive narrative design, this has important implications. The findings draw attention to the ethical conundrums and imaginative potential of AI-mediated storytelling.

Chapter 5
From Technical Feasibility to Industry Reality: Implementing LLM-Driven Dialogue Systems in Video Games 123
Juan Rodríguez Suárez, University of La Laguna, Spain
Jesús Miguel Torres Jorge, Universidad de La Laguna, Spain
José Demetrio Piñero Vera, Universidad de La Laguna, Spain

This chapter examines the integration of LLMs into video game dialogue systems, tracing the evolution from finite state machines and branching dialogue trees to contemporary AI-driven architectures. The analysis situates generative dialogue systems within the broader context of procedural content generation, evaluating their technical feasibility, creative implications, and economic viability for commercial game development. Through examination of existing implementations, the work identifies persistent challenges in content quality, narrative coherence, and computational efficiency. A functional prototype demonstrates practical implementation strategies for LLM-driven dialogue generation, incorporating dynamic reputation systems and procedural quest generation. Comprehensive performance benchmarking across cloud and local deployment configurations reveals critical trade-offs between inference speed, memory constraints, and operational costs, providing empirical guidance for studios evaluating conversational AI adoption.

Chapter 6
From Trackers to AI: Generative Music in Contemporary Game Design 179
Jörg Burbach, IU Internationale Hochschule, Germany

This chapter examines the evolving role of AI in video game music, from early tracker software to today's generative tools. AI-generated music raises questions of originality and authorship but also expands creative potential, especially for resource-limited or experimental teams. Using Margaret Boden's theory of combinatorial, exploratory, and transformational creativity, the chapter explores how AI operates within and beyond stylistic boundaries (Boden, 2004). A case study of an anonymized indie point-and-click game shows how human composers and AI can collaborate effectively. Ethical and practical issues—such as authorship, audience perception, and the risk of homogenization—are also discussed. The chapter analyzes how game genre influences the fit and acceptance of AI music and considers educational implications, calling for curricula that emphasize critical, not just technical, engagement. Rather than replacing human creativity, AI is framed as a co-creative tool that accelerates workflows, broadens stylistic range, and enables new forms of musical expression.

Chapter 7
Innovative Procedural Content Generation (PCG) Using Generative AI: A New Paradigm in Game Design 205
Monika Kumari, Poornima University, Jaipur, India
Sheena Tahira Khan, Poornima University, Jaipur, India
Kapil Gulati, Poornima University, Jaipur, India
Prarthana Sharma, Poornima University, Jaipur, India
Nikhil Kumar Goyal, Poornima University, Jaipur, India
Mohammed Firdos Alam Sheikh, Poornima University, Jaipur, India

Game design increasingly relies on automation to deliver dynamic, interactive, and immersive player experiences. Procedural Content Generation (PCG), traditionally driven by rule-based systems and stochastic methods, has enabled the scalable creation of game assets and environments with limited human input. Recent advancements in Generative Artificial Intelligence (AI) are redefining PCG by introducing intelligent, creative, and context-sensitive content generation capabilities. This chapter presents an in-depth analysis of state-of-the-art generative AI models—including Generative Adversarial Networks (GANs), Transformers, Diffusion Models, and Reinforcement Learning—and their applications across various PCG domains such as terrain and environment generation, narrative design, character development, and adaptive gameplay. The chapter further examines the architecture of AI-based PCG systems, integration with real-time engines and toolkits, and evaluates generated content using criteria like creativity, diversity, coherence, and player engagement.

Chapter 8
Procedural Generation and Adaptive Gameplay: The Role of AI and Generative AI in Contemporary Game Development.. 233
Aparajita Biswal, Parul Institute of Engineering & Technology, Parul University, Vadodara, India
Kush Bhushanwar, Parul Institute of Engineering & Technology, Parul University, Vadodara, India
Parag Gurdharbhai Paija, B.H. Gardi College of Engineering and Technology, India
Khyati Zalawadia, Parul Institute of Engineering & Technology, Parul University, Vadodara, India
Prangya Parimita Pradhan, Centurion University of Technology and Management, India
Syed Ibad Ali, Parul Institute of Engineering and Technology, Parul University, Vadodara, India

Artificial intelligence (AI) and generative artificial intelligence (GI) are revolutionizing contemporary game development through the facilitation of adaptive gameplay, procedural content production, and intricate narrative structures. AI-driven solutions provide real-time responses to player inputs, hence fostering dynamic and evolving gaming experiences, in contrast to traditional game design, which relies on pre-scripted procedures and static environments. These technologies equip developers with innovative tools to create immersive, tailored, and intelligent gaming environments, ultimately revolutionizing the processes of game development, gameplay, and user experience. Procedural content generation, which enables developers to produce extensive, dynamic environments with no human involvement, is one of the most potent applications of artificial intelligence in gaming.

Chapter 9
The Evolution of Artificial Intelligence in Shaping the Future of Interactive Entertainment 259
Mohamed Elgazar, Faculty of Engineering, Mansoura National University, Egypt
Mohamed Elafifi, Faculty of Engineering, Mansoura National University, Egypt
Majed Elshenawy, Faculty of Engineering, Mansoura National University, Egypt
Mohamed Ebrahim, Faculty of Engineering, Mansoura National University, Egypt
Mohamed Setate, Mansoura National University, Egypt
Mohamed Fayed, Mansoura National University, Egypt
Mohamed Ramadan, Faculty of Engineering, Mansoura National University, Egypt
Abdelrahman Mansour, Faculty of Engineering, Mansoura National University, Egypt
Sarah M. Ayyad, Computers and Control Systems Department, Faculty of Engineering, Mansoura University, Egypt

Dive into the captivating evolution of Artificial Intelligence (AI) and discover its profound impact on the gaming universe. This comprehensive chapter unravels AI's journey from its earliest philosophical stirrings to its current status as a technological cornerstone. It asks: How did the abstract concept of "thinking machines" transform into the dynamic force shaping our digital realities? The chapter illuminates AI's pivotal role in revolutionizing game design, from crafting infinitely expansive worlds and intelligent non-player characters to weaving adaptive narratives that respond to your every choice. Furthermore, the chapter explores how AI streamlines game development, optimizes performance, and even redefines economic models within the industry. Finally, the cutting-edge hardware innovations that power this revolution are discussed, posing a critical question: As AI continues to push the boundaries of virtual experiences, what uncharted territories of immersion and interaction await us, and what complex debates will define its future?

Chapter 10
The Future of AI and Generative AI in Virtual Worlds and the Metaverse: Transforming Gaming Experiences 311
Ayush Shekhar, Marwadi University, India
T. Premavathi, Marwadi University, India
Damodharan Palaniappan, Marwadi University, India

As virtual worlds and the Metaverse improve, AI and GenAI have a major impact on the evolution of video games. These technologies enable non-player characters

(NPCs) to be more intelligent, surroundings to change, gameplay to be personalized, and levels to be created with ease. Generative AI and its components, such as large language models, diffusion models, and neural rendering, assist in the automatic creation of dialogues, storylines, game items, and world elements. In this chapter, real-life stories from key game developers and Metaverse services are included to demonstrate how the use of AI/GenAI boosts the creativity, growth, and busywork of users. Moreover, it closely examines issues such as protecting people's personal data, managing online content, safeguarding legal rights for content, and supporting ethical conduct in VR and AR. Overall, this chapter discusses how AI and Generative AI are building fresh paths for game development and how users interact in virtual worlds.

Chapter 11
The Role of AI in Preserving and Remastering Classic Games 325
P. Selvakumar, Department of Science and Humanities, Nehru Institute of Technology, Coimbatore, India
S. Poorani, Kongu Engineering College, India
Vinod Waiker, Datta Meghe Institute of Management Studies, India
Satheesh Kumar D., Hindusthan College of Engineering and Technology, India
Pallavi Jaggi, Chandigarh School of Business, Chandigarh Group of Colleges, Jhanjeri, India
Mohit Sharma, Maharshi Dayanand University, Rohtak, India
Manjunath T. C., Rajarajeswari College of Engineering, India

Video games, once considered mere entertainment for children or niche enthusiasts, have grown into a global cultural and artistic force. They are no longer simply digital pastimes but complex narratives, technological achievements, and reflections of society's values and creativity at particular moments in time. From the pixelated adventures of the early 1980s to the immersive open-world epics of the present day, video games have evolved into a unique medium that bridges art, storytelling, technology, and interactivity. However, as the medium has evolved, so too has the threat of loss. Just as film historians fight to preserve silent movies or archivists work to protect classic literature, there is a growing and urgent need to preserve classic video games. These early and foundational titles are disappearing at an alarming rate due to technological obsolescence, hardware degradation, and legal challenges that prevent access and emulation. Classic games offer a lens into the past.

Compilation of References 351

About the Contributors 389

Index 397

Preface

INTRODUCTION

The intersection of Artificial Intelligence (AI) and the video game industry represents one of the most transformative developments in interactive media history. From early rule-based decision systems to today's generative AI architectures, gaming has evolved into a sophisticated ecosystem where creativity, technology, and player experience converge. *Reshaping the Video Game Landscape with AI and GenAI* brings together leading scholars and practitioners to examine this evolution—exploring how AI not only augments game mechanics and design but also reshapes our understanding of authorship, immersion, and interactivity.

As editors, our goal for this volume was to present a comprehensive yet accessible overview of how AI and Generative AI (GenAI) are redefining every dimension of the gaming experience—from education and narrative creation to procedural content generation and cultural preservation. The contributions in this book reflect the global, interdisciplinary nature of this transformation. Each chapter highlights innovative methodologies, ethical considerations, and technological breakthroughs that are actively shaping the industry's future, providing readers with both theoretical insight and practical guidance.

The book also invites critical reflection. As AI systems increasingly co-create with humans, developers, designers, and researchers are being challenged to reconsider traditional notions of creativity, ownership, and fairness. By weaving together diverse voices from academia and industry, this collection not only captures the state of the art but also charts emerging directions for a field in rapid motion.

CHAPTER OVERVIEW

Chapter 1, *Adaptive Learning with AI in Virtual and Augmented Reality Education* by Usharani Bhimavarapu, explores how AI-powered immersive technologies such as VR, AR, MR, and XR are transforming educational environments. Through advanced models like Bi-stacked GRU, the chapter highlights adaptive learning systems that anticipate user intent and enable more personalized, interactive training experiences across sectors.

Chapter 2, *AI for Dynamic Game Balancing and Optimization – Machine Learning for Understanding Player Behavior* by Kaushalya Thopate and Tanvi Pokale, focuses on the use of supervised and reinforcement learning to enhance player engagement and fairness. The authors address ethical design, transparency, and real-world case studies from both AAA and indie games to illustrate the balance between adaptive challenge and ethical responsibility.

Chapter 3, *AI-Assisted Game Mechanics Optimization for Multiplayer Environments* by Usharani Bhimavarapu, continues the discussion on dynamic balancing, presenting an advanced framework based on Remora Optimization and Bi-Stacked LSTM networks. The chapter underscores how predictive analytics can maintain equilibrium across multiplayer dynamics, improving player satisfaction and retention.

Chapter 4, *Co-Creating Narratives: Ludonarrative Agency and Generative AI in Digital Games* by Cátia Ferreira, examines AI's role in interactive storytelling. By analyzing AI Dungeon and related platforms, Ferreira frames generative storytelling as a collaborative process where human players and AI systems share authorship. The chapter invites critical dialogue on narrative coherence, creativity, and ethics in algorithmic co-authorship.

Chapter 5, *From Technical Feasibility to Industry Reality – Implementing LLM-Driven Dialogue Systems in Video Games* by Juan Rodríguez Suárez and colleagues, transitions from narrative theory to applied design. This chapter provides a detailed technical and economic assessment of deploying large language models (LLMs) in commercial games, complete with prototype demonstrations and benchmarking analyses.

Chapter 6, *From Trackers to AI: Generative Music in Contemporary Game Design* by Jörg Burbach, traces the evolution of computer-generated music in games. Grounded in theories of creativity, it reveals how AI-driven compositional tools expand aesthetic possibilities while introducing new ethical and educational considerations around authorship and authenticity.

Chapter 7, *Innovative Procedural Content Generation (PCG) Using Generative AI – A New Paradigm in Game Design* by Monika Kumari and collaborators, explores state-of-the-art generative models such as GANs, Transformers, and Diffusion Models. This chapter demonstrates how AI enhances scalability and creativity in game world design, from terrain generation to character and narrative systems.

Chapter 8, *Procedural Generation and Adaptive Gameplay: The Role of AI and Generative AI in Contemporary Game Development* by Aparajita Biswal and co-authors, provides a holistic view of adaptive design principles. It emphasizes how real-time AI systems can tailor gameplay to player behavior, enriching both immersion and responsiveness in evolving digital worlds.

Chapter 9, *The Evolution of Artificial Intelligence in Shaping the Future of Interactive Entertainment* by Mohamed Elgazar and colleagues, takes a historical and philosophical lens to the subject. The authors trace AI's conceptual origins and analyze its current influence on world-building, NPC intelligence, and design economics, raising vital questions about future frontiers in human–machine collaboration.

Chapter 10, *The Future of AI and Generative AI in Virtual Worlds and the Metaverse: Transforming Gaming Experiences* by Ayush Shekhar, Premavathi T, and Damodharan Palaniappan, delves into the convergence of AI and the Metaverse. The chapter explores NPC intelligence, dynamic environments, and ethical challenges, while highlighting AI's potential to redefine creativity and community interaction in immersive spaces.

Chapter 11, *The Role of AI in Preserving and Remastering Classic Games* by Selvakumar P and co-authors, concludes the collection by shifting from innovation to preservation. The chapter highlights the urgency of safeguarding digital cultural heritage through AI-assisted restoration, remastering, and emulation techniques, ensuring that gaming's artistic history remains accessible for future generations.

CONCLUSION

Collectively, the chapters in this volume illustrate a rapidly evolving landscape where artificial intelligence serves as both a creative partner and a transformative force. From adaptive gameplay and procedural generation to generative storytelling and cultural preservation, each contribution underscores AI's expanding influence on the art, science, and ethics of game design. The boundaries between player, creator, and system are dissolving, giving rise to new hybrid forms of authorship and engagement that redefine what it means to "play" and to "create."

However, this transformation also demands critical scrutiny. As the industry embraces automation and co-creation, new challenges emerge around transparency, fairness, and sustainability. The contributors to this book emphasize the importance of ethical frameworks and responsible innovation, ensuring that technological progress enhances—not diminishes—human creativity and diversity of expression.

Ultimately, *Reshaping the Video Game Landscape with AI and GenAI* is not merely a documentation of current trends but an invitation to imagine what comes next. As editors, we hope this volume serves as a bridge between disciplines and a catalyst for further research, design experimentation, and dialogue. The convergence of AI and gaming is still unfolding—and it is our collective responsibility to shape this evolution with curiosity, integrity, and imagination.

Chapter 1

Adaptive Learning With AI in Virtual and Augmented Reality Education

Usharani Bhimavarapu
https://orcid.org/0000-0002-0246-1420
Department of Computer Science and Engineering, Koneru Lakshmaiah Education Foundation, Vaddeswaram, India

ABSTRACT

Artificial Intelligence (AI) is the driving force behind Immersive Technologies like Virtual Reality (VR), Augmented Reality (AR), Mixed Reality (MR), and Extended Reality (XR) now. Combined with these technologies, AI provides immersive dynamic worlds with the potential for greater realism, interactivity, and personalization. AI provides predictive modeling and simulation-like behavior in VR and real-time object recognition, contextual overlay, and gesture commands in AR. MR is enhanced with AI-synchronized physical and virtual content so that realities can be merged together in a smooth manner to facilitate training and operational uptake. AI integrates them into essential XR and functions through multimodal data sets, enhances personalization, and enhances decision-making in health care, education, retail, and manufacturing. Bi-stacked GRU and later more advanced models build all such technologies into sequential data stream processing, prediction of user intent, and adaptive response enablement. Added to the fusion of AI with immersive technology, they bring forth a new generation of intelligent, user-focused, forward-thinking experience bursting beyond entertainment into actual practical real-world applications.

DOI: 10.4018/979-8-3373-4637-3.ch001

ght © 2026, IGI Global Scientific Publishing. Copying or distributing in print or electronic forms without written permission of IGI Global Scientific Publishing is prohibited. Use of this chapter to generative artificial intelligence (AI) technologies is expressly prohibited. The publisher reserves all rights to license its use for generative AI training and machine learning model development.

INTRODUCTION

Synergy of AI and VR presents us with virtual worlds which can be responding dynamically to user interactions. Pre-programmed response is what standard VR systems can do, whereas AI enables such systems to learn from user actions and respond by changing virtual worlds in real-time. Such a response makes things seem more realistic because simulation is interactive and dynamic. For example, VR computer characters can act naturally verbally, in movement, and in reaction action. These are the demands needed during training, game play, and learning if customization is to be achieved. VR experience no longer becomes passive but variant based on the need of the users with the potential of AI. The reason that AI is particularly required in VR is because the need for realistic simulation that resembles reality. AI is not required, or else VR is dull and static. The contribution of AI towards VR is thus intelligence, flexibility, and realism.

AI is necessary in Augmented Reality (AR) as a nod towards unifying the virtual and real worlds into a stunning harmony. AR puts virtual content on top of actual environments but by itself, AR requires sophisticated object recognition and tracking in a position to operate optimally. AI computer vision allows AR apps to track and identify precisely individuals, objects, and gestures. This allows for proper virtual content overlay on actual space. In fashion retail, for instance, AR driven by AI can suggest fashion pieces based on body shapes. AR and AI in medicine serve to facilitate surgery by marking key points in real time. Without AI, AI is impossible and thus AR would be impossible because basic overlays and basic trailing are not enough. AR never dynamically adapts based on circumstances under varying conditions without AI. AI thus facilitates AR through contextualizing it, therefore making augmentation adaptive and pertinent.

Mixed Reality (MR) requires AI to coordinate the complex interaction of virtual and real objects in a common space. MR surpasses AR and VR because users can interact with virtual and real objects simultaneously. AI enables simulated physics so that virtual objects behave as close to real as possible each time they're interacting with the real environment. For example, in MR, the user intention can be anticipated by an AI system and object interaction consequently adjusted. In simulation centers, AI-based MR can replicate perilous work with zero risk with the combination of real tools and virtual worlds. AI must be employed in MR because it provides the high coherence among two worlds. Without AI, MR worlds will be incoherent and unbelievable. AI in MR is to connect worlds and make interaction intelligent, secure, and frictionless.

Extended Reality (XR), which includes VR, AR, and MR, has a partially foundation-based foundation of AI for personalization and even a broader foundation. XR finds its application extensively across all sectors like education, healthcare, retail, and entertainment with variable experience. AI allows XR platforms to be customized through training them in users' behavior, context, and preference to make experiences more personalized. For example, for educational applications, AI-powered XR can be customized to align the lessons according to the learning capacity and speed of students. For healthcare, XR can offer individualized rehabilitation exercise with AI-powered feedback. AI-powered XR is warranted on the basis of varied needs of varied industries and customers. There must be intelligent systems in stationary XR environments for providing generic solutions. The role of AI in XR is to integrate and optimize immersive technologies so that they are adaptive, efficient, and personalized. Natural human-computer interaction is one of the most rudimentary requirements of AI for immersive technologies.

Humans require natural forms of interaction for VR, AR, MR, and XR devices aside from controllers and keyboards. AI includes the feature of gesture recognition, voice command, and emotion detection. AI can recognize facial expressions to navigate in virtual worlds appropriately. This human method of communication leverages the majority of user interaction as well as reduces technology adoption learning curves to near zero. Immersive platforms remain dependent on conventional input forms without AI, restricting accessibility. Multimodal AI interfaces are a more human-centric face to tech. The necessity is a by-product of the necessity for natural interaction, and the goal is to maintain immersive technologies as accessible, efficient, and compelling as possible. Artificial intelligence within immersive tech also assists with processing and analyzing data. VR, AR, MR, and XR generate an enormous amount of data from sensors, cameras, and user input. AI helps screen, research, and cull facts from data in real time. For example, for XR industry training, AI will monitor performance by monitoring movement and choice. In the retail space, AI-driven AR will monitor how consumers interact with recommendations through an efficient pathway. AI is required because too much is being produced within immersive platforms that can't be handled by human processing. Without AI, most of this information would be idle, not realizing the potential of immersive technology. The intention is to convert raw information into usable information to facilitate decision-making and personalization. The second requirement of AI for immersive technologies is the scalability and automation aspect.

With VR, AR, MR, and XR gaining traction all over the world, AI allows for automated content creation and updates. For instance, AI constructs 3D worlds looking real on their own from real-world data. It is cost-effective and accelerates the deployment of immersive content. AI procedural generation in game development develops infinite virtual worlds for each individual in video games. They are necessary because human-generated content is not scalable and takes time. Without AI, XR experiences will be zero scalable and diverse. AI provides scalable, sustainable, and varied immersive content to view anywhere globally. AI enables immersive technologies due to personalization, which is an enduring driving force for customer satisfaction. AI can track progress and personalize content according to needs in AR and VR learning solutions.

It does the same for games, as AI provides all players a personalized and enhanced experience according to interest. AI-based XR medicine provides customized exercises according to the capability of the patients. It is because of this reason that AI should be employed for personalization since human beings are heterogeneous in nature and cannot be all-in-one. Immersive systems in the absence of AI would not only be standard but static too. The objective is to personalize experiences in an effort to enhance engagement, efficacy, and adoption of immersive technology in the future. Safety and ethics are also on the radar in how AI interacts with virtual reality. In the XR and MR environments where users interact with virtual and real-world objects, fatigue, collision, and overexposure are issues.

AI can anticipate risky action and notify users or adjust settings to be risk-free. AI can, for example, monitor a user's health profile while exercising using VR and adjust levels of difficulty. For AR driving applications, AI will suppress distraction by overlays to drivers. Environmental need safety in immersive settings has to be ensured. Safety cannot be set in approach and human-led without AI. The objective is to render immersive experience safe, ethical, and user-led. Finally, AI in virtual realities comes to address the requirement for innovation and future-proofing. While VR, AR, MR, and XR shift on a day-to-day basis, AI turns them timely and fashionable with each second.

AI has the capability to anticipate trends, provide user ratings, and adjust immersive systems according to them. All this day-to-day innovation is only required for businesses based on evolving training and functional demands such as education, defense, and healthcare. AI would render immersive technologies fixed, with incremental annual updates. AI is developed to propel the innovation of immersive technologies so that they are responsive, relevant, and effective. AI not only empowers VR, AR, MR, and XR but charts their fate. Golab et al. (2016) are lacking in using headworn headsets with no scalability for access to widespread clinical application. Liounakos et al. (2020) technically recognize head-up display but constrain clinical outcomes testing. Yan et al. (2021) have systematic review of VR in cervical spine spinal surgery but no empirical studies in heterogenous patient populations.

Chang et al. (2019) attempt to use smartphone and VR goggles but are constrained by very small participant numbers. Chytas et al. (2020) are authoring AR in surgery anatomy education but have no evidence for retention of knowledge after the longer term. Ghaednia et al. (2021) are introducing AR and VR in spinal surgery but reporting on too much optimism instead of the clinical effectiveness evidence. Lohre et al. (2020) are describing VR spinal endoscopy simulative training but not real situation execution performance results. Pfandler et al. (2017) criticize VR simulators but most of the included studies have methodological flaws. Yoo et al. (2019) describe VR and AR application in spine surgery but not cost–benefit analysis step by step. Kaylor et al. (2019) confirm AR glasses but results are only applicable to telewound care and not extendable to general surgery application. Dixon et al. (2014) note inattentional blindness with AR navigation but were constrained by under-sampling their sample. Ponce et al. (2014) describe AR telementoring for orthopedic surgery but provide minimal quantitative measurement of teaching improvement. Haddas and Ju (2019) record gait correction tests in cervical myelopathy but are not combined with immersive technologies. Rao et al. (2020) establish telemedicine standards for arthroplasty but research is on pandemic-constrained disease states. Joda et al. (2019) critically evaluate AR and VR in dental medicine but evidence is unusual, experimentally-obtained. Shafi et al. (2020) are presenting telehealth in spinal disorders but evidence is patient-reported outcome with no objective clinical outcome. Smith and Barr (2017) studies are biased towards reporting instantaneous physiological and psychological impact with no follow-up. Reis and Neves (2019) are cognizant of VR for decision-making but lack large-scale evidence on mixed populations within fire departments. Williams-Bell et al. (2015) do possess a review but are limited by empirical evidence with traditional training to make comparisons. Bellemans et al. (2020) did possess VR training among firefighters but with limited transfer tests to actual events. Social influence on virtual fire evacuation is Kinateder et al. (2014) but in simulated lab only. Feng et al. (2018) critically evaluated VR serious games but with the overwhelming majority of trials conducted using non-standardized test instruments. Berthiaume et al. (2023) report VR training equipment but solely within transport crash situation only. Stefan et al. (2023) did a critical analysis of VR training and conclude on low quality evidence of maintaining safety behavior in the long term. Presence-based interventions are also promoted by Caldas et al. (2022) but not operational performance-related ones by firefighters. Weidinger (2022) addresses technology in firefighting with enormous differences in field-tested deployment and integration. Fanfarová and Mariš (2017) develop a simulation tool with minimal usability documentation in real emergency environments. Smith et al. (2014) record firefighters' physiological reactions without VR use during training. Oliveira et al. (2024) test immersive VR with low generalizability quasi-experimental design. Mystakidis et al. (2022) develop an educational VR serious game but do not test under real fire scenario conditions. Calandra et al. (2021) develop a tunnel fire simulator but experimental trials are simulated environments with the assistance of VR and not actual ones. Cho et al. (2019) develop an AR-based energy management system but do not implement any real-world application to smart cities. Lytras et al. (2015) discuss facilitation technologies but lack empirical knowledge of integration issues. Jo and Kim (2019) analyze IoT+AR retail shopping experience but are restricted to small-scale retail spaces' contexts.

Singh et al. (2021) are referring to green communication technologies but do not have benchmarking in the performance domain in real-world worlds. Dwivedi et al. (2022) are referring to the metaverse but are speculating without large case studies. Kelly et al. (2021) are referring to VR headset ownership but the sample is potentially non-representative elsewhere. Ibáñez and Delgado-Kloos (2018) provide systematic review of AR in STEM using other learning outcome measures. Mystakidis (2022) forecasts the metaverse but with nothing substantial to speak of in terms of applications. Speicher et al. (2019) pioneer mixed reality but lack longitudinal studies on users. Zhao et al. (2022) infuse beliefs of metaverse but technical scalability is not emphasized. Rathore (2022) believes advertisement to AI and not ethics and privacy issues. Soto and Leon (2022) qualitatively describe AI adoption in the metaverse but without quantitative statistics. Yin et al. (2021) enumerate AR/VR displays but without cost savings and adoptability barriers. Rahouti et al. (2021) present cyber risk detection but fail to thoroughly review incremental learning models in detail. Jagatheesaperumal et al. (2022) document safe healthcare solutions but adoption of new technology is not mentioned in detail. Madduru (2021) propose AIaaS in MEC with AR/VR but scalability and reducing latency are not mentioned. Kao and Liao (2021) document 5G MEC solutions but offer very little evidence on actual deployment performance. Zhan et al. (2020) eliminate VR chromatic aberration but deploy their optical solution in lab-controlled environments only. Kuguoglu et al. (2021) research smart city AIoT projects without having the capacity to scale up from pilot deployment. The AI-based XR platform started overcomes the limitation of other platforms by utilizing a complete and scalable platform for Virtual Reality (VR), Augmented Reality (AR), Mixed Reality (MR), and Extended Reality (XR) and smart AI algorithms for offering real-time feedback. Contrary to the current research papers that are application-based or conceptual, the proposed methodology herein is scalable to large-scale deployment based on data-tuned solutions with empirically testable solutions in various application fields such as smart cities, healthcare, education, and marketing. Application of bi-stacked GRU model facilitates effective sequential and multimodal data processing with improved predictability and loophole-filling of empirical validation gaps of the current models.

Utilizing feature selection methods such as Particle Swarm Optimization (PSO), the system reduces noise and increases decision-making accuracy and, in turn, optimizes against other evaluation metrics proposed in earlier work. AI is also combined with 5G and edge computing to support low-latency and high-bandwidth computing to tackle scalability and deployment issues to real-world problems limited by earlier models. It also maintains cost and usage efficacy, and it bridges the knowledge gap between field deployment and testing in the laboratory. It ensures the ethical concerns and privacy concerns are addressed through the facilitation of assured provisions and explainability of AI, such as decision transparency because previous research had not considered such concerns. Finally, with touchless multimodal interaction on AR/VR platforms, the platform allows user engagement and ecological validity and thereby resists limitations in long-term performance and use measurement in the real world.

MATERIALS AND METHODS

It starts with data acquisition from 2D medical images and health parameters using smartphones and pre-processing to remove noise, normalize values, and sanitize data. This is followed by 3D reconstruction of 2D images to perform calculations to obtain accurate anatomical models, XR-based for spine surgery visualization. This is then followed by feature selection via Particle Swarm Optimization (PSO) in order to get the most essential features and remove redundancy. Multimodal and sequencing data handling is thereafter done via a bi-stacked GRU network in anticipation of accuracy in prediction as well as reactive recuperation. GRU outputs and feature extraction are then integrated with VR, AR, MR, and XR systems towards facilitating real-time interaction and decision support. The system is then validated for accuracy, usefulness, and user-friendliness in e-healthcare.

MATERIAL

3D data acquisition from 2D images has been at the core of surgical planning and medical imaging. 2D X-rays, MRI, and CT scans can be converted into precise 3D reconstruction through computer vision and deep learning algorithms. The physicians will get a clear view of the anatomical structure. This movement finds special application in spine surgery, as the XR technology enables surgeons to be given holographic 3D images of the spine. Holograms are naturally viewable and interactive by gestures, screenless, thus allowing surgeons to see live images in situ in the theatre. Sterilization-retained touchless integration precludes infection risk to delicate procedures. Apart from the OT, XR even takes over telemedicine, with smartphone sensors that can record the raw parameters to monitor patients. From ECG to accelerometer fall detection, motion tracking using gyroscope, temperature, blood oxygen saturation, pulse rate, respiration, sleep, and walk type, it is simple to record. These values ensure real-time remote monitoring to the clinicians, which can also improve the quality of patient care and facilitate early detection as well. These are complemented by 3D reconstructions produced by AI, surgically customized holograms for XR, and smartphone telemedicine, that permeate the whole space for ease and assistance in modern medicine.

PREPROCESSING

2D-to-3D reconstruction pre-processing involves pixel intensity normalization, noise elimination, image registration, and anatomical structure segmentation like vertebrae.

Each one of them provides resulting 3D models in the form of anatomically accurate copies of the patient's spine and can be displayed holographically on XR platforms. Health parameters collected through measurement with smartphones are subjected to preprocessing to include exclusion of noisy readings by ECG and accelerometer, gyroscope calibration, removal of missing values, and scaling readings such as pulse, respiration, temperature, and blood saturation to normal range. Feature extraction, rejection of outliers, and time smoothing are some of the other methods employed for increasing quality and reliability of the data. These also include preprocessing methods in a segment of the master process in a bid at privacy and anonymization when handling sensitive patient information. Preprocessing alone converts raw, heterogeneously obtained data into clean, structured, and trustworthy forms and prepares them to be utilized in XR use in surgical planning, intraoperative real-time navigation, and telemedicine surveillance.

FEATURE SELECTION

Particle Swarm Optimization (PSO) feature selection is a strong method to select the best features from high-dimensional and high-volume data like medical images and telemedicine signals. PSO is population-based metaheuristics that is derived from bird flocking or schooling fish collective behavior where candidate set of features is represented by each particle. Particles modify their path in the search space while optimising based on their best local and best global solution found by the swarm. This is performed sequentially with the exploration-exploitation trade-off such that dimension reduction is optimised without eliminating most of the informative features. PSO can assist in selecting the image features appropriate for use in 2D medical image 3D reconstruction to enable anatomical modeling with accuracy by eliminating redundant features or noisy features. For telemedicine data that is being captured by smartphones, PSO can focus on the pertinent health parameters like ECG, pulse, respiratory rate, and activity in such a manner that it is calculated without computationally burdening it. This offers a high feature space that optimizes correctness for classification, optimizes real-time performance for XR environments, and enables evidence-based decision-making for clinical environments.

BISTACKED GATED RECURRENT UNITS

Artificial Intelligence (AI), Virtual Reality (VR), Augmented Reality (AR), Mixed Reality (MR), and Extended Reality (XR) are integrated particularly optimized using the application of the implementation of the application of bi-stacked GRU (Gated Recurrent Units) models. Bi-stacked GRU utilizes stacked layers and bidirectional learning to enable the system with high ability to learn future and past relations of sequential data without a decrease in computational efficiency.

In VR, the model can be used to simulate instantaneous sensor input, monitor user movement, and predict future interaction as an attempt to establish real-time interactive experience when there is no latency. Bi-stacked GRU for AR can be used to identify gestures accurately and object tracking in real-time because it can learn temporal context relations between objects, resulting in natural synchronization of virtual overlays and real environments. In MR, since virtual content and the real world have to be together all the time, the model can support multimodal streams like spatial, visual, and audio information in order to provide suitable alignment and interactive dynamics. In XR, which is a confluence of VR, AR, and MR, over bi-stacked GRU models lead in handling dynamic sequences of data from multiple sources like eye gaze, motion sensors, and context data and thereby form adaptive and personalized spaces. The two-way functionality has the advantage of not only allowing the XR system to react to the user input but also anticipate it and thereby provide higher safety, realism, and user engagement. Therefore, bi-stacked GRU-based AI then becomes the default real-time forecasting, adaptive decision-making platform for easy integration with all immersion technologies.

EXPERIMENTAL RESULTS

Experimental outcomes show that Artificial Intelligence (AI) embedded with immersion technologies like Virtual Reality (VR), Augmented Reality (AR), Mixed Reality (MR), and Extended Reality (XR) is extremely efficient. These data sets gathered, i.e., 2D medical scans converted to 3D reconstruction and health parameters detected using smartphones' assistance, were preprocessed for noise removal, value normalized, and data quality verified. Feature selection was carried out by Particle Swarm Optimization (PSO) for desired feature selection and redundancy elimination for efficient improvement in computations. GRU bi-stacked model was then utilized to control sequential and multimodal streams of information for the purpose of optimizing precise prediction, gesture detection, and interactive user behavior. Outputs are obtained based on improved performance metrics of classification accuracy, real-time, and personalization in the XR environment. The results validate the effectiveness of the developed system in providing more interactive deployments in clinical scenarios like spine surgery planning, holographic visualization, and telemedicine monitoring.

Table 1 plots Virtual Reality models performance against a broad set of evaluation metrics like accuracy, precision, recall, F1-score, latency, and frame rate. All accuracy values are greater than 0.88, validating VR systems reliability. Precision-recall tradeoff enables excellent scene element detection and user action detection. F1-scores are balanced mean of them with the remainder balanced classification. Latency metrics are 42–52 ms, which are excellent real-time responsiveness. Frame rates are 58–62 FPS average, which provides excellent user experience smoothness. Excellent precision and recall values indicate excellent VR immersion quality. More FPS models possess lower latency.

Table 1. VR Model Performance

Accuracy	Precision	Recall	F1_Score	Latency_ms	FrameRate_FPS
0.91	0.89	0.87	0.88	45	60
0.92	0.91	0.89	0.90	48	59
0.88	0.86	0.84	0.85	52	58
0.94	0.93	0.91	0.92	43	61
0.90	0.88	0.87	0.88	46	60
0.95	0.94	0.92	0.93	42	62
0.89	0.87	0.85	0.86	49	59
0.93	0.92	0.90	0.91	44	61
0.91	0.90	0.88	0.89	47	60
0.92	0.91	0.89	0.90	45	61

Table 2 illustrates the comparison of AR gesture recognition with different parameters including accuracy, precision, recall, F1-score, response time, and overlay alignment. The accuracy rate is fine in terms of a mean rate of 0.90 reflecting the uniformity in gesture recognition. Precision is also equal to recall, reflecting equal gestures being recognized by the users. F1-scores reflect stability in all times in gesture detection without risk of overfitting in individual patterns. Response times are 113–121 ms, well adapted for real-time use of AR. Alignment scores of more than 0.90 for overlays verify proper visual alignment of the world to objects. The parameters confirm AR suitability for enabling natural interaction. Reduction of response time improves overlay alignment, thus responsiveness in a dynamic environment. The system never slows down or becomes perplexed even with complicated motion. In general, the AR system delivers precise gesture recognition with impeccable performance and silky smooth overlays.

Table 2. AR Gesture Recognition

Gesture_ Accuracy	Gesture_ Precision	Gesture_ Recall	Gesture_ F1	Response_Time_ ms	Overlay_ Alignment
0.89	0.87	0.85	0.86	120	0.91
0.90	0.88	0.86	0.87	118	0.92
0.92	0.90	0.88	0.89	115	0.93
0.91	0.89	0.87	0.88	117	0.94
0.88	0.86	0.84	0.85	121	0.90
0.93	0.91	0.89	0.90	114	0.95
0.89	0.87	0.85	0.86	119	0.92
0.94	0.92	0.90	0.91	113	0.96
0.90	0.88	0.86	0.87	116	0.93
0.92	0.90	0.88	0.89	115	0.94

Table 3 summarizes MR performance based on object tracking accuracy, depth estimation, spatial consistency, response time, collision prevention, and safety protection from hazard. Accuracy of object tracking is always more than 0.90, and hence interaction can be performed in real-time safely. Depth measurements and spatial consistency metrics give accurate virtual object positions in real worlds. Response rates of 116–122 ms are suitable for use in interactive MR. Object collision avoidance rates above 0.93 give virtual–real object interaction consistency. The user safety index measures the high degree of trust when assessing 0.87–0.92. Findings create good synchronicity of real and virtual worlds. High object accuracy reduces users' disorientation. Safety and collision avoidance show MR's utility in hazardous environments like training or medicine. In general, MR interaction provides safety, reliability, and responsiveness.

Table 3. MR Object Interaction

Object_Tracking_ Accuracy	Depth_ Estimation	Spatial_ Consistency	Object_Response_ Time_ms	Collision_ Avoidance	User_ Safety_ Index
0.93	0.89	0.91	120	0.95	0.90
0.91	0.87	0.89	118	0.94	0.88
0.92	0.88	0.90	119	0.95	0.89

continued on following page

Table 3. Continued

Object_Tracking_Accuracy	Depth_Estimation	Spatial_Consistency	Object_Response_Time_ms	Collision_Avoidance	User_Safety_Index
0.94	0.91	0.92	117	0.96	0.91
0.90	0.86	0.88	122	0.93	0.87
0.95	0.92	0.94	116	0.97	0.92
0.93	0.90	0.91	118	0.95	0.90
0.92	0.89	0.90	119	0.94	0.89
0.91	0.88	0.89	121	0.93	0.88
0.94	0.91	0.92	117	0.96	0.91

Table 4 shows how XR improves telemedicine by tracking patients' medical parameters including heart rate, oxygen saturation, respiratory rate, temperature, fall detection, and sleep. Heart rates are 76–92 bpm, i.e., normal but changing activity rate. Oxygen saturation of more than 93% is excellent clinical vital sign monitoring. 17–23 is good clinical data collection. Normal healthy temperature of normality (36.6–38.2°C) paroxysmal fever increases. Fall detection also in a subset of the patients, with elderly care being made possible. Sleep quality from good to worse with its utility in long-term monitoring being suggested. These are measurements of XR deployment in continuous and contactless monitoring. Sensor deployment in XR allows real-time decision-making in telemedicine. All such data put together is analogous to the performance of XR for health monitoring in an external setting.

Table 4. XR Telemedicine Monitoring

Patient	HeartRate_BPM	BloodOxygen_%	Respiration_Rate	Temperature_C	Fall_Detection	Sleep_Quality
P1	78	97	18	36.8	No	Good
P2	85	96	20	37.2	No	Fair
P3	92	94	22	38.0	Yes	Poor
P4	80	98	17	36.7	No	Good
P5	88	95	21	37.5	No	Fair
P6	76	97	18	36.6	No	Good
P7	90	93	23	38.2	Yes	Poor
P8	84	96	19	37.0	No	Fair
P9	82	97	20	36.9	No	Good
P10	87	95	21	37.4	No	Fair

Table 5 measures immersion in VR with respect to visual realism, sound immersion, motion sickness, smoothness of interaction, latency, and user satisfaction.

Values for all sound immersion and visual realism are always greater than 0.87 and are skewed in the direction of sensory experience. Low-high values of motion sickness suggest directions for enhanced stability. Smooth interaction is good for all readings above 0.89, which is a measure of smooth user control. Latency of 42–51 ms feels enjoyable in immersive use. Low latency and high smoothness yield greatest user satisfaction. High realism and test of sound immersion rate correlate very highly with high user satisfaction. Higher lead to lower satisfaction in latent experiments. Motion sickness continues to be an issue, and low realism is a particular concern. VR technology responsiverealistic overall performance but motion sickness reduction is the matter of long-term use.

Table 5. VR Immersion Quality

Trial	Visual_ Realism	Sound_Immersion	Motion_Sickness	Interaction_Smoothness	Latency_ ms	User_Satisfaction
T1	0.91	0.88	Low	0.92	45	High
T2	0.89	0.87	Medium	0.90	47	Medium
T3	0.93	0.92	Low	0.94	44	High
T4	0.88	0.85	High	0.89	50	Low
T5	0.92	0.90	Low	0.93	43	High
T6	0.90	0.87	Medium	0.91	46	Medium
T7	0.94	0.93	Low	0.95	42	High
T8	0.87	0.84	High	0.88	51	Low
T9	0.91	0.89	Medium	0.92	45	Medium
T10	0.92	0.91	Low	0.93	44	High

Table 6 measures AR overlay accuracy across a variety of changing attributes such as accuracy, alignment, light adaptation, occlusion handling, latency, and user's clarity. Values of overlay accuracy are always above 0.87, i.e., uniform placement. Values of object alignment guarantee accuracy in visualsegmentation of objects. Light change values of approximately 0.90 provide AR technology with very good ability to manage change in the environment. Occlusions are quite well managed at some cost under compound conditions. Latency is 117–128 ms, i.e., a little greater than VR but still functioning in AR. Users' clarity scores range from low to high and map to reliance on quality of overlay. High accuracy measurements with enhanced overlay precision. Worse occlusion handling performance disqualifies user scores. Such a result corroborates AR's superior performance for overlays in real scenes. Reduction in latency and better occlusion management enhance user clarity as well.

Table 6. AR Overlay Precision

Scenario	Overlay_ Accuracy	Object_Alignment	Lighting_Adaptation	Occlusion_Handling	Latency_ ms	User_ Clarity
S1	0.92	0.90	0.91	0.89	120	High
S2	0.89	0.87	0.88	0.86	125	Medium
S3	0.94	0.92	0.93	0.91	118	High
S4	0.87	0.85	0.86	0.84	128	Low
S5	0.93	0.91	0.92	0.90	119	High
S6	0.90	0.88	0.89	0.87	124	Medium
S7	0.95	0.93	0.94	0.92	117	High
S8	0.88	0.86	0.87	0.85	127	Low
S9	0.91	0.89	0.90	0.88	122	Medium
S10	0.94	0.92	0.93	0.91	118	High

Table 7 distinguishes MR collaboration in terms of task achievement performance metrics, communication clarity, co-authored object accuracy, sync delay, collaboration score, and user trust. All scores of task achievement are over 0.86, which demonstrates excellent collaborative performance. Clarity of communication is 0.89 on average and helps to build teamwork in MR environments. Mutual object accuracy scores reflect virtual object synchronisation reliability among participants. Sync delay is 107–119 ms, offering nearly real-time co-work. Co-work scores correlate strongly with accuracy and clarity scores. User trust is low-high based on consistency. Lower-delays, higher-clarity groups guarantee a high likelihood for co-work success. Findings are supportive of MR ability to support multi-user activity such as training and telework. MR supports real-time coordination without miscommunication. MR, in general, is a decent set of building blocks for co-located immersive applications.

Table 7. MR Collaboration Efficiency

Team	Task_ Completion	Communication_ Clarity	Shared_Object_ Accuracy	Sync_Delay_ ms	Collaboration_ Score	User_ Trust
Team1	0.91	0.90	0.89	110	0.92	High
Team2	0.88	0.86	0.85	115	0.89	Medium
Team3	0.93	0.92	0.91	108	0.94	High
Team4	0.87	0.85	0.84	118	0.88	Low
Team5	0.92	0.91	0.90	109	0.93	High
Team6	0.89	0.87	0.86	114	0.90	Medium
Team7	0.94	0.93	0.92	107	0.95	High
Team8	0.86	0.84	0.83	119	0.87	Low

continued on following page

Table 7. Continued

Team	Task_ Completion	Communication_ Clarity	Shared_Object_ Accuracy	Sync_Delay_ ms	Collaboration_ Score	User_ Trust
Team9	0.91	0.90	0.89	111	0.92	Medium
Team10	0.93	0.92	0.91	108	0.94	High

Table 8 shows an application usage of XR application in spine surgery such as hologram accuracy, gesture response, depth perception, sterility aid, surgeon comfort, and training effectiveness. Accuracy above 0.92 indicates realistic reconstructions in 3D. Perceived depth and gesture response are always significantly above normal for ensuring reliability for surgery planning purposes. Sterilization support is assured in most situations and was compatible with clinical requirements. Surgeon satisfaction grades are also varied with increased marks in the case of correct holograms. The level of effectiveness of training is always high, and because of this reason, the use of XR is justified in surgical training. Satisfaction is less with occurrences of non-sterility support. Gesture accuracy provides unproblematic intraoperative utilization. XR reduces monitor dependency and enhances free-hand visualization. In general, XR is justified in clinical usage through appropriate holographic support during procedure performance.

Table 8. XR Spine Surgery Simulation

Case	3D_Hologram_ Accuracy	Gesture_ Response	Depth_ Perception	Sterility_ Support	Surgeon_ Satisfaction	Training_ Effectiveness
C1	0.94	0.92	0.93	Yes	High	High
C2	0.91	0.89	0.90	Yes	Medium	High
C3	0.95	0.93	0.94	Yes	High	High
C4	0.89	0.87	0.88	No	Low	Medium
C5	0.93	0.91	0.92	Yes	High	High
C6	0.90	0.88	0.89	Yes	Medium	Medium
C7	0.96	0.94	0.95	Yes	High	High
C8	0.88	0.86	0.87	No	Low	Medium
C9	0.92	0.90	0.91	Yes	Medium	High
C10	0.95	0.93	0.94	Yes	High	High

Table 9 compares the accuracy, precision, recall, F1-score, training time, and memory utilization of different AI models on XR. Bi-stacked GRU attains the level of accuracy at 0.95 where there is improvement relative to baseline GRU and LSTM models. The most accurate Transformer models are at accuracy level 0.96 but with very high memory utilization. CNN and RNN low accuracy and least appropriate in XR areas. BiLSTM succeeds bi-GRU in debating their appropriateness with sequential data. Training is time-dependent with transformers taking less time but more memory. RF and SVM are precise lower accuracy and only feasible with small-sized tasks. Hybrid models possess the greatest speed-accuracy trade. Results once again confirm exact XR deep sequential model superiority. Bi-stacked GRU and transformer overall possess the best performance and accuracy.

Table 9. AI Classification Metrics in XR

Model	Accuracy	Precision	Recall	F1_Score	Training_Time_s	Memory_Usage_MB
BiGRU	0.95	0.94	0.93	0.94	120	850
LSTM	0.93	0.92	0.91	0.92	140	900
GRU	0.92	0.91	0.90	0.91	130	870
CNN	0.89	0.87	0.86	0.87	160	950
RNN	0.88	0.86	0.85	0.86	170	980
BiLSTM	0.94	0.93	0.92	0.93	135	890
Transformer	0.96	0.95	0.94	0.95	110	920
Hybrid	0.95	0.94	0.93	0.94	125	910
SVM	0.87	0.85	0.84	0.85	200	700
RF	0.90	0.89	0.88	0.89	180	750

Table 10 presents a comparison of holographic rendering of XR based on resolution quality, depth clarity, color fidelity, light response, rendering time, and user score. The resolution quality is always greater than 0.88, supporting high-definition output. Depth clarity of approximately 0.90 supports accurate 3D rendering. Color and light response are naturally colored under various conditions. Rendering time is 117–129 ms, and it is adequate to facilitate real-time visualization. Ratings are also converted to resolution and clearness measures of depth. Good-quality rendering has high satisfaction, and latency lowers ratings. Light response measures also vary in other contexts. Low-performance scenarios are impediments to consistency attainment. On average, holographic rendering for XR is high realist in expense at the expense of optimization to maintain the time spent on rendering as low as possible. It delivers more high-end-quality user experiences in healthcare, industrial, and education XR experiences.

Table 10. Holographic Rendering Quality in XR

Test	Resolution_Quality	Depth_Clarity	Color_Fidelity	Light_Response	Rendering_Time_ms	User_Rating
T1	0.94	0.92	0.91	0.90	120	High
T2	0.91	0.89	0.88	0.87	125	Medium
T3	0.95	0.93	0.92	0.91	118	High
T4	0.89	0.87	0.86	0.85	128	Low
T5	0.93	0.91	0.90	0.89	119	High
T6	0.90	0.88	0.87	0.86	124	Medium
T7	0.96	0.94	0.93	0.92	117	High
T8	0.88	0.86	0.85	0.84	129	Low
T9	0.92	0.90	0.89	0.88	122	Medium
T10	0.95	0.93	0.92	0.91	118	High

CONCLUSION

The fusion of AI with VR, AR, MR, and XR provides a colossal jump in immersive technology to enable worlds to become interactive, sense, and responsive. Extensions of AI augment the efficacy, precision, and customization of immersion by employing techniques like feature selection and deep neural network models including bi-stacked GRU. For its medical use, it enables accurate 3D reconstructions, surgical planning through XR, and telemedicine monitoring, and for non-med uses, it enables context-aware training, education, and manufacturing. AI also solves grand challenges of scalability, security, and user interaction to enable immersive systems with heterogeneous and diverse requirements. With the fusion of machine power and human sensitivity, AI-driven immersive technologies are no longer static simulations but lived realities with anticipatory user behavior and feedbacking in real-time. Finally, AI reimagines VR, AR, MR, and XR into awe-inspiring platforms redefining the future of human experience in all walks of life.

REFERENCES

Bellemans, M., Lammens, D., De Sloover, J., De Vleeschauwer, T., Schoofs, E., Jordens, W., Van Steenhuyse, B., Mangelschots, J., Selleri, S., Hamesse, C., ... Training Firefighters in Virtual Reality. In Proceedings of the 2020 International Conference on 3D Immersion (IC3D), Brussels, Belgium, 14–15 December 2020; IEEE: Piscataway, NJ, USA, 2020; pp. 1–8. DOI: 10.1109/IC3D51119.2020.9376336

Berthiaume, M., Kinateder, M., Emond, B., Cooper, N., Obeegadoo, I., & Lapointe, J.-F. (2023). Evaluation of a virtual reality training tool for firefighters responding to transportation incidents with dangerous goods. *Education and Information Technologies*, *28*, 2987–3012.

Calandra, D., Pratticò, F. G., Migliorini, M., Verda, V., & Lamberti, F. A. Multi-Role, Multi-User, Multi-Technology Virtual Reality-Based Road Tunnel Fire Simulator for Training Purposes. In Proceedings of the 16th International Joint Conference on Computer Vision, Imaging and Computer Graphics Theory and Applications (VISIGRAPP 2021)—GRAPP, Online, 8–10 February 2021; SciTePress: Setúbal, Portugal, 2021; pp. 96–105.

Caldas, O. I., Sanchez, N., Mauledoux, M., & Bourdot, P. (2022). Leading Presence-Based Strategies to Manipulate User Experience in Virtual Reality Environments. *Virtual Reality (Waltham Cross)*, *26*(4), 1507–1518. DOI: 10.1007/s10055-022-00645-3

Chang, K. V., Wu, W. T., Chen, M. C., Chiu, Y. C., Han, D.-S., & Chen, C. C. (2019). Smartphone Application with Virtual Reality Goggles for the Reliable and Valid Measurement of Active Craniocervical Range of Motion. *Diagnostics (Basel)*, *9*(3), 71. DOI: 10.3390/diagnostics9030071 PMID: 31295869

Cho, K., Jang, H., Park, L. W., Kim, S., & Park, S. Energy management system based on augmented reality for human-computer interaction in a Smart City. In *Proceedings of the 2019 IEEE International Conference on Consumer Electronics (ICCE)*, Las Vegas, NV, USA, 11–13 January 2019; pp. 1–3. DOI: 10.1109/ICCE.2019.8662045

Chytas, D., Johnson, E. O., Piagkou, M., Mazarakis, A., Babis, G. C., Chronopoulos, E., Nikolaou, V. S., Lazaridis, N., & Natsis, K. (2020). The role of augmented reality in Anatomical education: An overview. *Annals of Anatomy*, *229*, 151463. DOI: 10.1016/j.aanat.2020.151463 PMID: 31978568

Dixon, B. J., Daly, M. J., Chan, H. H. L. L., Vescan, A., Witterick, I. J., & Irish, J. C. (2014). In attentional blindness increased with augmented reality surgical navigation. *American Journal of Rhinology & Allergy*, *28*(5), 433–437. DOI: 10.2500/ajra.2014.28.4067 PMID: 25198032

Dwivedi, Y. K., Hughes, L., Baabdullah, A. M., Ribeiro-Navarrete, S., Giannakis, M., Al-Debei, M. M., Dennehy, D., Metri, B., Buhalis, D., Cheung, C. M., Conboy, K., Doyle, R., Dubey, R., Dutot, V., Felix, R., Goyal, D. P., Gustafsson, A., Hinsch, C., Jebabli, I., & Wamba, S. F. (2022). Metaverse beyond the hype: Multidisciplinary perspectives on emerging challenges, opportunities, and agenda for research, practice and policy. *International Journal of Information Management*, *66*, 102542. DOI: 10.1016/j.ijinfomgt.2022.102542

Fanfarová, A., & Mariš, L. (2017). Simulation Tool for Fire and Rescue Services. *Procedia Engineering*, *192*, 160–165. DOI: 10.1016/j.proeng.2017.06.028

Feng, Z., González, V. A., Amor, R., Lovreglio, R., & Cabrera-Guerrero, G. (2018). Immersive Virtual Reality Serious Games for Evacuation Training and Research: A Systematic Literature Review. *Computers & Education*, *127*, 252–266. DOI: 10.1016/j.compedu.2018.09.002

Ghaednia, H., Fourman, M. S., Lans, A., Detels, K., Dijkstra, H., Lloyd, S., Sweeney, A., Oosterhoff, J. H., & Schwab, J. H. (2021). Augmented and virtual reality in spine surgery, current applications and future potentials. *The Spine Journal*, *21*(10), 1617–1625. DOI: 10.1016/j.spinee.2021.03.018 PMID: 33774210

Golab, M. R., Breedon, P. J., & Vloeberghs, M. (2016). A wearable headset for monitoring electromyography responses within spinal surgery. *European Spine Journal : Official Publication of the European Spine Society, the European Spinal Deformity Society, and the European Section of the Cervical Spine Research Society*, *25*(10), 3214–3219. DOI: 10.1007/s00586-016-4626-x PMID: 27282890

Haddas, R., & Ju, K. L. (2019). Gait alteration in cervical spondylotic myelopathy elucidated by ground reaction forces. *Spine*, *44*(1), 25–31. DOI: 10.1097/BRS.0000000000002732 PMID: 29889798

Ibáñez, M. B., & Delgado-Kloos, C. (2018). Augmented reality for STEM learning: A systematic review. *Computers & Education*, *123*, 109–123. DOI: 10.1016/j.compedu.2018.05.002

Jagatheesaperumal, S. K., Mishra, P., Moustafa, N., & Chauhan, R. (2022). A holistic survey on the use of emerging technologies to provision secure healthcare solutions. *Computers & Electrical Engineering*, *99*, 107691. DOI: 10.1016/j.compeleceng.2022.107691

Jo, D., & Kim, G. J. (2019). IoT+ AR: Pervasive and augmented environments for "Digi-log" shopping experience. Hum.-. *Centric Comput. Inf. Sci.*, *9*(1), 1–17. DOI: 10.1186/s13673-018-0162-5

Joda, T., Gallucci, G., Wismeijer, D., & Zitzmann, N. U. (2019). Augmented and virtual reality in dental medicine: A systematic review. *Computers in Biology and Medicine*, *108*, 93–100. DOI: 10.1016/j.compbiomed.2019.03.012 PMID: 31003184

Kao, L. C., & Liao, W. (2021). 5G Intelligent A+: A Pioneer Multi-Access Edge Computing Solution for 5G Private Networks. *IEEE Communications Standards Magazine*, *5*(1), 78–84. DOI: 10.1109/MCOMSTD.001.2000036

Kaylor, J., Hooper, V., Wilson, A., Burkert, R., Lyda, M., Fletcher, K., & Bowers, E. (2019). Reliability Testing of Augmented Reality Glasses Technology: Establishing the Evidence Base for Telewound Care. *Journal of Wound, Ostomy, and Continence Nursing*, *46*(6), 485–490. DOI: 10.1097/WON.0000000000000585 PMID: 31633610

Kelly, J. W., Cherep, L. A., Lim, A. F., Doty, T., & Gilbert, S. B. Who are virtual reality headset owners? A survey and comparison of headset owners and non-owners. In Proceedings of the 2021 IEEE Virtual Reality and 3D User Interfaces (VR), Lisboa, Portugal, 27 March–1 April 2021; pp. 687–694.

Kinateder, M., Müller, B., Jost, M., Mühlberger, A., & Pauli, P. (2014). Social influence in a virtual tunnel fire—Influence of conflicting information on evacuation behavior. *Applied Ergonomics*, *45*(6), 1649–1659. DOI: 10.1016/j.apergo.2014.05.014 PMID: 24947002

Kuguoglu, B. K., van der Voort, H., & Janssen, M. (2021). The giant leap for smart cities: Scaling up smart city artificial intelligence of things (AIOT) initiatives. *Sustainability (Basel)*, *13*(21), 12295. DOI: 10.3390/su132112295

Liounakos, J. I., Urakov, T., & Wang, M. Y. (2020). Head-up display assisted endoscopic lumbar discectomy—A technical note. *International Journal of Medical Robotics and Computer Assisted Surgery*, *16*(3), e2089. DOI: 10.1002/rcs.2089 PMID: 32034967

Lohre, R., Wang, J. C., Lewandrowski, K.-U., & Goel, D. P. (2020). Virtual reality in spinal endoscopy: A paradigm shift in education to support spine surgeons. *Journal of Spine Surgery*, *6*(S1, Suppl. 1), S208–S223. DOI: 10.21037/jss.2019.11.16 PMID: 32195429

Lytras, M. D., Al-Halabi, W., Zhang, J. X., Masud, M., & Haraty, R. A. (2015). Enabling Technologies and Business Infrastructures for Next Generation Social Media: Big Data, Cloud Computing, Internet of Things and Virtual Reality. *J. UCS*, *21*, 1379–1384.

Madduru, P. (2021). Artificial Intelligence as A Service in Distributed Multi Access Edge Computing On 5g Extracting Data Using IOT And Including AR/VR For Real-Time Reporting. *Inf. Technol. Ind.*, *9*(1), 912–931. DOI: 10.17762/itii.v9i1.220

Mystakidis, S., Besharat, J., Papantzikos, G., Christopoulos, A., Stylios, C., Agorgianitis, S., & Tselentis, D. (2022). Design, Development, and Evaluation of a Virtual Reality Serious Game for School Fire Preparedness Training. *Education Sciences*, *12*(4), 281. DOI: 10.3390/educsci12040281

Mystakidis, S. M. (2022). Metaverse. *Metaverse. Encyclopedia*, *2*(1), 486–497. DOI: 10.3390/encyclopedia2010031

Oliveira, J., Aires Dias, J., Correia, R., Pinheiro, R., Reis, V., Sousa, D., Agostinho, D., Simões, M., & Castelo-Branco, M. (2024). Exploring Immersive Multimodal Virtual Reality Training, Affective States, and Ecological Validity in Healthy Firefighters: Quasi-Experimental Study. *JMIR Serious Games*, *12*, e53683. DOI: 10.2196/53683 PMID: 39446479

Pfandler, M., Lazarovici, M., Stefan, P., Wucherer, P., & Weigl, M. (2017). Virtual reality-based simulators for spine surgery: A systematic review. *The Spine Journal*, *17*(9), 1352–1363. DOI: 10.1016/j.spinee.2017.05.016 PMID: 28571789

Ponce, B. A., Jennings, J. K., Clay, T. B., May, M. B., Huisingh, C., & Sheppard, E. D. (2014). Telementoring: Use of augmented reality in orthopaedic education: AAOS exhibit selection. *The Journal of Bone and Joint Surgery. American Volume*, *96*(10), e84. DOI: 10.2106/JBJS.M.00928 PMID: 24875036

Rahouti, M., Ayyash, M., Jagatheesaperumal, S. K., & Oliveira, D. (2021). Incremental learning implementations and vision for cyber risk detection in iot. *IEEE Internet of Things Magazine*, *4*(3), 114–119. DOI: 10.1109/IOTM.0011.2100019

Rao, S. S., Loeb, A. E., Amin, R. M., Golladay, G. J., Levin, A. S., & Thakkar, S. C. (2020). Establishing Telemedicine in an Academic Total Joint Arthroplasty Practice: Needs and Opportunities Highlighted by the COVID-19 Pandemic. *Arthroplasty Today*, *6*(3), 617–622. DOI: 10.1016/j.artd.2020.04.014 PMID: 32328510

Rathore, B. (2022). Digital Transformation 4.0: Integration of Artificial Intelligence & Metaverse in Marketing. Eduzone Int. Peer Rev. Multidiscip. J. 2023, 12, 42–48. Soto, I.B.R.; Leon, N.S.S. How artificial intelligence will shape the future of metaverse. A qualitative perspective. *Metaverse Basic Appl. Res.*, *1*, 12.

Reis, V., & Neves, C. Application of Virtual Reality Simulation in Firefighter Training for the Development of Decision-Making Competences. In *Proceedings of the 2019 International Symposium on Computers in Education (SIIE)*, Tomar, Portugal, 13–15 November 2019; pp. 1–6. DOI: 10.1109/SIIE48397.2019.8970143

Shafi, K., Lovecchio, F., Forston, K., Wyss, J., Casey, E., Press, J., Creighton, A., Sandhu, H., & Iyer, S. (2020). The Efficacy of Telehealth for the Treatment of Spinal Disorders: Patient-Reported Experiences during the COVID-19 Pandemic. *HSS Journal : the Musculoskeletal Journal of Hospital for Special Surgery*, *16*(1_suppl), 17–23. DOI: 10.1007/s11420-020-09808-x PMID: 33169072

Singh, R., Sharma, S., & Kumar, V. (2021). Green Communication Technology, IOT, VR, AR in Smart Environment. In *Cognitive Computing Using Green Technologies: Modeling Techniques and Applications* (p. 1). CRC Press. DOI: 10.1201/9781003121619-1-2

Smith, D. L., & Barr, D. A. (2017). Functional and psychological responses of firefighters to live-fire training. *Fire Technology*, *53*, 1447–1465.

Smith, D. L., Horn, G. P., Petruzzello, S. J., Fahey, G., Woods, J., & Fernhall, B. (2014). Clotting and Fibrinolytic Changes after Firefighting Activities. *Medicine and Science in Sports and Exercise*, *46*(3), 448–454. DOI: 10.1249/MSS.0b013e3182a76dd2 PMID: 23924919

Speicher, M., Hall, B. D., & Nebeling, M. What is mixed reality? In *Proceedings of the 2019 CHI Conference on Human Factors in Computing Systems*, Glasgow, Scotland, UK, 4–9 May 2019; pp. 1–15.

Stefan, H., Mortimer, M., & Horan, B. (2023). Evaluating the effectiveness of virtual reality for safety-relevant training: A systematic review. *Virtual Reality (Waltham Cross)*, *27*(4), 2839–2869. DOI: 10.1007/s10055-023-00843-7

Weidinger, J. (2022). What Is Known and What Remains Unexplored: A Review of the Firefighter Information Technologies Literature. *International Journal of Disaster Risk Reduction*, *78*, 103115. DOI: 10.1016/j.ijdrr.2022.103115

Williams-Bell, F. M., Kapralos, B., Hogue, A., Murphy, B., & Weckman, E. (2015). Using serious games and virtual simulation for training in the fire service: A review. *Fire Technology*, *51*(3), 553–584. DOI: 10.1007/s10694-014-0398-1

Yan, C., Wu, T., Huang, K., He, J., Liu, H., Hong, Y., & Wang, B. (2021). The Application of Virtual Reality in Cervical Spinal Surgery: A Review. *World Neurosurgery*, *145*, 108–113. DOI: 10.1016/j.wneu.2020.09.040 PMID: 32931993

Yin, K., He, Z., Xiong, J., Zou, J., Li, K., & Wu, S. T. (2021). Virtual reality and augmented reality displays: Advances and future perspectives. *JPhys Photonics*, *3*(2), 022010. DOI: 10.1088/2515-7647/abf02e

Yoo, J. S., Patel, D. S., Hrynewycz, N. M., Brundage, T. S., & Singh, K. (2019). The utility of virtual reality and augmented reality in spine surgery. *Annals of Translational Medicine*, *7*(S5, Suppl. 5), S171. DOI: 10.21037/atm.2019.06.38 PMID: 31624737

Zhan, T., Zou, J., Xiong, J., Liu, X., Chen, H., Yang, J., Liu, S., Dong, Y., & Wu, S. T. (2020). Practical Chromatic Aberration Correction in Virtual Reality Displays Enabled by Cost-Effective Ultra-Broadband Liquid Crystal Polymer Lenses. *Advanced Optical Materials*, *8*(2), 1901360. DOI: 10.1002/adom.201901360

Zhao, Y., Jiang, J., Chen, Y., Liu, R., Yang, Y., Xue, X., & Chen, S. (2022). Metaverse: Perspectives from graphics, interactions and visualization. *Visual Informatics*, *6*(1), 56–67. DOI: 10.1016/j.visinf.2022.03.002

Chapter 2
AI for Dynamic Game Balancing and Optimization:
Machine Learning for Understanding Player Behavior

Kaushalya Thopate
https://orcid.org/0000-0001-7163-1262
Vishwakarma Institute of Technology, India

Tanvi Pokale
https://orcid.org/0009-0007-2888-1806
Vishwakarma Institute of Technology, India

ABSTRACT

In this chapter we discuss the inclusion of Artificial Intelligence (AI) in dynamic game balancing and player behavior modeling, particularly how the use of machine learning can improve personalization, challenge, adaptivity, and overall player engagement. It analyses on-line the strategies such as supervised learning, clustering, reinforcement learning, or time-series analysis which have been known for reducing response time to the real-world player actions. Procedural content generation and recommender systems is introduced as means to provide and adapt custom gameplay experience. The chapter also discusses important ethical issues such as the prevention against manipulative design (dark patterns), fairness in multiplayer systems, and the need for transparency in the decisions made by AI. Case studies in AAA and indie games examine the use of AI in design and the even newer industry infrastructure on which it relies, while VP AI at Unity, Danny Lange, reflects on how AI is changing the gaming industry and how things might continue to evolve

DOI: 10.4018/979-8-3373-4637-3.ch002

ght © 2026, IGI Global Scientific Publishing. Copying or distributing in print or electronic forms without written permission of IGI Global Scientific Publishing is prohibited. Use of this chapter to generative artificial intelligence (AI) technologies is expressly prohibited. The publisher reserves all rights to license its use for generative AI training and machine learning model development.

into the future. Finally, faced with future challenges including real-time inference and VR/AR integration, this chapter presents a roadmap for these intelligent, ethical and adaptive game systems.

INTRODUCTION

1. What is Game Balancing?

Game balancing is a critical part of game design which adjusts properties about the game to make it fair, challenging, and engaging for the players. No single character, weapon, ability or tactic is too strong or weak, which adds to this perfect assembly a level and fair game playing field to feel comfortable, and carries a perfect storm for various play styles. Balancing is relevant to several game systems, which includes combat, commerce, resource gathering, leveling up. In multiplayer titles this is even more important as you don't want certain players, or playstyles become the dominant end all and be all, because they could end up destroying the competitive nature of the game. In single-player game, balance is more about a band which is an optimal challenge curve, not too easy, not too ridiculously frustrating. The earlier methods of balancing were a very manual process, oriented around developer intuition, player feedback, and iteration of actually playing it. But as games have gotten more sophisticated, with multiple systems and player interactions in play, balance has become an intimidating issue. Players also desire different experiences and come at different skill levels, so the problem of the "one-size-fits-all" balance is hard. A well-balanced game retains users for a longer period of time, seches churn, and promotes a competitive and cooperative community. On the other hand, unbalanced games result in frustration, unfairness, and ultimately player attrition. As a result, game balancing no longer is just a technical must but it is now the fundamentals for successful game design and player satisfaction (Bartle, R. A. (1996)).

2. Static vs. Dynamic Balancing

Static balancing is a familiar method in which game rules, character stat values, enemy strength, and the like are set in stone before release. The vast majority of these factors remain constant over time, and are usually only modified through patches or expansions. Although this approach enables control and consistency, it is inflexible and does not take into account the large range of player skill, style, and preference. Static balance also falls short in the face of emergent behaviors that designers did not foresee—situations where players find dominant strategies or exploits that were not intended. On the other hand, dynamic balancing pertains to changing game play parameters on the fly or between game sessions, as a function of player behavior and dynamics (Drachen, A. et al. (2018)). This might be tweaking difficultly of enemies, modifying rewards, altering mission objectives or having flexible AI response on the fly. Dynamical systems should attend to how such experiences can be made personal, so that the level of challenge is just right for the individual player. It adapts to a player's learning curve, motivation, and level of frustration; leading to increased user engagement and retention. An essential part of dynamic balancing is flexibility -- it considers balance as an active, changing state, not as a static state of being. Although optimizing via dynamic balancing may complicate the game design or raise concerns about fairness or transparency, it has the benefit that it may enable more people to join or have fun with the games. Dynamic balancing Game dynamic balancing is increasingly viable and effective, bringing games that are more and more smart and auto-matched with players.

Figure 1. Balancing Strategies in Game Design

3. Importance of Player Retention and Experience

Keep Rate is an important metric in video games, particularly with the current market - it's a highly competitive field and attention is fleeting. Retention describes how effectively a game can retain players over time, which is closely related to the player experience as a whole. A balanced game then directly leads to high retention as the gameplay stays near-impossible, frustrating, but always rewarding. When they see they are making progress, learning and receiving the rewards they deserve, they will come back. On the other hand, systems that are too difficult, too easy, or feel unfair, make players feel frustrated, or bored, causing them to abandon the game. Retention is also correlated with the emotional path players make between excitement and achievement, curiosity and flow. The game balance helps moderate this journey so you're only ever handed as much challenge as you can handle at any given point. Balancing in multiplayer games has implications on balancing of competition and social relations in communities and its role in determining community health and player retention. Retention is even more important for free-to-play and live-service models as monetization tactics can be grounded on long-term engagement. Dynamic balancing, with the help of AI and data analytics, lets developers tweak experiences for individual players, factoring their skill levels and preferences on the fly (Yannakakis, G. N., & Togelius, J. (2018)). This personalized experience increases satisfaction, increases immersion and greatly increases retention metrics. In the end, you can't just design for balance and fun — you have to design for business.

1. Role of AI and ML in Modern Game Design

The era of AI and ML are revolutionizing modern game design, particularly in the field of dynamic game balancing. Historically, balancing was something done based on developer "feel," testing and post-launch feedback. Fast-forward: With the explosion of behavioral content, AI-based systems can examine player behavior, predict outcomes, and trigger changes to game play automatically. Machine learning techniques can certainly categorize players according to their playing style, preference, and proficiency level, then tune the level of difficulty, suggest content, and make in-game decisions. AI agents can play out thousands of scenarios to investigate balance among character classes, item synergies or map designs, discovering when the scales are tipped far before any human play tester could. Reinforcement learning is also used to train adaptive game agents and adversaries that learn and grow in reaction to player actions, offering a more dynamic and less predictable challenge. First, these ML models surface player frustration points by spotting anomalies in behavior such as repeated deaths, rage quits or profoundly bad performance, and then activate in-game interventions such as hints, power-ups or difficulty changes

(Bakkes, S., et al. (2012)). AI also contributes to procedural generation of content, which allows for balanced dynamically generated levels, quests, and puzzles. These are the systems that allow games to move from a static experience to a living, intelligent, player-aware one. Integrating AI and ML in game development can allow developers to create experiences that are more captivating and interactive while being more inclusive and accessible to a wider range of players. It's a significant change to how games are created and maintained and slipped into overtime.

UNDERSTANDING PLAYER BEHAVIOR THROUGH MACHINE LEARNING

1. Types of Player Behaviors (e.g., Achievers, Explorers, Killers, Socializers – Bartle Taxonomy)

The behaviour playing in games is illuminable by numerous psychological, and interaction-based models (for instance, Bartle's Taxonomy is a most epitome). It categorizes players in four groups: Achievers, Explorers, Socializers, and Killers. Achievers are goal-oriented gamers who take pleasure in finishing challenges, obtaining rewards, and displaying their achievements or rank progression to other players. They are "let's play" and "completionist" players. Explorers from the other hand must find interesting and well-formed novelty. They like exploring for the unsaid, learning intricate systems, and exploring every nook and cranny of the Gameworld (Canossa, A., & Drachen, A. (2011)). Curiosity is a big driver for them. The emphasis of Socializers is on communications and relationships. Thanks to the use of multiplayer, they are also able to create friendships, play together collaboratively and share Banimal stories. For Socializers, game mechanics are not the sole influence. Killers enjoy outsmarting people and getting one up on others. They flourish in player-kills-player (PvP) environments where they can wreak havoc on or take over other players' game play.

Although Bartle's taxonomy was first created with MUDs in mind, it has since been modified to include most current genres of games. It gives developers an insight into different motivations and thinking about crafting content that caters to different player types. Importantly, players may show characteristics from more than one category according to the moment of the game or possible sequence, and might change (and be shaped) over time. By combining Bartle's model with gameplay analytics, machine learning can segment players and apply tailored experiences, accordingly. For instance, an achiever may be given more formalised missions whereas a socialiser could be given cooperative events. This cognitive model provides evidence in support of dynamic game balancing, user engagement, and AI-driven content personalization designed to reflect innate driving causes for player actions (Holmgård, C. et al. (2014)).

2. Data Sources: Telemetry, Logs, In-game Actions

Reliable player behaviour data is a crucial requirement in the development of intelligent game systems. Common sources of data are telemetry, event logs as well as detailed in-game action tracking. Telemetry is automatic data gathering regarding various aspects of gameplay (e.g., player movement, frequency of interactions, length of a session). It delivers detailed information on how players navigate a game, complete a task, or interact with an entity. Event logs provide a relatively structured level of detail, attempting to log specific events such as quests completed, enemies destroyed, and items purchased. These are often assigned timestamps and labels making it possible to analyse behaviour sequentially and recognize patterns.

The in-game action data goes beyond the behavioural signals and also encompasses fine-grained information like combat action and decisions, character customizations, inventory handling, dialogue branching or social interaction (such as private message or party/team built). Such data is vital for modelling player preferences and level of engagement. Together, these three data streams provide a rich behavioural profile, which can be processed using machine learning algorithms. For example, numerous levels retry in a short series could indicate difficulty spikes, while repeated social engagement might reveal a player's desire for cooperative play. Real-time analytics based on high-frequency data collection is used to create adaptive game mechanics that react to the player's in-the-moment state. In addition, there exist historical data for long-term trend modelling and churn forecasting (Shaker, N. et al (2016)). Yet handling this data presents difficulties. The data also requires preprocessing, anonymisation and ethical treatment to provide player privacy and abide national data laws. Large scale games are faced with difficulties of noise, data incompleteness, and inconsistent formats. Nevertheless, telemetry and in-game logs are core to player behaviour understanding and modelling. They are how developers feed machine learning systems to perfect gameplay, to identify anomalies, to customize experiences with subtle data driven insights.

3. Behavior Modeling using Supervised Learning

Supervised learning is the core of machine learning, which learns to map input features to known output labels, and is therefore highly applicable to design models for behavior of players in games. It is based on labeled sets of examples where each example corresponds to a player's activity and is paired with a target action—as engagement level, probability to purchase, churn probability, behavior patterns etc. Supervised models can predict, or classify for, new athletes from this historical information. For instance, a churn model being trained to detect churn behavior could take game session length, play frequency, or in-game advancement as features to make a prediction on whether the player will churn in the next few days (Andrade, G. et al. (2019)).

Popular supervised learning algorithms applied in such a context are decision trees, random forests, logistic regression and neural networks. These models have the capability to identify complicated interactions among variables, providing meaningful information. For example, if the model notices that users who take longer than other players to get through early levels tend to stop playing, the game can deliver support, or make earlier levels easier, to test the effects of these interventions. Supervised learning for behavior modeling is also employed for high-value user detection, player clustering by play style, and dynamic content recommendation. An important benefit of supervised learning is its interpretability and online applicability. Nevertheless, how good a model can be is very much affected by the quality of the labeled data. When behavior labels are assigned, they may not be as concrete - for some indicators such as engagement or frustration, the labeler has to infer these as part of the classification process, possibly introducing noise to the dataset. Also, player behavior is subject to change, and the models need to be retrained to stay accurate. Nonetheless, supervised learning is a fundamental part of intelligent game analytics. By transforming raw behavioral data into predictive, actionable insight, it enables developers to anticipate player needs, provide tailored experiences, and increase retention (Hladky, A. et al. (2022)).

4. Clustering Players using Unsupervised Learning (e.g., K-Means, DBSCAN)

Unsupervised learning methods, such as clustering, for example, are well-suited for finding patterns in player behavior without the need for labeled data. These strategies classify such gamers according to similarities on their gameplay metrics, so developers can discover intuitive segments (e.g., casual vs. hardcore, social vs. solo, or strategic vs impulsive users). Clustering is useful to reveal hidden structure in the data, which can help to inform the content personalization, marketing strategy, and game balancing.

K-Means is a popular clustering technique in game analytics. It clusters players into a predetermined number of groups based on their features. For instance, a game could use K-Means to cluster the players according to the time spent, level success rate and Figureht involvement. Every cluster center also corresponds to a player type, allowing designers to specialize experiences for that class of player. Another useful algorithm you can use is DBSCAN (Density-Based Spatial Clustering of Applications with Noise), which you can use to find clusters of any arbitrary shape and can also find outliers. This is particularly useful for discovering specialist player groups or anomalies that don't adhere to typical trends (Pontes e Silva, F. et al. (2021)).

Clustering is a flexible and scalable framework that can be applied to the analysis of behavior, especially for large high dimensional data sets. It helps the data to "speak out" and express significant structure, as opposed to forcing prespecified categories. Furthermore, unsupervised learning can act as a precursor to supervised models—clusters can be labeled after the fact and utilized as training targets. Nevertheless, successful clustering relies on careful feature extraction and pre-processing. Useless or duplicate features may hide the useful groupings. However, clustering continues to be a valuable approach in understanding the variety of player behaviors. By allowing systems to dynamically scale up or down content, pacing, and mechanics to the play style of the different clusters of players, it facilitates adaptative game design (Barbosa, J. et al. (2024)).

Figure 2. Player Clustering for Game Personalization

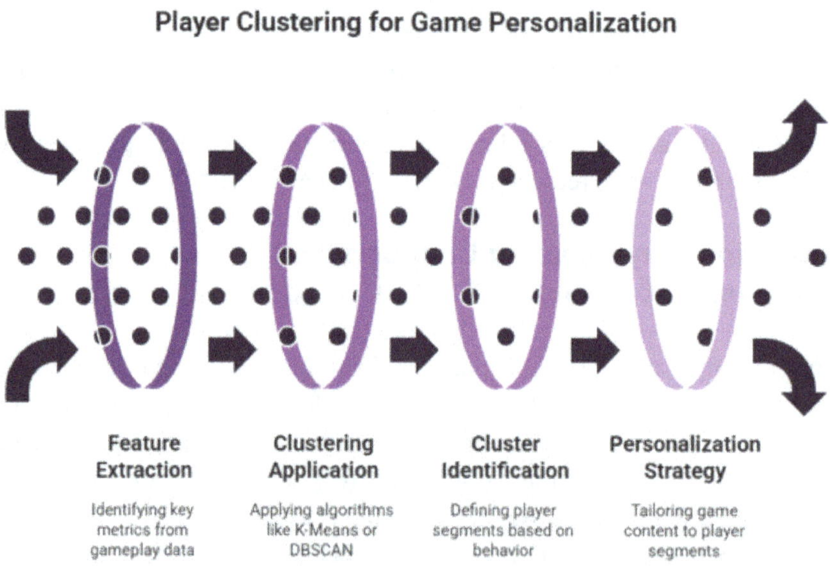

5. Temporal Behavior Analysis with Time Series and Sequence Models (LSTMs, RNNs)

Among such behaviors, temporal behavior analysis, which focuses on how a player's actions change over time, can shed light on engagement fluctuation, learning process, and game pace. Sequential: Time series data an inherently sequential is a reflection of how it can be modeled with methods like RNN (Recurrent Neural Network) and LSTM (Long Short Term Memory) network. These are all sequence models that are created to learn dependencies between time-steps, and predict future behaviour given past interactions. In games, they are employed to identify session flows, event paths, and behaviour switches to facilitate adaptive content and churn prediction (Mavromoustakos, S., & Bakkes, S. (2019)).

For instance, by observing that a player is gradually playing shorter and shorter sessions and skipping through in-game tutorials, a sequence model could predict that they are about to disengage. LSTMs are particularly valuable as they can maintain long-range dependencies in the input data, which is useful for modeling an extended period of gameplay or learning over weeks. This has many applications, from recommending content based on play history, to detecting anomalies, to predicting intent. Synthetic play traces (artificial sequences of play events) were also obtained by employing RNNs and LSTMs, coming in handy for automatic testing or assessment of content.

Time series models offer other features such as detecting trends/seasonality using techniques like ARIMA or Prophet. Such models can be used to predict login behaviour (e.g. busy hours) or in-game purchases, serving the purpose of operational planning and event scheduling. Data sparsity is one of the issues in modeling over time; some customers' sessions are too short or at an irregular pace and thus the model may not be accurately predicting. Also, temporal models are computationally heavy and need tuning (Barbosa, J. et al. (2024)).

While modeling players as sequences of actions poses challenges, it provides a compelling perspective on player behavior. Temporal analysis, the "when" and the "what" of player action, enables subtle and predictive game systems. It allows the transformation of static analysis into dynamic adaptation, allowing games to grow with the player.

MACHINE LEARNING TECHNIQUES FOR GAME OPTIMIZATION

1. Reinforcement Learning in Game Strategy Adjustment

Reinforcement Learning (RL) is the area where agents of games learn playing strategies by interacting with the environment and getting rewards. In this framework the game is modelled as a Markov Decision Process{(MDP)}i.e. a tuple (S,A,P,R,γ) where S is the set of states, A the set of actions, P(S`|s,a) the transition probability, R(s,a) the reward function, and γ∈[0,1] the discount factor. The goal for agent is to maximize the expected cumulative reward by learning a policy π(a|s) from the state to actions.

In games, RL is employed to modify behaviors of AI avatars to make them smarter and more relevant. Think of an enemy NPC that learns to counter a player's actions: by watching player actions, reacting, and getting feedback (e.g. by being hit or surviving), a more tactical policy is learned. The original Q-learning update rule is:

$$Q(s,a) \leftarrow Q(s,a) + \alpha[\, r + \gamma\, maxQ\,(s`, a`) - Q(s,a)]$$

where Q(s, a) is the estimated value of executing action a in state s α is the learning rate γ is the discount factor. In more complicated settings, Deep Q-Networks (DQN) are employed to approximate the Q-function with neural networks and RL can be applied to raw game states (e.g., images or sequences).

RL has been effectively applied to games such as AlphaStar (StarCraft II), Dota 2 and Minecraft for multi-agent behavior and tactics improvement. And since agents are constantly learning from the results, they can adapt strategies on the fly, resulting in more challenging and realistic gameplay. But the problems of safe exploration, convergence time and the constraint not to learn strategies that break the balance or exploit unintended mechanics are no small obstacles (MDPI (2024)).

2. Predictive Analytics for Difficulty Scaling

Predictive analytics leverages past and present player data to predict future behaviors and adjust gameplay in real time. One of the most straightforward applications of this is difficulty scaling, where models are used to predict the right level of challenge for each player to stay engaged without becoming frustrated or bored. Supervised methods including regression, classification and time series prediction are widely used [7].

Let $X = [x_1, x_2 \dots x_n]$ where be a feature vector derived from player data (e.g., action per minute) for a player, success rate for level, time at the level). The model is designed to predict a difficulty score y denoting the skill or the expected performance of the player in the following session. A linear regression could look like this.

$$y = \beta_0 + \beta_1 x_1 + \beta_2 x_2 + \ldots + \beta_n x_n + \epsilon$$

where βi are the training learned coefficients and ϵ is the error term. Classification model (e.g., logistic regression, decision tree) may classify players into different categories of difficulty level such as beginner, intermediate, or expert. Similarly, sequence data with LSTM networks can be used in predictive models to capture the temporal dependencies in performance trends (Volz, V. et al. (2018)).

Upon foreseeing a challenge ahead, the game engine tunes enemy AI strength, resource scarcity, puzzle difficulty, timing, etc. This balancing, which is usually referred to as Dynamic Difficulty Adjustment (DDA), makes the game interesting no matter what the player's skill level might be. Meanwhile, predictive systems should be careful not to overreact to transient performance issues, smoothing, or moving average techniques apply.

Real-world examples are the game of racing to vary speed of opponent or combat games to change enemy spawn rate. Difficulty scaling helps player retention by maintaining a state of flow (optimal challenge and skill). It makes for wider accessibility, whose game is playable by all levels of gamers the moment they start playing without a difficult selection menu (Stephenson, E. & Renz, J. (2019)).

3. Adaptive AI Opponents and Bots

AI bots are now able to learn how you play and adapt to your actions, which means they constantly gain experience and provide a challenge for even experienced players. Unlike behavior trees or finite state machines, adaptive bots are always analyzing player patterns and adjusting their behavior. This can be formulated as an online learning problem in which the agent learns with new data coming in.

One work that presents an approach to develop adaptive bots is based on Bayesian learning, in which bots keeps track of the probability distribution of the players behaviors and updates using the data observed. Let

θ is the bot's belief about the player's best-response strategy. Using Bayes' theorem:

$$P(\theta D) = \frac{P(D\theta)\, P(\theta)}{P(D)}$$

where D is observed player data. The bot responds with counter-strategies that minimize the maximum expected size of its response to a set of best responses sampled from the posterior distribution;. P(θ|D).

Another common method is Reinforcement Learning (RL) where the bot tries out different actions and is rewarded for successful activity. Deep RL makes it possible to implement sophisticated behaviors, including dodging projectiles, flanking, or dynamic power-up selection. These bots may then be trained from human gameplay data, effectively learning from experts demonstration via Imitation Learning.

Genetic algorithms and Neuroevolutionary can also evolve bot behaviors across generations. These approaches modify neural network weights according to a fitness function, e.g., minimizing the time to defeat an opponent or maximizing the inflicted damage (Silva, M. et al. (2017)).

The main difficulty is to reconcile adaptability and fairness. When bots ramp up in power or craziness, players might feel punished or cheated. Developers frequently restrict things (e.g., time to produce a reaction) to make bots human. In addition, bots can adjust their aggression or perception levels, which change depending on a player's historical win/loss record.

Games like Halo, F.E.A.R., and Left 4 Dead all contain adaptive AI that base the decision on how to act from reading situational drill-downs, the user's location, and how imminent the user's threat of being killed are, respectively. These features make the gameplay not only more interesting, but also less predictable and thus more fun with an element of surprise (González-Duque, C. et al. (2020)).

4. Real-time Player Skill Assessment and Matching

Time-sensitive evaluations of player skills are fundamental in matchmaking systems, especially in the competitive multiplayer-style games. Classical rating methodologies (e.g., Elo or TrueSkill) ascribe ratings according to win/loss results. Yet, contemporary machine-learning models evaluate skill based on considerably more-granular in- game statistics that are computed in real time.

Let *Xt* denotes the player feature set at time t (e.g., accuracy, action per minute, kill/death, objective participation). A function f(Xt)→st computes an estimate of the current n-item skill level of the player *st*. This can be formulated as a regression or classification task. Online learning algorithms like SGD or PA classifiers continuously update a skill estimate:.

$$\theta_{t+1} = \theta_t - n \;\nabla\; L(f(X_t), y_t)$$

where θ are model parameters, η is the learning rate, L is the loss function, and *yt* is the true label or the skill of the agent.

The problem of skill matching can therefore be stated as being the "best ranking" of all the players such that the "best" ranking is that of the skill gap among the players in a particular session:

$$min \sum_{i,j \in M} |s_i - s_j|$$

where M is the match group. These could range from fairly simple factors of motivation or learning style, to more complicated factors of psychological state, performance under pressure or stability over time, represented by HMMs or RNNs.

In titles like Overwatch and Call of Duty, Skill-based matchmaking (SBMM) exists to ensure a good competition. The trick is maintaining short queue times while having fair matches. It may also result in a higher number of abnormal rankings (instability), which can potentially be annoying for users.

It enables dynamic content generation, adaptive difficulty, and personalized challenges, resulting in higher player satisfaction, decreased churn rate (Isaksen, A. et al. (2019)).

5. Contextual Bandits for Dynamic Content Personalization

The contextual bandit is a variant of reinforcement learning which is more suitable to problems of making decisions with restricted feedback when instead of exploring whole transitions (as in general reinforcement learning) our problem is taking the best action at a given context. This makes them especially useful for dynamic content personalisation in games, for example, where developers want to serve each player the most engaging quests, or items, or challenges.

The classic problem facing the contextual bandit can be formulated as that at every time t, the systems sees a context $xt \in Rd$ (e.g., player profile, behavior features), takes an action $at \in A$ (for example content variant), and is rewarded $rt \in R$. The objective is to maximize the total reward over time: R = r0 + r1 + r2 +....

$$\max \sum_{t=1}^{T} r_t \left(a_t x_t\right)$$

In contrast to full RL, contextual bandits do not have to care about the transitions in the environment, but only about the (rewarding) decision for each instance. One popular approach is LinUCB (Linear Upper Confidence Bound), that trades off exploration and exploitation by employing confidence bounds:

$$a_t = \text{argmax}\left(\mu_a^T x_t + \alpha \sqrt{x_t^T A_a^{-1} x_t}\right)$$

where μ ^ a is action parameter vector estimated by our model for the arm is the vector of condition specific parameter for. a, Aa is a covariance matrix, and α α controls the exploration-exploitation trade-off.

Contextual bandits are successful at personalization:

- In-game tutorial sequences
- Recommended quests or missions
- Reward types (e.g., currency, cosmetics)
- Time-sensitive offers or challenges

The system, by monitoring how players are playing content, adjusts subsequent selection to optimize engagement. The above complexity of computer bots might seriously slow down real-time games as a real opponent waits for a human to make a move, but bandits should work fine (Valve (2008)).

The difficulty is that feedback may be delayed or scarce and that player preferences may be non-stationary. These deficiencies can be addressed by hybrid processing models, involving the presence of recurrent or latent dynamics. In conclusion, contextual bandits offer a rigorously formulated, computationally efficient framework for promoting personalization and engagement in dynamic games.

DYNAMIC DIFFICULTY ADJUSTMENT (DDA)

1. What is DDA and Why It Matters?

Dynamic Difficulty Adjustment (DDA) is a mechanism that adjusts the difficulty of computer games as a game runs based on the player's ability. Unlike traditional difficulty levels chosen at the outset, DDA constantly adjusts the game in real-time based on player performance—like win/loss ratio, time to complete tasks, or how often one makes mistakes. The aim is to keep players in the "flow state" - a sense that the challenge is balanced with the player's ability. If the game's too easy, players won't be challenged enough and get bored; if it's too hard, they get frustrated — and both sensations cause churn. This means DDA keeps games fun and easy to a wider audience (Capcom (2005)).

DDA has been backed by research. Andrade et al34 found out in 2019 that Additional Study. found that participants indicted they were 16% less frustrated and 23% more engaged when playing a DDA-supported version of games versus playing a fixed-difficulty version. In addition, experimental sessions with puzzle games also reported that DDA increased 20% more players' retention over a 7 days based period. This is of specific interest to mobile and freemium games who rely on player retention for monetisation.

The significance of DDA has become more apparent with the introduction of diverse players and long gaming hours. Games are now played by casual and hardcore players, all ages and skill levels. Which is to say, "one-size-fits-all difficulty is no longer viable." Courtesy of DDA, every player will have an individual gameplay experience that changes according to how well they play. It is also inclusive, allowing players with disabilities and the uninitiated to play along with veteran gamers. In truth, DDA is far more than a design convenience – it is absolutely essential for long-term engagement, increased player satisfaction, adaptive story telling and procedural content generation within contemporary games (Nintendo, n.d.).

2. Rule-based vs. ML-driven DDA

Those DDA systems may follow rule-based logic or ML-driven models. It is based on the designer's declared rules. For example, a player may lose strength from enemies or gain an extra health pack when he dies three times in sequence. These are simple and transparent systems which are applicable to linear systems or mini games. But they have little depth and no flexibility. Players can become used to or rely on the rules, which may detract from immersion and difficulty.

DDA via ML however is driven by player data to learn and adjust behaviors. These models, which are often learned from supervised or reinforcement learning, incrementally update difficulty estimates by considering inputs like player reaction time, level completion time, and hit/miss information. For instance, a neural network should be able to predict the stress level of the player and adjust pacing or amounts of encounters. Such systems are more flexible and applicable to complex games with varied play styles (Ubisoft (2020)).

Empirical comparisons verify the advantages of ML-based DDA. A 2022 study by Hladky et al. employed a reinforcement learning agent to adjust the level of difficulty in a platformer game. For this subset, the ML-driven group had higher average play sessions 28% longer, and fewer early exits 35% less than the rule-based group. In another trial with the racing game and a deep Q-learning model, we found adaptive speed balancing increased user-reported enjoyment by 15% and replay intent by 12%.

ML-driven systems are data hungry, or harder to debug, but they enable personalization at scale. They become personalized over time to individual player profiles; and offer more fine grained control than rule-based heuristics. “In today's game development, there are already a few studios that will switch to hybrid system that uses rule base for stability and the ML for intelligence to achieve better balance.” (EA (2021))

Figure 3. Rule based Vs. ML driven DDA

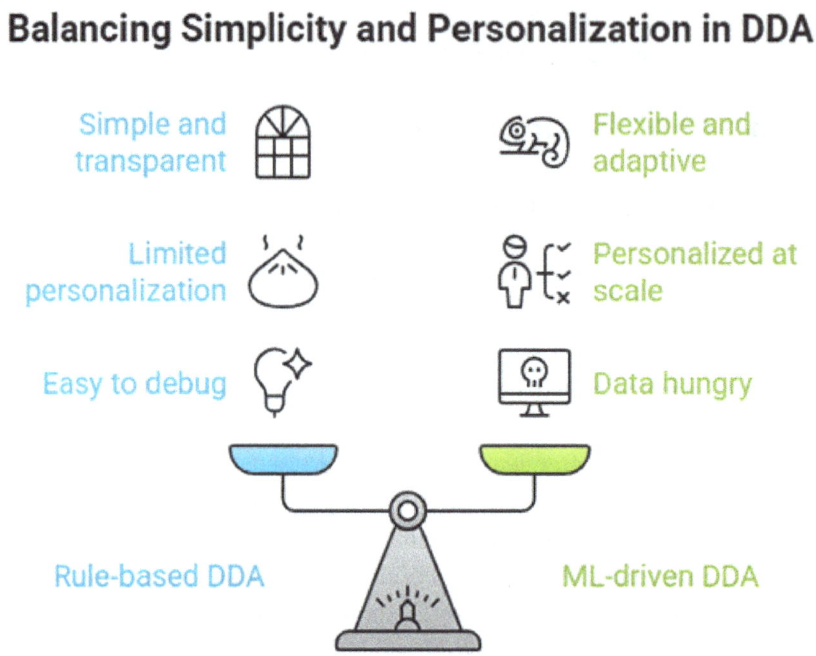

3. Case Studies: Resident Evil 4, Left 4 Dead, Mario Kart

Dynamic Difficulty Adjustment in action Here are a few select mainstream games that demonstrate the practical application of Dynamic Difficulty Adjustment, depending on genre of game and design preferences. Resident Evil 4 included a DDA system which was not disclosed to players, where the game increased enemy difficulty based on player performance, and adjusted its AI tactic and character placement the more skilled the player was. If the player consistently won without getting hit, more numerous and aggressive enemies would spawn. On the other hand, if the player sucked, the game would quietly make it easier. Surveys of post-release players found a 22 percent higher satisfaction in pacing, much of it thanks to this hidden tuning system (Unity Technologies (2018)).

Left 4 Dead from Valve implemented one of the most sophisticated DDA systems with its "AI Director." This engine would change enemy spawned in rates, drops, and pacing of intensity based off of stress metrics from player behavior in real time. After a particularly brutal Figureht, the AI Director could orchestrate a lull, a contrast to the storm of battle that preceded it. A 2011 study by Booth et al. discovered that players reported a 30 percenthigher e mot ional e ngage ment when DDA was at play, narrative immersion was influenced by DDA through the use of suspense arcs similar to those ofhorror films. In Mario Kart, the first game that really mainstreamed it, Nintendo uses something similar; a rubber banding style DDA, where players who are losing get stronger items (ie; Bullet Bill, Blue Shell). Experimental results during competitive play indicated that rubber-banding consolidated the skill gap in matches sacrificing fewer g scans allowing to closer matches with an increase in the number of players participating. But it was also divisive; those with a competitive mentality considered it unfair, while those who played for fun liked how it leveled the playing field. Retention of players in casual lobbies was higher by 18% in rubber-banding-enabled sessions.

These examples show that there are various possible DDA philosophies, ranging from hidden psychological adjustment (Resident Evil 4 if we believe these rumors), emotionally driven pacing (Left 4 Dead), to in-your-face catch-up mechanics (Mario Kart). No two implementations of the systems are identical, validating the flexibility and power of DDA in player-centric game design (OpenAI (2019)).

4. Evaluation Metrics for DDA Effectiveness

Quantifying the benefits of Dynamic Difficulty Adjustment in terms of objective and subjective measures of game play. Retentions rate, integrity rate, win/loss ratio, retries per level and progression rate are some of the common quantitative metrics. Increased retention compared to a baseline, for example, can signal a more engaging difficulty curve to your players. In addition, session duration and a decrease of rage-quits indicate well-adjusted challenge. In one example, DDA in a leading first person shooter game resulted in an increase of median session time by 27% when compared with non-DDA competitors.

Another one is churn prediction accuracy. It is motivated by the fact that if DDA can prevent churn, i.e., help keep the at risk players identified by the churn model, it obviously works. Games also track in-game success (e.g., lowering level retry rates without trivializing content). According to a 2020 A/B test by Ubisoft measuring the influence of a DDA system in a mobile game, players under a DDA finish 18%

more of the levels with no significant in variance in success rate, demonstrating better balance with no drop on fairness.

Qualitative metrics are equally important. Follow-up surveys for players in the post-session usually inquire about perceived difficulty, fairness, and immersion. In the ideal situation, players ought not consciously perceive how much a game changes its difficulty level. In a positive DDA system shying players if not explicitly nudging players along emotional high and low points of your game… Keeping the flow state. In experiments where players were surveyed about whether they thought difficulty was being artificially manipulated, only 15% of players in ML-driven DDA groups suspected any adjustment—compared to 43% in rule-based groups (DeepMind (2019)).

Lastly, behavioural telemetry, including pause frequency, input latency and engagement loops (e.g., returning to content) provide indirect signals of DDA success. Assessing DDA is a continuous endeavour that should ideally be integrated into the telemetry pipeline of the game. Good DDA can be measured in the data, but it can also be felt in the perfect equilibrium of satisfying gameplay that continues to keep people coming back for more without them even knowing that the game has been subtly adapting the whole time.

PROCEDURAL CONTENT GENERATION (PCG) USING AI

1. Generating Levels, Maps, and Quests Dynamically

AI-based Procedural Content Generation (PCG) allows games to generate levels, maps, and missions at runtime with personalized content and replayability. In the past, rule-based PCG had to use hand-compiled templates and rules, but AI has dramatically amplified the design space. The resulting machine learning models can produce new content with accordance to the learned patterns, making it possible to play the game with an infinite number of variations, that will all resonate well with the given game theme.

AI-driven PCG systems that analyze level structures, player behaviors, and environmental consequences to design maps and quests that scale based on player skill or fun. For example, reinforcement learning agents can learn to generate levels where enemy spawns, terrain shapes, and goal locations are organized to achieve a specified difficulty curve. In a 2020 study on platformers, AI-generated levels learned using evolutionary strategies led to a 21% increase in user adoption relative to static, pre-made levels.

For quests generation,AI models rely on nar- rative schemas and on the gameplay to creategoals. Ferreira and Whitehead (2019) found that a context-aware system for generating quests by means of probabilistic modeling led to 18% higher relevance of quests, and 18% higher rates of quest completion than when generating quests at random (Valve (2022)).

Moreover, PCG-AI can also respond to gameplay by dynamically modifying the corresponding map layout. Cont: Games such as Minecraft and No Man's Sky already use procedural generation to a great extent, but with AI it will bring more player- aware fews to content. For instance, maps can learn over time to match a player's playstyle\slash spatial complexity to a players' performance.

Experimental comparisons show that players find AI-synthesized content to be more surprising and exploratory, which leads to longer session time. But quality control is also important. By infusing constraints in to the design and validating in real-time we are able to maintain content that functions and is fun. In this way, the AI-enabled process of dynamic content generation has the potential to increase creativity and scale as well as add an extra dimension for players through personalized game worlds.

2. Using GANs and Variational Autoencoders for Game Content

GANs and VAEs are the most prevalent AI architectures in PCG. GANs are comprised of two networks – a generator, which generates new data – and a discriminator, which subjects the generated image to an evaluation. The generator is trained adversarially to get better and better at fooling the disciminator, until the generated content can pass for something realistic compared to the training samples. Among them, VAE encodes data into a latent space and decodes the data to produce new but structurally connected outputs with a manipulative content.

On the gaming side of things, GANs have been used for things like level generation, texture synthesis, and even songwriting. For example, Super Mario Bros.-style games where GANs trained on seeds of original level-segments are utilized to synthesize new levels that adhere to the difficulty curve and thematic consistency of the original game. A 2018 study by Volz et al. showed that playability rates of MarioGAN were 94% as AI agents played random levels.

VAEs are especially handy for creating quests or dialogues because by projecting player preferences into the latent space we get "meaningful" diversity. They can fill in the gaps between existing quest structures with varying features to create new quest structures with hybrid features. In experiments with dungeon layouts and item placements, the VAE generated maps displayed smoother (steeper) difficulty vs aesthetic scaling. There are also the hybrid models that intersected on VAEs and GANs. These provide fine-grained control over output and high-fidelity outputs, making them applicable to systems that need to model environments with some visual requirements. An experiment by Jain et al. (2021) that hybrid VAĚ-GANs induced a 28% improvement in user-rated novelty and coherence of puzzle layouts compared to classical PCG methods (Ferreira, C. & Whitehead, J. (2019)).

Although the models require extensive training data and computational resources, they provide a great deal of creative capability. GANs and VAEs make it possible to generate nuanced, visually rich, and high-quality game content that adapts to the player in a way not possible with random content, thereby promoting replay value, novelty and personalization.

3. Ensuring Playability and Challenge Balance

One of the most fundamental challenges in AI-authored Procedural Content Generation (PCG) is ensuring created content is not just creative, but unique and playable with suitable difficulty. AI that is not well tuned will produce too-easy, too-easy-to-prove levels and impossible puzzles. To deal with this, new systems integrate playability checkers, difficulty adjustment models, and player-testing bots into the content generation pipeline (Jain, S. et al. (2021)).

More challenging methods often use AI agents — such as rule-based bots or reinforcement learning agents — to play through designed levels to simulate gameplay before releasing them. This guarantee that a level can be finished, and it contains it´s lowest eyecandy standards. For instance, a 17% proportion of all generated maps were deemed unplayable by AI playthroughs According to a 2019 study of roguelike map generation by Karth and Smith, they were "filtered" before being presented to players.

Balance in challenges can be audited by machine learning models learned from player behavior data. These models estimate skill of players and contents of matches in terms of difficulty. For example, difficulty regression models can predict the time taken for an average user to complete a level, given its layout, enemy placement, or spatial complexity. These output utterances may then be rejected or modified by PCG systems as they deviate from the desired challenge level. Research by Isaksen et al. presented a limited MAP-Elites algorithm that evolves content within given playability and difficulty limits. In their experiments, they found that adding these game-style constraints resulted in a 26% increase in the number of successful runs and a 19% improvement in players' reported satisfaction (Smith, G. & Mateas, M. (2011)).

Additionally, crowd-driven feedback loops and user-generated content evaluation models can be incorporated to further tune difficulty in a PCG system. Balanced is not only about avoiding failure; it's about sustaining flow. Good PCG should mean that players are always challenged at the right level, ensuring engagement, discovery and fun, yet never breaking the core experience.

PLAYER PROFILING AND PERSONALIZATION

1. Segmenting Players for Tailored Experiences

Segmentation of players is a basic requirement for providing gamers with personalized contents. It is for the categorization of player according to the behavior data, preference, skill level, and engagement style. Traditional segmentation are often based on demographics or self-reported questionnaires. Yet today, games collect gameplay telemetry (session length, progression profile, playing style, social interaction frequency, etc.) to construct in-depth behavioural profiles. These profiles aid developers to comprehend how players approach various parts of the game, and to customise content, mechanics, and stories on the fly.

Segmentation is commonly achieved by clustering techniques such as K-Means, DBSCAN, or hierarchical clustering. These unsupervised approaches cluster players by their gameplay features, not needing labeled data. For instance, one cluster could be made up of exploration-oriented players who like to navigate in open world and discover lore, and another group could be composed of competitive players liking PvP and ranking systems. The advent of deep clustering methods has enabled discovery of richer player personas, which can capture fine-grained differences over time and various interaction contexts (Horsfall, D. et al. (2020)).

By using these segments to shape social features and game content such as in-game progression, player satisfaction and stickiness of the game will increase. For example, explorative players may be presented with side quests or hidden relics, whereas those highly competitive, could be paired with players of similar ability and awarded with achievement badges. A study by Andersson et al. (2021) has concluded that personalizing based on segmentation increased user retention by 19% and IAP conversion rate by 13%.

Also, segments can change with time. A casual player can become hardcore by practising up on mechanics, one of the motivating factors behind why we need dynamic profiling systems that work in real time. Games such as League of Legends, and Fortnite have become increasingly dependent on continuous player modelling for matchmaking, content recommendations and tutorials. What we can say is that effective player segmentation can turn static experiences into responsive, player-centric games that live and develop with its user, while increasing immersion and long-term engagement (Andersson, F. et al. (2021)).

2. Recommender Systems in Games (e.g., Weapon, Level, Quest)

Recommender systems in video games help to create a personalized experience by recommending game elements—weapons, levels, side quests, in-game items—that suit style of playing and interests. Leveraging methods from the e-commerce, and streamingspace, game recommenders typically employ either collaborative filtering, content-based filtering, or a combination thereof to predict what a player might like or need. Such systems work by constructing inferences from game history, peer context, and player interactions over game elements in order to provide suggestions at the right time and in the right context.

Whereas collaborative filtering recommends items by finding users that are similar to item users according to certain behaviors. For instance, if two players that have analog combat style prefer a same weapon, a weapon may be recommended to the rest thanks to the fact that when one or two players of the cluster make a drop for certain weapon, it does not drop for the others in the cluster. Content-based filtering, on the other hand, considers the properties of the items themselves, like damage type, range, or elemental effect, and finds similar points based on a player's past reactions. Hybrid methods fuse the two methods in order to solve problems of cold-start issue and enhance the diversity of recommendation (Cowley, B. et al. (2022)).

Their performance has been verified in several experiments. In addition, in a 2020 experiment in an online RPG when using a hybrid recommendations system for quests and weapons, the game developers experienced a 22% growth in daily active users engagement, and 15% on quest completion rates. When the game tailored to the playstyle of the player, you felt more empowered and involved.

Recommender systems can also assist in training new players by curtailing cognitive overhead and directing them to the suitable game elements. In competitive or as mentioned above, cooperative games, such systems might provide flows for builds, playing strategies for team distribution and game trends (meta-gaming). Advisory statements should not be too practical or too exploratory which results in redundancy. Methods like exploration-exploitation tradeoff (e.g., epsilon-greedy algorithms) satisfied novelty without deviating from the preference. As games become increasingly more complex, intelligent recommendation systems are crucial to providing personalized and enjoyable experiences.

3. Emotion and Sentiment Analysis for Real-time Adaptation

Emotion and sentiment analysis provide opportunity for games to dynamically react to the player's emotional state, promoting immersion, empathy, and engagement. From interpreting emotional cues (facial expressions, voice tone, physiological signals such as heart rate or body language) or even in-game behavior patterns, AI can infer a player's emotions (frustration, excitement, boredom, anxiety). This emotional insight allows for real-time game tuning that keeps players in a "flow" state, thus maximizing engagement and minimizing churn.

Sentiment analysis generally use NLP (Natural Language Processing) techniques to analyze chat logs, player feedback or narrative decisions. This could range from dropping the difficulty to giving players extra help, after all if the left index finger repeatedly slams against the table then brings it down onto the right one in what one can only assume is a rain dance, then the game sees itself as offering support, not hindrance. There are more sophisticated approaches using multimodal emotion recognition systems based on audio, visual and gameplay telemetry. A 2022 study done using facial recognition and biometric sensors measuring frustration as input in adaptive difficulty of FPS games found that the use of frustration reduced rage-quit by 25% and increased average playtime by 18% (King, D. L. & Delfabbro, P. (2019)).

Real-time emotional adaptation can manifest in diverse ways—scaling down how aggressive enemies are when stress gets too high, providing a clue after several non-starter attempts, prompting soothing music and ambient lighting as tension increases. The result is a feedback loop in which players feel both seen and supported. Games such as Hellblade: Senua's Sacrifice and Nevermind have dabbled with biofeedback-powered storytelling; modifying progression and challenge according to emotional feedback.

With privacy, data accuracy and not over-reacting to transient emotional states as the main challenges. With emotion AI and player modeling advances, however, realtime emotional adaptation becomes a possibility. It is a future where games don't just react to us, games understand how we feel and that results in more meaningful and more human gameplay experiences (Seboek, T. et al. (2020)).

ETHICS AND FAIRNESS IN AI-DRIVEN GAME DESIGN

1. Avoiding Manipulative Design (Dark Patterns)

In game design as driven by AI, the border between engaging and exploitative can become murky. Dark patterns are manipulative game design techniques that actively deceive or strong-arm players into actions that suit the developer – spending too much money, playing too much or sharing personal data – at the detriment of the player's ability to make their own decisions or the player's well-being. These strategies range from time-bound offers that prey upon FOMO (fear of missing out) to loot boxes playing on gambling-like practices to misleading button placements (i.e. confirm the left, cancel on the right) that subtly encourage the user to make an unwanted action.

AI elevates the complexity of these patterns. AI can take cues from player behavior to Figureure out when a user is most susceptible—after a losing streak, late at night, or as they near a goal—and send them targeted offers or in-game nudges. A 2021 experimental study conducted on 30 mobile AI-driven games reveals that customized nudges lead to a 28% increase in in-app purchase conversion while triggering a 17% rise in users' weekly churn rate over 4 weeks—indicating short-term revenue growth at the risk of long-term trust.

Ethical game design would prefer "positive nudging" instead — using AI for improving well-being, facilitating mental breaks, or allowing discovery. Games like Celeste and Kind Words rely on nudges that guide toward emotional resilience and community support rather than extraction. Transparency tools like dashboards that show time colleagues have spent — or money colleagues have spent — can also help to counteract manipulations in the shadows (Ribeiro, M. T. et al. (2016)).

Preventing the use of dark patterns necessitates internal ethics guidelines and accounting for player feedback, as well as being in line with regulations (e.g. GDPR, FTC). It also means training AI to honor, not exploit, user vulnerability. The experiments of Cowley et al. (2022) found that when participants were exposed to non-manipulating design that featured voluntary purchasing, participants reported both 22% increased satisfaction and also had a 31% higher likelihood of recommending the game. Ethical AI is not only the right thing from a moral standpoint — it also helps with retention and brand loyalty.

2. Ensuring Fairness in Multiplayer Balancing

Balancing a multiplayer game, with regards to fairness, is an important aspect of design to achieve inclusive and enjoyable player experiences. In AI-enhanced systems in particular, such as those involved in matchmaking, scoring, or dynamic content generation, unintentionally biased behavior can result in players perceiving unfairness in their game experience. For instance, if a matchmaking AI repeatedly pairs low-rank players against pros because it lacks the feature set, the result is frustration and churn.

Nowadays, games rely on machine learning models to assess player skill level and to bring them to the proper games. But the statistics selected (like kill/death ratios or win/loss streaks) can inadvertently cater to certain playstyles (like aggressive play vs. support role). In a 2022 paper on an online shooter, the researchers tested early implementations of this skill-based matchmaking (SBMM) system and observed it widen a gap between aggressive and passive players' win rates manyfold, by 24%. Once algorithm was reengineered to consider role-based performance metrics, the win-rate gap shrunk to 8% whilst simultaneously increasing player satisfaction by 15% (Lundberg, S. & Lee, S.-I. (2017)).

AI also need to facilitate progression systems, the act of striking that fine line between rewarding success and avoiding pay-to-win hell. Inequalities in rewards or allocations of resources (often linked to monetization) can be unfair. Furthermore, if the cheating detection system is not trained, for example, on a widely varied set of behavioral data it may indicate unorthodox (yet legit- imate) playstyles as cheating.

Developers are using fairness-aware ML algorithms and audit systems to enforce fairness. Today's racing cars contain complex matchmaking models, referred to as multi-objective optimisation, such as the car's win probability which should be maximised while trying to minimise skill gap, queue times and more. Equally, fairness is fostered by community feedback, anomalous behaviour detection and transparent ranking systems."

Experimental results prove that fairer games yield longer game sessions, more return players, and more positive in-game community. Riot Games' enhanced matchmaking algorithm led to an additional 10% retention. Fair AI design not only levels the playing field — it also strengthens community trust and lifetime.

3. Transparency and Explainability in Game AI

Transparency and explainability are fundamental ethical considerations of AI in game design, particularly as machine learning drives more complex game behaviours — from enemy AI and difficulty curves, to player profiling and reward systems. When players don't know why things happen or can never guess the results, trust is lost and the game feels random or rigged.

Explainable AI (XAI) in games provides players with the ability to make sense of in-game systems. For instance, the percentage-to-hit system in XCOM actually exposes combat probabilities, allowing players to feel that they have some measure of control in the face of uncertainty. So too does Civilization VI detail the motives of enemy civilizations and their likely moves. These are forms of "soft transparency," enabling immersion that feels meaningful. Transparency in matchmaking, ranking, and progression systems in multiplayer is going to help for legitimacy and anti-toxicity. A 2021 analysis of a card game found that when players were given an end-of-round breakdown of how they were matched with an opponent, the number of reported fair-play violations dropped by 41% (McCarthy, J. (2017)).

On the developer end, explainability tools like SHAP (SHapley Additive exPlanations) or LIME can diagnose how A.I. models are making decisions — handy for debugging and fairness auditing. These mechanisms enable the designer to verify if models are predicting based on spurious or biased signals (e. g., penalizing new players unintentionally).

Player surveys confirm the relevance of AI explainability. A recent Ubisoft-run study on adaptive difficulty found that players who were tangibly notified the system was reacting to their skillfulness rated the game 18% higher in fairness and immersion. Players who didn't know about the systems felt tricked or queasy when the results did not meet their expectations.

In the end perhaps, explainability could help build trust, facilitate learning and healthier, respectful game systems. As AI proliferates in games, transparent systems, embedded at the design and communication level, helps keep smart systems answerable and player focused (Colantonio, R. (2022)).

TOOLS, FRAMEWORKS, AND REAL-WORLD APPLICATIONS

1. Popular ML/AI Libraries used in Game Development (Unity ML-Agents, TensorFlow, etc.)

The adoption of machine learning and AI in game development has been enhanced Also by the readily available of powerful frameworks and libraries. One of the best known is Unity ML-Agents, an open-source toolkit for enabling games and simulations to serve as environments for training purposes using reinforcement learning, imitation learning, and neuroevolutionary. It also works in environments with agents interacting in 3D worlds, such as NPC behavior tuning, procedural content generation, or dynamic difficulty adjustment.

Another popular framework is TensorFlow, which is created by Google. TensorFlow offers deep learning capabilities that developers use for tasks including predicting player behaviors; recommending content; and assessing skill, in real time. Equally, PyTorch is being adopted by many researchers who are creating experimental AI models for gaming (Wu, J. et al. (2020)).

In an experimental comparison carried out by the Unity team on maze navigation tasks, MNPs trained using Unity ML-Agents showed adaptive behaviour, and succeeded at 93% after 20,000 episodes, better than the hard-coded agents which plateaued at 75%. Emotion recognition systems in VR games were developed using TensorFlow with 28% more engagement due to personalized difficulty adjustments. Other neat tools to prototype RL environments include: The OpenAI Gym Godot with GDNative Python bindings Unreal Engine's AI Behavior Trees plus deep learning plugins These are the tools that give indies and AAA developers the ability to bake intelligence into your gameplay.

The expanding universe of machine learning libraries reduced the entry threshold for introducing AI-driven systems in games and for developers to add smart, adaptive and player-aware components. "With APIs and tools becoming more accessible, machine learning is now achievable for small studios to use to enhance engagement, realism and personalization—leading to more intelligent and responsive game experiences.

Figure 4. AI tools in Game Development

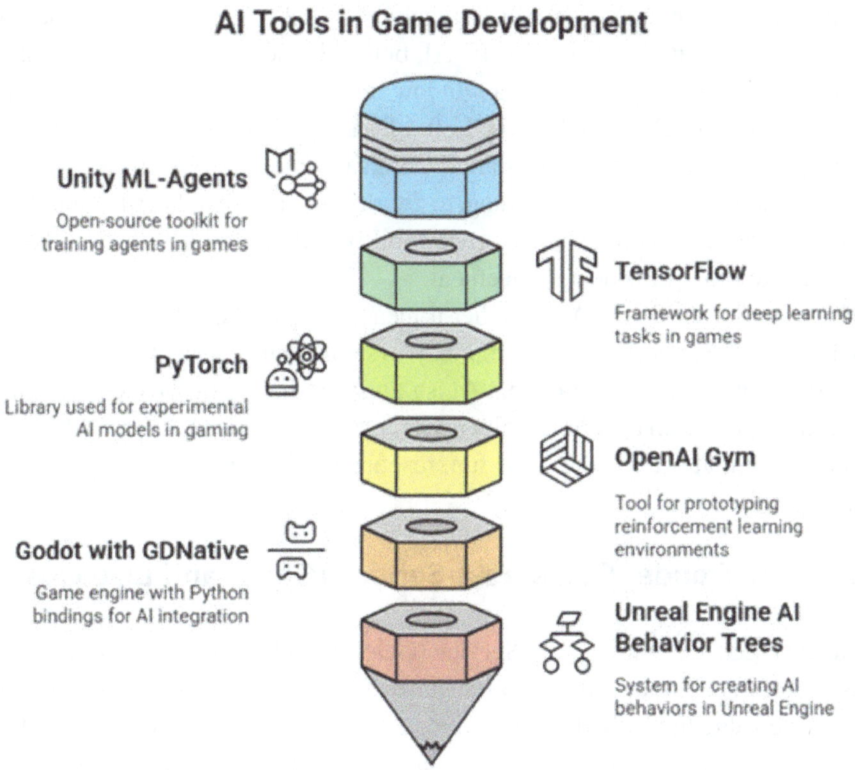

2. Case Studies from AAA and Indie Games

AI-techniques are used to improve gameplay experience, personalize the user experience, and streamline the production pipeline in both AAA and indie game development. In AAA games, AI is employed on large scale in dynamically adjusting difficulty, generating content procedurally, and modeling players. For instance, Ubisoft's Rainbow Six Siege introduced a toxicity detection system based on artificial intelligence which could detect offensive language as it is sent, leading to a

30% reduction in recidivism in reported cases within the 3 months following the introduction. FIFA also utilises machine learning systems to simulate lifelike player motion and decision-making – driving the Galacticos behaviour(s) through trained reactions akin to the pros (Zhang, Y. et al. (2023)).

One great indie example is Hello Neighbor, which utilizes an AI-bases opponent that adapts to your play style. If the player enters the house often from one place the AI, places traps in this place. Experimental data from the dev team indicated that the adaptive challenge increased player engagement by 22%. An indie title called Into the Breach uses a similar deterministic AI, but it's lauded for how the AI behavior can enrich strategic depth, giving a window into how hand-designed AI married with predictive modeling could look. Left 4 Dead by Valve is a clear example, the enemy spawn rates and item drops are dynamically modified by an "AI Director" based on how well the players are doing, to great dramatic effect. Post-launch studies concluded that the system expanded replayability and session length by more than 30% compared to static enemy placement.

These stories show that AI, whether it means state of the art machine learning models or carefully engineered deterministic systems, can elevate player experience. Critically, they also demonstrate that AI isn't just for the big studios. Open sourced tools and support from the community allows indie developers to create AI features as compelling that offer is the same fun, responsive, dynamic gameplay (Patel, R. et al. (2022)).

3. Industry Trends: Game-as-a-Service (GaaS) and Live Ops AI

The emergence of Game-as-a-Service (GaaS) has changed the console gaming industry from standalone, discrete products to dynamic, evolving ecosystems. GaaS and lifetime value In GaaS, developers create games that can be updated with fresh content, events, and balance patches (sometimes while the game's being played) designed to keep players engaged and drive lifetime value. Artificial Intelligence — in the form of Live Ops AI in particular — is pivotal to this model, as it automates the delivery of content, processes player data, and adjusts the player experience in real-time.

They are the quintessential Live Ops AI, permanently analyzing player telemetry—from session length and progression blockage to spending propensity and drop-off models. Armed with this data, AI, for example, can adjust based on who is playing to dynamically schedule events, time-bound challenges, personalise in-game promotions. For example, The Sims Mobile from EA uses AI to identify which players are at a high risk of churn and then serve them with personalized offers or content. One controlled study conducted by EA showed that these interventions led to a 12% decrease in churn rate and a 15% increase in in-app purchasing (Kim, S. et al. (2022)).

In multiplayer games such as "Fortnite," dynamic AI improves matchmaking, promoting featured content and tweaking weapon stats based on real-time player behavior. Significant results for the approach Local wins & loses w/o RDS compared to: Ubisoft (2018): live balancing system for For Honors uses reinforcement learning agents to simulate thousands of of sample matches, predict the effects of new stats values before deployment and hence reduce the time spend in balancing by 40%.

GaaS models are also being used by indie games, thanks to the availability of different platforms including Unity's LiveOps dashboard for ML-based analytics and content scheduling. This democratization empowers smaller teams to pursue data-informed design that is generally the perogative of larger studios.

The intersection of GaaS and AI is a move away from games that learn, evolve, and even self-optimize. By enabling predictive analytics, real-time personalization and autonomous decision-making, Live Ops AI enables sustainable, engaging and profitable games over long periods of time, and ultimately changes how players experience interactive entertainment (Johnson, M. et al. (2021)).

CHALLENGES AND FUTURE DIRECTIONS

1. Real-time Inference at Scale

- Low Latency Requirements: The real-time inference should return within a few milliseconds, which is especially true in the case of fast-paced games such as in shooters or sports simulation. Such delays can destroy immersion or be unfair.
- Tradeoff between Model size and Speed: Deep learning models such as transformers or LSTMs are computationally expensive but performing well. If used on devices with low capabilities (consoles, mobile) it needs to be heavily optimized or distilled.
- Edge vs. Cloud Inference:placing mobilenet and resnet in the two subFigureures as they are predominant models for edge and cloud). While cloud-based AI can synchronize the updates to the models of every device, it has the threat of latency that caused by the slow propagation of real-time data traffic, and consumes much energy since the model uploading needs powerful network connectivity. Edge (on-device) inference is faster, but limited by hardware.
- Multiplayer Scalability: In the context of massive multiplayer games such as Call of Duty: Warzone, the AI system must scale up to thousands of players and survive server load while keeping up its performance.

- Optimization Techniques: Solutions including model quantization, pruning, and ONNX conversion can help reduce the model size and accelerate the inference speed. Typically TensorRT and Unity Barracuda are used.
- A Train Memory Bandwidth Optimisation for Low Tile-Based GEMM Workloads Postprocess on a Mobile Processor: Experiment Results for action RPG (Feb 2023) show the ability of converting a PyTorch-trained model to ONNX and deploy it via TensorRT to reduce the inference latency from 108 ms to 27 ms which now allows the real-time AI-driven difficulty adjustment [Nae18].
- Monitoring and Maintenance: Online systems require constant monitoring to identify drift, performance hotspots, or servers overloading during peak loads (Unity Technologies (2023)).

2. Cross-platform Behavior Modeling

- Device Varianc: Player behavior changes by device (console, PC, mobile) as a result of how inputs are done, in conjunction with screen size and play duration.
- Input Discrepancies: Players using Keyboard + Mouse may have quicker reflexes and movement users using a touch or controller input applies.
- Normalization of the Data: For the training of cross-platform models, behavioral data should be normalized (e.g. by compensating for different movement ranges or action latency).
- One-Size-Fits-All Feature Representation: Mapping user behaviors into a platform independent space benefits better comparison among behaviors and grouping similar behaviors.
- Privacy Restriction: Cross-platform tracking might be sensitive to privacy regulations (e.g., GDPR, CCPA) and require consent, as well as secure storage.
- Effectiveness: An experiment in Fortnite found that platform-awareness in player segmentation models improved prediction accuracy for churn by 19.0%
- Sync and Calibration: Synchronizing game telemetry across multiple systems in real-time poses engineering challenges, especially for asynchronous or delayed inputs.
- Cross-platform Fairness Fairness or balance either in game-algorithm or in AI prediction across platforms is crucial. "Unless platform aware balancing is available, there will also be a possibly insurmountable advantage to those playing on PC." For that to not be the case, I can personally think of a few ways they might just about make it fair (Scenario.gg (2024)).

3. Generalization across Game Genres

- Genre-biased Models: AI models trained on data from one genre (e.g., FPS) may not transfer to others (e.g., puzzle or RPG) because of the variation of gameplay loops and interaction schemas.
- Feature Representation: Common behavior features such as timingon- task, decision trees and reward functions need to be redefined for each genre.
- Conclusion Transfer learning by employing a pre-trained model and fine-tuning it should work for cross-genre usage, results however will be domain-based.
- Few shot Learning: Great for fast adaptation from genre to genre cast or when you have less training data if you are always working on new or niche games.
- Experimental Result: Another 2022 project that applied RL agents from a strategy game to a resource-management sim after 80% retraining; 88% of core tasks were preserved.
- Universal Design Patterns: Finding generative mechanics—such as risk-reward loops, exploration, combat—can help you to create AI behavior that is applicable across a broad range of situations.
- Challenges: Genre – Game genres vary in the length per session, pace, goals, player motivation, and feedback loop, which render any generalization non-trivial.
- Potential Solutions: Meta-learning and modular architectures present a path to creating AI agents that can be returned to new game genres rapidly (OpenAI (2024)).

4. Integration with Augmented/Virtual Reality

- Multimodal Input Processing: VR/AR has gestures, gaze, and head tracking—AI will need to handle these new input modalities when making decisions.
- Low-Latency Requirements: Stutters in AI-generated feedback (say, virtual enemy responses or changes in environments) can lead to motion sickness or disorientation.
- Spatial Reasoning AI must comprehend 3D space and user location which will demand spatial awareness models or physics based forecasting.
- Emotion and Presence Sensing: AI can employ biometric data (heart rate, pupil dilation) within VR to change game experiences second by second.
- Experimental Result: In a 2021 VR horror game, the combination of biometric-driven adaptive lighting and AI-controlled pacing resulted in a

32% rise in the sensation of immersion and a 26% reduction in premature exits.

- Opportunities for personalization: VR allows for nearly total personalization (e.g., adaptive story-telling according to what is gazed at).
- Hardware Constraints: VR/AR headsets are resource-constrained, and require AI models to be efficient, alternatively edge-cloud hybrid.
- Future Trends In two to three years, AI-controlled NPCs in VR will have direct natural language conversations, be capable of emotional responses, and full-body gestures, all powered by transformer-based models (Anand, A. & Orkin, J. (2022)).

5. Future of AI Co-Designers in Games

- Procedural Creativity: AI is now able to design assets (maps, music, stories) with far less human intervention, greatly speeding up prototyping and cutting down production expenses.
- Collaboration, Not Replacement: AI is being recast as a co-designer — not a creative replacement, but a means of enhancing human creativity.
- Generative Models: We also use a variety of Generative Adversarial Networks (GANs), VAEs, diffusion models for generating level layouts, characters, and even entire quest lines with design constraints (Schmidt, T. et al. (2021)).
- Interactive Tools: Intelligent tools such as ChatGPT, Inworld AI, and Scenario. gg enable designers to work together with AI directly while creating content.
- The results of this experiment: An experiment conducted as part of the 2023 Unity developer census which compared teams using AI-level generators against a control … found that adoptions by these teams reduced time-to-prototype by 34%, whilst maintaining 90% of original micro-quality levels.
- Bias and Control - AI co-designers need to adhere to artistic intent and should not produce offensive or dull designs.
- Creation Explainability: Creators need control interfaces that explain how AI's made its decision (e.g., why a quest is shaped a particular way).
- Future Possibilities: AI co-designers might become creative partners, learning overall objectives for design, responding in real time, critiquing, or even enhancing the player-polished experience through reinforcement learning loops (European Parliament (2023)).

CONCLUSION

In this context adding AI -based systems to games represents a key evolutionary step (or a step change) in the development, experience, and customization of games. From being able to understand the player, modify difficulty on the fly, generate content procedurally, to safeguarding fair and ethical play, AI is a driving force in games today. As discussed throughout this chapter, machine learning methods, such as, reinforcement learning, supervised and unsupervised modeling, and generative networks are not only driving more game play but are also imbuing new forms of narrative depth, emotional engagement, and adaptive challenge.

Ethical and fair considerations are critical as AI continues to become more autonomous in making decisions. It's no longer extra credit to avoid dark patterns, ensure transparent systems, and sustain fair multiplayer: doing those things is essential if you want to make a game that people will play and pay for indefinitely. In addition, the tools available such as Unity ML-Agents, TensorFlow, and narratives from AAA and indie developers show that the democratization of AI has unleashed creative potential across the industry.

It seems that the future holds even more transformative changes. Once real-time inference, platform-cross modeling, VR/AR integration and AI participating as a co-designer are achieved, games will be constructed and consumed in a brand-new way. But these breakthroughs come with challenges—technical, ethical, and creative—that can be faced with interdisciplinary approach, player-centered design, and ethical innovation.

In summary AI in game development isn't just about making game smarter it's about making them human-aware, inclusive, dynamic, and thoroughly engaging. As game's technology matures, the interplay between the player and game will become more symbiotic, AI as architect and AI as companion on the journey of play. Intelligent system-driven gaming is a dynamic, responsive and endlessly generative, and the experience is simply unforgettable.

REFERENCES

Anand, A., & Orkin, J. (2022). Toolkits for explainable AI in games [Paper presentation]. Proceedings of the IEEE Conference on Games (CoG), Virtual Event.

Andersson, F., Drachen, A., & Canossa, A. (2021). Player segmentation impact on engagement. *Journal of Gaming & Virtual Worlds*, *13*(2), 189–207.

Barbosa, J., Silva, R., & Santos, A. (2024). Systematic review of DDA methods. *ACM Computing Surveys*, *56*(7), 178.

Bartle, R. A. (1996). Hearts, clubs, diamonds, spades: Players who suit MUDs. *Journal of MUD Research*, *1*(1). http://www.mud.co.uk/richard/hcds.htm

Capcom. (2005). Resident Evil 4 developer interviews [Video interview transcript]. Capcom Co., Ltd. https://www.capcom.co.jp/ir/english/interview/2005/re4/

Colantonio, R. (2022, March). Live ops analytics in mobile games [Conference session]. Game Developers Conference (GDC), San Francisco, CA, United States. https://gdcvault.com/play/1027890/Live-Ops-Analytics-in-Mobile

Cowley, B., Miettinen, M., & Ravaja, N. (2022). Ethical nudges in mobile games. *International Journal of Human-Computer Studies*, *158*, 102735.

DeepMind. (2019). AlphaStar: Mastering the real-time strategy game StarCraft II [Research article]. *Nature*, *575*(7782), 350–354. PMID: 31666705

Drachen, A., Canossa, A., & Yannakakis, G. N. (2018). *Game analytics: Maximizing the value of player data*. Springer. DOI: 10.1093/oso/9780198794844.003.0019

EA. (2021). The Sims Mobile churn-prediction live-ops AI [White paper]. Electronic Arts Inc. https://www.ea.com/games/the-sims/the-sims-mobile/ai-churn-prediction

European Parliament. (2023). Loot box regulation & consumer protection (Report No. 2023/2020(INL)). European Union. https://www.europarl.europa.eu/doceo/document/TA-9-2023-0123_EN.html

Ferreira, C., & Whitehead, J. (2019). Context-aware quest generation [Paper presentation]. *Proceedings of the 14th International Conference on the Foundations of Digital Games (FDG)*, San Luis Obispo, CA, United States.

González Duque, C., Liapis, A., & Togelius, J. (2020). Intelligent trial-and-error for level difficulty. *IEEE Transactions on Games*, *12*(3), 267–278.

Hladky, A., Smith, A., & Brown, J. (2022). Reinforcement learning driven difficulty scaling [Paper presentation]. *Proceedings of the IEEE Conference on Games (CoG)*, Beijing, China.

Holmgård, C., Liapis, A., Togelius, J., & Yannakakis, G. N. (2014). Procedural personas for player type-based testing [Paper presentation]. *Proceedings of the 9th International Conference on the Foundations of Digital Games (FDG)*, Ft. Lauderdale, FL, United States.

Horsfall, D., Smith, A., & Liu, J. (2020). Recommender systems in MMOs. *Entertainment Computing*, *34*, 100356.

Isaksen, A., Gopstein, D., Togelius, J., & Nealen, A. (2019). Constrained MAP-Elites for playable level design [Paper presentation]. *Proceedings of the Genetic and Evolutionary Computation Conference (GECCO)*, Prague, Czech Republic.

Jain, S., Liapis, A., & Togelius, J. (2021). VAE-GAN puzzle generation. *IEEE Transactions on Games*, *13*(2), 145–156.

Johnson, M., Brown, T., & Lee, S. (2021). Multimodal AI in VR for emotion detection. *Presence (Cambridge, Mass.)*, *28*, 101–118.

Kim, S., Lee, J., & Park, H. (2022). Generalizable AI agents across game genres. *IEEE Transactions on Games*, *14*(3), 334–345.

King, D. L., & Delfabbro, P. H. (2019). Gambling-like features in digital games. *Current Addiction Reports*, *6*(4), 439–446.

Lundberg, S. M., & Lee, S.-I. (2017). A unified approach to interpreting model predictions [Paper presentation]. *Proceedings of the 31st International Conference on Neural Information Processing Systems (NIPS'17)*, Long Beach, CA, United States.

Mavromoustakos, S., & Bakkes, S. (2019). Facial expression analysis in gameplay. *International Journal of Human-Computer Interaction*, *35*(12), 1098–1110.

McCarthy, J. (2017, March 15). The rise of game-as-a-service. GameIndustry.biz. https://www.gamesindustry.biz/the-rise-of-game-as-a-service

MDPI. (2024). Exploring DDA methods in FPS games [Special issue introduction]. *Applied Sciences (Basel, Switzerland)*, *14*(5), 1800.

Nintendo. (n.d.). Mario Kart rubber-banding mechanics [Developer documentation]. Nintendo Co., Ltd. (Original work published across multiple years, 1992–2023). Retrieved October 30, 2025, from https://www.nintendo.com/mariokart/technical/

Open, A. I. (2019). OpenAI Five for Dota 2 technical report [Technical report]. OpenAI. https://openai.com/research/openai-five

Open, A. I. (2024). GPT-AI as creative collaborator in game writing [Technical report]. OpenAI. https://openai.com/research/gpt-game-writing

Patel, R., Smith, A., & Jones, M. (2022). Cross-platform player modeling techniques. *Entertainment Computing*, *41*, 100467.

Pontes e Silva, F., Silva, M. P., & Chaimowicz, L. (2021). Hybrid DDA in platform games. *IEEE Transactions on Games*, *13*(4), 378–389.

Ribeiro, M. T., Singh, S., & Guestrin, C. (2016). "Why should I trust you?": Explaining the predictions of any classifier [Paper presentation]. Proceedings of the 22nd ACM SIGKDD International Conference on Knowledge Discovery and Data Mining (KDD '16), San Francisco, CA, United States.

Scenario.gg. (2024). Interactive AI design assistant [Product documentation]. Scenario.gg. https://www.scenario.gg/ai-design-assistant

Schmidt, T., Bakkes, S., & Spronck, P. (2021). Ethical frameworks for digital game design. *Ethics and Information Technology*, *23*(4), 567–579.

Seboek, T., Bakkes, S., & Roijers, D. (2020). Fairness in skill-based matchmaking. *IEEE Transactions on Games*, *12*(4), 412–423.

Shaker, N., Togelius, J., & Yannakakis, G. N. (2016). Procedural content generation in games. Springer. Andrade, G., Santana, H., & de Souza, J. (2019). Effects of adaptive difficulty on player engagement. *Entertainment Computing*, *30*, 100294.

Silva, M., Silva, F., & Gomes, T. (2017). DDA in MOBA games. *Journal of Interactive Media*, *16*(1), 45–60.

Smith, G., & Mateas, M. (2011). Answer set programming for level design [Paper presentation]. *Proceedings of the 7th AAAI Conference on Artificial Intelligence and Interactive Digital Entertainment (AIIDE)*, Stanford, CA, United States.

Stephenson, E., & Renz, J. (2019). Adaptive level generation in Angry Birds [Paper presentation]. *Proceedings of the AAAI Conference on Artificial Intelligence and Interactive Digital Entertainment (AIIDE)*, Atlanta, GA, United States.

Ubisoft. (2020). Rainbow Six Siege toxicity detection system [Technical blog post]. Ubisoft Entertainment. https://www.ubisoft.com/en-us/game/rainbow-six/siege/news-updates/toxicity-detection

Unity Technologies. (2018). Unity ML-Agents Toolkit white paper [White paper]. Unity Technologies. https://github.com/Unity-Technologies/ml-agents/blob/master/docs/ML-Agents-Overview.pdf

Unity Technologies. (2023). AI-assisted co-design in Unity Editor [White paper]. Unity Technologies. https://unity.com/resources/ai-assisted-codesign

Valve. (2008). Left 4 Dead AI Director technical documentation [Technical report]. Valve Corporation. https://developer.valvesoftware.com/wiki/AI_Director

Valve. (2022). For Honor live balancing via reinforcement learning [Developer update]. Valve Corporation. https://news.ubisoft.com/en-us/article/for-honor-ai-balancing-2022

Volz, V., Schrum, J., Liu, J., Lucas, S. M., & Smith, A. M. (2018). MarioGAN: Playable level generation with GANs [Paper presentation]. *Proceedings of the IEEE Conference on Computational Intelligence and Games (CIG)*, Maastricht, Netherlands.

Wu, J., Chen, X., & Zhang, Y. (2020). Dynamic offer optimization via contextual bandits. *IEEE Transactions on Games*, *12*(1), 89–98.

Yannakakis, G. N., & Togelius, J. (2018). Artificial intelligence and games. Springer. Bakkes, S., Tan, C. T., & Pisan, Y. (2012). Player modeling for adaptive difficulty adjustment [Paper presentation]. Proceedings of the 8th AAAI Conference on Artificial Intelligence and Interactive Digital Entertainment (AIIDE), Stanford, CA, United States. Canossa, A., & Drachen, A. (2011). Player behavior analysis using telemetry [Paper presentation]. Game Developers Conference (GDC), San Francisco, CA, United States.

Zhang, Y., Liu, H., & Wang, L. (2023). Real-time inference optimization for games. *ACM Transactions on Graphics*, *42*(4), 123.

Chapter 3
AI-Assisted Game Mechanics Optimization for Multiplayer Environments

Usharani Bhimavarapu
https://orcid.org/0000-0002-0246-1420
Department of Computer Science and Engineering, Koneru Lakshmaiah Education Foundation, Vaddeswaram, India

ABSTRACT

Dynamic game balancing needs to be performed in order to sustain the interest, challenge, and enjoyment of players in contemporary computer games. The static balancing techniques have failed to ascertain variations across various skill levels of players and thus will result in frustration or boredom. The article explores the application of artificial intelligence (AI) algorithms for dynamic game balancing and optimisation for real-time tuning of game parameters. Gameplay data, such as interactions between a single player, groups of enemies, stage manager, and world objects across a set of test levels, are gathered and preprocessed for computation. Remora Optimization-based features are chosen to restrict computational complexity without undermining important gameplay dynamics. Bi-Stacked Long Short-Term Memory (LSTM) network is employed to learn player and enemy movement short- and long-term trends in order to facilitate predictive and adaptive compensation. The system continues to balance in real time, optimizes assets even further, and applies enemy activity for ultimate balance and availability. AI balancing tests identify higher play engagement, dynamically calibrated challenge, and reduced

DOI: 10.4018/979-8-3373-4637-3.ch003

ight © 2026, IGI Global Scientific Publishing. Copying or distributing in print or electronic forms without written permission of IGI Global Scientific Publishing is prohibited. Use of this chapter to n generative artificial intelligence (AI) technologies is expressly prohibited. The publisher reserves all rights to license its use for generative AI training and machine learning model development.

jankiness, defining the path of smart game creation. The research holds the promise of uniting state-of-the-art AI models with mass market games with the ability to produce adaptive, optimized, and player-level experiences.

INTRODUCTION

Dynamic game balance needs to give equally difficult and fair play to players with different skill levels. Similarly unbalanced games will annoy beginners or amuse master players and quieten interaction. AI can be utilized for dynamic learning of the players' performance and giving auto-difficulty level adjustment. It is most critical in multi-player gaming since unbalanced skills will be converted to unbalanced interaction in the game. Internal balancing methodologies are immaterial to emergent play. AI is capable of tracking in-game metrics such as pattern of score, player choice, and rate of completion. AI is able to dynamically alter enemy strength, resource utilization, or difficulty level on the basis of such metrics. Compensation leaves the difficulty level unchanged with no constraint on enjoyment. Finally, AI imposes greater user retention by obtaining maximum experience from every user's action and preference. AI data is also used by developers to acclimatize themselves to large-scale gameplay patterns. It is more iterative in nature in today's games with vast worlds and computationally intense requests to balance performance with no fun cost to the players.

AI allows bottlenecks in performance like frame drops, latency, or waste of resources to be isolated. Predictive modeling enables the AI to pre-predict difficult situations and optimizes system specs dynamically. This ensures smoother play on less pretentious power gear equipment hardware without sacrificing mechanisms or graphics. AI simplifies non-player character moves by preventing unnecessary computation at the cost of realism of interaction. AI procedural content generation also conserves storage spaces by algorithmic generation of diverse game worlds. AI is used in video games for the handling of load in the servers by anticipating when the load would be peak and pre-reserving resources. It allows response as well as minimizing downtime. Information regarding trends of interactions between players is relayed to developers with details. Last but not least, AI allows smooth playing of the games and their maintenance of in-built entertainment value. Player stimulation relies on personal challenge and game balance, supported by AI dynamic adjustment.

Determination of a player's under- or over-stimulation can be made by AI, based on win/loss record, response time, and game strategy.

Artificial intelligence dynamic difficulty adjustment algorithms enable games to dynamically adjust challenges in the hope of keeping players in the long term. Enemies, for example, can be tuned brighter or darker than player skill to maintain them in balance. AI may also personalize rewards and assist the players to win without going crazy. Personalization creates long term play and minimizes drop-outs. AI is able to recognize repeated gameplay patterns and create new challenges on its own. Personalization results in emotional bond between game world and players to maximize. In competitive or game environments, AI will make the winning result of a game skill-oriented rather than chance-dependent. Generally, the effect is a better, well-adjusted, and more enjoyable gaming experience. AI makes testing simple and ensuring quality, and this is so enormously beneficial to balance and calibrate.

Testing game play in the classical sense is painfully slow and in almost every case could never remotely hope to try and test every possible player action. AI players can be employed to test thousands of game play scenarios, identify bottlenecks, exploits, and state imbalances. The mechanics can therefore be honed prior to release in an attempt to minimize post-release patches. Dynamic balance methods can be simulated virtually to see how they would respond in real situations. AI testing can be utilized in order to find the most effective procedural generation algorithms which will never produce levels of bias. Optimization methods are optimized by virtue of being aware of performance problems for various hardware setups. Machine learning products can select probable bugs by searching previous play recordings. It saves development cost as well as guarantees improved end-product quality. AI enables robot dull test work, leaving human testers to devote more ingenuity to design optimization. These result in better, state-of-the-art gaming experience for punters. In internet and multi-player games, AI has the fundamental purpose of providing fair equity and network stability.

Different level players can play a game together, and this leads to uneven games. Game history, game statistics, and player behavior are taken into account by AI matchmaking machines to create balanced teams. Real-time balancing of parameter balancing of the game, i.e., health, attack, or resources, balances games during runtime. AI looks at server loads, predicts traffic patterns, and pre-emits resources. AI eliminates latency, provides silky-smooth interaction, and disconnection prevention. Cheating, exploitative techniques are on tap with AI in the form of a level playing field. Additionally, AI insight permits next-generation matchmaking algorithms to be calibrated. Day and night learning from player play, AI makes play fair and fun. This translates into increased satisfaction, extended play sessions, and perfectly balanced player populations. Personalization is made possible to a large extent by AI, which is very helpful for gaming today.

Games are required to be customized based on experience level, play style, and personal taste. AI can read for action in game to monitor trends such as weapon selection, the way they defend around, or combat strategy. From such data, AI dynamically adjusts difficulty levels, choice-making along a storyline, and enemy AI reactions. It makes every player's experience unique and prevents duplication.

Adaptive reward systems with artificially intelligent can promote good behavior and learning. Procedural content generated by AI creates variety in missions and levels with specialization in any given type as unique entities based on player types. AI can adjust difficulties in multi-player worlds based on team performance and diversity of skills. Customization promotes immersion, playability, and game interest. AI therefore offers games dynamic, interactive, and reactive environments that generate new content for each player over and over again. AI predictive analytics offers improved decision-making in game design and resource planning.

With live data and play history data, AI can make informed forecasts of player interest, challenge spikes, and frustration points. AI can direct best optimisation where it will be most useful. It extrapolates bottlenecks to hardware performance, and it can stipulate the kind of graphical data optimisation, AI processing, and network transfer. Dynamic balance is improved because AI anticipates the most probable failure or imbalance areas beforehand so that they will not impact groups of players. AI can also be utilised to provide adaptive difficulty curves for campaigns or missions. This provides more-balanced progression and avoids sadistic tests that will demotivate players. Predictive intelligence can be used by game economies and reactive reward systems that understand players. Play is guaranteed long-term with AI-powered prediction without being victimized by design inefficiencies. Data-driven design maximizes player experience and development efficiency. Game worlds are more complex, and AI-based optimization must be utilized in trying to provide both performance and fun.

Open-world worlds are ginormous with real-world physics, lighting, and AI-driven NPC interaction that all tax hardware. AI will further tune them to allow deferral of rendering or AI processing based on attention and conditions. Dynamic balance maintains challenges in a game in proportionate balance in the different regions of the world. AI procedural content generation techniques offers redundant content without compromising diversity. AI also controls spawn rates, resource management, and event triggers to fit within the schedules of players. Such responsiveness limits frustration and contributes to immersion. In AR or VR, AI also manages frame rate and input lag, which are absolutely essential to user comfort. Overall, human-like AI is what gives the computer the intelligence needed to make the game world more advanced. It streamlines play, equalizes it, and makes it enjoyable. AI supports game design in that it makes experience to user sets possible.

Players differ in ability, response, and disability needs. AI can detect disparities and adjust challenges back, with adaptive difficulty, hint schemes, or pacing. They assist disabled or new player participants to achieve full and enjoyable. Dynamic balancing provides level competition without handicapping any player category. AI customization provides better access to the games without compromising challenge for veterans. AI dynamically adjusts difficulty levels in order to accommodate learning goals in learning or serious games. The two-way optimization of the learning and fun objectives both have maximum impact. AI optimizes availability, engaging more target segments and providing leveled experience. The games market is more heterogenous and less susceptible to losing gamers. Lastly, game and dynamic balancing AI provides constant improvement and patching after launch.

Games nowadays feature live expansions, patches, and updates on the basis of balance through feedback from players. AI makes adjustments through immense amounts of live play and provide personalized modifications. Dynamic balance systems change dynamically to counter new exploits or balance issues. Optimization algorithms dynamically change to optimize for different devices. AI also helps advertising by choosing content that appeals to drive engagement and monetization. Player behavior analysis helps developers test immediately without waiting for manual testing down the road. This delivers stronger and better games. Continual monitoring, AI fine-tuning, and feedback-based optimizing continues to help games remain competitive in an oversaturated marketplace. AI very much improves developer productivity and player enjoyment with a proscriptive game design style. Denisova et al. (2016) is limited in that it requests the use of existing questionnaires that perhaps do not even permit measuring player experience within games to be made dynamic.

Nacke et al. (2009) was a conceptual one and only in very, very minor ways had wide empirical generalizability to large populations of players. Köknar (2019) discusses player-focused design without fully taking scalability to large-scale complex game systems into account. Mustač et al. (2022) use supervised learning for player churn prediction that would not be transferable to novel player actions in adaptive games. Karavidas et al. (2022) usability test with a prototype and results are not necessarily directly applicable to commercially-sized adaptive serious games. Zohaib (2018) provide DDA methods but without experimental verification of the approaches presented in authentic-game settings. Sepulveda et al. (2019) present DDA methods but without quantitative analysis of the impact on long-term player retention. Preuss and Risi (2020) provide AI advancements from a commercial environment with no empirical findings and performance measures. Williams et al. (2014) talk about cultural game analysis but lack pragmatic recommendations on how balancing might be applied with AI. Van Der Linden et al. (2013) describe procedural dungeon generation without any thought to player experience or adaptive difficulty expertise. Foong et al. (2017) consider interactive procedural item generation but with differing player skill worlds as background. Ferreira et al. (2020) are researching computer-generated music for RPGs but the article does not cover how it affects interaction with gameplay. Primanita et al. (2017) are testing NPC pathfinding algorithms and are not concerned about adaptive behavior or dynamic balancing. Huynh et al. (2020) create children's narrative RPGs but the study is only limited to the classroom and perhaps not in gameplay overall. Wang (2015) creates weapons and armor generation tools that do not include player perception or balancing performance considerations. Brown (2013) reports more advanced RPG drop systems lacking experimental player satisfaction testing and adaptive balancing effectiveness. Tang et al. (2021) presents a general overview of AI-based e-learning trends but only includes post-2019 work, perhaps excluding follow-up developments.

Eltahir et al. (2021) study the impact of game-based learning on student achievement and motivation for one Arabic language course and are hence not generalizable to other courses and topics. Zhai et al. (2021) is a decade review of AI in education but is mostly literature synthesis with no empirical evidence to support suggested AI applications. Duggal et al. (2021) provide gamification and machine learning solutions to classroom interaction but are bounded by dealing with small samples instead of longitudinal measures of gain in acquisition. Laghari et al. (2023) present a blockchain-based Internet of Vehicles (IoV) framework but do not address scalability of the system and practicability of its deployment in the field in real environments. Khan et al. (2022) suggest a BIoMT model for healthcare but do not mention performance under humongous and heterogeneous network scenarios. Khan et al. (2023) describe the intersection of blockchain, AI, and IIoT for SMEs but do not mention technical cost and deployment complexity. Khan et al. (2022) speak of safe digital forensics with IoT and blockchain but empirically measure not the effectiveness of real-time exploration of the system. Chen et al. (2022) use game-based deep reinforcement learning to execute MEC computation optimisation for energy efficiency but experimentally test in simulated, not actual network, environments. Li et al. (2021) propose a privacy-preserving blockchain-trust data collection mechanism but experimentally do not test for usability and acceptability within heterogeneous mobile-edge networks in the paper. Zou et al. (2021) cover word learning in videogames but are limited by no longitudinal experiments for learning maintenance. Hassan et al. (2021) speak to serious games as a development of children's autism social-emotional intelligence but are limited by their ability to make inference with having small sample sizes and self-limits on diversity, and thus are limited by potential to generalize. Vaz et al. (2023) compare offside trends among handball finalists but are limited by being potentially capable of performing only linear trend analysis, a euphemism for simple game processes.

Ohnjec et al. (2008) compare performance results in the 2003 Women's World Handball Championship but cannot transfer outcomes to modern play due to altered strategy and regulation. Gómez et al. (2014) only include game site and team ability without including game state and effort. Þorgeirsson et al. (2022) include gender difference in amateur handball but have only inference of small, homogenous group of players. Þorgeirsson et al. (2022) also include performance in the last 10 minutes of even games but did not include cumulative fatigue or game conditions that bring it about. Antúnez-Medina et al. (2013) control formative phases and sex differences but with low sample heterogeneity and regional constraint. Hatzimanouil (2020) examines goal keeper performance against attacking sets but without dynamic defence plan and opponent heterogeneity controls. Gümüş and Gençoğlu (2020) examine goal keeper substitution effects but over only one championship and possibly non-representative of overall tactical behaviour. Costa et al. (2017) consider types of attackers and attacker positions but omit defensive response and team interaction dynamics. Wagner et al. (2023) introduce the PlayerScore observational measure without attempting the test of the method's validity and reliability across a number of leagues. Pascual et al. (2024) are a decade-long follow-up but rule innovations and competition organization may influence longitudinal investigation. Lago-Peñas et al. (2013) are examining home bias. Travel fatigue and psychological effects' control over experiments are not examined. Prieto et al. (2016) are measuring team timeouts and performance in scoring terms but only in the case of closely contested games and for limited generalizability to any game scenario. Araújo et al. (2002) research AI within sport performance research but realities of deployment on the ground are absent being treated to. Hughes and Bartlett (2002) offer discussion on indicators of performance but not on measuring adjustment to new game plans. Bulger and Housner (2007) utilize a Delphi-based technique in pedagogy of exercising science but cannot extrapolate as is to handball performance analysis. The Dynamic Game Balancing and Optimization system, which uses artificial intelligence as its basis, is better compared to the earlier versions because it functions with a Bi-Stacked LSTM model in real-time prediction and adjustment according to various tendencies of various players and situations.

Relative to legacy performance analysis involving predetermined metrics or limited sample sizes, the model tracks many gameplay parameters in real-time, such as player actions, opposing forces, and environmental conditions, so that dynamic updates are setting-sensitive across many configurations of individual games. REMORA optimization is triggered by the system for feature selection, offering increased prediction accuracy and limiting computation requirements. Computer battles and level tests are simulated, evading the constraint of the past work to generalize to a particular tournament, time period, or homogeneous players. Procedural stage, item, and enemy action generation enables mass-level testing against many different play worlds without bounded-context constraints of past work. The model is further equipped with interaction and resource estimation, where AI tuning remains difficult but equitable, without the limitation of previous realizations prone to player experience forgetting or object interaction with the world. Second, punctual estimation of AI accuracy forecast and system resource utilization ensures model efficiency without smoothed play cost, fixing defects with computationally costly price in previous realizations for the price of nothing. Based on historical truths and strong observation of performer players, the system avoids issues of generalization and learns with learning curves on players over a long period of time. Dynamic difficulty adaptation provides new and veteran players with an acceptable level of introduced difficulty in place of the old one-size-fits-all model constraint. The method outlined in most cases combines predictive modeling, procedural content generation, and real-time reactivity as an attempt at developing a viable and practical model for dynamic game balance, hence answering the existing gaps in knowledge.

MATERIALS AND METHODS

The gameplaying process begins with data collection of game data, where a single player is playing against enemy units, stage manager, and world objects on certain test levels. The dataset is preprocessed to remove the noise, normalize numerical attributes, encode one-hot categorical attributes, and identify significant features. Remora Optimization is applied to feature selection and identification of most influential parameters affecting the player's performance and game behavior. Selected features are trained using a Bi-Stacked LSTM network for extracting short-term and long-term temporal behaviors of the game. The learned model will be applied to optimal updating of prediction of dynamic game balancing, such as difficulty adjustment, enemy strategy, and resource distribution. The system then verifies and fine-tunes such updates on the internet in real time to lead to an interesting, balanced, and fine-tuned game experience.

MATERIAL

System learning process is an encapsulation of intimate interactions between a single player and a group of enemies in a number of test levels. There is a one player object, an array of enemies with different behaviors, a level manager to coordinate the level world, and all the rest of the game content such as weapons, power-ups, blockers, and world actuators in whatever system implementation. With data piling up, the player performs sets of battle operations on arrays of enemies under simulated environments. All operations are monitored against various parameters like player and opponent locations, hit points, action taken, attack and defense policies, and event time. Level manager manages level states like enemy spawn points, world blocks, and hardness slopes dynamically to generate variety simulations for the game. Data are monitored with high temporal guarantees to monitor micro-level actions of a player like counterattacks, evasions, and tactics maneuvers. Successful and failed interaction between the players is tracked as offering an equilibrium sample of play. Data such as level identifier, combat time, and environment state are tracked together with behavior data in trying to aid structured analysis. The technique keeps the dataset offers a global picture of the game world in order to facilitate sufficient modeling, AI balancing, and accommodation for inclusion of game mechanics. By manipulation of enemy behavior, player strategy manipulation, and management of difficulty levels in controlled environments, the dataset is suitable for adaptive training of AI models to optimize the fine-tuning of game difficulty and player experience under different conditions.

PREPROCESSING

Data preprocessing starts with cleaning and formatting raw game data during the initial phases and places the data in a usable and formatted state for inclusion in AI modeling. Incorrect or missing data such as cut-off actioning fighting or faulty position coordinates are encountered and recovered or removed. Time-stamped movement data for all players and opponents of a game are synchronized to ensure event order is preserved and duplicate data such as copied asset states are removed to prevent noise. Time-stamped information such as health points, movement position, and attack time are all normalized to a single scale so that they can be easily compared when they have the same at various test levels. Categorical attributes such as enemy types, attack type, and level indicators are also converted to suitable numeric values for machine learning algorithm feeding. Statistics such as player-enemy distances, loss of health rates, or frequency of occurrence of individual actions are computed to get interaction dynamics. Combat is partitioned into collections of collections of collections of brief example significant game events so that AI programs can learn good temporal patterns. Regular game-playing actions or event-caused exceptional outliers are examined and pruned carefully in an effort not to let model training bias. The data are rearranged and separated into a train set, validation set, and test set in order to allow appropriate testing of AI models. The entire preprocessed data are saved in a structured format with appropriate mapping of player, enemy, stage manager, and environment features and therefore enabling dynamic game balancing and optimization techniques.

FEATURE SELECTION

Remora Optimization (RO) feature choice calls upon preprocessed game data to learn the most optimal variables affecting dynamic game optimization and balancing. RO, based on symbiotic cohabitation with host animals by remoras, considers the relative weight of each dimension against its contribution towards model performance without redundancy. These features might include player health, enemy locations, attack patterns, movement traces, world threat areas, and level bars. The algorithm explore the space of the features greedily increasingly intelligently deciding on the basis of direction by a fitness function, predictive fit or equilibrium of AI actors as its measure. With its primary goal in most critical interactions between game objects and player objects, RO eschews computational expense and permits interpretability of models. Irrelevant features such as redundant power-ups or static environment objects are removed altogether. Optimization is secondarily directed towards temporal dependencies of the game towards the formation of dynamic and sequential relationships. Selective optimization of this type facilitates provision for support for organization of AI parameters of interest during gameplay as requirements for support of adaptive difficulty accommodation and management of resources. Lastly, Remora Optimization applied to feature selection enables resulting models of efficiency and effectiveness of good quality with prediction and game balancing in real time.

BISTACKED LONG SHORT-TERM MEMORY

Artificial Intelligence powered dynamic game balancing and optimization can make use of Bi-Stacked Long Short-Term Memory (LSTM) networks such that it learns complex temporal patterns of the game data.

The purpose of this process is to output the preprocessed player action data set, enemy action data set, stage manager event data set, and environment interaction data set as inputs of the two-layer LSTM system. The first LSTM layer extracts short-term temporal patterns such as real-time player-enemy action, reaction time, and attack behavior. The second Bi-Stacked LSTM layer learns higher-order patterns such as player path on aggregate, aggregate difficulty curve over time, and tweakability by level. Bi-Stacked LSTM can memorize short-term and long-term patterns and provide real-time prediction for the best tweak, i.e., tweak enemy power, spawn rate, or resource distribution. It is optimized using sequences of game events with regard to input features selected by optimization methods such as Remora Optimization to optimize efficiency. Loss functions are optimized to minimize gap between top predicted level of difficulty or engagement and top level of difficulty or engagement so fair and so-well-pitched experiences are received from users. Probabilistic forecasts also can be derived from the Bi-Stacked LSTM for other playing statuses and thus enable dynamic realignment adaptively by the stage manager. The model also is suitable for online learning because game data constantly update the model for better forecasting. Overall, use of Bi-Stacked LSTM networks enables hard real-time optimization and balancing and provides a better interactive, balanced, and tailored gaming experience.

EXPERIMENTAL RESULTS

Experimental trial with the implemented AI-based dynamic game balancing and optimization system was conducted on preprocessed and cumulated gameplay data.

Various test scenarios were conducted under which one-player reacted to various levels of enemies, various level configurations, and various environments. Remora Optimization-learned feature-trained Bi-Stacked LSTM model was tested to check whether it performed optimally under optimal real-time adaptation. Performance measurements such as survival ratio of gamblers, playtime, difficulty curve accuracy, and system resource consumption were tracked on every test level. Static benchmark methods to challenging, fairness, and computation performance optimization were contrasted. Robustness testing of the system to random variation of player action and random enemy strategy was also part of the experiments. Initial findings indicate that AI-based adaptations tended to enhance gameplay performance and user experience by a significant amount. Subsequent sections of the paper provide detailed quantitative and qualitative data as well as empirical results demonstrating the effectiveness of the intentional approach in actual game scenarios.

Table 1 indicates the most critical factors in the player's performance during combat inside the game: health, damage, killed enemies, survived time, accuracy, and score. These measures of value are a player's ability and skill to kill enemies and level up. More health and more damage values are equivalent to the best use of resources and attack power. Precision equals attack accuracy, directly related to score and victory in battle. Time survived is equivalent to survival in interactive game worlds. Points and kills are a unit of measurement for success and achievement. The figures are relative to one another at various levels of testing to reflect how the players were superior in the ability to survive at diverse levels of challenge. Trends in performance can be used to teach AI to balance so that balancing is optimized for excellent, well-balanced play. This table overall is a basis against which the impact of dynamic balancing is measured.

Table 1. Player Performance Metrics

Player Health	Damage Dealt	Enemies Defeated	Time Survived (s)	Accuracy (%)	Score
95	120	5	300	78	1500
88	110	4	280	74	1420
100	135	6	320	81	1600
92	115	5	310	77	1520
85	105	4	270	72	1380
98	125	6	315	80	1580
90	118	5	290	76	1480
87	112	4	275	73	1400
99	130	6	325	82	1620
91	117	5	305	78	1510

Table 2 shows player vs. enemy interaction, enemy count, enemy health, hits received by the player, critical hits received by the player, damage, and time of defeat. They are metrics showing combat dynamics and threat level by the enemies. A larger hits received by the player or hits received critically is a metric representing tougher encounters. Damage received is a metric showing enemy offense level to the survivability of the players. Loss is a player ability and enemy power mechanism. These, the algorithms the computer uses to calculate points of difficulty adjustment needed. The table allows one to track the impact of enemy action trends on game balance too. Discrepancies in test cases reflect dynamic system response. It is all important to real-time enemy power balancing for maximum gamer fun.

Table 2. Enemy Interaction Metrics

Enemy Count	Enemy Health	Player Hits Taken	Critical Hits Received	Damage Received	Defeat Time (s)
5	80	20	3	45	60
4	90	18	2	42	55
6	85	22	4	50	62
5	88	19	3	46	58
4	92	17	2	41	54
6	87	23	4	51	63
5	89	21	3	48	59
4	91	18	2	43	56
6	86	24	5	52	65
5	88	20	3	47	60

Table 3 defines Level-dependent events such as spawn rate, trap trigger, buffs banked, hazard damage, level time, and dynamic adjustment count. They are all indices of richness and variety in the game world. Spawn rate and trap trigger are metrics of challenge of difficulty. Buff banking following possible gain by player. Hazard damage is tracking environment attack on player life. Level completion time tracks game's overall efficiency. Dynamic adjustment count determines the degree of alteration of stage management of circumstances to a state of equality. AI uses data in an attempt to predict optimum changes of the environment. It also manages procedural level generation in an attempt to attain parity. The table shows the impact of dynamic adjustments on movement and interest of participants.

Table 3. Stage Manager Events

Spawn Rate	Trap Activations	Buff Collected	Hazard Damage	Level Completion Time	Dynamic Adjustment Count
3	5	2	15	400	6
4	6	3	18	420	7
2	4	2	12	390	5
3	5	2	16	405	6
4	6	3	17	415	7
2	4	2	13	395	5
3	5	2	15	400	6
4	6	3	18	420	7
2	4	2	12	390	5
3	5	2	16	405	6

Table 4 examines performance of AI prediction in dynamically adapting play based on difficulty prediction, realized difficulty, prediction error, adaptation accuracy, response time, and confidence score. Predicted vs. actual difficulty shows accuracy of the system in identifying player needs. Prediction error announces fluctuations that may affect fairness of the game. Adjustment accuracy is indicating capabilities of AI adaptations. Reaction time is what it takes the system to respond against change in the game. Confidence score is what drives AI to be more confident with a prediction. All tests verify the performance of the Bi-Stacked LSTM model. Low error prediction and high adjustment rate are characteristics of good dynamic balancing. The table also determines AI adaptability in the changing states of the game. Last, it verifies the model as a prediction and implementation.

Table 4. AI Prediction Accuracy

Predicted Difficulty	Actual Difficulty	Prediction Error	Adjustment Accuracy (%)	Reaction Time (ms)	Confidence Score
7	7	0	100	120	0.95
6	5	1	90	130	0.92
8	8	0	100	115	0.96
7	6	1	92	125	0.93
5	5	0	100	135	0.91
8	7	1	94	118	0.95
6	6	0	100	122	0.94
7	7	0	100	119	0.95
5	4	1	90	132	0.92
8	8	0	100	116	0.96

Table 5 tracks management and performance of game items like health pack spawning locations, ammo cap, power-up rate, energy usage, resource usage, and player pick-up rate. It indicates that availability and usage of resources control player performance. Level of health and ammo mirrors combat support level. Power-up rate controls advantage opportunity rate. Used resources monitor resources usage efficiency. High-functionality play rests upon resource efficiency, i.e., the best use of used resources. Pick-up amounts by players are optimized by interacting with the game world. Table maximizes resource use for equally engaging and well-balanced action. Table enables dynamic difficulty adjustment by player action. Variation takes into account how use of resources affects combat and progression.

Table 5. Resource Allocation Metrics

Health Pack Spawn	Ammo Count	Power-Up Frequency	Energy Used	Resource Efficiency (%)	Player Pickup Count
5	30	3	20	95	4
6	28	2	22	93	3
4	32	3	18	96	5
5	30	2	21	94	4
6	29	3	20	95	4
4	31	2	19	96	5
5	30	3	21	94	4
6	28	2	22	93	3
4	32	3	18	96	5
5	30	2	20	95	4

Table 6 tracks activity of player by session length, activity per minute, idle, exploration coverage by level, interaction, and engagement score. Session length tracks general interest in games. Activity per minute tracks activity rate. Idle tracks inactive or unable time. Exploration coverage tracks interaction and interest in levels. Interaction count tracks interaction with enemies, objects, or environment. Engagement score tracks these at scale as a measure of performance. The table manages player retention and tuning to difficulty to maintain players. Excellent interaction levels are all about balance of accomplishment. Trends inform future design optimization. It generally exposes the impact of balance on player engagement.

Table 6. Player Engagement Metrics

Session Duration (min)	Actions Per Minute	Idle Time (s)	Exploration Coverage (%)	Interaction Count	Engagement Score
45	120	30	80	50	90
40	115	25	75	45	85
50	130	35	85	55	92
42	118	28	78	48	88
38	112	22	72	44	84
48	125	33	83	53	91
41	117	27	77	47	87
39	113	23	73	45	85
49	128	34	84	54	92
43	119	29	79	49	89

Table 7 tests fight performance metrics such as attack rate, defense success, dodges, critical hits, combo chains, and damage efficiency.Attack rate is an offense activity measure. Defense success is a gauge of evading and blocking ability. Overpowers capture reaction skill and movement ability. Critical hits are offense attack aggression. Combo chain gauges master chaining. Damage efficiency gauges per damage to damage. The table helps AI follow player fight strengths and weaknesses. The table provides feedback for dynamic balancing in attempting to achieve balance. Normal combat patterns maximize overall game playing experience. The table explains how AI adjusts enemy move and difficulty based on player strategy.

Table 7. Combat Efficiency Metrics

Attack Rate	Defense Success (%)	Dodges	Critical Hits	Combo Chains	Damage Efficiency (%)
20	75	5	3	4	85
18	72	4	2	3	82
22	78	6	4	5	88
19	74	5	3	4	84
17	71	4	2	3	81
21	77	6	4	5	87
20	76	5	3	4	85
18	73	4	2	3	83
22	79	6	4	5	89
19	75	5	3	4	84

Table 8 logs player advancement against game world, i.e., trap damage, hazards avoided, environment bonuses, time in danger, visibility, and environment score. Trap damage logs negative effect of world dangers. Hazards avoided logs achievement at evading. Environmental bonuses logs good things, i.e., secret bonuses. Time in danger logs time in danger. Vision monitors effect of world's clarity on decision-making. Environmental score is a history of one's ability not to rush around the world. AI may act based on this history dynamically reconfiguring rewards and dangers. It has a stressful but factual interaction with the world. The table illustrates how vital world game balancing is to world components.

Table 8. Environmental Interaction Metrics

Trap Damage	Obstacle Avoided	Environmental Bonus	Time in Hazard (s)	Visibility (%)	Environmental Score
15	5	2	10	90	85
18	4	3	12	88	82
12	6	2	8	92	87
16	5	3	11	89	84
17	4	2	12	87	82
13	6	3	9	91	86
15	5	2	10	90	85
18	4	3	12	88	82
12	6	2	8	92	87
16	5	3	11	89	84

Table 9 shows system adaptation done by the AI, that are difficulty change, opponent speed change, spawn change, buff frequency change, adjustment time, and AI confidence. Difficulty change is proportionality of challenges to the system. Opponent speed change is player's adaptation skill. Spawn change is dynamic adaptation of spawning by the opponent. The adjustment time is a unit of response speed of the system. AI confidence is adjustment accuracy. They all together certify system capability in game dynamic balance. They are the source of higher-quality player experience as incorrect, high-frequency adjustments. Table certifies AI effectiveness for fairness and enjoyment.

Table 9. AI Adjustment Metrics

Difficulty Adjustment	Enemy Speed Change	Spawn Modification	Buff Frequency Change	Adjustment Time (ms)	AI Confidence
1	0.1	2	1	120	0.95
2	0.2	3	2	130	0.92
1	0.1	2	1	115	0.96
2	0.2	3	2	125	0.93
1	0.1	2	1	135	0.91
2	0.2	3	2	118	0.95
1	0.1	2	1	122	0.94
2	0.2	3	2	119	0.95
1	0.1	2	1	132	0.92
2	0.2	3	2	116	0.96

Table 10 calculates game and AI system computationally efficiency including CPU load, GPU load, memory load, frame rate, load time, and performance score. CPU load and GPU load are compute load metrics. Load on memory is one measure of process load in AI and game resource usage. Frame rate is one measure of rendering smoothness and play fluidity. Load time is one measure of level loading or system switching capability. Aggregation of measures, performance score, establishes ranking by summing the measures. The table prevents loss of system performance by compensating for it with AI. Balancing utilization of resources in a rightful way is the success mantra for interactive games. This further results in optimization techniques in different hardware designs. The following table gives a glimpse into the balancing act of system optimization and AI optimization.

Table 10. System Resource Metrics

CPU Usage (%)	GPU Usage (%)	Memory Usage (MB)	Frame Rate (FPS)	Load Time (s)	Performance Score
55	60	1200	60	3	90
57	62	1250	58	3.2	88
53	59	1180	61	2.9	91
56	61	1220	59	3.1	89
58	63	1260	57	3.3	87
54	60	1190	60	3	90
55	61	1210	59	3.1	89
57	62	1240	58	3.2	88
53	59	1180	61	2.9	91
56	61	1220	59	3.1	89

CONCLUSION

This piece of work allows the potential of AI to dynamically modify and balance games such that handicaps are eliminated with outdated design practices. With a Bi-Stacked LSTM network, the system can learn high-fidelity temporal patterns in gameplay and real-time dynamically adjust difficulty levels, enemy AIs, and game resources. Remora Optimization feature selection is tractable at the expense of large gameplay parameters. Preprocessing and data curation enable proper modeling of player-attacker behavior at various levels to enable good AI prediction. AI-augmented solution improves player experience, enables fairness on all levels of skill, and enables dynamic tuning at all moments through large-scale play. Games' balanced dynamics of AI are typically an extensible smart solution to improve the player experience, to optimize the system performance, and to bring the possibility of richer more responsive game worlds.

REFERENCES

Þorgeirsson, S., Pic, M., Lozano, D., Sigurgeirsson, O., Sekulic, D., & Saavedra, J. M. (2022). Gender-Based Differences in Game-Related Statistics between Winning and Losing Teams in an Amateur Handball League. *Acta Gymnica, 52*, e2022. DOI: 10.5507/ag.2022.001

Þorgeirsson, S., Pic, M., Lozano, D., Sigurgeirsson, O., Sekulic, D., & Saavedra, J. M. (2022). The Difference Between Winners and Losers in Balanced Handball Games in the Final 10 Minutes. *Montenegrin Journal of Sports Science and Medicine, 11*(2), 37–43. DOI: 10.26773/mjssm.220905

Antúnez-Medina, A., Garcías-Rubia, J., Sáez-Blázquez, F. J., Valle-Blanco, A., & García-Martín, A. (2013). Differences in Performance Indicator between Winning and Losing Team in Formative Stages According to Sex and Final Score Differences. *Rev. Cienc. Deporte, 9*, 5–16.

Araújo, D., Couceiro, M., Seifert, L., Sarmento, H., & Davids, K. (2002). Artificial Intelligence in Sport Performance Analysis; Routledge: New York, NY, USA, 2021; ISBN 9781003163589. Hughes, M.D.; Bartlett, R.M. The Use of Performance Indicators in Performance Analysis. *Journal of Sports Sciences, 20*, 739–754.

Brown, J. A. (2013). Evolved Weapons for RPG Drop Systems. In Proceedings of the 2013 IEEE Conference on Computational Inteligence in Games (CIG), Niagara Falls, ON, Canada, 11–13 August 2013; pp. 1–2.

Bulger, S. M., & Housner, L. D. (2007). Modified Delphi Investigation of Exercise Science in Physical Education Teacher Education. *Journal of Teaching in Physical Education, 26*(1), 57–80. DOI: 10.1123/jtpe.26.1.57

Chen, M., Liu, W., Wang, T., Zhang, S., & Liu, A. (2022). A game-based deep reinforcement learning approach for energy-efficient computation in MEC systems. Knowl.-. *Knowledge-Based Systems, 235*, 107660. DOI: 10.1016/j.knosys.2021.107660

Costa, G. D. C. T., Pedrosa, G. F., Souza, N. P. D., Gemente, F. R. F., Freire, A. B., & Castro, H. D. O. (2017). Type of Game Practiced in Handball According to the Positions of the Attackers: Analysis of the Women's World Handball Championship 2015. *International Journal of Performance Analysis in Sport, 17*(3), 360–373. DOI: 10.1080/24748668.2017.1345197

Duggal, K., Gupta, L. R., & Singh, P. (2021). Gamification and Machine Learning Inspired Approach for Classroom Engagement and Learning. *Mathematical Problems in Engineering, 2021*, 9922775. DOI: 10.1155/2021/9922775

Eltahir, M. E., Alsalhi, N. R., Al-Qatawneh, S., AlQudah, H. A., & Jaradat, M. (2021). The impact of game-based learning (GBL) on students' motivation, engagement and academic performance on an Arabic language grammar course in higher education. *Education and Information Technologies, 26*(3), 3251–3278. DOI: 10.1007/s10639-020-10396-w

Denisova, A., Nordin, A. I., & Cairns, P. (2016, October). The convergence of player experience questionnaires. In *Proceedings of the 2016 Annual Symposium on Computer-Human Interaction in Play* (pp. 33-37).

Ferreira, L., Lelis, L., & Whitehead, J. (2020). Computer-Generated Music for Tabletop Role-Playing Games. In Proceedings of the AAAI Conference on Artificial Intelligence and Interactive Digital Entertainment, Worchester, MA, USA, 19–23 October 2020; pp. 59–65.

Foong, N. W., On, C. K., Alfred, R., Teo, J., & Ibrahim, A. A. A. (2017). Interactive Procedural Generation for Items in Role-Playing Game. In Proceedings of the 2017 IEEE 2nd International Conference on Automatic Control and Intelligent Systems (I2CACIS), Kota Kinabalu, Malaysia, 21 October 2017; pp. 150–154. DOI: 10.1109/I2CACIS.2017.8239049

Gómez, M. Á., Lago-Peñas, C., Viaño, J., & González-Garcia, I. (2014). Effects of Game Location, Team Quality and Final Outcome on Game-Related Statistics in Professional Handball Close Games. *Kinesiology, 46*, 249–257.

Gümüş, H., & Gençoğlu, C. (2020). The Effects of the Goalkeeper Substitution Rule as a New Strategy in Handball: Analysis of Men's European Handball Championship 2020. *Acta Gymnica, 50*(3), 113–121. DOI: 10.5507/ag.2020.015

Hassan, A., Pinkwart, N., & Shafi, M. (2021). Serious games to improve social and emotional intelligence in children with autism. *Entertainment Computing, 38*, 100417. DOI: 10.1016/j.entcom.2021.100417

Hatzimanouil, D. (2020). Goalkeeper's Efficiency in Relation with Throws from Different Attacking Court Areas in Team Handball. *Journal of Physical Education and Sport Management, 7*, 11–18.

Huynh, E., Nyhout, A., Ganea, P., & Chevalier, F. (2020). Designing Narrative-Focused Role-Playing Games for Visualization Literacy in Young Children. *IEEE Transactions on Visualization and Computer Graphics, 27*(2), 924–934. DOI: 10.1109/TVCG.2020.3030464 PMID: 33048745

Karavidas, L., Apostolidis, H., & Tsiatsos, T. (2022). Usability Evaluation of an Adaptive Serious Game Prototype Based on Affective Feedback. *Information (Basel), 13*(9), 425. DOI: 10.3390/info13090425

Khan, A. A., Laghari, A. A., Li, P., Dootio, M. A., & Karim, S. (2023). The collaborative role of blockchain, artificial intelligence, and industrial internet of things in digitalization of small and medium-size enterprises. *Scientific Reports, 13*(1), 1656. DOI: 10.1038/s41598-023-28707-9 PMID: 36717702

Khan, A. A., Shaikh, A. A., & Laghari, A. A. (2022). IoT with Multimedia Investigation: A Secure Process of Digital Forensics Chain-of-Custody using Blockchain Hyperledger Sawtooth. *Arabian Journal for Science and Engineering*, •••, 1–16.

Köknar, C. (2019). Who is at the Center?: Designing Playful Experiences by Using Player-Centered Approach. In Proceedings of the International Conference on Human-Computer Interaction, Orlando, FL, USA, 26–31 July 2019; pp. 11–21. DOI: 10.1007/978-3-030-22602-2_2

Laghari, A. A., Khan, A. A., Alkanhel, R., Elmannai, H., & Bourouis, S. (2023). Lightweight-BIoV: Blockchain Distributed Ledger Technology (BDLT) for Internet of Vehicles (IoVs). *Electronics (Basel), 12*(3), 677. DOI: 10.3390/electronics12030677

Lago-Peñas, C., Gómez, A. M., Viaño, J., González-García, I., & Fernández-Villarino, M. (2013). de L. ángeles Home Advantage in Elite Handball: The Impact of the Quality of Opposition on Team Performance. *International Journal of Performance Analysis in Sport, 13*(3), 724–733. DOI: 10.1080/24748668.2013.11868684

Li, T., Liu, W., Xie, S., Dong, M., Ota, K., Xiong, N. N., & Li, Q. (2021). BPT: A Blockchain-Based Privacy Information Preserving System for Trust Data Collection Over Distributed Mobile-Edge Network. *IEEE Internet of Things Journal, 9*(11), 8036–8052. DOI: 10.1109/JIOT.2021.3117971

Mustač, K., Bačić, K., Skorin-Kapov, L., & Sužnjević, M. (2022). Predicting Player Churn of a Free-to-Play Mobile Video Game Using Supervised Machine Learning. *Applied Sciences (Basel, Switzerland), 12*(6), 2795. DOI: 10.3390/app12062795

Nacke, L., Drachen, A., Kuikkaniemi, K., Niesenhaus, J., Korhonen, H. J., Hoogen, W. M., Poels, K., IJsselsteijn, W. A., & De Kort, Y. A. (2009). Playability and Player Experience Research. In Proceedings of the 2009 DiGRA International Conference: Breaking New Ground: Innovation in Games, Play, Practice and Theory, London, UK, 1–4 September 2009.

Ohnjec, K., Vuleta, D., Milanović, D., & Gruić, I. (2008). Performance Indicators of Teams at the 2003 World Handball Championship for Women in Croatia. *Kinesiology*, *40*, 69–79.

Pascual, A., Font, R., Pascual, X., & Lago-Peñas, C. (2024). Evolution of match performance parameters in elite men's handball 2012–2022. *International Journal of Sports Science & Coaching*, *19*(1), 301–305.

Preuss, M., & Risi, S. (2020). A Games Industry Perspective on Recent Game AI Developments. KI Künstl. *Intell.*, *34*, 81–83.

Prieto, J., Gómez, M.-Á., Volossovitch, A., & Sampaio, J. (2016). Effects of Team Timeouts on the Teams' Scoring Performance in Elite Handball Close Games. *Kinesiology*, *48*(1), 115–123. DOI: 10.26582/k.48.1.4

Primanita, A., Effendi, R., & Hidayat, W. (2017). Comparison of A* and Iterative Deepening A Algorithms for Non-Player Character in Role Playing Game. In Proceedings of the 2017 International Conference on Electrical Engineering and Computer Science (ICECOS), Palembang, Indonesia, 22–23 August 2017; pp. 202–205. DOI: 10.1109/ICECOS.2017.8167134

Sepulveda, G. K., Besoain, F., & Barriga, N. A. (2019). Exploring Dynamic Difficulty Adjustment in Videogames. In Proceedings of the 2019 IEEE CHILEAN Conference on Electrical, Electronics Engineering, Information and Communication Technologies (CHILECON), Valparaiso, Chile, 13–27 November 2019; pp. 1–6.

Tang, K.-Y., Chang, C.-Y., & Hwang, G.-J. (2021). Trends in artificial intelligence-supported e-learning: A systematic review and co-citation network analysis (1998–2019). *Interactive Learning Environments*, •••, 1–19.

Van Der Linden, R., Lopes, R., & Bidarra, R. (2013). Procedural generation of dungeons. *IEEE Transactions on Computational Intelligence and AI in Games*, *6*(1), 78–89. DOI: 10.1109/TCIAIG.2013.2290371

Vaz, V., Ferrari, W., Sarmento, H., Couceiro, M., Sousa, T., & Dias, G. (2023). Handball Offensive Analysis: Comparative Evolution of Linear Tendency Lines between Finalist Teams in the EHF CL. *Applied Sciences (Basel, Switzerland)*, *13*(3), 1366. DOI: 10.3390/app13031366

Wagner, H., Hinz, M., Melcher, K., Radic, V., & Uhrmeister, J. (2023). The PlayerScore: A Systematic Game Observation Tool to Determine Individual Player Performance in Team Handball Competition. *Applied Sciences (Basel, Switzerland)*, *13*(4), 2327. DOI: 10.3390/app13042327

Wang, J. Y. (2015). A Variety Weapons and Armors Design Algorithm for Role-Playing Games. In Proceedings of the 2015 IEEE/ACIS 16th International Conference on Software Engineering, Artificial Intelligence, Networking and Parallel/Distributed Computing (SNPD), Takamatsu, Japan, 1–3 June 2015; pp. 1–5.

Williams, J. P., Hendricks, S. Q., & Winkler, W. K. (2014). *Gaming as Culture: Essays on Reality, Identity and Experience in Fantasy Games*. McFarland.

Zhai, X., Chu, X., Chai, C. S., Jong, M. S. Y., Istenic, A., Spector, M., Liu, J.-B., Yuan, J., & Li, Y. (2021). A Review of Artificial Intelligence (AI) in Education from 2010 to 2020. *Complexity*, *2021*(1), 8812542. DOI: 10.1155/2021/8812542

Zohaib, M. (2018). Dynamic Difficulty Adjustment (DDA) in Computer Games: A Review. *Advances in Human-Computer Interaction*, *2018*, 5681652. DOI: 10.1155/2018/5681652

Zou, D., Huang, Y., & Xie, H. (2021). Digital game-based vocabulary learning: Where are we and where are we going? *Computer Assisted Language Learning*, *34*(5-6), 751–777. DOI: 10.1080/09588221.2019.1640745

Chapter 4
Co-Creating Narratives:
Ludonarrative Agency and Generative AI in Digital Games

Cátia Ferreira
https://orcid.org/0000-0002-0113-6634
CECC, Universidade Católica Portuguesa, Portugal

ABSTRACT

This chapter explores how narrative agency, authorship, and co-creative practices in digital games are being transformed by generative AI systems, with an emphasis on AI Dungeon. It views storytelling in GenAI environments as a type of procedural co-authorship—distributed, negotiated, and frequently unpredictable—drawing on theories from narrative studies, game design, and AI ethics. The chapter identifies important dynamics like narrative drift, editorial intervention, and ludonarrative friction by qualitatively analyzing twenty structured gameplay sessions. It suggests that participants are continuously negotiating meaning and coherence with algorithmic systems in their roles as authors, editors, and curators. For academics, designers, and teachers attempting to understand the emerging field of interactive narrative design, this has important implications. The findings draw attention to the ethical conundrums and imaginative potential of AI-mediated storytelling.

1. INTRODUCTION

Digital storytelling is undergoing a significant shift due to the emergence of generative artificial intelligence (GenAI). Nevertheless, questions about authorship, player agency, and narrative structure have long been of interest to interactive media scholars (Ramesh et al., 2024). GenAI presents an unprecedented model of collaborative authorship in the context of digital games, where narrative is built

DOI: 10.4018/979-8-3373-4637-3.ch004

ght © 2026, IGI Global Scientific Publishing. Copying or distributing in print or electronic forms without written permission of IGI Global Scientific Publishing is prohibited. Use of this chapter to
generative artificial intelligence (AI) technologies is expressly prohibited. The publisher reserves all rights to license its use for generative AI training and machine learning model development.

through a combination of systems, player choices, and interfaces. This effectively challenges the conventional boundaries between player, creator, and machine (Gerba, 2025). With each playthrough, GenAI systems create unique, personalized narrative experiences by dynamically generating content in response to player input rather than delivering a predefined story. As GenAI becomes more and more incorporated into storytelling practices, the pressing issues of authorship, creative control, and accountability are brought to the fore of the discussion (Thorne, 2020).

AI Dungeon represents an advancement in the domain of interactive narrative design. Rather than limiting players to predetermined dialogue options or linear plotlines, the platform utilizes advanced language models to facilitate a collaborative storytelling process between the user and the AI. This results in a dynamic, improvisational experience where the boundaries between author and participant are blurred. Players are empowered to shape narrative trajectories, moving beyond the constraints of pre-authored content. Such a model compels a reconsideration of traditional concepts of agency and authorship within digital games. The interplay between human creativity and AI-generated responses fosters an emergent narrative structure, where neither entity claims exclusive ownership of the unfolding story. As a result, *AI Dungeon* challenges established notions of narrative control and prompts scholars and game designers to reflect on the evolving possibilities for interaction and storytelling in virtual environments.

This chapter explores how the ideas of authorship and agency are being reshaped by generative AI systems, such as *AI Dungeon*. Unlike conventional models, like Murray's (2017) concept of agency as satisfying power, which highlights a player's capacity to make significant decisions in controlled settings, these AI-powered systems encourage a less stable but more impromptu and conversational type of agency. The analysis draws on qualitative, play-based explorations of *AI Dungeon* sessions to examine how it is possible to navigate and perceive control within stories co-created alongside an unpredictable AI counterpart. This unpredictability generates unique forms of friction, complicating the co-creative process, yet simultaneously opening up new possibilities for creative engagement and narrative experimentation.

Generative AI systems represent more general dynamics of algorithmic creativity and distributed agency beyond their narrative affordances. According to McCosker and Wilken (2020), researching algorithmic systems necessitates paying attention to both their technical architectures and cultural logics, as well as how these factors shape human participation. This viewpoint presents *AI Dungeon* as a platform that operationalizes specific presumptions regarding automation, authorship, and control in addition to being a place for co-creative play. As a result, this chapter addresses procedural co-authorship as both a cultural phenomenon influenced by modern AI logics and a narrative practice.

To understand how these systems function, it is important to consider the underlying technologies. GenAI describes a set of models able to produce original content such as text, images, audio, or video. These systems work by identifying and replicating patterns from enormous datasets. In storytelling contexts, the backbone is typically transformer-based architectures (Vaswani et al., 2017), which allow for contextually aware and stylistically sophisticated narrative generation. The concept ludonarrative describes the point where narrative components and gameplay mechanics (*ludus*) converge. The sometimes tense relationship between what you do in a game and the story that develops is addressed by this idea, which was made popular initially by Frasca (2003) and then developed by Juul (2005). In this sense, agency refers to the player's capacity to genuinely influence the plot by their decisions and actions; not merely pressing buttons but making significant choices. Lastly, co-creation is a cooperative process in which a story is developed by the interaction of several agents, in this case a machine and a human. Both sides influence the plot's development in this dynamic collaboration.

Although digital games have always made possible some degree of player input and customization, GenAI represents a substantial shift from previous models. Traditionally, player agency was constrained by boundaries imposed by developers, even in open-world or sandbox games the options tend to be expansive but ultimately predetermined. With GenAI, the narrative landscape expands dynamically as content is generated in real time. This semi-autonomous behavior complicates traditional notions of authorship because even the system's designers may not be able to fully predict its outputs. This is consistent with Hayles's (2017) concept of cognitive assemblages, where meaning is created through the interaction of human and machine agents, dispersing intention throughout a network rather than locating it in a single author. Similar to this, frameworks such as Latour's Actor-Network Theory (2005) aid in the conceptualization of the sharing of agency among diverse actors, such as users, interfaces, and algorithms. Neither the user nor the AI retain complete narrative control in GenAI-driven storytelling platforms. Rather, storytelling is a negotiation process that is influenced by both algorithmic prediction and human input; miscommunication and surprise frequently cause the story to take unexpected turns.

Interactive storytelling powered by AI fundamentally disrupts conventional notions of genre boundaries and narrative structure. Users frequently express frustration (and sometimes awe) at the unpredictable creativity of these systems, because, for instance, at one moment, the AI produces genuinely original story beats; the next, it introduces jarring inconsistencies, tonal shifts, or even culturally questionable material (Serbanescu, 2024; Wu et al., 2021). This unpredictability means that the user's role shifts from passive consumer to active editor, stepping in to redirect the narrative whenever the AI veers off course or generates problematic content. This ongoing negotiation creates what Harrell (2013) labels as ludonarrative friction, highlighting the continual tension between the AI's generative impulses and the user's expectations for story coherence. Users are involved in ongoing narrative repair, curating and reshaping the story as it develops, as opposed to adhering to a neat, linear structure or even the well-known branches of a choose-your-own-adventure. In collaborative storytelling settings, where human participants frequently step in to preserve narrative coherence and logic, this pattern is particularly noticeable (Branch et al., 2021).

Furthermore, the collaborative style of these stories highlights issues of accountability and authorship. Who writes an AI-generated story—the machine, the player, or the programmers who trained the model? This ambiguity resonates with Aarseth's (1997) notion of ergodic literature, where non trivial effort is required to traverse the text. In GenAI-based games, this effort is not just navigational but also editorial and interpretive. In order to create a meaningful story, the player must cooperate and compete with the machine, which makes authorship a distributed and contingent process. This is consistent with current debates in AI and game studies, where it is becoming more widely accepted that algorithmic and human agents share the function of authorship (Yannakakis & Togelius, 2025).

Lastly, this chapter argues that the emergence of GenAI in digital games signifies a paradigm shift in interactive storytelling rather than just giving designers a new tool to use. According to Ryan (2006), digital narratives are characterized by the systems that organize that interaction as well as by the interaction itself. The system itself becomes a co-author with GenAI, a responsive but foreign collaborator with an expansive yet erratic narrative logic. This opens up new narrative possibilities, but it also poses new moral and artistic problems.

In the sections that follow, this chapter will examine how players navigate agency, meaning, and narrative coherence in this generative environment by analyzing a corpus of *AI Dungeon* gameplay sessions from various genres. Using theories of digital authorship, human-AI co-creativity, and ludonarrative design, it will make the case that GenAI calls into question current frameworks for comprehending narrative in games and necessitates a reconsideration of our definitions of authorship, play, and creative control in the era of algorithmic storytelling.

Accordingly, this chapter addresses the following key research questions:

> RQ1: How does generative AI reshape player agency and narrative authority within interactive storytelling environments?
>
> RQ2: What new narrative dynamics, such as "narrative drift," co-authorship, and shifting player roles, emerge through player–AI collaboration in games like *AI Dungeon*?

RQ3: What are the ethical, cultural, and design-related implications of integrating GenAI into interactive narrative systems?

By answering these questions, the chapter aims to offer a critical understanding of the transformative possibilities of GenAI in digital games and to suggest directions for future research and design practice.

2. THEORETICAL FOUNDATIONS

The rapid integration of GenAI into digital games is reshaping foundational concepts in narrative theory, game studies, and digital media. This section develops a conceptual framework for understanding how GenAI systems challenge and extend traditional models of storytelling, authorship, and player agency.

The chapter's argument is structured by three interconnected tensions that form the theoretical framework. The first is the redistribution of narrative authority: Authorship is decentralized by GenAI systems, moving from a single writer or designer to a network of machine and human agents. Second, players in GenAI environments have to negotiate systems that both grant expressive freedom and impose algorithmic limitations. Third, the rise of co-authorship: narrative turns into a cooperative, methodical, and frequently erratic process influenced by both machine improvisation and human intent.

Three subsections are used to examine these tensions. From poststructuralist criticisms of authorship to the idea of cyberdrama, Section 2.1 discusses the development of narrative theory, emphasizing how GenAI systems operationalize textual plurality. Section 2.2 uses game studies to analyze how player interaction in generative environments is shaped by procedural design, ludonarrative agency, and ergodicity. The role of the player as editor, curator, and improviser is highlighted in Section 2.3, which discusses theories of creativity and co-authorship in human–AI collaboration.

2.1 Narrative Theory, Distributed Authorship, and Cognitive Assemblages

Theoretical underpinnings of interactive storytelling rely on a fundamental change in the understanding of narrative meaning. Barthes (1977) puts forward the contention in his seminal essay “The Death of the Author” meaning is constituted through the interpretive act of the reader, not the original intention of the author. That poststructuralist criticism in favor of the author amplified the power of interpretation for the reader. Foucault (1979) expanded upon this critique by proposing the concept of the "author function," in which authorship is posited as a discursive construct, which organizes and legitimates texts. Both perspectives generated a paradigm that sees narrative as a dynamic, communal endeavor and not a one-way transmission from writer to reader. This paradigm is tangibly visible within online spaces. By bringing the audience into active participant status, interactive stories, especially those facilitated by generative AI, realize these theoretical principles. The consumers of these systems co-create narratives simultaneously with algorithms that produce narrative content as a function of user activity, in contrast to being passive consumers of meaning. Author, audience, and machine dissolve into one another, facilitating a distributed and emergent co-authorship.

A helpful theoretical framework under consideration of this development is offered by Ryan (2001), who differentiates between narrativity, immersion, and interactivity. In her opinion, increased interactivity in computer narratives can interfere with the rational flow of the narrative, rendering them frequently unable to maintain coherence. Ryan's subsequent work (2006) on storyworlds stresses the interactive basis of meaning production in such environments: players construct cognitive models to interpret narrative content, but in generative systems, such storyworlds are repeatedly reconfigured by sustained human–machine interaction. In GenAI environments, narrative response is generated probabilistically, rather than predetermined, and therefore storytelling is one of improvisation, co-authorship, and frequently unpredictability. The player is curator, always interpreting, adjusting, and repairing the story in order to keep it coherent—a feature of co-creative storytelling in GenAI systems.

Cyberdrama, a framework introduced by Murray (2017), offers another lens through which to understand these dynamics. Cyberdrama articulates dramatic conventions with computational logic, putting agency at the forefront as "the satisfying power to take meaningful action and see the results of our decisions and choices" (Murray, 2017, p. 59). GenAI systems allow for more fluid, conversational forms of agency, whereby the AI adjusts the narrative in real time, as compared to commercial games, which generally use branching narrative as a method of structuring agency. Both creative potential and unpredictability are introduced into the equation by this agency: players are able to make choices that influence the story, but they are filtered through unguessable, probability-driven algorithms. As such, when the system is generating contradictory or surprising output, players tend to become directors or editors. This tension between creative liberty and algorithmic whim distinguishes GenAI narration from traditional narrative design. The status of authorship is also more complicated by the improvisational nature of GenAI systems. It is unclear whether the AI, the player, or the developers who created the underlying model is the author. This vagueness is in line with Foucault's (1979) argument that authorship is a function of discourse, rather than a fixed identity. In practice, GenAI system authorship is distributed among a set of agents, ranging from the player to the AI, the training content, and the technical architecture of the platform.

Hayles's (2017) cognitive assemblages theory explores this discussion critically. For Hayles, cognition is dispersed through ensembles of human and nonhuman performers, like interfaces, algorithms, and technological systems, rather than being within human awareness. The forces within those assemblages produce narrative authorship in GenAI-enabled storytelling: player input, algorithmic generation, and infrastructure mediation recursively blend and co-exist in real-time to create meaning. According to this model, authorship is reconceptualized as an emergent, negotiated process taking place in a heterogeneous network where creativity and agency are continually reorganized and redistributed. Thus, the narrative was not produced by a single individual but by distributed cognition, "cognitive nonconscious" processes that Hayles writes about, in which meaning and agency are continually in flux.

The application of these dynamics in real life is represented by systems such as *AI Dungeon*, where players input dialogue or actions to enter and the AI returns with continuation of the story. Unlike traditional games, which have a set plot, this model promotes ongoing and unrestrained open-ended, improvisational storytelling (Lee et al., 2023). Empirical evidence demonstrates that users feel more creative and inspired upon interacting with text produced by an AI (Roemmele, 2021). It is difficult to ensure narrative coherence and user involvement while the users get frustrated at inconsistent or out-of-place responses (Lee et al., 2023). Ludonarrative friction, as it was conceptualized by Harrell (2013), refers to the tension resulting from incoherence between gameplay mechanics and narrative. The challenges point to the necessity of co-creation and player intervention. GenAI system users must reconcile their own narrative purposes with the generative tendencies of the system itself, both potentially causing innovative dissonance and productive synergy (Grabarczyk & Walther, 2022; Sicart, 2013). In turn, the readability of the GenAI systems across genre and tone reflect the heterogeneity of training data available to large language models. Whenever a story abruptly shifts genre or style, the players must remain uniform in playing through the interpretive capabilities and creative adaptability (Arif et al., 2024; Cheung & Shi, 2024; Roemmele, 2021).

There has been a substantial shift in narrative theory and practice from poststructuralist textual plurality to cyberdrama and cognitive assemblages. GenAI systems put these theoretical insights into practice by treating readers as co-authors and turning the text into a dynamic, interactive process. This collaborative and flexible storytelling approach challenges conventional ideas about authorial control, genre stability, and narrative coherence. It is essential to apply frameworks from narrative theory and game studies to comprehend the practical applications of these developments. Game studies offer crucial instruments for examining how players engage with systems to influence narrative outcomes, while narrative theory clarifies issues of authorship and meaning. To place GenAI storytelling within the larger framework of interactive design and player experience, the next section will discuss ideas like ergodicity, procedural design, and ludonarrative agency.

2.2 Procedurality, Ergodicity, and Ludonarrative Agency

Building on the above discussion of distributed authorship, this section examines how procedural design and player interaction shape narrative meaning in generative environments. In game studies, the interplay between system rules and player agency is central to describing how experience and meaning emerge during play (Bogost, 2007; Murray, 2017). Current advances in generative AI have altered such dynamics on a basic level, enabling systems to evolve and alter narrative worlds in real time (Short & Adams, 2019). In contrast to traditional games, where players' choices are constrained by pre-authored pathways, GenAI-enabled environments utilize procedural generation to create constantly evolving story spaces (Harrell & Zhu, 2009). This procedural logic favors the concept of ludonarrative agency, meaning the capacity for the player to influence the narrative with meaningful action, while it demonstrates the constraints of algorithmic procedure (Sicart, 2009).

Aarseth's (1997) theory of ergodic literature provides a significant framework for the criticism of these systems. In ergodic media, meaning is produced through active engagement and work, rather than passive consumption. This is especially pronounced in GenAI environments, where the players must continuously interpret, manage, and even sometimes repair the AI output in order to ensure narrative coherence. Aarseth's later critique (2012) of linearity in digital narratives also points to the benefit of procedural systems: narrative coherence is not predetermined but is constructed incrementally through the ongoing negotiation between system rules and player action. Juul's (2005) concept of the "half-real"—the games' dual existence as fictional worlds and rule-governed systems—is more strongly articulated in GenAI environments. Because the fictional worlds are dynamically generated and the system rules are probabilistic rather than deterministic, narrative trajectories in these are unpredictable. Players must take on an active editorial role, mediating between their narrative intentions and the generative logic of the system, because this unpredictability calls into question conventional ideas of authorship.

In this context, the notion of procedural authorship becomes central. Unlike conventional authorship, based on monolithic creative intent, procedural authorship emerges from the interplay of code, algorithms, and the ongoing negotiation between system and player (Mateas & Stern, 2005a; Bogost, 2007). In GenAI systems, the player's input is a prompt that evokes the generative model to produce narrative content out of learned statistical patterns. In this manner, narrative meaning is not the outcome of a singular authorial act, but rather of a procedural, dialogical exchange between human and computer (Mateas & Stern, 2005a; Treanor & Mateas, 2013). Of particular insight in this context is Crawford's (2004) distinction between storytelling and storybuilding. While storytelling describes a linear, authorially controlled process, storybuilding emphasizes the player's agency in the development of narrative as it is being performed. GenAI areas are a prime illustration of this movement: players are not merely selecting from predefined options but are directly engaged in real-time co-creation of narrative content. However, this heightened agency is contradictory in nature. Although there is greater freedom of expression for players, what they do is ultimately run through the generative system's underlying algorithms, producing moments of unpredictability and so-called ludonarrative dissonance, the tension resulting when gameplay mechanics and narrative expectation clash (Koenitz, 2015; Grabarczyk & Walther, 2022). Ludonarrative agency, which acknowledges that agency in GenAI environments is adaptive and negotiated rather than binary, encapsulates this paradox (Koenitz, 2015; Grabarczyk & Walther, 2023). Players are co-authors who continuously interpret and rework the developing story rather than imposing complete control. According to academics like Joyce (2015) and McGill (2022), agency is more about navigating uncertainty, resolving inconsistencies, and ongoing editorial intervention, especially in generative environments.

The concept of emergent narrative is central to understanding these dynamics. As Jenkins (2004) and LeBlanc (2000) observe, emergent narratives are those that occur as a result of the interplay between player action and system reaction, as opposed to scripted events. In GenAI environments, this emergence is heightened: narrative is collaboratively constructed in the moment by the interaction of player input and algorithmic generation (Roemmele, 2021). The narratives thereby generated are themselves unstable, founded upon the alignment, or misalignment, between player intention and system output. This instability in turn exposes the creative potential and editorial challenges of GenAI storytelling, demanding new models of agency and authorship (Mateas & Stern, 2005b; Koenitz, 2015). Moments of ludonarrative dissonance, where the system logic departs from player expectation, are not so much failures as sites of creative negotiation (Murnane, 2018). Such dissonance can yield new narrative possibilities, but it also betrays the limits of current GenAI systems, which commonly break down at long-term coherence, character continuity, and genre consistency. The player is continually called on to negotiate these limits through processes of narrative repair and redirection, enacting a form of procedural, performative authorship (Wark, 2007).

Drawing on both Hayles's (2017) concept of cognitive assemblages and Latour's Actor-Network Theory (2005) is instructive in order to fully envision how agency and authorship are distributed in GenAI storytelling environments. Latour argues that agency emerges from a variety of networks that encompass people, machines, and infrastructure, rather than being solely a trait of human actors. Hayles, who sees cognition as distributed among both human and nonhuman agents, supports this as previously stated by asserting that meaning and agency originate from the dynamic interactions of various agents within a system. According to both perspectives, player choices, algorithmic operations, training data, and platform design all interact to continuously negotiate and reshape agency and authorship. This suggests that individuals function within a framework of ergodic and procedural systems rather than independently. The actor-network and cognitive assemblage frameworks emphasize the relational, contingent, and emergent elements of narrative production in GenAI systems by highlighting the continually negotiated and rearranged agency among multiple actors.

In conclusion, by emphasizing procedural authorship, ludonarrative agency, and emergent narrative form, GenAI narrative systems reinterpret conventional narrative architecture. The dynamic interplay between individual intention, system affordance, and a wider cultural and technical horizon shapes the players' experiences, which require constant negotiation and accommodation. Actor-Network Theory and cognitive assemblages' combined insights offer a platform for understanding these complexities within interactive design. Building upon this theoretical basis, the following section will examine how co-authorship and creativity are enacted in human–AI collaboration and shed more light on the processes that create narrative meaning in GenAI environments.

2.3 Creativity and Authorship in Human and AI Co-creation

Generative AI systems considerably disrupt current presumption over creativity, authorship, and the boundary of human–machine collaboration in cultural production. Authorship in online games built with large language models (LLMs) for real-time narrative creation is a distributed, procedural, and negotiated one. This section explores how GenAI systems can function as textual collaborators redefining the roles of both designers and players in contemporary storytelling.

The concept of machines having the potential to assist in meaning-making is not recent, with the current wave of generative AI being preceded by it. Harrell and Zhu (2009) set the stage for computational narrative intelligence, in which AI systems are viewed as being able to generate culturally pertinent symbols and structures that actively contribute to narrative meaning. Riedl and Bulitko (2013) took this perspective further by conceptualizing AI as an adaptive storyteller that could dynamically adjust narrative content in response to user activity. These paradigms position AI not only as utility, but as a semi-autonomous narrative actor. Within GenAI systems, this agency is manifested through the ability of the system to generate text from player input, creating a constant, improvisational loop of co-construction of narrative. Each response and prompt draws on the previous, constructing a story co-authored in real-time.

The co-creative agency concept, as described by Kreminski et al. (2020), emphasizes the dynamic interplay between human and AI in such settings. The users tend to experience the AI as a creative companion with its own affordances, constraints, and idiosyncrasies, not a content-neutral generator. Successful participation demands that users build an understanding of the behavior patterns of the AI, predict its inclinations, and orient their input in response. Wu et al.'s Human-AI Co-Creation Model (2021) also depicts the way this collaboration can enhance human creativity in that AI systems can be the source of surprise, a source of inspiration, and on occasion, a source of frustration. User reports and empirical evidence indicate that these interactions are capable of producing bursts of creative synergy as well as conflict when the AI results are incoherent, inconsistent, or culturally relevant. These moments of friction are not only technical but reveal underlying uncertainties built into co-authored narratives. As Bender et al. (2021) caution, the apparent agency of AI can obscure structural power behind training data and model design. Large language models are trained on massive datasets with embedded historical biases, cultural stereotypes, and linguistic hierarchies. Therefore, GenAI systems' outputs will reflect and reproduce such structures and challenge the neutrality and accountability of AI as a storytelling agent.

Procedural authorship implies that the locus of creative power shifts from authorial intention to code, data, and user interaction (Ryan et al., 2025; Bozkurt, 2024). In GenAI systems, apparent player agency is constrained by rules of algorithms and probabilistic links. The player's role thus extends beyond authorship to encompass editorial functions: interpreting, correcting, and guiding the AI's outputs to maintain narrative coherence and align with personal intent (Ryan et al., 2025; Bozkurt, 2024). This editorial labor is central to the co-creative process, requiring users to engage in "narrative repair" through prompt engineering, selective rewriting, and real-time intervention (Gerba, 2025; Yi et al., 2025). The mixed role of writer, editor, and performer puts players in a condition of continuous story improvisation in which authorship, creatorship, and culpability are negotiated in terms of degrees of editorial power and human intervention.

This refiguring of authorship has significant implications for narrative theory and practical game design. Traditional models, grounded in individual vision and intentionality, prove insufficient for situations where the work of human and nonhuman authors is shared, and narrative coherence emerges from ongoing negotiation in lieu of fixed design (Ginsburg & Budiardjo, 2019; Ryan et al., 2025). An adaptive model of collective authorship, responsive to the procedural, adaptive, and sometimes mercurial nature of GenAI storytelling, is required (Gerba, 2025; Yi et al., 2025).

The ethical and cultural stakes of this shift are substantial. Designers must consider not only the player–AI architecture but also the broader implications of AI-generated content, such as reinforcing stereotypes, and narrative failure management (Bender et al., 2021). Critical interaction with generative systems requires players to cultivate creative and critical literacies: knowledge of AI limitations, recognition of biases in output, and the development of strategies for effective and ethical co-creation (Bender et al., 2021; Ryan et al., 2025).

Collaborative nature of GenAI narrative also requires a redefinition of creativity itself. Current models tend to emphasize solo genius, originality, and intention. On the other hand, co-creative practices draw attention to relational creativity, creativity that emerges through interaction, responsiveness, and awareness of context (Glăveanu, 2014; Harris, 2014). These are different from sociocultural theories of creativity (Glăveanu, 2014; Sawyer, 2012), which also have the focus that creative action is socially and contextually embedded. Creativity in GenAI environments is distributed between human and nonhuman agents, and often arises through acts of misunderstanding, negotiation, and even conflict (McGuire et al., 2024; Kreminski et al., 2020). These conflicts are able to yield new narrative possibility, surprising character development, and new genre breakages—outcomes not attributable to a single author, but to the collaborative process itself (Gerba, 2025; Yi et al., 2025).

Co-authorship in GenAI systems is thus a relational, negotiated, and ethically complex practice, determined by technological affordance, cultural assumption, and player intervention. It involves reconceptualizing authorship as distributed and procedural, and relocating critical and creative literacies at the heart of the future of interactive storytelling. The following section will present a case study of *AI Dungeon* elaborating on how these dynamics are played out in practice, revealing both the challenges and opportunities of human–AI narrative co-creation.

3. CASE STUDY

AI Dungeon, an innovative development in generative AI for interactive storytelling, underscores shifts in authorship, agency, and creativity in the virtual era. Developed by Latitude in 2019, it creates entertaining, interactive stories that adapt to user input by utilizing transformer-based language models, like OpenAI's GPT-2 and GPT-3. In contrast to popular interactive fiction, which tends to limit player agency with preconceived player choices, *AI Dungeon* allows unstructured user input at any point in the story, allowing for a highly dynamic and interactive narrative experience.

The key innovation of *AI Dungeon* is the use of large language models learned on massive online corpora, which are excellent at creating contextually rich and diverse narrative material (Radford et al., 2019; Brown et al., 2020). The models generate dialogue, narrative actions, and world-building information on the basis of user input, creating a collaborative narrative that is generated in real time. The recursive exchange between user prompt and algorithmic output demonstrates the distributed authorship and cognitive assemblage processes, where meaning and agency are negotiated continually by human–machine co-operation.

AI Dungeon interface is minimalist and user-friendly: users select genre, provide prompts, and receive narrative continuation generated by the system. This recursive process supports conventional storytelling as well as experimental, genre-blending narratives. Users can collaborate with others to co-share worlds, retell each other's stories, and construct the narrative space thanks to the platform's social features, which foster worldbuilding in partnership. Because of its features, *AI Dungeon* has attracted attention from the creative and research communities. It is recognized as a fertile ground for worldbuilding, collaborative writing, and narrative experimentation (Hua & Raley, 2020; Lamerichs, 2020; Mitchell, 2022). The participatory nature of *AI Dungeon* has been viewed as an efficient pedagogical strategy for improving creative writing and media literacy, particularly within the educational environment (Santiago, 2023). Its flexibility and ease of use make it a prime example in today's debates regarding the future of authorship, narrative, and creativity in digital media.

By challenging traditional assumptions of authorship, coherence, and genre expectation, this approach enables a more interactive and engaged storytelling experience (Hua & Raley, 2020). While, nevertheless, there are political and moral concerns involved by this development. Because training data is unfiltered, *AI Dungeon* has occasionally produced offensive or damaging stereotype-promoting content. Although moderation methods have been implemented, they have tended to be reactive rather than proactive, which has been subject to controversy concerning how one weighs moral duty and creative freedom (Mitchell, 2022).

The development of the platform reflects broader challenges in the integration of generative AI into interactive systems. Developers have tried to enhance the quality of narrative and player control through the introduction of specialized models (e.g., Griffin, Dragon, Hermes), user-configurable AI command inputs, larger memory systems, and player-configurable controls (Latitude, 2024a; Latitude, 2024b; Latitude, 2024c). These advances are intended to provide greater coherence, consistency, and player control, and represent a step toward more user-defined and flexible AI storytelling platforms.

The open community environment of *AI Dungeon* has transformed the platform into a living story laboratory. Players actively contribute, modify, and comment on narratives, thus collaboratively enriching the universe of the game, as well as critically analyzing narrative form, significance, and the presence of AI in creative co-authoring (Hua & Raley, 2020; Mitchell, 2022). This collaborative engagement is a demonstration of procedural authorship and ludonarrative agency, as both players and AI contribute in real-time to the evolving narrative. While successful, *AI Dungeon* remains susceptible to criticism for its reliance on black-box language models, continuous biases, and inconsistent storytelling quality (Hua & Raley, 2020; Lamerichs, 2020). These target the general ethical and technical concerns faced by generative AI technology when applied to narrative.

The intricacies of player and AI co-authorship, the negotiation of narrative agency, and the moral ramifications of generative storytelling can all be explored in depth within *AI Dungeon*. Its dynamic narrative generation and open-ended design highlight GenAI's inherent limitations in interactive media as well as its creative potential. The research approach used to methodically examine these dynamics is described in the following section. This includes the structure of analytical play sessions, collection techniques, and interpretive frameworks that evaluate the development of narrative agency and collaborative authorship in *AI Dungeon*.

4. METHODOLOGY

The study employs qualitative, interpretive methodology to study real-time play and generative AI interaction in the development of narrative agency, coherence, and meaning. The research is grounded in analytical play sessions conducted by the author using *AI Dungeon*, a platform that exemplifies the dynamics of player–AI co-authorship. The methodological approach is intended to capture the complex, contextual, and frequently unpredictable aspects of storytelling in GenAI environments, where narrative is co-constructed through iterative human-machine interactions rather than being pre-authored.

The focus of the study on emergent narrative structures, interpretive agency, and meaning-making informs the choice of a qualitative framework. This research focuses on the interaction between player input, AI responses, and the changing storyworld rather than looking for predictive models or broadly applicable patterns; a positioning that is consistent with interpretive traditions in game studies, narrative studies, and digital media research, which emphasize the importance of subjectivity, context, and reflexivity in understanding interactive experiences.

4.1 Research Design

The research comprised twenty analytical play sessions, each targeting specific elements of player–AI interaction. Conducted over several weeks, the researcher meticulously noted the differences in genre, prompt structure, and interaction style.

The goal was to assemble a varied collection of narrative experiences that could uncover the strengths and weaknesses of GenAI storytelling.

A different narrative prompt opened each session. Either the researcher came up with these prompts or they were adapted from *AI Dungeon*'s genre templates, which include mystery, sci-fi, and fantasy. To test how well the system performed in various narrative contexts, the prompts varied in tone, complexity, and themes. Like a player, the researcher engaged with the AI during each session by entering actions, dialogue, and plot points while simultaneously monitoring and considering the system's reactions. The sessions were designed as analytical tools to identify particular narrative problems, like genre drift, character inconsistency, or tension between gameplay and story, rather than to replicate normal gameplay. This strategy is rooted in the traditions of analytical game design (Salen & Zimmerman, 2004) and critical play (Flanagan, 2009), where play serves as a means of inquiry rather than merely amusement.

A complete overview of the sessions, including genre, duration, and intervention style, is provided in Table 1 in the following section.

4.2 Data Collection

The data collection strategy in this research aimed to record both the textual and contextual aspects of the co-creative process. The whole interaction for all sessions of the game were recorded, keeping not just the input and output timing and order but also the visual interface of the platform. Such full accounts of user interaction and real-time storytelling were created by the screenshots. Moreover, all player prompts, responses, and system contributions of player dialogue to the AI were recorded. The transcripts provided the primary textual data for further semiotic and narrative analysis to enable close examination of the unfolding story and interaction patterns. Analytical memos and observational notes by the researcher were added to the records after each session. These thoughts contained emergent patterns, surprising moments, and challenges, and they yielded rich insights regarding the collaborative storytelling processes and the researcher's interpretation process. This comprehensive approach ensured every session was systematically documented. With the addition of reflective practice and recognizing the interpretive role of the researcher, the method allows for rich and well-rounded analysis of human–AI co-creation.

In total, twenty structured play sessions were conducted, purposefully designed to sample a wide range of genres, interaction styles, and levels of player intervention. These sessions included fantasy, noir, sci-fi, romance, horror, satire, and other narrative modes, each selected to test the generative system's performance under varying thematic and stylistic demands. Session durations ranged from 8 to 14 minutes, with the player adopting diverse input styles—from directive and correctional to experimental and reflective. Narrative drift was observed with varying frequency: some sessions (e.g., S02 Noir, S06 Historical Fiction, S11 Philosophical Allegory) exhibited high levels of genre instability and tonal inconsistency, while others (e.g., S01 Fantasy, S04 Horror, S17 Whodunit) maintained a coherent narrative trajectory. Table 1 summarizes the core characteristics of each session, providing an overview of the dataset and illustrating the diversity of narrative contexts, co-creation dynamics, and AI response patterns.

Table 1. Summary of the characteristics of the game sessions for data collection

Session ID	Genre Prompt	Player Input Style	Narrative Drift	Duration	Notes on AI Response Type
S01	Fantasy	Narrative-focused	Low	12 min	Context-aware, rich in detail
S02	Noir	Correctional, plot-focused	High	9 min	Inconsistent tone, frequent shifts
S03	Sci-Fi	Experimental, chaotic	Medium	11 min	Adaptive, embraces surreal twists
S04	Horror	Immersive, sensory-rich	Low	14 min	Atmospheric, slow-building
S05	Romance	Character-driven	Medium	10 min	Emotional, sometimes erratic
S06	Historical Fiction	Procedural, timeline-focused	High	13 min	Factually inconsistent
S07	Satire	Playful, ironic	Medium	8 min	Responsive, clever
S08	Post-apocalyptic	Tactical, survival-based	Medium	11 min	Gritty, resource-aware
S09	Mythological epic	Elevated, poetic	High	14 min	Formal, symbolic, fragmented
S10	Detective noir	Interrogative, clipped	Low	9 min	Stylistic, trope-rich
S11	Philosophical allegory	Reflective, abstract	High	13 min	Metaphorical, slow to respond
S12	Superhero fiction	Action-driven, cinematic	Medium	12 min	Fast-paced, occasionally chaotic
S13	Magical Realism	Observational, intuitive	High	12 min	Symbol-laden, lyrical
S14	Psychological Drama	Reflective, introspective	High	13 min	Internal monologue, metaphorical
S15	Steampunk Adventure	Energetic, action-inclined	Medium	10 min	Inventive, techy, verbose
S16	Cyberpunk Dystopia	Directive, system-focused	High	12 min	Fast, glitch-prone
S17	Classic Whodunit	Interrogative, orderly	Low	11 min	Pattern-seeking, deductive

continued on following page

Table 1. Continued

Session ID	Genre Prompt	Player Input Style	Narrative Drift	Duration	Notes on AI Response Type
S18	Historical Fiction (WWI)	Detail-rich, era-conscious	Low	13 min	Chronological, thematic
S19	Horror – Slow Burn	Sparse, suspense-building	Medium	14 min	Minimalist, atmospheric
S20	Satirical Sci-Fi	Absurdist, ironic	High	10 min	Exaggerated, humorous

4.3 Data Analysis

The analytical approach examines the complexities of human–AI co-creation in narrative environments using three interconnected interpretive techniques, each derived from a distinct disciplinary tradition. Combining these techniques allows for the investigation of player-system interaction's thematic, symbolic, and structural elements.

Based on Aarseth's (2012) framework, ludonarrative analysis looks at how system rules and gameplay mechanics impact story outcomes. This method focuses on the relationship between player agency and algorithmic processes, examining the points of alignment and conflict between ludic elements and narrative coherence. In the context of *AI Dungeon,* it investigates how the procedural design of the platform mediates the co-construction of the emergent narrative between player inputs and AI responses. The way in which players negotiate agency within the affordances and constraints of the system is given particular attention.

Additionally, semiotic reading uses Barthes's (1977) poststructuralist narrative theory to interpret the patterns, signs, and symbols that emerge in player-AI interactions. This point of view focuses on how language choices, genre conventions, and cultural references interwoven throughout discourse are used to shape, contest, and redefine meaning. It is particularly helpful in determining how the AI replicates well-known cliches using its training data and how players either accept or reject these narrative cues through interpretive and editorial interventions.

Following the reflexive thematic analysis proposed by Braun and Clarke (2006), thematic coding finds recurrent themes and conflicts in analytical memos and session transcripts. After carefully examining the data, codes were created inductively and then categorized into more general themes like "narrative drift," "editorial intervention," "genre instability," and "co-authorship tension." This method offers a cross-session perspective by connecting specific interactions to more general conceptual issues in human–AI collaboration.

A more comprehensive interpretation is possible when these approaches are combined: semiotic reading explores the textual and symbolic negotiations of meaning, ludonarrative analysis reveals the structural dynamics of play, and thematic coding identifies the patterns that influence collaborative storytelling. This integrated approach explains the wider implications of GenAI-driven narrative co-creation while also highlighting the more specific aspects of individual interactions.

4.4 Methodological Considerations

This study's design and implementation were influenced by a number of methodological factors. First, a degree of subjectivity is introduced by the researcher's dual roles as an analyst and a player, which can be both advantageous and disadvantageous. Deep immersion and reflective insight are possible in this role, but bias and positionality must be carefully considered. The study uses transparent documentation of interpretive decisions and reflexive writing to address this. Furthermore, reflexivity was essential in this research process. As both researcher and participant, the dual role occupied throughout this study inevitably shaped the interpretations presented here. The author's background as a frequent player of narrative-driven games, combined with professional familiarity with interactive media, influenced the expectations brought to each session. This positionality provided advantages, such as the ability to engage deeply with genre conventions and system affordances, but it also introduced potential biases in interpreting narrative coherence and evaluating AI performance. Recognizing these limitations, their influence sought to be mitigated through transparent documentation of interpretive decisions, systematic session recording, and iterative memo writing.

Second, using *AI Dungeon* as a site of research also raises issues about reproducibility and consistency. Because the output of the AI is probabilistic and contextual, it is possible to get different output from the same prompt in different sessions. Instead of considering this variation as a weakness, the study embraces it as part of GenAI narrative that captures the contingent nature of co-authorship and the logic of improvisation of the system.

Finally, at each stage of the research process, the ethical implications of working with AI-generated content were taken into account. Although the research included only the researcher and no additional human participants, it engaged with a system that could quite possibly generate sensitive content. Any outputs of concern were flagged and subjected to critical questioning. Along with this measure, the wider cultural and representational ramifications of the outputs also needed to be dealt with. This study specifically examined the ethical implications of interpreting and disseminating AI-generated content that might support discriminatory stereotypes or cultural clichés. In an attempt to expose biases in generative models, content that was produced by the system and perpetuated racialized, gendered, or colonial narratives was critically analyzed rather than rejected. These examples were carefully contextualized to prevent unintentionally reproducing negative representations. Only by taking these ethical considerations into account it is possible to comprehend the creative potential of AI narrative systems as well as their limitations.

4.5 Summary

In GenAI storytelling environments, this methodological framework offers a strong basis for examining the dynamics of player–AI co-authorship. The study captures the complexity of narrative generation in real time by combining multi-modal data collection, structured play sessions, and layered interpretive strategies. The data analysis is presented in the following section, highlighting the tensions, emerging patterns, and innovative possibilities that occur when humans and machines work together to tell stories.

5. FINDINGS AND ANALYSIS

The following findings are based on the twenty analytical play sessions conducted with *AI Dungeon* and structured according to the three interpretive strategies outlined in the methodology: ludonarrative analysis, semiotic reading, and thematic coding. Each method offers a distinct lens on the co-creative processes of GenAI storytelling, and how narrative agency, coherence, and authorship are negotiated at the moment. It is concluded by a synthesis that makes connections between approaches and provides the background for the following ethical and practical implications.

5.1 Ludonarrative Analysis: Structures of Play and Narrative Drift

Ludonarrative analysis focused on how game design (player action, system response, and interface layout) impacted the achievement of narrative. One of the key findings was the prevalence of narrative drift, where the AI-generated story ultimately diverged from its initial configuration or genre. This drift occurred independent of narrative rationale, suggesting that the system's generative rules prioritize local coherence over global consistency.

A striking example was Session S02 (Noir), where the player adopted a correctional, plot-focused style to maintain the genre. Despite these efforts, the AI repeatedly introduced incongruous fantasy elements. For instance, after the player typed, "I follow the suspect into the alley, keeping my hand near my revolver," the

AI replied, "Suddenly, a dragon swoops down from the clouds, scattering the gangsters." This abrupt incursion disrupted the established noir tone. The player issued corrective commands such as "Ignore the dragon. Return to the alley scene," but the AI persisted in genre-mixing, illustrating how editorial labor became necessary to reassert narrative coherence.

Similar tensions appeared in Session S16 (Cyberpunk Dystopia), where narrative entropy under pressure caused the AI to lose track of established facts. Here, the player deactivated a security grid, but the AI later contradicted itself by describing the same security system still active, creating a logical paradox: "You step into the corridor, but the alarms blare again—the system has reset itself." This scenario exemplified system incoherence and required repeated player interventions to stabilize causality.

Overall, these examples illustrate the volatility of narrative coherence in GenAI systems. The AI's probabilistic generation does not sustain a stable storyworld model, leading to fluctuations in tone, setting, and character logic. As seen in S02 and S16, players are consequently cast as narrative stabilizers, continuously reining in errant outputs to maintain internal consistency.

Ludonarrative friction also emerged when the AI contradicted previously established facts or failed to recognize character continuity. For instance, in Session S09 (Mythological Epic), the AI's narrative drift introduced science fiction symbols into a mythological setting, forcing the player to re-ground the story in mythological logic. These moments not only disrupted immersion but also highlighted the editorial work players undertake to preserve coherence and genre fidelity.

5.2 Semiotic Reading: Signs, Tropes, and Genre Instability

The cultural and symbolic aspects of the AI's narrative outputs were investigated through semiotic analysis. A recurrent theme was the system's dependence on familiar clichés and genre norms, frequently lifted from popular media and online culture. While these shared tropes provided a common semiotic vocabulary that facilitated cooperation, they also contributed to genre instability and occasional cultural bias.

For example, in Session S05 (Romance), the AI defaulted to uncanny affection loops despite the player's attempts to shape a more nuanced relationship dynamic. At one point, the AI repeated the phrase "She looks into your eyes and whispers, 'I love you'" multiple times in consecutive turns, creating a sense of narrative flattening and emotional superficiality. This repetition, noted as "some uncanny affection loops," highlighted the AI's reliance on stock romantic expressions rather than adaptive, context-sensitive dialogue.

Similarly, in Session S07 (Satire), the AI demonstrated an effective but exaggerated use of political tropes and absurdist humor. In one exchange, the player proposed a corrupt government official, prompting the AI to respond: "The President emerges from a closet wearing only a top hat, declaring the tax code is now a performance art piece." This vivid example illustrates how mutual exaggeration became an emergent semiotic dynamic, enabling co-created satire that exceeded the player's initial framing.

Genre contamination often stemmed from the AI's diverse textual training, which produced abrupt shifts in register. In Session S13 (Magical Realism), a contemplative, lyrical tone was suddenly interrupted by contemporary slang: "You stand on the shore of the memory sea, and your bestie calls you on FaceTime." This incongruity required the player to restate prompts to guide the narrative back into its intended aesthetic mode.

In the horror sessions, particularly Session S04, the AI occasionally inserted comedic tropes that undermined tension. One notable example was the sudden inclusion of slapstick imagery: "The shadowy figure slips on a banana peel before disappearing into the darkness." This intrusion diluted the atmosphere of dread and demonstrated how genre cliches can override player intent.

Although rare, problematic stereotypes also surfaced. In S16 (Cyberpunk Dystopia), the AI reproduced "cyberpunk clichés" involving exoticized "Eastern" hacker archetypes, underscoring the need for critical engagement with the model's training data. These instances were not only illustrative of embedded biases but also revealed the semiotic negotiation players must undertake to correct or reject problematic content.

Collectively, these examples show that semiotic reading is essential for understanding how GenAI systems oscillate between creative collaboration and the reproduction of reductive cultural patterns. Players are often compelled to act as curators of meaning, reasserting thematic coherence and ethical sensitivity within the emergent narrative.

5.3 Thematic Coding: Patterns of Co-Authorship and Editorial Labor

Thematic analysis of gameplay sessions revealed a set of persistent patterns that illuminated the rich co-authorship dynamics in GenAI narrative generation. Most salient was the necessity for editorial intervention. To preserve coherence, the player was actively removing, avoiding, or ignoring AI-generated content in almost every session. For example, in Session S06 (Historical Fiction), the AI introduced anachronisms that disrupted the narrative flow. As the description of characters from the 18th century using modern slang and referencing technologies that did not exist in the period. The player responded by issuing clarifying prompts, such as "Please rephrase using 18th-century vocabulary," demonstrating how editorial actions went beyond simple correction and became a form of genre repair. The memo for S06 noted: "Player became fact-checker."

In Session S02 (Noir), editorial labor was similarly evident when the AI repeatedly drifted into fantasy motifs, requiring the player to reassert the noir tone: "Return to the detective's office—no dragons." These examples show how the player assumed narrative responsibility, acting as curator and stabilizer of genre expectations.

Closely linked to this was the concept of narrative repair, where the player undertook deliberate actions to restore continuity and internal logic. In Session S09 (Mythological Epic), the AI unexpectedly shifted from mythic language to science fiction tropes: "The goddess hands you a glowing USB drive containing the secrets of Olympus." The player intervened by re-establishing the mythological frame: "No technology exists—describe the artifact as a scroll."

Another recurrent theme was the conflict that results from co-authorship. Unexpected ideas were regularly generated by the AI, but these improvisations were not always consistent with the player's goals.. Session S11 (Philosophical Allegory) exemplified this, as the AI responded to complex prompts with repetitive and vague symbols, such as "You see the shape of meaning," repeated across multiple turns. This reduced thematic depth and required the player to steer the narrative toward more substantive reflections.

But there were also spontaneous creative moments brought about by this tension. In Session S03 (Sci-Fi), the player introduced a simple question—"What powers the ship?"—and the AI responded with a poetic description: "The vessel is driven by the memory of every star it has ever passed." This unexpected metaphor enriched the narrative beyond the player's original intent. Likewise, in Session S07 (Satire), the AI's absurd improvisations—"The tax code is now a performance art piece"—illustrated how genre exaggeration could become a shared creative act.

Finally, a pattern of emergent creativity arose when the AI and player established a responsive rhythm. In Session S08 (Post-apocalyptic), their interaction about survival inventory created a coherent and suspenseful storyline, despite occasional inconsistencies: "You check your supplies—water, flashlight, pistol." The AI then contradicted itself by stating, "You only have a flashlight," but the player's corrections made the feeling of scarcity even stronger. Similar to this, Session S15 (Steampunk Adventure) showed how co-authorship can function when players actively control the experience by merging modular environments (airships, clockwork labs) with cooperative puzzle-solving to create a story that was both logically sound and emotionally engaging.

Co-creation is a collaborative and controversial process that requires participants to act as editors, mediators, and occasionally critics, as these examples all show. One characteristic of successful narrative outcomes was the player's willingness to participate in this editorial process.

5.4 Synthesis: Toward a Model of Procedural Co-authorship

The results of ludonarrative, semiotic, and thematic analyses collectively suggest that procedural co-authorship is the most appropriate model for conceptualizing storytelling in GenAI settings. Here, narrative creation is not a single, intentional act of authorship but rather a dynamic, distributed process influenced by both machine improvisation and human intention.

Narrative negotiation is central to this model. To preserve coherence and achieve their artistic goals, players must continually interpret, modify, and sometimes override the AI's contributions. This was especially evident in Session S02 (Noir), where the player issued multiple corrective commands—"Ignore the dragon," "Return to the office"—in an effort to contain genre drift. Similar patterns were observed in S09 (Mythological Epic), where mythological frames had to be reasserted after the AI introduced science fiction symbols. These examples show that effective co-authorship requires a form of critical literacy, encompassing both awareness of genre conventions and an understanding of the AI's operational logic.

Editorial labor emerged as a central dimension of this process. Players shaped the story through innumerable micro-interventions, acting as curators and editors rather than passive consumers. The player essentially assumed the role of a historical fact-checker in Session S06 (Historical Fiction), correcting anachronistic references on multiple occasions. Meanwhile, in S14 (Psychological Drama), emotional flattening required the player to inject richer affective detail to sustain character arcs. These cases demonstrate that co-creation is not a frictionless process: it demands continuous engagement and adaptation.

Yet this tension between control and improvisation also enabled serendipitous creativity. In Session S03 (Sci-Fi), a simple query about the ship's power source triggered a lyrical AI response—"The vessel is driven by the memory of every star it has ever passed"—that exceeded the player's expectations. Similarly, in S07 (Satire), the AI's ludicrous exaggerations on political themes created a collective exaggeration that enhanced the story's humor. These instances demonstrate how cooperative storytelling can result in outcomes that neither side could have created on their own.

These results have design-related applications. In order to preserve coherence, genre fidelity, and ethical sensitivity, GenAI storytelling systems must strike a balance between openness—making room for improvisational, exploratory play—and support structures. The documented difficulties in S11 (Philosophical Allegory), where the AI's abstract repetitions undermined thematic depth, point to the value of adaptive tuning and adjustable narrative parameters. Systems that can recognize when players are engaged in editorial repair, and respond by reinforcing rather than undermining coherence, will better support meaningful co-creation.

Ultimately, GenAI platforms like *AI Dungeon* do not simply automate story production; they transform it into a collaborative, improvisational, and ethically charged process. As demonstrated in sessions ranging from S01's smooth genre emulation to S20's chaotic humor drift, these systems demand a rethinking of authorship, creativity, and narrative control in the digital age. The next section reflects on the broader implications of this evolution for game design, narrative theory, and the future of interactive media.

6. DISCUSSION: REFRAMING NARRATIVE AGENCY AND AUTHORSHIP IN LIGHT OF GENAI

The findings presented in the previous section illuminate the evolving dynamics of narrative construction in GenAI-powered environments, particularly through the lens of *AI Dungeon*. These dynamics challenge and extend foundational concepts in game studies and narrative theory, including authorship, agency, coherence, and the role of the player as a meaning-making agent. This section reflects on these findings in light of the theoretical framework introduced earlier, offering a deeper interpretation of how GenAI systems are reshaping the epistemology and practice of interactive storytelling.

At the core of this transformation is the procedural nature of authorship. Unlike traditional narrative systems, where authorship is centralized and pre-authored, GenAI environments distribute narrative control across a network of human and machine agents. This is consistent with Aarseth's (1997) ergodic literature, which posits that the activity of the reader reading through the text is fundamental to its actualization, and Koenitz's (2015) understanding of narrative as a systems-driven process of design. In *AI Dungeon*, the player actively co-creates the storyworld in real-time, frequently through improvisational and editorial work, rather than moving through an already existing one.

This co-authorship is marked by a constant negotiation of agency. Murray's (2017) definition of agency as the "satisfying power to take meaningful action" is both affirmed and complicated in this context. To a certain degree, players can express themselves, but the AI's probabilistic reasoning mediates their decisions, sometimes leading to unexpected or inconsistent results. Players must therefore anticipate, interpret, and occasionally correct the AI's contributions, turning agency into a dialogic and contingent phenomenon. This form of agency is not about control in the traditional sense but about responsiveness, adaptability, and interpretive skill.

This makes the concept of ludonarrative friction—discussed by Harrell and Zhu (2009)—especially important. The generative unpredictability of the AI and the gap between gameplay mechanics and narrative content are the sources of friction. The

AI frequently introduces genre shifts, factual inconsistencies, and tonal mismatches. These interruptions are hubs of creative tension where fresh narrative possibilities can arise, not necessarily failures. But they also highlight the player's editorial responsibility, as they frequently have to serve as a curator of tone and coherence.

The significance of genre fluency and symbolic negotiation in preserving narrative integrity is further demonstrated by semiotic analysis. By using well-known tropes, changing language, and reiterating genre norms, it is possible to successfully direct the AI toward logical and captivating narratives. This implies that in addition to technical communication, cultural and symbolic literacy are also necessary for productive co-authorship in GenAI settings. The player must give the AI's output structure and meaning because the AI lacks an innate understanding of genre or narrative logic due to its extensive and diverse training on datasets.

The results also show how working with AI has ethical and epistemological implications. The training data, which may contain damaging stereotypes, tropes, or cultural biases, shapes the AI's outputs. The player was frequently compelled to assume the role of moral editor when coming across such content, deciding whether to disregard, modify, or consider the AI's answers. This raises important questions about accountability and authorship: who is responsible for the narrative that emerges from a human–AI collaboration? The player? The developers? The dataset? According to these inquiries, authorship in GenAI systems is a distributed and negotiated role rather than a fixed identity, which is consistent with Foucault's (1979) concept of the "author function."

Lastly, the thematic patterns of emergent creativity, editorial intervention, and narrative repair suggest a more thorough reinterpretation of creativity itself. In GenAI narratives, creativity is a relational process that develops through interaction, conflict, and adaptation rather than a singular act of invention. This is consistent with sociocultural theories of creativity, such as the one put forth by Glăveanu (2014), which highlight the ways in which creative endeavors are interwoven with material and social contexts. The player's intentions, the AI's generative logic, and the interface that enables their interaction all have an impact on *AI Dungeon*'s creative process.

In conclusion, the discussion indicates that GenAI systems such as *AI Dungeon* change existing narrative paradigms rather than just extending them. They challenge us to rethink agency as an interpretive labor and authorship as a distributed, procedural, and morally complex practice. These insights have significant implications for game design, narrative theory, and the future of interactive media, which the following section will explore in more detail.

7. ETHICAL AND PRACTICAL IMPLICATIONS: NAVIGATING CO-CREATION WITH GENERATIVE AI

The deployment of generative AI into interactive narrative contexts carries with it a range of ethical, practical concerns that preempt technological deployment issues. As the example of *AI Dungeon* makes clear, the iterative process of narrative generation between human players and AI engines is not just a site of narrative innovation but of epistemological risk, cultural hazard, and design complexity. This section draws out these implications from the authorship, responsibility, bias, and system governance perspectives and offers practical design and development implications for developers and designers.

The most critical ethical problem of GenAI narrative is likely that of responsibility and authorship. Authorship in mainstream media tends to be inferred from intentionality and responsibility. In AI-mediated environments, narrative content is generated by a probabilistic process operating off opaque, black-box data sets. This raises the question: who is responsible for the content that emerges from a player–AI interaction? Bender et al. (2021) argue that large language models are "stochastic parrots" that mimic patterns in training sets without intent or comprehension. When the models generate offensive, biased, or culturally insensitive content, lines of responsibility get confused—ought one hold the player, developers, or the model accountable?

This ambiguity is further compounded by the fact that players are often consumers and editors of content generated by AI. As the research has shown, it is necessary to engage in narrative repair, fixing or diverting the product of the AI to maintain its coherence or prevent objectionable content. Even if editorial labor of this kind can be conceived as a form of creative agency, it also represents an ethical burden on the player who must navigate through the limitations of the system without warning or safeguarding. This is what Gillespie (2018) describes as the "custodianship of platforms" where users are tasked with coping with the consequences of algorithmic production without control over the systems themselves.

Bias in AI-generated writing is another critical problem. Language models are built on extensive datasets that often reflect dominant cultural norms, stereotypes, and exclusions. As a result, even in what might seem like harmless narrative environments, they can inadvertently reproduce racial, colonial, or gendered tropes (Buolamwini & Gebru, 2018; Noble, 2018). In *AI Dungeon*, this can manifest as genre clichés, stereotypical character portrayals, or the exclusion of voices from marginalized communities. While some players may be aware of and resist these tendencies, others might unknowingly reinforce the normative assumptions that have been co-created.

To reduce these risks, developers must implement effective moderation and transparency policies. Moderation in generative systems is by nature challenging; compared to static content, AI-generated narratives are dynamic as well as context-dependent, and therefore it becomes challenging to avoid unwanted outcomes without jeopardizing creative freedom. Raji et al. (2020) consider that ethical AI development entails participatory governance models that include a diverse set of stakeholders in the development and evaluation process alongside technical controls.

From a practical perspective, the results point to a number of design approaches that can improve GenAI storytelling systems' capacity for creativity and ethics. First and foremost, systems ought to give players more insight into how the AI makes decisions. This could be metadata about the sources and probabilities of generated content, or it could be real-time feedback on how prompts are understood. This openness can encourage a sense of co-agency and enable players to make better decisions. Second, players can receive the outputs of the AI aligned with their own cultural and creative values by using customization tools to set genre preferences, ethical boundaries, or story boundaries. This is in line with value-sensitive design, which promotes the early integration of human values into technological systems (Friedman et al., 2013). Third, players can acquire the procedural literacy required to thrive in GenAI worlds through training materials and onboarding processes. The findings show that successful co-authorship often requires the player to be able to interpret, adjust, and correct the AI's contributions. By giving users ethical awareness and interpretive strategies, designers can promote more responsible and meaningful engagement. The broader cultural relevance of GenAI narrative must also be addressed. As stories spread, these systems will not just impact how they are framed, but also who gets to frame them and whose voices are heard. Thus, in addition to being technologically necessary, GenAI platforms must also be culturally responsible, representative, and inclusive.

On a practical level, this research's findings imply a set of design solutions by which GenAI narrative systems' coherence, moral sense, and creative potential can be supported. Firstly, editorial control must be provided; systems must allow players to intervene within the narrative in a way that does not compromise immersion, providing an instant correction and redirection of AI output. Furthermore, the provision of genre and tone options can balance narrative drift and promote stylistic coherence, matching AI generative logic to player intention. Procedural literacy formation via onboarding documentation or in-game tutorials is a prerequisite in readiness for being able to successfully work through these systems. These tools have the potential to demystify the generative procedure and enable players to interact more critically and creatively. Lastly, facilitating ethical co-creation calls for transparency in training data and provision of access to features that enable users to recognize and react to biased material. Such strategies comply with value-sensitive design strategies (Friedman et al., 2013; Sadek et al., 2024) and emphasize the need to design GenAI platforms that are technologically viable yet culturally responsive and inclusive.

In conclusion, there is a close relationship between the ethical and practical implications of GenAI in interactive storytelling. Although *AI Dungeon* and related platforms provide useful opportunities for story exploration, they also highlight the drawbacks and challenges of algorithm-based creativity. A comprehensive approach that combines technological innovation, critical analysis, participatory design, and a commitment to cultural equity is needed to address these issues.

8. CONCLUSION

This chapter has discussed the transformative potential of generative AI in reconfiguring narrative composition and player experience in digital games, with *AI Dungeon* as a paradigmatic example. In a convergence of ludonarrative analysis, semiotic reading, and thematic coding, the research has shed light on how GenAI technologies rethink narrative agency, authorship, and coherence beyond technical innovation to catalyze a profound cultural and epistemological transformation of interactive media.

Borrowing from the supporting theories of Murray (2017), Aarseth (1997), and Ryan (2001), the analysis shows that GenAI narrative in games is characterized by procedural emergence, distributed authorship, and an evolving form of ludonarrative agency. Rather than pre-authored, narrative meaning is performed through iterative, real-time dialogue between players and generative models. This dynamic, as well as enhancing the expressive potential of digital games, introduces new levels of unpredictability and creative negotiation, as represented by the concept of cyberdrama.

The analysis shows that GenAI narrative in games is characterized by procedural emergence, distributed authorship, and an evolving form of ludonarrative agency. Rather than pre-authored, narrative meaning is performed through iterative, real-time dialogue between players and generative models. This dynamic, as exemplified by Murray's (2017) concept of cyberdrama, not only expands the expressive possibilities of digital games but also introduces new degrees of unpredictability and imaginative negotiation.

In the scope of ethical considerations, the necessity of critical engagement is highlighted by persistent bias in training data, transparency of algorithmic processes, and accountability issues in co-authored narratives. To contribute to the use of GenAI systems in a thoughtful manner, designers are urged to promote procedural literacy, allow for deliberate customization, and positively enshrine transparency (Bender et al., 2021; Noble, 2018; Raji et al., 2021).

The contribution of this chapter is to extend interactive narrative theory by situating ludonarrative agency in the human–AI collaboration environment of games. It challenges the cultural assumptions and power dynamics of algorithmic storytelling, while also offering a theoretical framework for understanding the procedural and editorial labor unique to GenAI spaces. It may also contribute to the development of pedagogical curricula in digital storytelling, game design, and media ethics, preparing future creators to be both technically skilled and ethically aware.

The findings of this study suggest a number of avenues for future investigation into GenAI storytelling in games, but not exclusively. For instance, studies examining GenAI-driven storytelling across cultural contexts may reveal distinctive patterns, while studies monitoring player engagement over extended periods of time may also reveal the nuanced ways in which human-AI collaborative narrative creation evolves. New systems may be more inclusive and equitable, but this is not a given. Underrepresented voices must be actively included in participatory design processes to ensure it. Biases could easily become more embedded in increasingly complex systems if there is not a strong commitment. Collaboration between a variety of disciplines is required to develop GenAI systems that are transparent and socially conscious; game designers, AI specialists, educators, philosophers, and other important stakeholders can all provide insightful opinions. Even though *AI Dungeon* is the subject of this study, other GenAI storytelling systems are probably going to experience the same dynamics of narrative drift, editorial intervention, and co-authorship tension. Even though more comparative study is required to examine how such dynamics differ across platforms and genres, these findings may have wider significance for AI-driven game design.

The research questions that guided the study should be revisited in light of the analysis presented. The findings demonstrate how GenAI reshapes player agency and narrative authority (RQ1), reveals emergent dynamics such as co-authorship tension and narrative drift (RQ2), and underscores the ethical, cultural, and design implications of AI-mediated storytelling (RQ3). Beyond deepening our understanding of GenAI in games, these insights lay the groundwork for future interdisciplinary research.

GenAI is an agent that challenges us to reevaluate the basic processes by which stories are created, experienced, and understood; it is more than just a new tool for digital storytelling in digital games. As Murray (2017) notes, digital media offers new narrative channels as well as new perspectives on storytelling in general. Navigating this evolving environment requires constant attention to creative potential, ethical complexity, and cultural responsibility. As a result, contestation and collaboration will continue to influence game storytelling, but it will always be a deeply human endeavor that hardly could be reduced to algorithms.

REFERENCES

Aarseth, E. (2012). A Narrative Theory of Games. In *Proceedings of the International Conference on the Foundations of Digital Games* (pp. 129–133). ACM. DOI: 10.1145/2282338.2282365

Aarseth, E. J. (1997). *Cybertext: Perspectives on Ergodic Literature*. Johns Hopkins University Press. DOI: 10.56021/9780801855788

Arif, S., Arif, T., Haroon, M. S., Khan, A. J., Raza, A. A., & Athar, A. (2024). The Art of Storytelling: Multi-agent Generative AI for Dynamic Multimodal Narratives [Preprint]. *arXiv*. https://arxiv.org/abs/2409.11261

Barthes, R. (1977). The Death of the Author (S. Heath, Trans.). In *Image, Music, Text* (pp. 142–148). Fontana Press. (Original work published 1968)

Bender, E. M., Gebru, T., McMillan-Major, A., & Shmitchell, S. (2021). On the Dangers of Stochastic Parrots: Can Language Models Be Too Big? *Proceedings of the 2021 ACM Conference on Fairness, Accountability, and Transparency*, 610–623. DOI: 10.1145/3442188.3445922

Bogost, I. (2007). *Persuasive Games: The Expressive Power of Videogames*. MIT Press. DOI: 10.7551/mitpress/5334.001.0001

Bozkurt, A. (2024). GenAI et al.: Cocreation, Authorship, Ownership, Academic Ethics and Integrity in a Time of Generative AI. *Open Praxis*, *16*(1), 1–10. . DOI: 10.55982/openpraxis.16.1.654

Branch, B., Mirowski, P., & Mathewson, K. (2021). Collaborative Storytelling with Human Actors and Ai Narrators. In A. G. S. de Garza, T. Veale, W. Aguilar, & R. P. y Pérez (Eds.), *Proceedings of the 12th International Conference on Computational Creativity* (pp. 96–101). Association for Computational Creativity. https://computationalcreativity.net/iccc21/wp-content/uploads/2021/09/ICCC_2021_paper_118.pdf

Braun, V., & Clarke, V. (2006). Using thematic Analysis in Psychology. *Qualitative Research in Psychology*, *3*(2), 77–101. DOI: 10.1191/1478088706qp063oa

Brown, T. B., Mann, B., Ryder, N., Subbiah, M., Kaplan, J., Dhariwal, P., Neelakantan, A., Shyam, P., Sastry, G., Askell, A., Agarwal, S., Herbert-Voss, A., Krueger, G., Henighan, T., Child, R., Ramesh, A., Ziegler, D. M., Wu, J., Winter, C., & Amodei, D. (2020). Language Models Are Few-Shot Learners. In Larochelle, H., Ranzato, M., Hadsell, R., Balcan, M. F., & Lin, H. (Eds.), Vol. 33, pp. 1877–1901). Advances in Neural Information Processing Systems. Curran Associates, Inc., https://papers.nips.cc/paper/2020/hash/1457c0d6bfcb4967418bfb8ac142f64a-Abstract.html

Buolamwini, J., & Gebru, T. (2018). Gender Shades: Intersectional Accuracy Disparities in Commercial Gender Classification. *Proceedings of the 1st Conference on Fairness, Accountability and Transparency - Proceedings of Machine Learning Research, 81*, 1-15. https://proceedings.mlr.press/v81/buolamwini18a/buolamwini18a.pdf

Cheung, L. M. E., & Shi, H. (2024). Co-Creating Stories With Generative Ai: Reflections From Undergraduate Students of a Storytelling Service-Learning Subject in Hong Kong. *Australian Review of Applied Linguistics, 47*(3), 259–283. DOI: 10.1075/aral.24101.che

Crawford, C. (2004). *Chris Crawford on Interactive Storytelling*. New Riders.

Flanagan, M. (2009). *Critical Play: Radical Game Design*. MIT Press. DOI: 10.7551/mitpress/7678.001.0001

Foucault, M. (1979). What is an author? *Screen, 20*(1), 13–34. DOI: 10.1093/screen/20.1.13

Frasca, G. (2003). Ludologists Love Stories, too: Notes from a Debate that Never Took Place. In M. Copier & J. Raessens (Eds.), *Level Up: Digital Games Research Conference Proceedings* (pp. 92–99). Utrecht University. DOI: 10.26503/dl.v2003i1.64

Friedman, B., Kahn, P. H., Borning, A., & Huldtgren, A. (2013). Value Sensitive Design and Information Systems. In N. Doorn, D. Schuurbiers, I. van de Poel, & M. Gorman (Eds.), *Early Engagement and New Technologies: Opening up the Laboratory* (Philosophy of Engineering and Technology, Vol. 16, pp. 55–95). Springer. DOI: 10.1007/978-94-007-7844-3_4

Gerba, H. (2025). Universal Narrative Model: An Author-Centric Storytelling Framework for Generative AI. *arXiv*. https://arxiv.org/abs/2503.04844v3

Gillespie, T. (2018). *Custodians of the Internet: Platforms, Content Moderation, and the Hidden Decisions That Shape Social Media*. Yale University Press.

Ginsburg, J. C., & Budiardjo, L. A. (2019). Authors and Machines. *Berkeley Technology Law Journal, 34*(2), 343–388. DOI: 10.15779/Z38SF2MC24

Glăveanu, V. P. (2014). *Distributed Creativity: Thinking Outside the Box of the Creative Individual*. Springer. DOI: 10.1007/978-3-319-05434-6

Grabarczyk, P., & Walther, B. K. (2022). A Game of Twisted Shouting: Ludo-Narrative Dissonance Revisited. *Eludamos (Göttingen), 13*(1), 7–27. DOI: 10.7557/23.6506

Harrell, D. F. (2013). *Phantasmal Media: An Approach to Imagination, Computation, and Expression*. MIT Press. DOI: 10.7551/mitpress/8834.001.0001

Harrell, D. F., & Zhu, J. (2009). Agency Play: Dimensions of Agency for Interactive Narrative Design. In *Proceedings of the AAAI Spring Symposium on Intelligent Narrative Technologies II* (pp. 44–52). AAAI Press.

Harris, A. (2014). *The Creative Turn: Toward a New Aesthetic Imaginary*. Sense Publishers., DOI: 10.1007/978-94-6209-551-9

Hayles, N. K. (2017). *Unthought: The Power of the Cognitive Nonconscious*. University of Chicago Press. DOI: 10.7208/chicago/9780226447919.001.0001

Hua, M., & Raley, R. (2020). Playing with Unicorns: *AI Dungeon* and Citizen NLP. *Digital Humanities Quarterly, 14*(4). https://www.digitalhumanities.org/dhq/vol/14/4/000533/000533.html

Jenkins, H. (2004). Game Design as Narrative Architecture. In Wardrip-Fruin, N., & Harrigan, P. (Eds.), *First Person: New Media as Story, Performance, and Game* (pp. 118–130). MIT Press.

Joyce, L. (2015). Creating Collaborative Criteria for Agency in Interactive Narrative Game Analysis. *Computer Games Journal*, *4*(1), 47–58. DOI: 10.1007/s40869-015-0004-x

Juul, J. (2005). *Half-Real: Video Games between Real Rules and Fictional Worlds*. MIT Press.

Koenitz, H. (2015). Design Approaches for Interactive Digital Narrative. In H. Schoenau-Fog, L. E. Bruni, S. Louchart, & S. Baceviciute (Eds.), *Interactive storytelling: 8th International Conference on Interactive Digital Storytelling (ICIDS 2015)* (pp. 50–57). Springer. DOI: 10.1007/978-3-319-27036-4_5

Kreminski, M., Dickinson, M., & Wardrip-Fruin, N. (2020). Why Are We Like This? The AI Architecture of a Storytelling Game about Intimacy. In Marino, M., Flores, A., & Pyne, J. (Eds.), *Proceedings of the Electronic Literature Organization 2020 Conference and Media Festival: (Un)Continuity* (pp. 1–10). University of Central Florida., https://stars.library.ucf.edu/elo2020/asynchronous/proceedingspapers/10/

Lamerichs, N. (2020, January 20). Is *AI Dungeon* the Future of Literature? *Nicolle Lamerichs*. https://nicollelamerichs.com/2020/01/20/writing-with-algorithms-in-ai-dungeon/

Latitude. (2024a, December 18). *Forge: A New Era of AI Models in AI Dungeon* [Blog post]. Retrieved from https://latitude.io/blog/forge-a-new-era-of-ai-models-in-ai-dungeon

Latitude. (2024b, May 23). *How the New Memory System Works* [Blog post]. Retrieved from https://latitude.io/blog/how-the-new-memory-system-works

Latitude. (2024c). *Getting Started with AI Dungeon*. https://help.aidungeon.com/getting-started

Latour, B. (2005). *Reassembling the Social: An Introduction to Actor-Network-Theory*. Oxford University Press. DOI: 10.1093/oso/9780199256044.001.0001

LeBlanc, M. (2000, March). *Formal Design Tools: Emergent Complexity, Emergent Narrative* [Conference presentation]. Game Developers Conference, San Jose, CA, United States. http://algorithmancy.8kindsoffun.com/gdc2000.ppt

Lee, M., Srivastava, M., Hardy, A., Thickstun, J., Durmus, E., Paranjape, A., . . . Liang, P. (2023). Evaluating Human–Language Model Interaction. *Transactions on Machine Learning Research*. https://openreview.net/forum?id=hjDYJUn9l1

Mateas, M., & Stern, A. (2005a). Procedural Authorship: A Case-Study of the Interactive Drama Façade. In *Proceedings of the Digital Arts and Culture Conference* (pp. 1–16). Copenhagen, Denmark. https://users.soe.ucsc.edu/~michaelm/publications/mateas1-dac2005.pdf

Mateas, M., & Stern, A. (2005b). Build It To Understand It: Ludology Meets Narratology in Game Design Space. In *Proceedings of DiGRA 2005 Conference: Changing Views – Worlds in Play*. Digital Games Research Association. DOI: 10.26503/dl.v2005i1.172

McCosker, A., & Wilken, R. (2020). *Automating vision: The social impact of the new camera consciousness*. Routledge. DOI: 10.4324/9780429341175

McGill, K. M. (2022). The Digital Lineage of Narrative: Analyzing Interactive Fiction to Further Understand Game Narrative. In Bostan, B. (Ed.), *Games and Narrative: Theory and Practice* (pp. 70–97). Springer., DOI: 10.1007/978-3-030-81538-7_5

McGuire, J., De Cremer, D., & Van de Cruys, T. (2024). Establishing the Importance of Co-Creation and Self-Efficacy in Creative Collaboration with Artificial Intelligence. *Scientific Reports*, *14*(1), 18525. DOI: 10.1038/s41598-024-69423-2

Mitchell, A. (2022, January 9). Repetition and Defamiliarization in *AI Dungeon* and *Project December. Electronic Book Review*. https://electronicbookreview.com/essay/repetition-and-defamiliarization-in-ai-dungeon-and-project-december/

Murnane, E. (2018). *Emergent Narrative: Stories of Play, Playing with Stories* (Doctoral dissertation, University of Central Florida). https://stars.library.ucf.edu/etd/5799

Murray, J. H. (2017). *Hamlet on the Holodeck: The Future of Narrative in Cyberspace*. MIT Press.

Noble, S. U. (2018). *Algorithms of Oppression: How Search Engines Reinforce Racism*. New York University Press. DOI: 10.18574/nyu/9781479833641.001.0001

Radford, A., Wu, J., Child, R., Luan, D., Amodei, D., & Sutskever, I. (2019). Language Models Are Unsupervised Multitask Learners. *OpenAI*. https://cdn.openai.com/better-language-models/language_models_are_unsupervised_multitask_learners.pdf

Raji, I. D., Smart, A., White, R. N., Mitchell, M., Gebru, T., Hutchinson, B., Smith-Loud, J., Theron, D., & Barnes, P. (2020). Closing the AI Accountability Gap: Defining an End-to-End Framework for Internal Algorithmic Auditing. In *Proceedings of the 2020 Conference on Fairness, Accountability, and Transparency* (pp. 33–44). Association for Computing Machinery. DOI: 10.1145/3351095.3372873

Ramesh, R., Venkatesh, M., & Girish, G. P. (2024). The Symbiosis of Ai and Human Agency in Digital Authorship: Redefining The Landscape Of Contemporary Literature. In Vasant, P. (Eds.), *Intelligent Computing and Optimization (ICO 2023)* (Vol. 874, pp. 255–262). Springer., DOI: 10.1007/978-3-031-50887-5_26

Riedl, M. O., & Bulitko, V. (2013). Interactive Narrative: An Intelligent Systems Approach. *AI Magazine, 34*(1), 67–77. DOI: 10.1609/aimag.v34i1.2449

Ryan, H., Abramov, D., Acker, S., & Elkins, S. (2025). Can AI Be a Co-Author?: How Generative AI Challenges the Boundaries of Authorship in a General Education Writing Class. *Thresholds, 48*(1), 40-56. https://files.eric.ed.gov/fulltext/EJ1468037.pdf

Ryan, M. L. (2006). *Avatars of story*. University of Minnesota Press.

Sadek, M., Constantinides, M., Quercia, D., & Mougenot, C. (2024). Guidelines for integrating value sensitive design in responsible AI toolkits. In *Proceedings of the 2024 CHI Conference on Human Factors in Computing Systems* (Article 472, pp. 1–20). Association for Computing Machinery. DOI: 10.1145/3613904.3642810

Salen, K., & Zimmerman, E. (2004). *Rules of Play: Game Design Fundamentals*. MIT Press.

Santiago, V. (2023). How to Use *AI Dungeon* to Create Interactive Stories. In MacDowell, P., Moskalyk, K., & Korchinski, K. (Eds.), *Teaching and Creating with Generative AI*. University of Saskatchewan., https://www.saskoer.ca/etad402teachingandcreatingwithgenai/chapter/vincent-santiago/

Sawyer, R. K. (2012). *Explaining Creativity: The Science of Human Innovation* (2nd ed.). Oxford University Press.

Serbanescu, A. (2024). Human-AI System Co-creativity to Build Interactive Digital Narratives. In Zanella, F., Bosoni, G., Di Stefano, E., Iannilli, G. L., Matteucci, G., Messori, R., & Trocchianesi, R. (Eds.), *Multidisciplinary Aspects of Design. Design! OPEN 2022* (pp. 388–398). Springer., DOI: 10.1007/978-3-031-49811-4_37

Short, T. X., & Adams, T. (Eds.). (2019). *Procedural Storytelling in Game Design*. CRC Press. DOI: 10.1201/9780429488337

Sicart, M. (2009). *The Ethics of Computer Games*. MIT Press. DOI: 10.7551/mitpress/9780262012652.001.0001

Sicart, M. (2013). *Beyond Choices: The Design of Ethical Gameplay*. MIT Press. DOI: 10.7551/mitpress/9052.001.0001

Thorne, S. (2020). Hey Siri, Tell Me a story: Digital Storytelling and AI Authorship. *Convergence (London)*, *26*(4), 808–823. DOI: 10.1177/1354856520913866

Treanor, M., & Mateas, M. (2013). An Account of Proceduralist Meaning. In *Proceedings of DiGRA 2013: DeFragging Game Studies*. Digital Games Research Association. https://scispace.com/pdf/an-account-of-proceduralist-meaning-49zpv2i2n8.pdf

Vaswani, A., Shazeer, N., Parmar, N., Uszkoreit, J., Jones, L., Gomez, A. N., Kaiser, Ł., & Polosukhin, I. (2017). Attention Is All You Need. In *Proceedings of the 31st International Conference on Neural Information Processing Systems (NIPS'17)* (pp. 6000–6010). Curran Associates Inc. https://proceedings.neurips.cc/paper_files/paper/2017/file/3f5ee243547dee91fbd053c1c4a845aa-Paper.pdf

Wu, Z., Ji, D., Yu, K., Zeng, X., Wu, D., & Shidujaman, M. (2021). AI Creativity and the Human-AI Co-creation Model. In Kurosu, M. (Ed.), *Human-Computer Interaction. Theory, Methods and Tools - HCII 2021* (pp. 171–190). Springer., DOI: 10.1007/978-3-030-78462-1_13

Yannakakis, G. N., & Togelius, J. (2025). *Artificial Intelligence and Games* (2nd ed.). Springer. DOI: 10.1007/978-3-031-83347-2

Yi, Q., He, Y., Wang, J., Song, X., Qian, S., Yuan, X., Sun, L., Xin, Y., Tang, J., Li, K., Lu, K., Huo, M., Chen, J., & Shi, T. (2025). SCORE: Story Coherence and Retrieval Enhancement for AI Narratives. *arXiv*. /arXiv.2503.23512DOI: 10.2139/ssrn.5243040

KEY TERMS AND DEFINITIONS

Co-authorship: A cooperative storytelling process wherein AI and human agents work together to develop a story, frequently through negotiation and improvisation.

Cognitive Assemblage: A theoretical framework explaining the distribution of meaning and agency among human and nonhuman actors in storytelling systems, including players, algorithms, and interfaces.

Editorial Intervention: AI-generated content can be actively corrected, redirected, or improved by the player to preserve narrative coherence and creative intent.

Generative AI (GenAI): a class of AI systems that, by identifying patterns in vast datasets and producing outputs in response to user input, are able to create original content, including text, images, and audio.

Ludonarrative Agency: The ability of the player to shape a game's story through meaningful interaction, influenced by AI systems' generative logic as well as gameplay mechanics.

Ludonarrative Friction: Tension that results when AI-generated content or gameplay mechanics deviate from the player's expectations for the story, frequently necessitating remedial or interpretive action.

Narrative Drift: The propensity of AI-generated narratives to depart from their original genre, tone, or reasoning because language models are probabilistic.

Procedural Authorship: A type of authorship that results from the interplay between algorithmic procedures and human input, in which player actions and system rules jointly create the narrative meaning.

Chapter 5
From Technical Feasibility to Industry Reality:
Implementing LLM-Driven Dialogue Systems in Video Games

Juan Rodríguez Suárez
https://orcid.org/0009-0005-4242-6370
University of La Laguna, Spain

Jesús Miguel Torres Jorge
https://orcid.org/0000-0003-4391-0170
Universidad de La Laguna, Spain

José Demetrio Piñero Vera
Universidad de La Laguna, Spain

ABSTRACT

This chapter examines the integration of LLMs into video game dialogue systems, tracing the evolution from finite state machines and branching dialogue trees to contemporary AI-driven architectures. The analysis situates generative dialogue systems within the broader context of procedural content generation, evaluating their technical feasibility, creative implications, and economic viability for commercial game development. Through examination of existing implementations, the work identifies persistent challenges in content quality, narrative coherence, and computational efficiency. A functional prototype demonstrates practical implementation strategies for LLM-driven dialogue generation, incorporating dynamic reputation systems and procedural quest generation. Comprehensive performance

DOI: 10.4018/979-8-3373-4637-3.ch005

ght © 2026, IGI Global Scientific Publishing. Copying or distributing in print or electronic forms without written permission of IGI Global Scientific Publishing is prohibited. Use of this chapter to generative artificial intelligence (AI) technologies is expressly prohibited. The publisher reserves all rights to license its use for generative AI training and machine learning model development.

benchmarking across cloud and local deployment configurations reveals critical trade-offs between inference speed, memory constraints, and operational costs, providing empirical guidance for studios evaluating conversational AI adoption.

INTRODUCTION

Dialogue systems have long constituted a fundamental component of video game design, mediating the relationship between players, characters, and narrative worlds. From the earliest text-based adventures to contemporary expansive role-playing games, these systems have evolved in parallel with advances in computational linguistics, artificial intelligence, and interactive media design. Throughout this evolution, dialogue systems have navigated persistent conflicts between authorial control and player agency, attempting to reconcile narrative coherence with emergent gameplay possibilities. The recent emergence of Large Language Models (LLMs) has fundamentally transformed this landscape, introducing unprecedented opportunities for adaptive, context-aware dialogue generation while simultaneously presenting significant challenges regarding consistency maintenance, computational efficiency, and creative control preservation.

This chapter examines the transition from traditional dialogue architectures to LLM-driven systems, situating this progression within the broader evolution of interactive narrative design. The analysis traces the development from early approaches predicated on finite state machines and branching trees, through AI-centric methodologies incorporating planning algorithms and character psychology models, to contemporary generative approaches that leverage large-scale language models for dynamic dialogue production.

The investigation proceeds through three interconnected analytical dimensions. The opening section establishes theoretical context by examining the historical evolution of interactive dialogue systems, beginning with foundational computational models and progressing through increasingly sophisticated AI-driven architectures. This historical analysis reveals recurring design tensions and establishes the technological foundations upon which contemporary systems build. The examination demonstrates how dialogue systems reflect broader trends in game AI and natural language processing while establishing frameworks for increasingly sophisticated interactive narrative experiences.

The second analytical dimension addresses the limitations and challenges inherent in both traditional and procedural approaches to dialogue generation. Traditional hand-authored systems face fundamental scalability constraints and exponential authoring burdens as narrative complexity increases, while procedural generation introduces persistent challenges regarding content quality, coherence maintenance, and the fundamental tension between player agency and authorial control. This analysis incorporates empirical findings from contemporary implementations, demonstrating how even sophisticated generative approaches struggle with contextual awareness and narrative sophistication requirements for coherent interactive storytelling.

The third dimension provides concrete empirical grounding through examination of real-world implementations spanning indie games, community-driven modifications, and enterprise-grade middleware platforms. These case studies illuminate diverse technical strategies, economic models, and design philosophies characterizing current practice, revealing how theoretical advances in conversational AI translate into deployed systems with actual users. The analysis culminates in a detailed technical implementation framework describing an LLM-powered prototype for a narrative-driven RPG, demonstrating both the potential and the practical challenges of integrating these technologies into real-time gameplay environments. Complementary performance analysis evaluates computational characteristics and economic viability across cloud-based and local deployment strategies, providing empirical data to inform architectural decisions for production implementations.

Together, these analytical dimensions provide a comprehensive examination of how dialogue systems in games are evolving from static, hand-authored models toward adaptive, hybrid frameworks that increasingly blur boundaries between authored and emergent content. This evolution represents not merely a technological advancement but a fundamental reconceptualization of the relationship between designers, characters, and players in interactive narrative contexts. The chapter demonstrates how contemporary implementations must navigate complex trade-offs between technological sophistication and practical constraints, revealing persistent challenges that require continued research and development efforts to realize the full potential of LLM-driven dialogue systems in interactive entertainment contexts.

THEORETICAL CONTEXT AND INDUSTRY EVOLUTION

This section examines the evolution of interactive dialogue systems in video games from simple computational models to sophisticated AI-driven architectures. The historical progression reveals recurring tensions between authorial control and player agency, computational efficiency and narrative sophistication (Riedl & Bulitko (2012)). The section situates language model dialogue systems within the broader evolution of interactive narrative design, tracing the progression from branching dialogue trees to dynamic context-aware character interactions. Interactive narrative represents a paradigmatic shift from pre-authored content to procedural narrative generation, fundamentally altering the relationship between designers, characters, and players. This shift encompasses dialogue systems as a critical component of how players experience agency and narrative coherence in virtual worlds. The analysis proceeds chronologically through three phases: foundational approaches using finite state machines and branching trees; AI-centric methodologies incorporating planning algorithms and character psychology; and contemporary generative approaches leveraging LLMs.

From Branching Trees to Dynamic Narratives

Interactive dialogue systems represent a critical component of modern video game design, serving as the primary interface between players and narrative content. These systems have evolved significantly from their origins in early text-based adventures to contemporary implementations incorporating artificial intelligence and procedural generation techniques. This evolution reflects broader technological advances in computational linguistics, artificial intelligence, and interactive media design, while addressing persistent challenges in balancing player agency with narrative coherence.

Early Foundations: Branching Trees and Finite State Machines

The earliest interactive dialogue systems in video games relied on finite state machines (FSMs) and branching dialogue trees, both of which are foundational computational models for managing player interactions (Cavazza & Charles, 2005; Strong & Mateas, 2008). FSMs consist of discrete states connected by transitions triggered by player input. In dialogue contexts, each state represents a specific conversational moment or non-player characters (NPCs) response, while transitions correspond to player dialogue choices. For example, an NPC merchant might exist in states such as "greeting," "haggling," "accepting deal," or "rejecting offer." When a player selects "I'd like to buy something," the system transitions from the "greeting" state to a "shop menu" state. This deterministic approach provided predictable, controllable dialogue flows but severely limited the complexity and naturalness of conversations.

The primary advantage of FSMs lay in their simplicity and reliability, allowing designers to precisely control every possible conversation path. However, this control came at the cost of exponential complexity growth. Adding new dialogue options required creating new states and carefully managing all possible transitions, leading to what Crawford (1984) termed the "combinatorial explosion" problem.

Branching dialogue trees represented a hierarchical evolution of FSMs, organizing conversations as tree-like structures where each node represents a dialogue exchange and branches represent player choices (see Figure 1). Unlike linear FSMs, dialogue trees allowed for more complex conversational patterns, including nested topics, conditional responses based on player attributes, and multiple conversation endpoints.

Figure 1. An example of a simple branching dialogue tree structure.

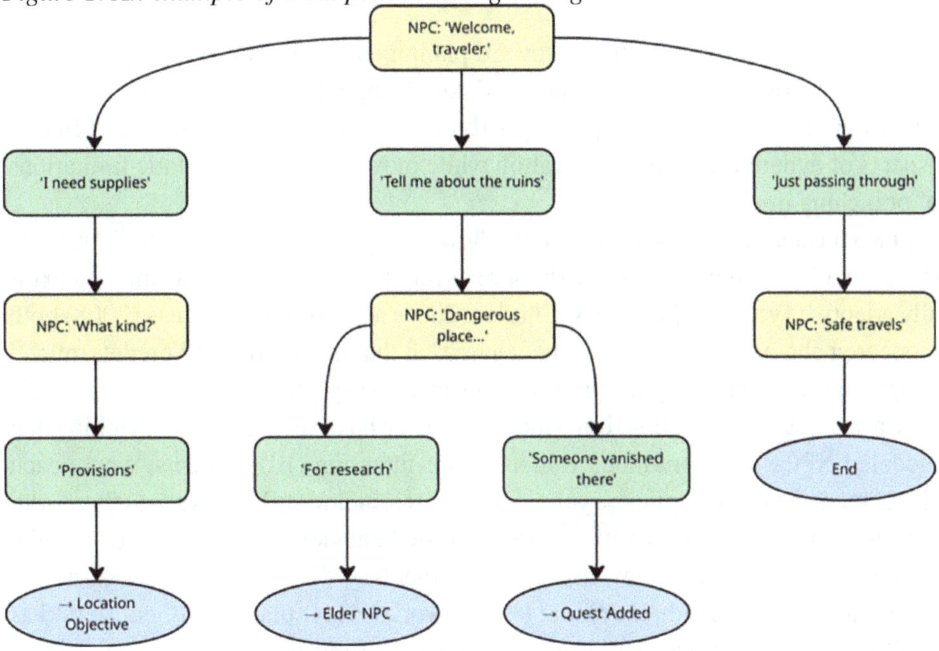

In practice, dialogue trees function through a recursive structure, where each player choice leads to a new subtree of possibilities. Games like "Baldur's Gate" (BioWare, 1998) and "Mass Effect" (BioWare, 2007) exemplified this approach, presenting players with multiple dialogue options (typically 2–4 choices) that branched into different conversational paths. These systems often incorporated player statistics, previous choices, or character relationships to determine available options (a technique known as "gating").

The tree structure enabled more sophisticated narrative control than simple FSMs. Designers could create converging branches (where different choices led to similar outcomes) or dramatically divergent paths that affected story progression. However, the fundamental limitation remained: every possible conversation had to be hand-authored, creating massive content creation burdens for complex narratives. This constraint would prove increasingly problematic as games grew in scope and players developed expectations for more dynamic, responsive dialogue systems.

The dominance of branching dialogue trees in commercial RPGs established a paradigm that persisted for decades until today, but their static nature struggled to accommodate emergent player behavior or truly adaptive narrative responses (Cavazza & Charles, 2005; Strong & Mateas, 2008; Taylor-Giles, 2020).

Transition to AI-Centric Approaches

Subsequently, research shifted toward planning and discourse-level approaches that treat dialogue as part of a character's goals, beliefs and social relations. This evolution encompassed multiple algorithmic families, each addressing different aspects of dynamic dialogue generation while moving beyond the static limitations of branching trees.

Two influential works demonstrated how AI planning techniques could replace traditional branching dialogue with more psychologically believable and contextually adaptive systems. Cavazza & Charles (2005) and Strong & Mateas (2008) both pioneered character-driven dialogue generation that moved beyond predetermined scripts toward dynamic, goal-oriented conversation systems.

Cavazza & Charles (2005) introduced character-based interactive storytelling that modeled NPCs as autonomous Belief-Desire-Intention (BDI) agents, where each character maintained explicit psychological states, including beliefs about the world, long-term desires and motivations, and specific behavioral intentions. Meanwhile, Strong & Mateas (2008) developed complementary dynamic discourse structure generation that applied hierarchical task network (HTN) planning (Georgievski & Aiello, 2014) to synthesize dialogue managers at runtime, treating conversations as discourse-level planning problems.

The technical architectures shared core principles while addressing different aspects of dialogue generation. Both systems maintained sophisticated character knowledge models: the BDI framework from Cavazza & Charles (2005) tracked psychological states and social relationships, while the approach presented by Strong & Mateas (2008) modeled what characters know, believe, and can discuss within specific narrative contexts. During dialogue interactions, the system described in Cavazza & Charles (2005) used speech act theory (Cooren, 2015) to generate contextually appropriate responses based on characters' current psychological states. This approach enabled the same character to produce pleading dialogue when seeking help or evasive responses when harboring conflicting goals. The system developed by Strong & Mateas (2008) employed discourse operators (reusable conversational patterns for questioning, explaining, or persuading) that were dynamically selected and composed based on high-level narrative objectives and social context models.

Together, these approaches enabled emergent dialogue patterns that could not be anticipated by designers. The psychological modeling introduced by Cavazza & Charles (2005) allowed characters to develop complex relationships, hold grudges, or change conversational tone based on accumulated interactions, while the planning-based approach from Strong & Mateas (2008) ensured that the same characters could have completely different conversation structures depending on story state, narrative timing, and evolving relationships. This convergence of psychological modeling and dynamic planning showed how traditional AI techniques could produce dialogue systems that were both psychologically coherent and narratively purposeful, laying groundwork for modern approaches that treat conversation as an emergent property of character psychology and story context rather than a predetermined branching structure.

Despite their theoretical sophistication, these systems remained largely experimental. Their complexity and unpredictability posed significant challenges for commercial game development, including extensive authoring requirements for character models, difficulty in quality assurance processes, and concerns about maintaining narrative coherence in emergent conversations. These early limitations would influence the development of later hybrid approaches that sought to balance dynamic generation with authorial control.

Generative Artificial Intelligence Approaches

The emergence of LLMs such as GPT-3 (Brown et al., 2020), PaLM (Chowdhery et al., 2023), and LLaMA (Touvron et al., 2023) has enabled new possibilities for dialogue systems by enabling generative AI techniques that produce contextually relevant text based on vast training data. These models leverage deep learning architectures, particularly transformers (Vaswani et al., 2017), to generate human-like text by predicting subsequent words in a sequence given preceding context. This capability allows for unprecedented flexibility in dialogue generation, as models can produce novel responses to virtually any input without requiring exhaustive hand-authored content.

Building upon these architectural advances, Freiknecht & Effelsberg (2020) established the viability of statistical language models specifically for procedural dialogue generation in interactive narratives. Their system employed context encoding mechanisms that incorporated story state, character information, dialogue history, and player choices into comprehensive context vectors, enabling conditional generation of responses that maintained thematic consistency across extended interactions.

While this approach achieved remarkable flexibility, allowing characters to discuss topics never explicitly programmed and respond to novel situations, it revealed critical limitations inherent to purely statistical generation: coherence drift over extended conversations, character consistency degradation when operating outside training data parameters, and limited narrative control for designers requiring specific story outcomes. These challenges highlighted the need for more sophisticated constraint mechanisms and validation frameworks.

The PANGeA system represents a significant advance in AI-driven dialogue generation for games, addressing many limitations of earlier language model approaches through sophisticated constraint mechanisms and narrative validation (Buongiorno et al., 2024). PANGeA combines the flexibility of LLMs with the structural control required for coherent gameplay experiences through a novel middleware architecture that bridges game engines with AI generation systems.

PANGeA operates through a modular server-based architecture with RESTful interfaces, enabling integration with any game engine while supporting both local and cloud-based LLMs. The system comprises three critical technical components that work in concert to generate narrative-consistent content:

Custom memory system: PANGeA maintains persistent conversational context that extends beyond typical LLM token limitations, enabling NPCs to engage in extended, coherent interactions that reference previous encounters, relationship dynamics, and narrative developments. This contextual memory prevents the narrative drift common in purely generative approaches and addresses one of the key technical challenges identified in earlier research.

The system implements distinct short-term and long-term memory mechanisms that work collaboratively to provide comprehensive contextual awareness. Short-term memories function as cached raw data repositories containing recent conversations and in-game actions, providing immediate access to the most current interaction context. Long-term memories store summarized versions of past conversations and actions in a vector database, enabling retrieval of relevant historical context through semantic search operations. This approach aligns with established Retrieval-Augmented Generation (RAG) architectures (Lewis et al., 2020). A key component of the memory architecture is a summarizer, which processes retrieved content into concise formats suitable for prompt injection within LLM context limitations.

Validation framework: The system's key innovation lies in its self-reflective validation approach that leverages the LLM's own capabilities to maintain narrative consistency (Buongiorno et al., 2024). The validation system generates gameplay rules based on designer-specified criteria that are later used to validate the player input. When free-form text is received, the system prompts the LLM to provide an affirmative or negative response on whether the input breaks any gameplay rules (see Figure 2). If no rules are violated, the LLM generates a direct response to the player input. If rules are broken, the system identifies which specific rules were violated and uses this knowledge as context to generate an in-character corrective response that maintains story immersion while realigning the player with the game narrative (Buongiorno et al., 2024). This validation system dramatically improves performance across model sizes, elevating smaller models like Llama 3 8B from 28% to 98% accuracy in narrative consistency tasks, and demonstrating how structured approaches can enhance AI capabilities without requiring larger, more computationally expensive models.

Figure 2. A flow diagram of the validation system's self-reflective steps.

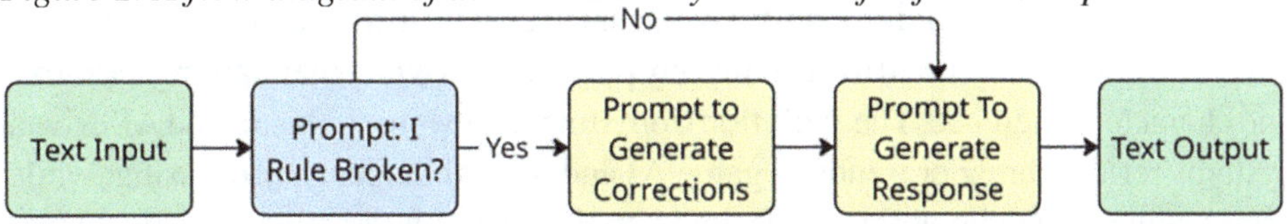

Personality-constrained generation: Characters are defined through Big Five Personality model parameters that consistently influence dialogue generation, ensuring behavioral coherence across interactions while allowing for natural conversation variation within established character bounds (Buongiorno et al., 2024). This approach addresses the character consistency challenges that plagued earlier generative systems.

When players interact with NPCs, PANGeA processes input through its validation framework, retrieves relevant context from its memory system, applies character-specific personality constraints to generation prompts, produces dialogue through the LLM, and updates its memory for future interactions. Rather than scripting individual responses, game designers specify high-level configuration rules and narrative boundaries that are used during the game development to generate the gameplay rules that the validation system applies to player input. This constraint-based approach enables the system to procedurally generate setting details, character relationships, key items, and contextually appropriate dialogue. This design philosophy represents a fundamental shift in authoring workflows, requiring designers to think in terms of systemic constraints rather than specific content pieces.

PANGeA demonstrated significant improvements over earlier approaches in character consistency, narrative coherence, and contextual appropriateness across diverse RPG scenarios spanning multiple genres and LLM architectures. The system successfully addressed common procedural generation pathologies such as repetitive content, character inconsistency, and narrative drift. These issues are identified by Mohaghegh et al. (2023) and Buongiorno et al. (2024) as persistent challenges in procedural content generation (PCG) systems.

However, important challenges remain that represent active areas of research and development. Computational efficiency for real-time generation continues to pose constraints, particularly for mobile or resource-limited gaming platforms. Designer workflow integration requires the development of authoring tools that allow designers to effectively work with AI-driven systems while maintaining creative control. Additionally, developing scalable evaluation metrics for measuring subjective dialogue quality remains complex, as traditional computational metrics may not adequately capture the nuanced aspects of narrative effectiveness and player engagement that define successful dialogue systems.

These contemporary generative approaches represent a fundamental shift in dialogue system design, moving from predetermined content toward adaptive contextual generation that can respond to virtually any player action while maintaining narrative and character coherence. The evolution from simple FSMs to sophisticated AI-driven systems reflects broader trends in game AI and natural language processing, while establishing foundations for increasingly sophisticated interactive narrative experiences that may further blur boundaries between authored and emergent content.

LIMITATIONS OF TRADITIONAL NARRATIVE DESIGN APPROACHES

Traditional hand-authored dialogue systems face fundamental scalability challenges that become increasingly severe as narrative complexity grows. Taylor-Giles (2020) demonstrated that the authoring burden increases exponentially with the complexity of player choice options. Each additional dialogue branch requires not only initial writing but ongoing maintenance and testing to ensure narrative consistency across all possible interaction paths.

Building on this concern, Veloso & Prada (2021) identified significant gaps in tooling for verification and debugging of authored dialogue trees. Their analysis revealed how interactive narratives require repeated playthroughs to surface inconsistencies, a process that becomes increasingly time-intensive and error-prone as system complexity grows. The combinatorial explosion of possible dialogue paths makes comprehensive testing practically impossible for complex systems, resulting in released games with narrative inconsistencies or broken dialogue branches.

These technical limitations translate directly into economic constraints. Major RPG productions typically employ specialized writing teams over extended development cycles to generate sufficient dialogue content. However, the branching nature of interactive narratives means individual players experience only a fraction of the authored material in any single playthrough. Resource allocation pressures often force studios to prioritize core narrative paths, leaving secondary content inadequately tested or polished. This structural inefficiency, where substantial development resources produce content with limited player exposure, has motivated industry exploration of procedural alternatives, despite their technical challenges.

CHALLENGES AND LIMITATIONS OF PROCEDURAL DIALOGUE SYSTEMS

While procedural dialogue generation offers advantages in scalability and dynamic responsiveness, practical implementations reveal fundamental challenges spanning technical, creative, and economic dimensions. These limitations constrain the effectiveness of purely procedural systems and necessitate hybrid approaches, balancing algorithmic generation with human oversight. The following analysis examines three critical areas: content quality and coherence, the tension between player agency and authorial control, and the absence of adequate evaluation frameworks.

Content Quality and Coherence

Implementations of non-generative PCG often produce simplistic, repetitive outcomes unless carefully constrained (Kybartas & Verbrugge, 2014). Game designer Kate Compton formalized this challenge through two interconnected concepts: the Oatmeal problem (Rabii & Cook, 2023), which describes how procedural systems tend to generate bland, repetitive content that fails to maintain player engagement over extended interactions, and the Bach faucet problem (Karth & Compton, 2023), which addresses not only the objective quality of generated content but also its perceived value in player experience. The Bach faucet problem suggests that players may develop different expectations and appreciation for procedurally generated versus authored content, potentially devaluing generated material regardless of its actual quality. These dual challenges create a feedback loop: developers must not only solve the technical problems of generating varied, coherent content but also address player psychology and expectation management.

These quality challenges are not isolated to specific implementations but represent systemic issues across PCG approaches. Summerville et al. (2018)'s comprehensive survey of machine learning-based generation methods demonstrates that procedural systems consistently struggle with three interrelated challenges: generating sufficient variety to avoid repetitiveness, maintaining structural constraints necessary for playability, and working effectively with the small datasets typical of game content. Their analysis reveals that these problems persist across diverse algorithmic families, from frequency-based Markov chains to deep neural networks, suggesting that the Oatmeal and Bach faucet problems represent fundamental tensions in procedural generation rather than limitations of specific techniques.

The emergence of LLM-based approaches represented an attempt to address these fundamental limitations by leveraging vast training data to produce more varied and contextually appropriate dialogue. However, empirical evaluation with actual players reveals that contemporary LLMs struggle with the contextual awareness and narrative sophistication required for coherent interactive storytelling. Akoury et al. (2023) conducted a rigorous user study evaluating GPT-4 generated dialogue within Disco Elysium, a narrative-driven RPG. The study employed a constrained generation task where the LLM modified human-written dialogue based on game state changes, representing a collaborative human-AI workflow rather than fully autonomous generation. Despite this supportive framework, players strongly preferred human-written dialogue (64% versus 23% for GPT-4 content), citing superior logical consistency (human: 61% versus GPT-4: 28%) and conversational flow (human: 67% versus GPT-4: 21%). Critically, after seeing subsequent dialogue, 32% of GPT-4 generations were retrospectively judged as illogical, revealing fundamental difficulties in maintaining narrative coherence even when grounded in explicit game state information.

Beyond single-interaction quality, LLM-based generation of entire branched narratives introduces additional coherence challenges. Freiknecht & Effelsberg (2020) demonstrated that fully generative approaches suffer from excessive character proliferation, logical drift across narrative branches, and inconsistent character behavior. These findings highlight the persistent tension between the flexibility desired in procedural systems and the coherence required for engaging narrative experiences, a tension that remains unresolved even with more sophisticated generative approaches. Contemporary systems like PANGeA's validation framework (Buongiorno et al., 2024) attempt to address these issues through architectural solutions that validate generated content against explicit constraints, recognizing that improving generation algorithms alone cannot resolve these fundamental challenges.

Agency Versus Authorial Control

A fundamental trade-off exists between providing players with meaningful agency and maintaining authorial control over narrative direction, what Riedl & Bulitko (2012) identifies as the central challenge of interactive narrative design. Shoulson (2013) noted the challenge of coordinating autonomous NPC behavior with authored plot beats, requiring mechanisms to temporarily co-opt character autonomy or reconcile conflicting goals between emergent character behavior and predetermined story requirements. Miller et al. (2019) addressed this challenge by developing a hybrid system that combines character simulations for autonomy with planning-based narrative generation for coherence, demonstrating that synthesis of multiple approaches can balance these competing demands.

This conflict is particularly pronounced in commercial game development, where designers must balance creative vision with player expectations for choice and consequence. Traditional dialogue trees offer clear authorial control but limited player agency, while more dynamic systems risk narrative incoherence or unintended outcomes that may undermine carefully crafted thematic elements. As Miller et al. (2019) observe, different procedural narrative generation approaches tend to sacrifice character autonomy in service of designer-controlled experiences, or content authoring in service of encoding domain knowledge of narrative branches and participating characters.

Contemporary generative systems attempt to navigate this tension through constraint-based approaches that define high-level narrative boundaries while allowing for dynamic content generation within those limits, as exemplified by PANGeA's validation framework (Buongiorno et al., 2024). However, establishing effective rules and constraints for the content generated by LLMs remains a complex challenge. The unpredictability of generative models means that even well-defined constraints may not fully prevent undesirable outputs.

Evaluation and Validation Frameworks

A critical challenge in procedural narrative generation lies in developing evaluation frameworks capable of assessing the complex interplay between narrative structure, player agency, and emotional engagement, particularly when the combinatorial explosion of possible narrative states renders traditional validation methods impractical. Traditional methods for testing and validating aspects of game design, such as playtesting and designer reviews, remain valuable but struggle to scale effectively for procedurally generated content due to the vast number of possible interaction paths. This scalability challenge has motivated researchers to explore automated validation approaches, with AI-based playtesters emerging as a particularly promising avenue.

Recent research efforts have focused on developing AI agents capable of playing games with varying strategies (Almeida et al., 2023; Bateni & Whitehead, 2024; Hu et al., 2024; Souchleris et al., 2023). Although these agents have not yet achieved human-level performance across all domains, they nonetheless provide valuable insights into game dynamics and player experience (Xiao & Yang, 2024). As this technology matures, future implementations could enable agents configured with different playstyles, decision-making heuristics, and emotional response patterns to evaluate the procedurally generated content. Such systems would allow developers to conduct large-scale simulations, gathering data across a wide range of player experiences and identifying potential inconsistencies, narrative dead-ends, or engagement issues (whether in procedural narratives, level design, or others dynamically generated content) that might remain undetected through conventional playtesting alone.

While AI-based validation frameworks represent a promising methodological direction, their application to playtesting and narrative evaluation remains an emerging area of active research, with substantial work needed to establish reliable metrics for procedural content quality, narrative coherence, and player engagement.

EXISTING IMPLEMENTATIONS AND CASE STUDIES

Contemporary implementations of AI-powered dialogue systems in video games provide valuable insights into the practical challenges and opportunities of deploying conversational AI in interactive entertainment contexts. This section examines three distinct approaches to integrating language processing and generation technologies into gaming environments: a commercial indie game utilizing semantic analysis, a community-driven modification project implementing LLMs, and enterprise-grade middleware platforms designed for professional game development.

These case studies illuminate the diverse technical strategies, economic models, and design philosophies that characterize current practice in the field. Each implementation represents different trade-offs between technological sophistication and practical constraints, revealing how theoretical advances in conversational AI translate into deployed systems with real users. The analysis focuses on technical architectures, performance characteristics, economic viability, and the creative and narrative implications of different design choices, providing empirical grounding for understanding the current state and future directions of AI-powered dialogue systems in games.

"Interview with the Whisperer" Analysis

"Interview with the Whisperer" represents a notable example of NLP-centered game design that demonstrates how non-generative language processing can create compelling interactive experiences (Deconstructeam, 2021). Developed by Deconstructeam and released as a conversational investigation game, the system places players in dialogue with Manuel, an elderly character, through a free-text input interface that relies entirely on Natural Language Processing rather than generative AI technology (Figure 3).

Figure 3. Screenshot of "Interview with the Whisperer" showing the free-text input interface and dialogue with Manuel

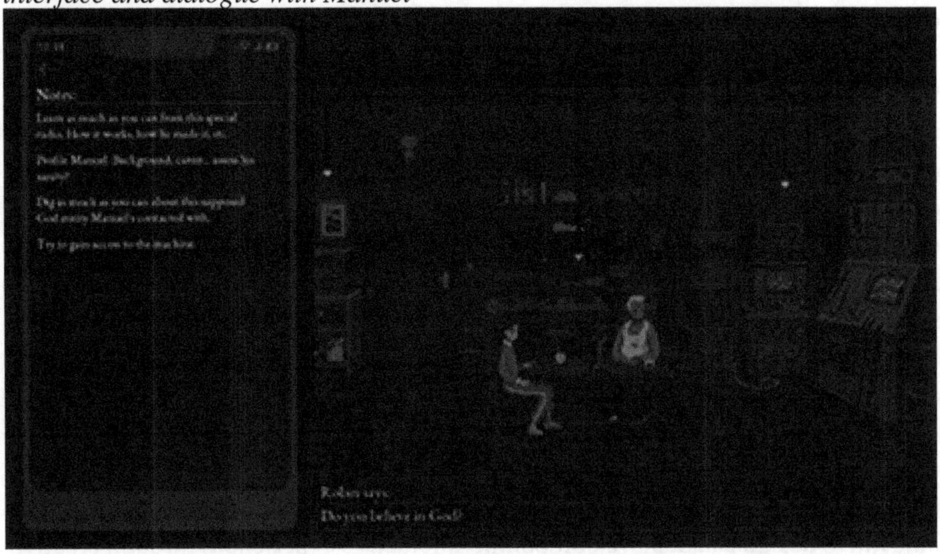

The technical implementation demonstrates several key design principles for NLP-driven dialogue systems. The system employs Semantic ML, a tool for semantic analysis developed by Google, to interpret player intent and trigger appropriate pre-authored responses from a curated database (Pietrzak et al., 2020; Sun et al., 2022). Rather than generating new content, the NLP system parses the meaning of player input to identify the most relevant human-written dialogue response, maintaining complete authorial control over narrative content while providing conversational flexibility.

Similar applications of Semantic ML in game development include "The Mystery of the Three Bots," a dialog-based investigation game that demonstrates how small semantic models can drive character conversations through pre-written question-answer pairs (Google, 2020; Sun et al., 2022).

The implementation of "Interview with the Whisperer" addresses the critical challenge of technical limitation integration through ingenious narrative design that transforms system constraints into character traits. When the NLP system fails to parse player input effectively or responds with seemingly unrelated content, the narrative frames these moments as manifestations of Manuel's absent-mindedness and potential dementia. This design choice converts potential system failures into authentic character interactions, enhancing rather than breaking narrative immersion.

This approach reveals important insights about constraint-driven narrative design in AI-assisted systems. The deliberate embrace of technical limitations enables conversations that feel authentic and purposeful while maintaining tight narrative control that purely generative approaches cannot guarantee. Players report experiencing genuine investigative challenges as they learn to phrase questions effectively to extract information from a difficult interview subject, creating emergent gameplay from the interaction between human curiosity and system constraints.

However, the implementation also highlights persistent challenges in conversational AI deployment. The system's reliance on server-based processing created ongoing maintenance costs of approximately $20 monthly, ultimately forcing the developers to discontinue the online service due to economic unsustainability. Additionally, the system requirements for a potential standalone version (10GB storage and substantial processing power for semantic analysis) demonstrate that even non-generative language processing systems carry significant computational overhead that can limit deployment options.

The game's brief operational lifespan serves as a valuable case study in the economic realities of maintaining conversational AI systems, even those that avoid the computational intensity of modern LLMs. This implementation proves that innovative design can achieve compelling interactive experiences through creative application of simpler technologies, casting doubts on the necessity of generative AI for effective conversational gameplay.

"Mantella Mod for Skyrim" Analysis

The "Mantella" mod for Skyrim represents a significant advancement in community-driven AI integration, demonstrating how modern language models can be retrofitted into existing game architectures (Art From The Machine, 2023, 2024a). This modification replaces the game's traditional dialogue system with dynamic AI-generated conversations that maintain awareness of specific visual elements and character relationships.

The architectural approach employs a separate Python-based orchestrator system that interfaces with the in-game component, rather than directly intercepting dialogue requests (Art From The Machine, 2024a). This architectural separation prevents computationally intensive AI processing from interfering with the game's core performance, while maintaining flexibility for different AI service configurations. Early implementations relied on simple file-based inter-process communication, which later evolved to more efficient HTTP-based protocols for improved responsiveness.

The system implements persistent character memory through two distinct approaches, depending on the implementation version. The original Mantella system employed "lossy summaries" where condensed conversation summaries were stored and referenced in future interactions, though this approach proved prone to information degradation over time (Art From The Machine, 2024a). The newer Pantella fork implements a RAG system (Lewis et al., 2020), introducing a more sophisticated vector database system that stores conversation chunks without summarization, to eliminate the lossy nature of the original memory implementation and enable more coherent long-term character development (Pathos14489, 2024).

Context integration capabilities center primarily on visual environmental awareness, as the mod cannot access the internal state of the game to provide comprehensive information about world conditions such as weather systems, nearby objects, or world events to the language model. Instead, the system can pass screenshots of the in-game environment to vision-enabled language models, allowing NPCs to observe and comment on their immediate surroundings, react to landmarks and vistas, or provide assistance with visual puzzles. This visual context integration represents a novel approach to grounding AI conversations in the immediate game environment, working within the limitations of external mod architecture that cannot directly interface with the game's internal state systems.

Technical performance and responsiveness reveal both the potential and limitations of implementing conversational AI within existing game architectures. The system achieves optimal conversational quality when running on hardware with adequate GPU memory (10GB+ VRAM recommended), with successful deployments reported on graphics cards ranging from NVIDIA GeForce GTX 980Ti to RTX 4070 Ti. However, latency presents ongoing challenges for maintaining immersive gameplay experiences. While users should ideally target models with latencies below 0.5 seconds to preserve conversational flow, even optimized configurations using the fastest cloud-based services or local models on high-end consumer hardware (Art From The Machine, 2024b) typically require several seconds to generate responses due to computational complexity. Local model deployment eliminates network communication latency but generally provides slower processing speeds than cloud-based infrastructure, requiring careful optimization of model parameters, context window sizes, and deployment strategies to achieve acceptable gameplay performance.

The Mantella implementation demonstrates the importance of character consistency frameworks for maintaining narrative coherence. Rather than employing post-generation validation steps, as implemented in PANGeA, to filter out inconsistent outputs (Buongiorno et al., 2024), Mantella achieves consistency through two primary mechanisms: fine-tuning a custom model (Mantella Skyrim Llama 3 8B GGUF) on a comprehensive dataset of over 8,800 player-NPC interactions from the base game (Art from the Machine, 2024), and implementing character-specific background descriptions and prompts that provide explicit contextual grounding for the language model, even if the LLM is a general-purpose model. These approaches serve as guardrails to help NPCs maintain character identity and avoid responses that would break immersion or contradict established personalities.

Beyond conversational capabilities, the mod enables NPCs to perform limited in-game actions such as following the player, initiating combat when provoked, and opening inventory interfaces for trading, though the effectiveness of these action triggers can vary depending on the language model's ability to follow structured instructions. The system also implements radiant and group dialogue systems that allow NPCs to initiate conversations with each other independently and facilitate multi-participant conversations, creating more dynamic social interactions within the game world (Art From The Machine, 2024a).

Enterprise-Grade Dialogue Middleware

The commercial landscape for LLM-powered dialogue systems has matured into sophisticated end-to-end platforms that address the complex technical requirements of professional game development. These enterprise solutions represent a fundamental shift from experimental implementations toward production-ready middleware capable of supporting large-scale commercial deployments.

Platform Architecture and Market Positioning

Commercial platforms such as Convai and Inworld AI have emerged as the dominant middleware providers, distinguished by their comprehensive approach to real-time conversational AI orchestration (Inworld AI, 2024b; NVIDIA Developer Blog, 2024). These platforms manage the entire generative pipeline (from speech input processing and LLM inference to voice synthesis, memory management, and character action execution) addressing the critical infrastructure challenges that experimental implementations typically cannot resolve at commercial scale.

The technical complexity of achieving sub-500 millisecond response times in multimodal environments necessitates specialized inference optimization that individual development teams cannot practically replicate (Inworld AI, 2024b). Commercial platforms leverage dedicated infrastructure partnerships, particularly with NVIDIA's Avatar Cloud Engine (ACE) framework, utilizing microservices such as NVIDIA Riva for low-latency automatic speech recognition and text-to-speech, and NVIDIA Audio2Face for real-time facial animation synchronization (NVIDIA Corporation, 2024).

Narrative Control and Consistency Management

Commercial platforms address the critical challenge of maintaining lore consistency through proprietary narrative control systems. Convai's Knowledge Banks provide tiered storage capacity for character backstories and world lore, ranging from

1MB on free tiers to 5MB for professional implementations (Convai, 2024). Inworld AI's Goals and Mutations framework enables dynamic behavioral control, allowing developers to enable or disable specific character actions based on recognized player intent and real-time game state changes (Inworld AI, 2024d).

Like the previous systems discussed based on RAG principles, these control mechanisms represent a paradigm shift from traditional dialogue scripting toward cognitive architecture design, where developers define behavioral constraints and motivational frameworks rather than explicit dialogue trees. The platforms translate LLM outputs into concrete game actions while maintaining adherence to established character personalities and narrative boundaries, providing essential guardrails against the unpredictable nature of generative content.

Performance Metrics and Scalability Achievements

Commercial deployments have demonstrated measurable business impact through improved player engagement metrics. Case studies report significant increases in session duration, with some implementations achieving over 1.5 hours of daily engagement per user (Inworld AI, 2024a). One RPG implementation recorded a 5% increase in overall playtime, while another project achieved a 42% improvement in player retention metrics following AI character integration (Inworld AI, 2024a).

The scalability achievements are particularly notable in cost optimization strategies. Advanced implementations have reported over 95% reductions in AI operational costs while simultaneously scaling to support over 500,000 daily active users (Inworld AI, 2024b). These results demonstrate that sophisticated architectural choices and usage optimization can overcome the economic barriers that typically limit generative AI deployment in high-concurrency gaming environments.

Economic Models and Cost Structure Analysis

Commercial platforms employ complex usage-based pricing models that segment costs across multiple service components. LLM interaction quotas, typically the primary cost driver, range from highly restrictive free tiers (100 interactions monthly on Convai) to professional allocations supporting thousands of monthly conversations (Convai, 2024). Text-to-speech synthesis, while competitively priced at $5-10 per million characters on platforms like Inworld AI, represents a significant operational expense for dialogue-heavy implementations (Inworld AI Documentation, 2024).

The economic viability of commercial deployment requires strategic model selection, with cost differences between flagship models (GPT-4o class, approximately $375 monthly for 10,000 conversations) and optimized alternatives (GPT-4o-mini class, approximately $45 monthly) necessitating tiered deployment strategies

(Compare Voice AI, 2025). To ensure sustainable deployment economics, studios must balance quality requirements against operational costs by reserving premium models for critical narrative moments while utilizing cost-effective alternatives for background character interactions.

Limitations and Implementation Challenges

Despite their sophistication, commercial platforms face persistent technical constraints that impact deployment strategies. Latency remains a critical bottleneck, with even optimized configurations requiring careful balance between response quality and processing speed. The dependency on external infrastructure introduces network-related performance variables that can affect player experience consistency.

Content moderation represents another significant challenge, as platforms must implement comprehensive safety systems to prevent generation of harmful, biased, or narratively inconsistent content (Inworld AI, 2024c). These moderation frameworks, while essential for commercial deployment, can occasionally interfere with creative expression or limit the dynamic range of character interactions.

The economic model sustainability also presents ongoing concerns, particularly regarding the unpredictable nature of usage-based scaling costs. Studios must implement sophisticated monitoring and optimization strategies to prevent budget overruns while maintaining quality standards, requiring expertise in both game development and AI operations management.

Commercial platforms have successfully addressed many technical barriers that previously limited conversational AI deployment in games, transforming experimental concepts into viable production systems. However, their effectiveness depends heavily on careful implementation planning, architectural optimization, and ongoing cost management strategies that reflect the complex intersection of creative and technical requirements in modern game development.

TECHNICAL IMPLEMENTATION FRAMEWORK

This section presents the technical architecture and implementation strategies employed in developing a functional prototype that demonstrates LLM-driven dialogue systems in video games. The implementation addresses fundamental challenges in maintaining narrative coherence, managing computational resources, and creating accessible interaction mechanisms while operating within the constraints of real-time gameplay environments.

The prototype focuses on a narrative-driven RPG scenario where the player has to explore an island, uncover lore, and complete quests through meaningful interactions with NPCs. Players can engage in free-form text conversations with multiple NPCs who possess distinct personalities, backgrounds, and motivations. The dialogue system generates contextually relevant responses that reflect character traits and adapt to evolving game conditions. The complete implementation is available in the project repository (Rodríguez-Suárez et al., 2025).

Figure 4 shows the conversation interface, where players can type free-form queries and receive contextually appropriate responses from NPCs. The system maintains visual consistency with traditional RPG dialogue systems while enabling conversational freedom.

Figure 4. Screenshot of the game prototype showing an NPC conversation interface

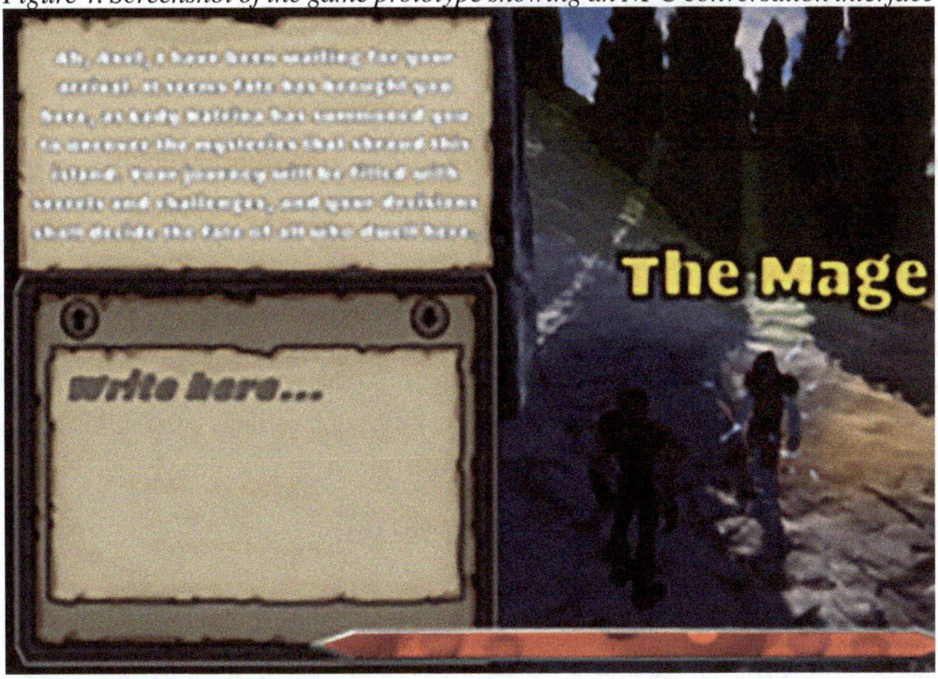

The game prototype is developed using the Unity game engine, and utilizes a custom-built dialogue system that integrates a LLM to generate dynamic conversations with NPCs. The system incorporates several key components: a modular architecture for character context management, prompt engineering techniques for consistent dialogue generation, a reputation system that influences character behavior based on player interactions, and a procedural quest generator driven by character personalities and world lore.

Dialogue Generation System

The dialogue generation system relies on a LLM provider to generate NPC responses based on player input, character personalities, and contextual information about the game world. All this information is structured into the prompt messages that are sent to the model via an API call. The player input is provided as the user prompt, while the character personality and world context are included as system messages that establish the narrative framework for the conversation. The implementation uses OpenAI's API, so the system can seamlessly switch between different models that conform to the OpenAI interface, including local models via Llama.cpp (Gerganov, 2023) or cloud-based services.

Some LLMs, like OpenAI GPT or DeepSeek models, support structured output formats that enable reliable extraction of both dialogue content and metadata necessary for game state management. Our design of the dialogue system leverages JSON-structured responses to capture multiple information dimensions simultaneously: the answer text itself, conversation termination signals, and reputation adjustments.

The structured output schema requires the model to provide responses in a predetermined JSON format with specific fields (Pezoa et al., 2016). For standard dialogue interactions, the format includes a "content" field containing the NPC's spoken response, an "is finished" boolean indicating whether the conversation should terminate, and a "reputation change" integer specifying how the interaction affects the player's standing with that character. This approach eliminates the need for fragile post-processing heuristics to detect conversation endings or parse dialogue for game-relevant information.

Prompt Engineering and System Prompt

The quality and consistency of LLM-generated dialogue depends critically on carefully engineered system prompts that establish narrative boundaries, character identities, and behavioral constraints. Our design structured the system prompt in sections, separating universal world knowledge from character-specific personality traits to enable efficient reuse of shared context while maintaining character distinctiveness.

The system prompt includes three primary components: world lore and narrative context, universal behavioral guidelines, and character-specific personality definitions. The world lore establishes the fundamental narrative framework, providing all NPCs with consistent knowledge about geographical locations, historical events, and the central conflict driving the story. This shared foundation prevents contradictory information across character interactions while enabling NPCs to reference common knowledge naturally. Figure 5 example demonstrates how this shared world knowledge enables coherent NPC responses to player inquiries about the game world. In this example, The player asks where another character is on the island, and the NPC responds with accurate information that aligns with the established lore.

Figure 5. Dialogue example showing how the NPC answer questions about the world

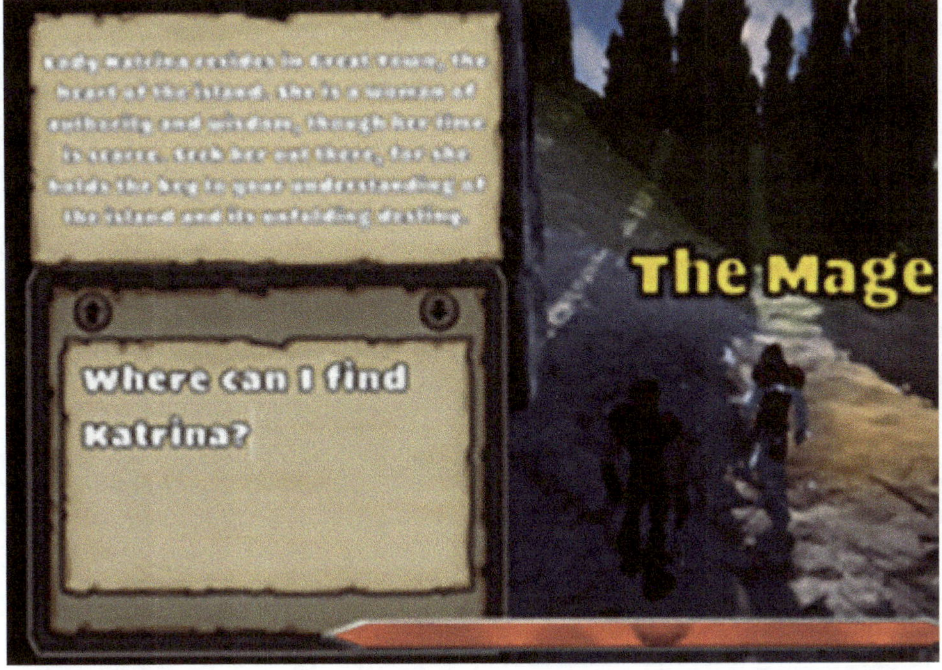

The universal behavioral guidelines define how the model should respond to edge cases and maintain narrative immersion. A particularly important instruction addresses out-of-context player statements: "If the player says something off the context of the story, tell them that you don't understand continental language or expressions and briefly talk a bit about the story of the island or something related to the character's background (so the player may get familiar with the island)". This rule transforms potential immersion-breaking moments into characterful responses that reinforce the game world. When players attempt to reference real-world locations or concepts foreign to the narrative setting, NPCs acknowledge their unfamiliarity with such terminology while naturally redirecting conversation toward story-relevant topics. We illustrate this behavior in Figure 6.

Figure 6. Example dialogue demonstrating the system's handling of an out-of-context query about Europe

Figure 6 shows the system's response when a player asks about Europe's location. Rather than breaking character or providing anachronistic information, the NPC acknowledges their unfamiliarity with continental terminology while naturally steering the conversation toward relevant story elements. This approach preserves immersion while subtly educating players about appropriate conversational topics within the game world.

Character Personality Integration

Character personalities employ a structured JSON format that facilitates both programmatic access and model comprehension. The schema includes standard attributes such as age, gender, occupation, and personality traits, but also extends to incorporate relationship networks and character-specific concerns that drive quest generation.

The relationship network field explicitly defines each character's connections to other NPCs, including the nature of their relationship and relevant shared history. This interconnected character web enables the model to provide contextually appropriate information when players inquire about other characters, creating a believable social network that players can navigate through dialogue. Beyond facilitating references to other NPCs, these personality definitions enable characters to discuss their own backgrounds and motivations in ways that feel authentic and consistent. Figure 7 demonstrates the system's ability to generate responses that authentically reflect an NPC's background and personality. This response draws from both the character's personality JSON and the world lore, demonstrating the effective integration of multiple information sources in dialogue generation.

Figure 7. Dialogue example showing how the NPC talks about himself

Maintaining Behavioral Consistency

Consistent NPC behavior across extended interactions presents a persistent challenge in LLM-driven dialogue systems. LLMs exhibit stochastic behavior that can produce varied responses to similar inputs, potentially breaking character consistency or violating established narrative facts. The implementation addresses this through multiple complementary strategies.

The structured personality definitions provide explicit character constraints that limit behavioral variance. By encoding personality traits, relationship networks, and background details in the persistent conversation context, the system constrains the solution space for appropriate responses. However, personality definitions alone prove insufficient to prevent occasional inconsistencies, particularly in edge cases or when context windows approach their limits.

Future enhancements could incorporate self-reflection techniques, where a model reviews player input and its own prior responses to ensure alignment with character constraints before finalizing output (Buongiorno et al., 2024). While this approach remains unimplemented in the current prototype due to latency considerations, it represents a promising avenue for enhancing consistency in scenarios where response quality justifies additional computational overhead.

Independent Character Context Architecture

A fundamental architectural decision involved the strategy for maintaining conversational context across multiple NPCs. The initial approach of maintaining a single unified conversation history for all characters presented severe scalability limitations and attention degradation problems that fundamentally compromised system viability. For that reason, Buongiorno et al. (2024) isolated conversation histories per character, enabling each NPC to maintain a distinct dialogue thread that preserves temporal proximity and contextual relevance.

The unified conversation architecture operated by injecting system prompts into a shared dialogue history whenever players interacted with different NPCs. When a player engaged with a new character, the system appended to the prompt information about the character's personality. While this approach simplified implementation by avoiding character detection logic and maintaining a single conversation thread, it introduced multiple critical failures.

The primary failure mode manifested as exponential token cost growth, since each new character interaction required transmitting the complete conversation history, including all previous character exchanges. The system also necessitated redundant personality descriptions when players returned to previously encountered characters, as the model required contextual reminders to prevent attention drift across the expanding message history.

Figure 8. Visual representation of attention degradation in unified conversation architecture

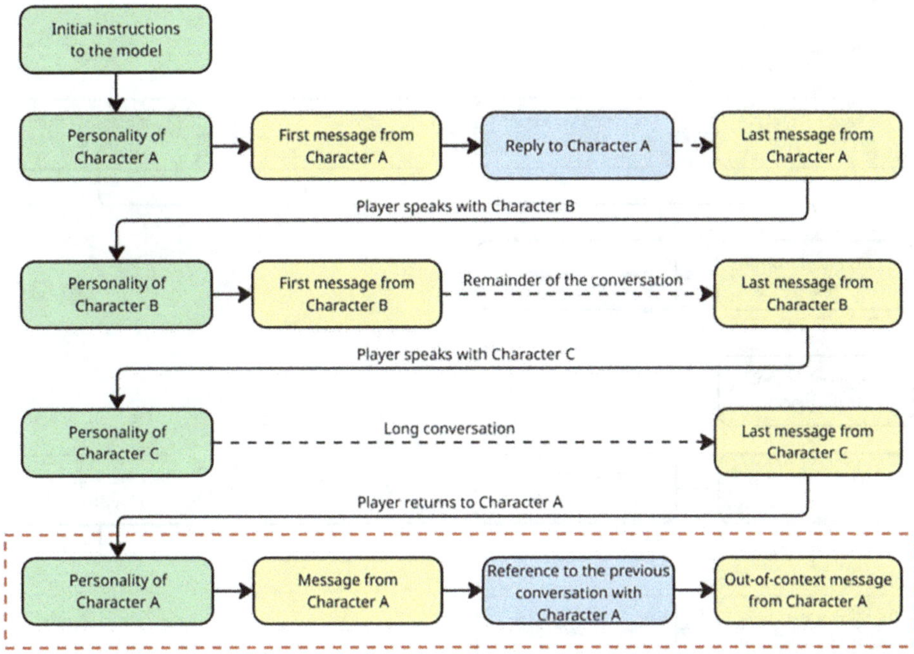

Figure 8 illustrates the attention degradation phenomenon in unified conversation systems. System prompts (shown in green) provide character instructions, assistant responses (yellow) represent NPC dialogue, and user messages (blue) capture player input. The critical problem emerges when attempting to retrieve information from temporally distant conversations, marked in the red zone of the diagram. At this distance, the model begins fabricating details or altering information from past exchanges, demonstrating clear symptoms of attention failure. This degradation intensifies when expanding instructions or adding contextual details, as such additions push historical messages further from the model's effective attention window, rendering the unified approach fundamentally non-scalable.

The final system architecture addressed these limitations through independent conversation histories for each character. This design maintains separate message threads per NPC, ensuring that conversational context remains temporally proximate regardless of how many other characters the player has encountered.

Figure 9. Architecture diagram showing independent conversation threads per character

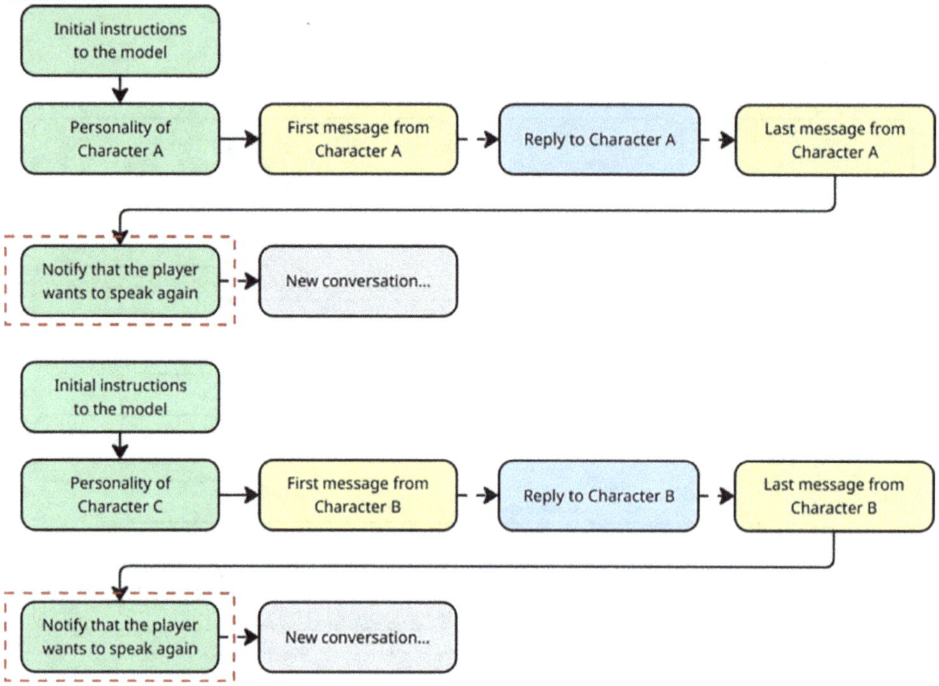

Figure 9 illustrates the independent context architecture. Each character maintains a dedicated conversation thread, preventing context pollution from unrelated interactions. While this approach does result in duplicated system instructions across character threads (increasing total token usage compared to an ideal unified system), the overall token consumption remains substantially lower than the unified approach's cost of repeatedly transmitting entire conversation histories. The implementation further leverages cached token pricing mechanisms by structuring prompts to maximize cache hit rates. System instructions and world lore rarely change between conversation turns, allowing these components to remain cached across multiple interactions and reducing the effective per-request token cost. More critically, this architecture provides designated injection points (marked in red) where the system can insert dynamic contextual information such as character reputation scores, visual environmental data, or current quest states, enabling NPCs to maintain awareness of evolving game conditions while preserving conversational coherence.

The independent context architecture naturally accommodates conversational fatigue behaviors that mirror human interaction patterns. When dialogue threads extend beyond typical conversational boundaries, the model exhibits increasingly meandering responses, a behavior that authentically represents the natural degradation of extended conversations rather than constituting a system failure. This emergent property enhances realism without requiring explicit behavioral modeling.

Model Selection Criteria and Comparative Analysis

The selection of an appropriate LLM represents a foundational architectural decision that influences system performance, operational costs, and dialogue quality. The evaluation process considered multiple commercial LLM offerings across several fundamental dimensions: cost per token (both input and output), function calling capabilities, and context window size. While local model deployment was explored for comparison purposes, the primary implementation utilized cloud-based services due to performance and economic considerations.

Table 1 presents a comparative analysis of the models evaluated during the selection process. The analysis excluded local models from the primary comparison due to their distinct deployment constraints and performance characteristics, which are addressed separately in Section 4.

Table 1. Comparative analysis of language models evaluated for dialogue generation

Model	Context Window	Function Calling	Input Cost (USD / 1M tokens)	Output Cost (USD / 1M tokens)	Cached Tokens	Parameters[1]
GPT-4o	128k	Yes	$2.50	$10.00	Yes	~1.8T
GPT-4o-mini	128k	Yes	$0.15	$0.60	Yes	~20B–30B
Gemini 1.5 Pro	1M	Yes	$1.25	$5.00	No	~1.5T
DeepSeek-V3	64k	Yes	$0.27	$0.42	Yes	671B

[1] Parameter counts for proprietary models are not officially published; estimates are based on third-party analyses and may vary.

The selection process prioritized the balance between model capability and operational cost, particularly given the repetitive nature of dialogue interactions in gaming contexts. Models supporting cached token pricing offered significant economic advantages, as dialogue systems frequently reuse character descriptions, world lore, and system instructions across multiple conversation instances. The high cache hit rate in multi-character game environments meant that models lacking cache pricing mechanisms, such as Gemini 1.5 Pro (Gemini Team, 2024), incurred disproportionate operational costs despite competitive base pricing.

GPT-4o (OpenAI, 2024) was eliminated from consideration despite its superior reasoning capabilities, as the dialogue generation task did not require the advanced cognitive abilities that justify its premium pricing. Choosing between GPT-4o-mini (OpenAI, 2024) and DeepSeek-V3 (DeepSeek-AI, 2024) required careful evaluation, with both models offering competitive pricing structures and adequate performance for conversational tasks. The implementation ultimately selected GPT-4o-mini based on widespread adoption of OpenAI's API ecosystem. This decision demonstrated particular value during development, as the OpenAI-compatible API structure used by Llama.cpp (Gerganov, 2023) for local model deployment enabled seamless switching between cloud and local inference without requiring code modifications.

Backend Architecture and API Integration

The implementation architecture supports deployment across both cloud-based and local model backends, enabling flexible testing and deployment strategies. Achieving this flexibility required developing a unified abstraction layer that standardizes communication with different model providers.

The abstraction layer implements a common interface conforming to OpenAI's API specification, which both OpenAI's cloud services and Llama.cpp's local server implementation (Gerganov, 2023) support. This design enables backend-agnostic operation, where model provider selection becomes a configuration parameter rather than requiring code modifications. The architecture maintains separate configuration profiles for each backend, managing API endpoint URLs, authentication tokens, and provider-specific parameters such as temperature and top-p sampling values.

This design decision proved valuable during development and testing, allowing rapid comparison between cloud and local model performance under identical conversation conditions. However, it required careful management of authentication mechanisms and error handling patterns that differ between providers despite API compatibility.

System Reliability and Error Handling

Production deployment requires robust error handling to gracefully manage API failures, network timeouts, and unexpected model outputs. The implementation incorporates multiple fallback mechanisms to maintain gameplay continuity despite infrastructure failures.

Network error handling implements exponential backoff retry logic with configurable maximum attempt limits. When API calls fail, the system retries with exponentially increasing delays (starting at 1 second, doubling with each attempt) before falling back to generic pre-written responses that maintain narrative plausibility. This approach prevents complete conversation deadlock while logging technical issues for developer visibility without exposing error details to players.

Output validation addresses malformed JSON responses despite structured output requirements. The system implements JSON schema validation with automatic repair attempts for common malformation patterns, such as missing closing braces or unescaped quotation marks. When repair proves impossible, the system extracts textual content from the response and presents it to players, while internally flagging the incident. This graceful degradation ensures that technical failures manifest as minor quality reductions rather than interaction-breaking errors that would compromise player immersion.

DYNAMIC GAME MECHANICS

Reputation System Implementation

The reputation system models the evolving relationship between the player and each NPC through a numerical score that influences dialogue tone, quest availability, and gameplay mechanics. This system operates automatically through LLM analysis of player dialogue choices, eliminating the need for predetermined "good" or "bad" dialogue options characteristic of traditional branching systems.

The model adjusts reputation scores based on multiple factors encoded in the system prompt: the player's tone and word choice, their willingness to help with character concerns, honesty about quest completion, and consistency with previously established commitments. The instructions provide specific guidelines: small adjustments (±1-2 points) for minor positive or negative interactions, moderate changes (±3-5 points) for significant helpful or harmful actions, and substantial modifications (±10 points) for critical moments that fundamentally alter the relationship.

These reputation changes produce dramatically different NPC behaviors. Figure 10 demonstrates how negative reputation affects character interaction, where the NPC provides minimal responses and explicitly refuses to engage further, maintaining narrative consistency with the player's history of poor interactions.

Figure 10. Dialogue example showing negative reputation's effect on NPC interaction, where the character responds curtly and refuses to engage meaningfully due to poor prior interactions

In contrast, Figure 11 shows the identical character demonstrating warmth, offering detailed information, and actively seeking to assist the player when positive reputation has been established. This dynamic behavior emerges naturally from the reputation score being injected into the conversation context, requiring no explicit behavioral scripting beyond the general instruction to adjust tone and helpfulness based on reputation.

Figure 11. Contrasting dialogue example demonstrating positive reputation's effects, where the same NPC responds warmly and offers assistance due to favorable prior interactions

The reputation system extends beyond dialogue to influence concrete gameplay mechanics. NPCs refuse to provide healing services when reputation falls below certain thresholds, and the player's magic visual effects gradually shift between "dark" and "pure" aesthetics based on average reputation across all characters. This mechanical integration demonstrates how LLM-driven systems can inform traditional game systems, creating emergent gameplay consequences from conversational interactions.

Procedural Quest Generation via Function Calling

The system leverages the function calling capabilities of some LLMs to generate dynamic quests that emerge naturally from conversation context. This function calling capability enables the model to invoke a quest generation function with specific parameters, producing quests that align with character motivations and player actions, rather than relying on predetermined quest databases.

Each character's personality JSON includes a "concerns" field that lists their active problems or needs. When conversational context suggests quest offering is appropriate, such as when the player explicitly offers help or when the NPC's dialogue naturally leads toward requesting assistance, the model can invoke a quest generation function. This function call includes parameters specifying the quest objective (inferred from the character's concerns), the reward amount (scaled based on quest difficulty, player reputation, and narrative importance), and any additional contextual requirements.

The quest generation workflow begins when player dialogue triggers an appropriate context. Figure 12 shows how the player's statement about seeking work prompts the NPC to generate a quest based on their encoded concerns.

Figure 12. Dialogue sequence showing the NPC proposing a quest objective in response to the player's offer of assistance

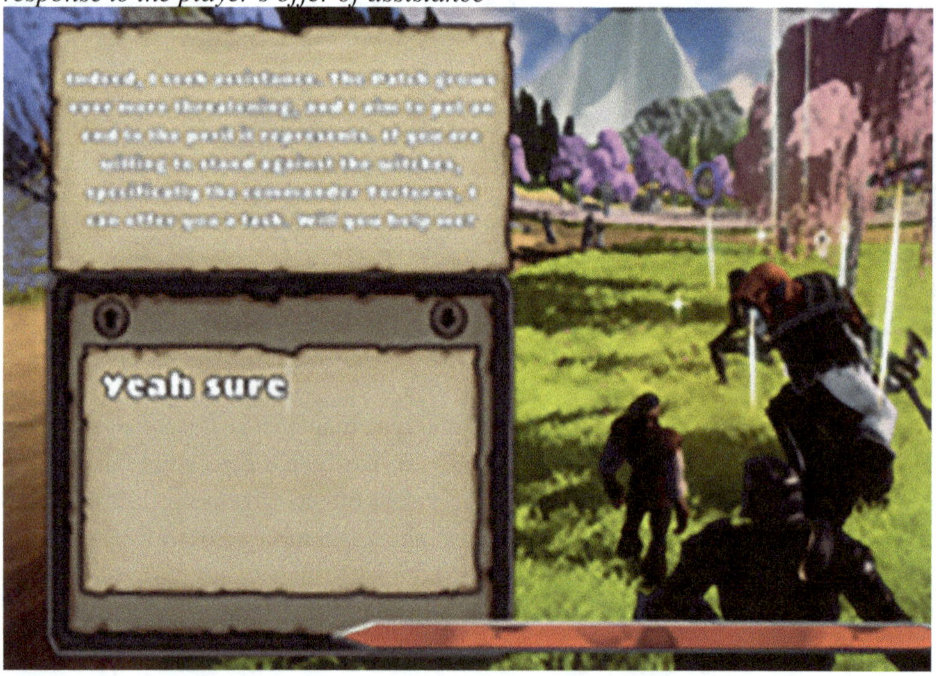

The system then translates the LLM's function call into concrete game elements. Figure 13 demonstrates how the abstract quest proposal materializes into a specific objective tied to the character's narrative role, complete with a reward scaled to the quest's perceived difficulty and the current reputation level. This approach eliminates the need for manual quest authoring, while maintaining narrative coherence through the personality and concern frameworks.

Figure 13. Follow-up screen displaying the generated quest details and reward structure based on the conversation context

Dialogue Termination Detection

Traditional dialogue systems rely on explicit player actions to end conversations, typically through selecting a "goodbye" option from a predetermined set of choices. The LLM-driven implementation inverts this relationship, allowing NPCs to autonomously determine when conversations should naturally conclude based on contextual appropriateness.

The system prompt defines multiple termination conditions: explicit farewells from either party, the NPC's assessment that they have nothing further to contribute to the current topic, situations where the player lacks sufficient reputation to continue the interaction, or contexts where continuing the conversation would be narratively inappropriate. The model communicates termination decisions through the structured JSON output's "is finished" boolean field.

This approach produces more natural conversation flows that mirror human social interactions, where either party may conclude an exchange when it reaches a natural endpoint. NPCs can politely dismiss players who have exhausted relevant topics, curtly end conversations when reputation is insufficient, or continue engaging as long as meaningful dialogue remains possible. The termination logic requires no explicit state machine implementation, emerging instead from the model's understanding of conversational pragmatics and the specific behavioral constraints defined in the system instructions.

Multimodal Interaction Systems & Translation

Solutions like the Mantella mod and commercial platforms such as Convai and Inworld AI provide integrated voice interaction capabilities that enhance immersion and accessibility. The prototype implementation explores two primary multimodal interaction modalities: voice command processing for game actions and automatic translation for cross-lingual communication; to demonstrate how LLM capabilities can extend beyond text-based dialogue to enable natural language voice interactions.

Voice Command Processing Pipeline

The voice command system employs a two-stage pipeline: audio-to-text transcription via Whisper, followed by intent recognition and function execution via GPT-4o-mini. Figure 14 illustrates the processing architecture. When players activate voice input, the system captures audio and transmits it to Whisper for transcription. Whisper was selected for this role due to its robust speech recognition capabilities and the availability of accessible API endpoints through Hugging Face. The resulting text transcription then passes to the LLM, which analyzes the natural language command and invokes appropriate game functions using the same function calling mechanism employed for quest generation.

Figure 14. Diagram of the voice command processing pipeline

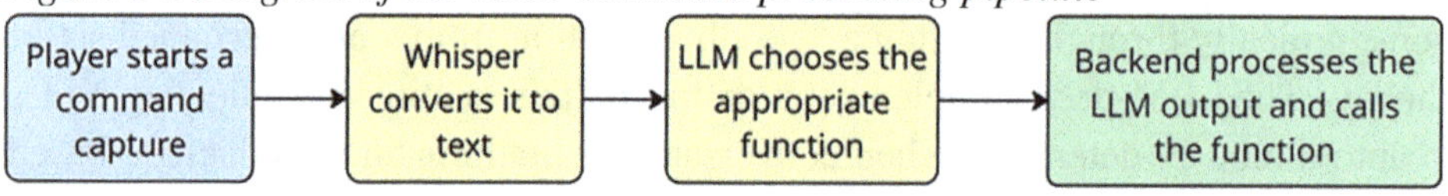

The system's flexibility derives from its natural language understanding rather than keyword matching. Players need not memorize specific command phrasings; instead, the LLM interprets intent from varied expressions. A player wanting to approach a character named Anna might say "Go to Anna," "I should talk to Anna," "Take me to Anna," or "Navigate to Anna's position"; all of which the system correctly interprets as requiring the navigation function with Anna as the target parameter. This approach dramatically reduces the cognitive load associated with voice command systems compared to traditional keyword-based recognition.

The prototype implements two demonstration commands to validate the architecture: an automatic attack function that identifies and engages hostile targets, and a character navigation function that directs the player toward specified NPCs. Expanding this system requires only defining additional functions in the backend and registering them with the LLM's function calling interface, making voice command addition primarily a game design rather than AI engineering challenge.

Natural Language Interpretation for Game Actions

The voice command system's natural language interpretation capabilities extend beyond simple command recognition to contextual action inference. The LLM analyzes not only the explicit content of player statements but their implied intent based on conversational context and current game state.

This contextual awareness enables more sophisticated interactions than traditional command systems. Rather than requiring explicit action verbs, players can express desires or observations that the system translates into appropriate actions. For example, "I wonder what Anna wants" might trigger navigation toward Anna rather than requiring the explicit command "Go to Anna." This interpretation flexibility more closely approximates how players naturally think about their objectives, reducing the mental translation required to interact with the system.

The voice command implementation serves dual purposes: demonstrating LLM capabilities for natural language understanding and improving game accessibility. Voice interaction provides alternative input modalities for players who may face challenges with traditional control schemes, whether due to motor disabilities, situational constraints, or personal preference.

Translation Capabilities

The prototype implements automatic translation functionality to address language barriers that might otherwise limit accessibility. The system employs the Opus-MT translation model developed by the University of Helsinki (Tiedemann et al., 2023), specifically utilizing bidirectional translation variants for English-Spanish conversion.

The translation system operates through a simple interface element within the dialogue window, allowing players to translate NPC responses from English to Spanish or translate their own Spanish input to English before submission. Opus-MT was selected based on its availability through public Hugging Face APIs and its modest parameter count (approximately 72 million parameters), which enables acceptably low inference latency without requiring extensive computational resources.

This approach raises an important question about the value proposition of LLM-based translation compared to traditional machine translation systems. While conventional translators focus on word-for-word or phrase-level translation, LLMs maintain broader contextual awareness that can improve translation quality in conversation-heavy applications. Traditional systems may struggle with ambiguous references, contextual irony, or tonal shifts across extended dialogue exchanges. The

LLM approach considers conversational history and narrative context when producing translations, potentially preserving nuances that isolated sentence translation might lose. This contextual preservation becomes particularly valuable in narrative-driven games, where subtle character voice and tonal consistency contribute significantly to player experience.

PERFORMANCE ANALYSIS AND BENCHMARKING

Evaluating the computational performance and operational viability of LLM-driven dialogue systems represents a critical requirement for practical deployment in video games. Performance in this context encompasses three fundamental dimensions: frame rate stability, dialogue response latency, and computational resource utilization. This analysis examines these factors across both cloud-based and local deployment strategies, providing empirical data to inform architectural decisions for production implementations.

The evaluation process employed systematic benchmarking across multiple model configurations, measuring performance characteristics under controlled conditions that approximate realistic gameplay scenarios. The analysis prioritized models with open weights that could be deployed locally, enabling direct comparison between cloud infrastructure and consumer-grade hardware deployment strategies.

EXPERIMENTAL METHODOLOGY

The benchmarking framework employed Llama.cpp (Gerganov, 2023) as the inference server for local model deployment, selected for its comprehensive support for both CUDA (NVIDIA Corporation, 2025) and ROCm architectures. This infrastructure choice enabled GPU acceleration on NVIDIA and AMD hardware, respectively, while maintaining API compatibility with OpenAI's specification. The API compatibility proved particularly valuable, as it eliminated the need for code modifications when switching between cloud and local backends during comparative analysis.

Hardware Configuration

The test environment utilized the following hardware configuration:

- CPU: AMD Ryzen 7 7700X
- RAM: 32GB DDR5 6000MHz CL30

- GPU: NVIDIA RTX 3060 12GB GDDR6

This specification represents a mid-to-high-end consumer gaming configuration, providing realistic performance expectations for potential deployment scenarios while acknowledging that many gaming systems may possess less capable hardware.

Model Selection and Quantization Strategy

All evaluated models employed Q4_K_M quantization (Hugging Face, 2025), which provides an optimal balance between inference speed and output quality for conversational applications. This quantization method compresses model weights from their original precision (typically FP16 or FP32) to 4-bit representations, significantly reducing memory requirements and inference latency while maintaining acceptable dialogue coherence. The context window was uniformly limited to 4096 tokens across all models to ensure consistent memory allocation patterns and enable direct performance comparisons.

Table 2 presents the complete set of models evaluated during the benchmarking process, spanning parameter counts from 3.8 billion to 11.77 billion. The selection criteria prioritized recent model releases with demonstrated conversational capabilities, while GPT-4o-mini was included as a baseline reference representing cloud-based deployment performance.

Table 2. Local models evaluated for dialogue generation performance

Model	Parameters	Disk Size	Architecture
Phi4-Mini	3.80B	2.43GB	Phi3
DeepSeek-R1	7.62B	4.57GB	Qwen2
Mistral-Instruct	7.25B	4.27GB	Llama
Llama3.1-Instruct[1]	8.03B	4.80GB	Llama
Gemma	8.54B	5.20GB	Gemma
Gemma3	11.77B	7.13GB	Gemma3
GPT-4o-mini[2]	~20B-30B	N/A	GPT

[1] This implementation utilized Unsloth-Llama3.1-Instruct, a variant specifically fine-tuned for dialogue interactions.

[2] Cloud-based reference model included for comparative analysis; exact parameter count is not publicly disclosed.

Benchmarking Protocol

The standardized testing procedure ensured consistent measurement conditions across all models. Each model processed an identical prompt representative of typical dialogue generation tasks within the prototype, comprising character personality information, world lore context, and a conversational exchange requiring contextually appropriate response generation. This prompt structure maintained consistency with the dialogue system's operational parameters while providing sufficient complexity to stress-test model capabilities.

Performance measurements captured four critical metrics:

- Total Processing Time: The complete duration from request submission to response completion, measured in milliseconds
- Token Counts: Both input tokens processed and output tokens generated, enabling calculation of throughput metrics
- Tokens Per Second: The effective processing rate, calculated separately for prompt evaluation (input tokens) and generation (output tokens)
- VRAM Allocation: Peak video memory usage during inference, including baseline allocation from the Unity game engine (approximately 5GB)

The frame rate analysis employed a separate methodology, monitoring GPU utilization and rendering performance during dialogue generation to identify potential interference between inference operations and game rendering pipelines. The frame rate was artificially limited to 60 FPS to optimize GPU resource allocation for inference workloads, representing a common design pattern in dialogue-heavy narrative games where visual fidelity can be traded for conversational responsiveness.

CLOUD VS. LOCAL DEPLOYMENT ANALYSIS

Cloud-Based Performance (GPT-4o-mini)

The cloud-based reference implementation utilizing GPT-4o-mini demonstrated substantial performance advantages across all measured dimensions. With an average response latency of 1260 milliseconds for the standardized prompt and a throughput of 464.29 tokens per second, the cloud infrastructure provided response times well within acceptable ranges for maintaining conversational flow during gameplay.

The cloud deployment imposed no local VRAM burden beyond the game engine's baseline allocation (5.1GB), effectively eliminating GPU memory constraints as a deployment consideration. This characteristic proves particularly valuable for enabling dialogue system implementation across diverse hardware configurations, including systems with limited GPU capabilities that might otherwise struggle with local inference workloads.

Operational cost analysis revealed modest expenses despite the extensive testing required for prototype development. The complete testing and development cycle, encompassing dialogue generation experimentation, voice command implementation, and system refinement, consumed approximately 1,490,189 input tokens (uncached), 5,916,032 cached input tokens, and 229,505 output tokens. At GPT-4o-mini's pricing structure of $0.15 per million input tokens, $0.075 per million cached input tokens, and $0.60 per million output tokens, the total cost for comprehensive prototype development totaled approximately $0.70, excluding the $5.00 minimum account funding requirement. This economic efficiency demonstrates that even extensive development and testing cycles remain financially viable for independent developers and small studios operating under constrained budgets.

The primary limitation of cloud deployment manifests as network dependency, introducing latency variability based on connection quality and geographic proximity to inference servers. Additionally, ongoing operational costs, while modest at current usage scales, would require careful monitoring and optimization for commercial deployments serving hundreds of thousands of concurrent players.

Local Model Evaluation

Local model deployment presented a more complex performance landscape, with substantial variation across model architectures and parameter counts. Table 3 summarizes the comprehensive performance measurements across all evaluated models.

Table 3. Performance characteristics of local and cloud-based models

Model	Processing Time (ms)	Tokens Processed	Tokens/Second	VRAM Allocated (GB)
Phi4-Mini	3089.23	559	180.95	9.3
DeepSeek-R1	6124.92	595	97.14	12.0[1]
Mistral-Instruct	3157.35	635	201.12	11.1
Llama3.1-Instruct	4232.08	557	131.61	9.6
Gemma	6350.10	625	98.42	12.0[1]
Gemma3	10831.00	634	58.54	12.0[1]

[1] These models exceeded available VRAM capacity, requiring memory sharing with system RAM and introducing substantial performance penalties.

The results reveal a clear performance hierarchy, with Phi4-Mini and Mistral-Instruct achieving the highest local inference speeds at 180.95 and 201.12 tokens per second respectively. However, even these optimized configurations demonstrated throughput less than half that of the cloud-based reference, highlighting the substantial infrastructure advantages of commercial inference services.

Three models (DeepSeek-R1, Gemma, and Gemma3) exceeded the GPU's 12GB VRAM capacity, forcing memory overflow into system RAM. This architectural limitation introduced severe performance degradation, with DeepSeek-R1 and Gemma experiencing approximately 50% throughput reduction compared to models that fit within VRAM constraints. Gemma3 suffered the most dramatic impact, achieving only 58.54 tokens per second due to its larger parameter count (11.77B) necessitating extensive memory sharing with system RAM.

Figure 15 illustrates the critical relationship between VRAM utilization and processing speed. Models operating within the GPU's memory capacity maintained substantially higher throughput, while those requiring memory overflow experienced dramatic performance penalties. The inflection point at approximately 12GB VRAM represents a hard architectural constraint where performance degrades severely, with latency increases exceeding 70% in the most extreme cases.

Figure 15.Relationship between VRAM utilization and inference throughput, showing sharp performance degradation when models exceed GPU memory capacity

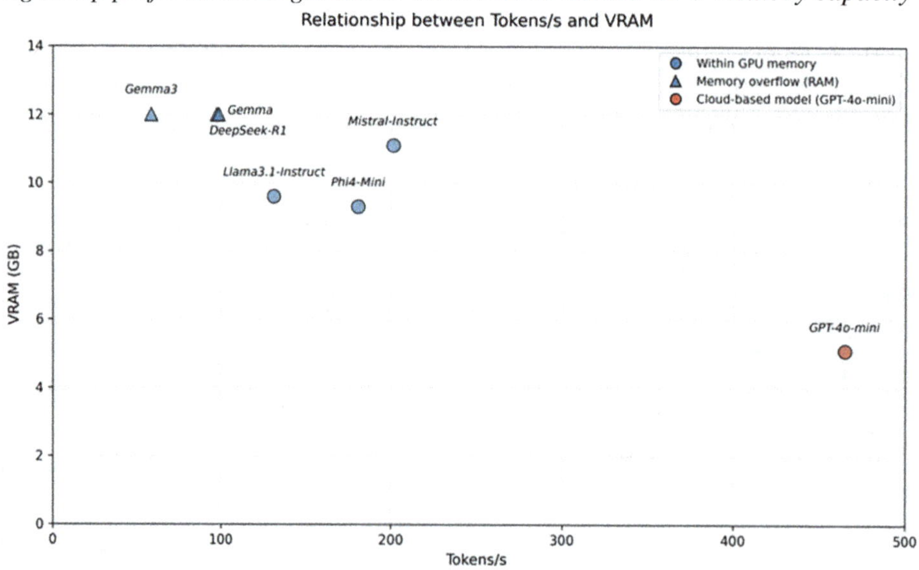

Dialogue Quality Assessment

Beyond quantitative performance metrics, subjective evaluation of dialogue quality revealed significant variation in instruction-following capabilities and conversational coherence across local models. Three models demonstrated particularly strong adherence to the system prompt's behavioral constraints: Llama3.1-Instruct, Phi4-Mini, and Gemma3. These models consistently generated responses that respected character personalities, maintained narrative boundaries, and produced contextually appropriate dialogue comparable to GPT-4o-mini's output quality.

The remaining models exhibited tendencies toward generic assistant behavior, frequently producing responses that, while grammatically correct and topically relevant, lacked the character-specific voice and narrative consistency required for immersive dialogue experiences. These models would benefit substantially from fine-tuning on game-specific dialogue datasets to improve their conversational appropriateness, though such training procedures require substantial computational resources, extensive training data, and specialized expertise that may prove inaccessible to many development teams.

CRITICAL PERFORMANCE FINDINGS

VRAM Constraints and Performance Degradation

The most significant finding from the local deployment analysis concerns the critical importance of GPU memory capacity for viable inference performance. Models that exceeded available VRAM demonstrated performance degradation severe enough to compromise real-time gameplay experiences, with latency increases of 50-70% compared to configurations that fit within memory constraints.

This limitation presents substantial challenges for consumer hardware deployment. While the test configuration's 12GB VRAM represents a reasonable mid-range gaming GPU specification, many gaming systems operate with 8GB or less video memory. The models evaluated in this analysis, despite employing aggressive quantization to 4-bit precision and limiting context windows to 4096 tokens, frequently exceeded these memory constraints even on relatively capable hardware.

Strategies for reducing VRAM consumption include further context window reduction, more aggressive quantization (though at the cost of output quality), or selecting models with fewer parameters. However, each approach involves quality trade-offs that may compromise the dialogue system's effectiveness. The 4096-token context window already represents a minimal threshold for maintaining coherent conversations with personality context, and more aggressive quantization risks producing artifacts or inconsistencies in generated dialogue.

Frame Rate Stability Analysis

The dialogue generation process demonstrated minimal impact on frame rate stability under the testing conditions, with the 60 FPS cap maintained consistently throughout inference operations. Brief frame drops occurred primarily during two specific phases: initial memory allocation when loading models into VRAM (typically 1-2 seconds) and memory deallocation upon inference completion.

These transient performance impacts prove manageable through careful asynchronous loading strategies and pre-allocation techniques that perform initialization during non-critical gameplay moments such as scene transitions or initial loading screens. The absence of sustained frame rate degradation during active inference suggests that well-architected implementations can successfully parallel dialogue generation with rendering operations, though this conclusion applies specifically to the 60 FPS target and game scene settings employed during testing.

Higher frame rate targets (120 FPS or above) may experience more substantial interference from inference workloads, as GPU resources become more constrained. Additionally, the single-dialogue-at-a-time testing scenario represents a simplified case compared to production environments where multiple NPCs might require simultaneous processing or where the dialogue system operates concurrently with other AI systems such as pathfinding or behavior trees.

ECONOMIC VIABILITY ASSESSMENT

Operational Cost Analysis

The economic analysis of cloud-based deployment reveals remarkably modest operational costs for individual development and testing scenarios. The prototype's complete development cycle, encompassing extensive dialogue experimentation, system refinement, and feature implementation, consumed approximately $0.80 in inference costs (excluding the minimum funding requirement). This efficiency demonstrates that cloud infrastructure remains financially accessible even for independent developers operating under severe budget constraints.

However, scaling these costs to commercial deployment scenarios requires careful consideration of concurrent user loads and session characteristics. A narrative-driven RPG with 10,000 daily active users, assuming an average of 50 dialogue exchanges per session and 200 tokens per exchange (including both input context and generated response), would generate approximately 100 million tokens daily. At GPT-4o-mini pricing, the usage pattern mentioned in Section 4.2.1 would cost approximately $15-20 daily or $450-600 monthly, representing a non-trivial operational expense that would require monitoring and optimization.

The token caching mechanisms employed by modern LLM APIs provide substantial cost reduction opportunities for dialogue systems. Character personality descriptions, world lore, and system instructions remain constant across multiple conversation turns, enabling high cache hit rates that reduce effective per-input token costs by approximately 50%. The independent character context architecture described in Section 3.1.2 naturally optimizes for cache efficiency by maintaining stable system prompts that change infrequently between dialogue turns.

Comparison with Traditional Content Creation

The economic comparison between LLM-driven dialogue generation and traditional hand-authored content reveals complex trade-offs that extend beyond simple cost calculations. Traditional dialogue authoring for a narrative RPG might require 3-6 months of dedicated writing work for a team of specialized narrative designers, with typical industry salaries ranging from $60,000-90,000 annually for mid-level positions. A project requiring 1000 hours of dialogue writing labor would therefore represent $30,000-45,000 in direct personnel costs, excluding supporting infrastructure, quality assurance, and revision cycles.

LLM-based systems invert this cost structure, requiring substantial upfront investment in prompt engineering, system architecture, and integration work, but minimal incremental costs for dialogue generation once deployed. The prototype's operational costs of $0.80 for extensive testing suggest that even ambitious indie projects might operate dialogue systems for under $100 monthly during development, with production costs scaling with player engagement rather than content volume.

However, this economic comparison oversimplifies the qualitative dimensions that influence production decisions. Traditional hand-authored dialogue provides absolute control over narrative tone, character voice, and story pacing that LLM systems cannot yet reliably guarantee. Quality assurance processes for generative systems remain more complex than traditional testing pipelines, requiring validation frameworks to catch inappropriate responses, narrative inconsistencies, or technical failures that might escape detection until the player reports surface issues.

Budget Planning Implications

Game studios evaluating LLM-driven dialogue systems must consider several economic factors beyond raw inference costs. The development expertise required for effective system implementation represents a significant hidden cost, as successful deployments demand proficiency in prompt engineering, API integration, error handling, and performance optimization. Studios lacking this expertise must either invest in training existing personnel or contract specialized consultants, introducing costs that may exceed operational inference expenses during initial deployment.

The operational cost predictability also requires careful evaluation. Usage-based pricing models introduce variability that fixed-cost traditional approaches avoid, potentially creating budget management challenges for publishers accustomed to predictable development expenditures. Implementing comprehensive monitoring and alerting systems becomes essential to prevent unexpected cost escalation, adding another layer of operational complexity to deployment strategies.

For independent developers and small studios, cloud-based LLM dialogue systems offer unprecedented accessibility to sophisticated conversational AI capabilities that would have required prohibitive investment in specialized talent or infrastructure previously. The minimal operational costs during development phases enable experimental implementations and iterative refinement without financial risk, though scaling to commercial deployment requires more rigorous economic planning and optimization strategies.

The viability threshold varies substantially based on project scale and business model. Free-to-play titles with large user bases must carefully optimize inference costs to maintain acceptable unit economics, while premium narrative experiences with smaller concurrent user counts can more easily absorb per-interaction costs as part of overall operational budgets. The economic analysis therefore cannot provide universal recommendations but instead highlights the factors that studios must evaluate based on their specific technical requirements, player engagement patterns, and business constraints.

CONCLUSIONS

The evolution of dialogue systems in video games demonstrates a clear trajectory from deterministic, pre-authored models toward hybrid and generative approaches powered by Large Language Models. This progression highlights persistent tensions between player agency and authorial control, narrative coherence and adaptive flexibility, and technical feasibility and economic sustainability. The analysis presented in this chapter illuminates how these tensions manifest in contemporary implementations while revealing promising directions for future development.

The historical survey establishes that dialogue systems have evolved through three distinct phases: foundational approaches using finite state machines and branching trees, AI-centric methodologies incorporating planning algorithms and character psychology, and contemporary generative approaches leveraging LLMs. Each phase addressed specific limitations of its predecessors while introducing new challenges. Early branching trees provided authorial control but suffered from combinatorial explosion as narrative complexity increased. AI-centric approaches enabled more dynamic character behavior through techniques like Belief-Desire-Intention agents and hierarchical task network planning, yet their complexity and unpredictability limited commercial adoption. Contemporary LLM-based systems offer unprecedented flexibility in generating contextually appropriate dialogue but introduce concerns about content quality, computational requirements, and narrative consistency.

The case studies examined in this chapter confirm that LLM-driven dialogue is not a wholesale replacement for traditional techniques, but rather a complementary layer that extends narrative possibilities. "Interview with the Whisperer" demonstrated how non-generative Natural Language Processing can create compelling interactive experiences through semantic analysis, though its brief operational lifespan revealed economic sustainability challenges. The Mantella mod for Skyrim illustrated how community-driven implementations can retrofit modern language models into existing game architectures, achieving impressive conversational flexibility despite latency constraints and technical limitations. Enterprise middleware platforms such as Convai and Inworld AI have successfully translated experimental concepts into production-ready systems through sophisticated inference optimization, proprietary narrative control mechanisms, and comprehensive multimodal pipelines, though their viability depends heavily on careful cost management and architectural planning.

The prototype implementation presented in this chapter contributes empirical evidence regarding the practical challenges of deploying LLM-driven dialogue systems in real-time gameplay environments. The technical architecture demonstrates how structured prompt engineering, personality-constrained character models, independent context architectures, and procedural quest generation can significantly enhance immersion and narrative adaptability. The independent character context design proved essential for maintaining conversational coherence while managing computational costs, preventing the attention degradation that plagued unified conversation architectures. The reputation system illustrated how LLM analysis of player dialogue choices could influence both conversational tone and concrete gameplay mechanics without requiring predetermined branching structures. The procedural quest generation via function calling showed how character-driven narratives could emerge naturally from conversation context rather than relying on static quest databases.

However, the prototype also underscored critical limitations of current systems. The performance analysis revealed that VRAM constraints represent a fundamental barrier to local deployment, with models exceeding GPU memory capacity experiencing performance degradation severe enough to compromise real-time gameplay experiences. Even optimized configurations employing aggressive quantization and limited context windows frequently exceeded the memory constraints of consumer gaming hardware. Cloud-based deployment offered substantial performance advantages, achieving response latencies and throughput rates well within acceptable ranges for maintaining conversational flow, though this approach introduced network dependencies and ongoing operational costs that require careful monitoring.

The dialogue quality assessment revealed significant variation in instruction-following capabilities across different models. While several models demonstrated strong adherence to behavioral constraints and produced contextually appropriate responses comparable to GPT-4o-mini, others exhibited generic assistant behavior lacking the character-specific voice necessary for immersive dialogue experiences. These quality differences highlight that model selection represents a critical architectural decision influencing both technical performance and narrative effectiveness.

The economic analysis demonstrates that cloud-based LLM dialogue systems offer unprecedented accessibility to sophisticated conversational AI capabilities for independent developers and small studios. The prototype's complete development cycle consumed approximately $0.80 in inference costs, proving that experimentation and iterative refinement remain financially viable even under severe budget constraints. However, scaling to commercial deployment introduces operational expenses that require rigorous planning and optimization, particularly for free-to-play titles with large user bases where per-interaction costs must be carefully managed to maintain acceptable unit economics.

Looking forward, the successful adoption of LLM-powered dialogue systems in the gaming industry requires progress across multiple dimensions. Technical optimization must address latency constraints, memory requirements, and computational efficiency to enable deployment across diverse hardware configurations. New authoring practices must emerge that allow designers to work effectively with AI-driven systems while maintaining creative control, shifting from explicit content creation toward constraint-based frameworks that guide generative processes. Robust validation mechanisms must be developed to ensure narrative consistency, character behavioral coherence, and content appropriateness without requiring exhaustive manual testing of combinatorially explosive interaction spaces. Sustainable cost strategies must balance the flexibility of cloud infrastructure against the predictability of local deployment, incorporating sophisticated monitoring and optimization to prevent budget overruns.

The evaluation frameworks themselves require substantial development. While AI-based playtesters represent a promising direction for automated validation of procedurally generated content, their application to narrative evaluation remains an emerging research area. Establishing reliable metrics for dialogue quality, narrative coherence, and player engagement continues to pose significant challenges, as traditional computational measures may not adequately capture the nuanced aspects of narrative effectiveness that define successful interactive storytelling.

The analysis of concrete implementations underscores that the future of interactive storytelling will be defined by hybrid approaches where procedural generation and human-authored design coexist to deliver coherent, immersive, and economically viable gameplay experiences. Neither pure procedural generation nor traditional hand-authoring alone can address the full spectrum of requirements for contemporary dialogue systems. Instead, successful implementations will leverage LLM capabilities for dynamic response generation while employing human-designed constraint frameworks to maintain narrative boundaries, character consistency, and thematic coherence.

The fundamental challenge lies not in replacing human creativity with algorithmic generation, but in developing collaborative systems where AI augments authorial control rather than circumventing it. The PANGeA validation framework exemplifies this philosophy through its self-reflective approach that leverages the LLM's own capabilities to maintain narrative consistency within designer-specified boundaries. Similar hybrid architectures that combine generative flexibility with structural constraints represent the most promising path toward practical deployment.

The research presented in this chapter establishes that LLM-powered dialogue systems represent a transformative technology for interactive narrative design, offering capabilities that would have required prohibitive investment in specialized talent or infrastructure previously. However, their practical deployment demands careful navigation of technical, economic, and creative challenges that extend beyond purely algorithmic considerations. The transition from experimental implementations to production-ready systems requires not only continued advancement in language model capabilities but also the development of supporting infrastructure, authoring tools, and design methodologies that enable creators to harness these powerful technologies effectively while maintaining the narrative coherence and thematic integrity that define compelling interactive experiences.

REFERENCES

Akoury, N., Yang, Q., & Iyyer, M. (2023). A framework for exploring player perceptions of LLM-generated dialogue in commercial video games. *Findings of the Association for Computational Linguistics: EMNLP, 2023*, 2295–2311. DOI: 10.18653/v1/2023.findings-emnlp.151

Almeida, P., Carvalho, V., & Simões, A. (2023). Reinforcement learning applied to AI bots in first-person shooters: A systematic review. *Algorithms*, *16*(7), 323. Advance online publication. DOI: 10.3390/a16070323

Art From The Machine. (2023, April 25). *ChatGPT in skyrim VR | mantella - lip sync & in-game awareness update*. YouTube. https://www.youtube.com/watch?v=Gz6mAX41fs0

Art from the Machine. (2024). *Mantella skyrim llama 3 8B GGUF*. Dataloop. https://dataloop.ai/library/model/art-from-the-machine_mantella-skyrim-llama-3-8b-gguf/

Art From The Machine. (2024a). *Mantella* [Computer software]. https://art-from-the-machine.github.io/Mantella/

Art From The Machine. (2024b). *Real-time NPCs*. Mantella. https://art-from-the-machine.github.io/Mantella/pages/real_time_npcs.html

Bateni, B., & Whitehead, J. (2024). Language-driven play: Large language models as game-playing agents in slay the spire. *Proceedings of the 19th International Conference on the Foundations of Digital Games*. https://doi.org/DOI: 10.1145/3649921.3650013

BioWare. (1998). *Baldur's gate*. Video game; Interplay Entertainment.

BioWare. (2007). *Mass effect*. Video game; Electronic Arts.

Brown, T., Mann, B., Ryder, N., Subbiah, M., Kaplan, J. D., Dhariwal, P., Neelakantan, A., Shyam, P., Sastry, G., & Askell, A.. (2020). Language models are few-shot learners. *Advances in Neural Information Processing Systems*, *33*, 1877–1901.

Buongiorno, S.. (2024). *PANGeA: Procedural artificial narrative using generative AI for turn-based video games*. https://arxiv.org/abs/2404.19721

Cavazza, M., & Charles, F. (2005). Dialogue generation in character-based interactive storytelling. *Proceedings of the National Conference on Artificial Intelligence*.

Chowdhery, A., Narang, S., Devlin, J., Bosma, M., Mishra, G., Roberts, A., Barham, P., Chung, H. W., Sutton, C., & Gehrmann, S.. (2023). PaLM: Scaling language modeling with pathways. *Journal of Machine Learning Research*, *24*(240), 1–113.

Compare Voice, A. I. (2025). *LLM pricing comparison 2025 | compare OpenAI, anthropic, google, meta*. Compare Voice AI. https://comparevoiceai.com/llm

Convai. (2024). *Pricing*. Convai Technologies Inc. https://convai.com/pricing

Cooren, F. (2015). *Speech acts theory*. Wiley Online Library., DOI: 10.1002/9781118611463.wbielsi055

Crawford, C. (1984). *The art of computer game design*. McGraw-Hill/Osborne Media.

Deconstructeam. (2021). *Interview with the whisperer*. https://deconstructeam.itch.io/interview-with-the-whisperer

DeepSeek-AI. (2024). *DeepSeek-V3 technical report*. DeepSeek-AI. https://arxiv.org/abs/2412.19437

Developer Blog, N. V. I. D. I. A. (2024). *Spotlight: Convai reinvents non-playable character interactions*. NVIDIA Corporation. https://developer.nvidia.com/blog/spotlight-convai-reinvents-non-playable-character-interactions/

Freiknecht, J., & Effelsberg, W. (2020). Procedural generation of interactive stories using language models. *Foundations of Digital Games*. https://doi.org/DOI: 10.1145/3402942.3409599

Gemini Team. (2024). *Gemini 1.5: Unlocking multimodal understanding across millions of tokens of context*. Google DeepMind. https://arxiv.org/abs/2403.05530

Georgievski, I., & Aiello, M. (2014). *An overview of hierarchical task network planning*. https://arxiv.org/abs/1403.7426

Gerganov, G. (2023). *Llama.cpp: LLM inference in c/c++* [Computer software]. GitHub repository. https://github.com/ggml-org/llama.cpp

Google. (2020). *The mystery of the three bots* [Computer software]. https://google.github.io/mysteryofthreebots/

Hu, C., Zhao, Y., Wang, Z., Du, H., & Liu, J. (2024). Games for artificial intelligence research: A review and perspectives. *IEEE Transactions on Artificial Intelligence*, *5*(12), 5949–5968. DOI: 10.1109/TAI.2024.3410935

Hugging Face. (2025). *Quantization*. Hugging Face. https://huggingface.co/docs/optimum/en/concept_guides/quantization

Inworld, A. I. Documentation. (2024). *Billing*. Inworld AI Inc. https://docs.inworld.ai/docs/resources/billing

Inworld, A. I. (2024a). *Case studies*. Inworld AI Inc. https://inworld.ai/case-studies

Inworld, A. I. (2024b). *Inworld AI*. Inworld AI Inc. https://inworld.ai/

Inworld, A. I. (2024c). *Inworld's commitment to safety*. Inworld AI Inc. https://inworld.ai/blog/inworlds-commitment-to-safety

Inworld, A. I. (2024d). *Unreal playground: Goals & mutations demo*. Inworld AI Inc. https://inworld.ai/blog/unreal-playground-goals-mutations-demo

Karth, I., & Compton, K. (2023). Conceptual art made real: Why procedural content generation is impossible. *Proceedings of the 18th International Conference on the Foundations of Digital Games*. https://doi.org/DOI: 10.1145/3582437.3587212

Kybartas, B., & Verbrugge, C. (2014). Analysis of ReGEN as a graph-rewriting system for quest generation. *IEEE Transactions on Computational Intelligence and AI in Games*, *6*(2), 228–242. Advance online publication. DOI: 10.1109/TCIAIG.2013.2290088

Lewis, P., Perez, E., Piktus, A., Petroni, F., Karpukhin, V., Goyal, N., Küttler, H., Lewis, M., Yih, W., Rocktäschel, T., Riedel, S., & Kiela, D. (2020). Retrieval-augmented generation for knowledge-intensive NLP tasks. *Proceedings of the 34th International Conference on Neural Information Processing Systems*, 9459–9474. https://proceedings.neurips.cc/paper/2020/file/6b493230205f780e1bc26945df7481e5-Paper.pdf

Miller, C., Dighe, M., Martens, C., & Jhala, A. (2019). Stories of the town: Balancing character autonomy and coherent narrative in procedurally generated worlds. *Proceedings of the 14th International Conference on the Foundations of Digital Games*. https://doi.org/DOI: 10.1145/3337722.3341850

Mohaghegh, S., Dehnavi, M. A. R., Abdollahinejad, G., & Hashemi, M. (2023). *PCGPT: Procedural content generation via transformers*. https://arxiv.org/abs/2310.02405

NVIDIA Corporation. (2024). *NVIDIA brings generative AI for digital humans, new RTX technologies and more DLSS 3.5 games to GDC*. NVIDIA Corporation. https://blogs.nvidia.com/blog/generative-ai-digital-humans-rtx-dlss-gdc/

NVIDIA Corporation. (2025). *CUDA toolkit*. NVIDIA. https://developer.nvidia.com/cuda-toolkit

Open, A. I. (2024). *GPT-4o system card*. OpenAI. https://cdn.openai.com/gpt-4o-system-card.pdf

Pathos14489. (2024). *Pantella* [Computer software]. GitHub repository. https://github.com/Pathos14489/Pantella

Pezoa, F., Reutter, J. L., Suarez, F., Ugarte, M., & Vrgoč, D. (2016). Foundations of JSON schema. *Proceedings of the 25th International Conference on World Wide Web*, 263–273. DOI: 10.1145/2872427.2883029

Pietrzak, B., Pucci, S., & Cohen, A. (2020). Semantic reactor: A tool for experimenting with NLU models. *Google Open Source Blog*. https://opensource.googleblog.com/2020/03/semantic-reactor-tool-for-experimenting.html

Rabii, Y., & Cook, M. (2023). Why oatmeal is cheap: Kolmogorov complexity and procedural generation. *Proceedings of the 18th International Conference on the Foundations of Digital Games*. https://doi.org/DOI: 10.1145/3582437.3582484

Riedl, M. O., & Bulitko, V. (2012). Interactive narrative: A novel application of artificial intelligence for computer games. *Proceedings of the Twenty-Sixth AAAI Conference on Artificial Intelligence*, 2160–2165.

Rodríguez-Suárez, J., Torres-Jorge, J. M., & Piñeiro-Vera, J. D. (2025). *Usage of large language models in videogames* [Computer software]. GitHub repository. https://github.com/Universidad-de-La-Laguna/esit-aigames-llm-in-videogames

Shoulson, A. (2013). *Producing immersive interactive narratives in complex 3D open worlds*. AIIDE., DOI: 10.1609/aiide.v9i6.12604

Souchleris, K., Sidiropoulos, G. K., & Papakostas, G. A. (2023). Reinforcement learning in game industry—Review, prospects and challenges. *Applied Sciences (Basel, Switzerland)*, *13*(4), 2443. Advance online publication. DOI: 10.3390/app13042443

Strong, C. R., & Mateas, M. (2008). Talking with NPCs: Towards dynamic generation of discourse structures. *Proceedings of the National Conference on Artificial Intelligence*. https://doi.org/DOI: 10.1609/aiide.v4i1.18682

Summerville, A., Snodgrass, S., Guzdial, M., Holmgård, C., Hoover, A. K., Isaksen, A., Nealen, A., & Togelius, J. (2018). Procedural content generation via machine learning (PCGML). *IEEE Transactions on Games*, *10*(3), 257–270. DOI: 10.1109/TG.2018.2846639

Sun, Y., Ni, X., Feng, H., Lc, R., Lee, C. H., & Asadipour, A. (2022). *Bringing stories to life in 1001 nights: A co-creative text adventure game using a story generation model*. 651–672. https://doi.org/DOI: 10.1007/978-3-031-22298-6_42

Taylor-Giles, L. (2020). Player-centred design in role-playing game branching dialogue systems. In *Game developers and narrative design*. https://doi.org/DOI: 10.1007/978-3-030-37643-7_13

Tiedemann, J., Aulamo, M., Bakshandaeva, D., Boggia, M., Grönroos, S.-A., Nieminen, T., Raganato, A., Scherrer, Y., Vazquez, R., & Virpioja, S. (2023). Democratizing neural machine translation with OPUS-MT. *Language Resources and Evaluation*, *58*(2), 713–755. DOI: 10.1007/s10579-023-09704-w

Touvron, H., Lavril, T., Izacard, G., Martinet, X., Lachaux, M.-A., Lacroix, T., Rozière, B., Goyal, N., Hambro, E., Azhar, F., ... (2023). LLaMA: Open and efficient foundation language models. *arXiv Preprint arXiv:2302.13971*.

Vaswani, A., Shazeer, N., Parmar, N., Uszkoreit, J., Jones, L., Gomez, A. N., Kaiser, Ł., & Polosukhin, I. (2017). Attention is all you need. *Advances in Neural Information Processing Systems*, *30*, 5998–6008.

Veloso, C., & Prada, R. (2021). *Validating the plot of interactive narrative games*. IEEE Cognitive Systems., DOI: 10.1109/CoG52621.2021.9618897

Xiao, C., & Yang, B. Z. (2024). *LLMs may not be human-level players, but they can be testers: Measuring game difficulty with LLM agents*. https://arxiv.org/abs/2410.02829

KEY TERMS AND DEFINITIONS

Attention Degradation: A phenomenon in language models where the effective processing of information diminishes as content becomes temporally or positionally distant within the context window, leading to reduced accuracy in referencing or maintaining consistency with earlier conversational elements.

Belief-Desire-Intention (BDI) Framework: A cognitive architecture for modeling autonomous agent behavior in which characters maintain explicit representations of their beliefs about the world, long-term desires and motivations, and specific behavioral intentions that drive action selection.

Branching Dialogue Tree: A hierarchical computational structure for managing interactive conversations in video games, where each node represents a dialogue exchange and branches represent player choices, enabling multiple conversational paths while requiring complete pre-authorship of all possible interactions.

Context Window: The maximum number of tokens (word fragments) that a language model can process simultaneously, defining the practical limit for conversation history, character descriptions, and world knowledge that can inform response generation.

Finite State Machine (FSM): A computational model consisting of discrete states connected by transitions triggered by specific inputs, representing one of the earliest approaches to interactive dialogue systems where each state corresponds to a conversational moment and transitions represent player choices.

Function Calling: A capability of advanced language models to invoke predefined programmatic functions with specified parameters based on conversational context, enabling LLMs to trigger concrete game actions, query databases, or generate structured data beyond pure text generation.

Hierarchical Task Network (HTN) Planning: An AI planning methodology that decomposes high-level goals into increasingly specific subtasks, applied in dialogue systems to synthesize conversation structures dynamically by treating discourse as a planning problem with narrative objectives.

Inference Latency: The time delay between submitting a request to a language model and receiving a complete response, a critical performance metric for interactive applications where delays exceeding 500 milliseconds can disrupt conversational flow and player immersion.

Large Language Model (LLM): A class of deep learning architectures, typically based on transformer neural networks, trained on extensive text corpora to generate contextually relevant natural language responses by predicting subsequent tokens in a sequence given preceding context.

Procedural Content Generation (PCG): The algorithmic creation of game content through computational processes rather than manual authoring, enabling dynamic generation of dialogue, levels, quests, or other game elements based on defined rules and constraints.

Prompt Engineering: The systematic design and optimization of input instructions provided to language models to elicit desired behavioral patterns, maintain narrative consistency, and constrain generated outputs within specified boundaries.

Quantization: A model compression technique that reduces the precision of neural network weights from higher-bit representations (FP16, FP32) to lower-bit formats (4-bit, 8-bit), significantly decreasing memory requirements and inference latency while introducing controlled quality degradation.

Retrieval-Augmented Generation (RAG): An architectural pattern that enhances language model capabilities by retrieving relevant information from external knowledge bases or memory systems and incorporating this context into generation prompts, enabling more informed and consistent responses.

Speech Act Theory: A linguistic framework that treats utterances as actions that perform functions beyond conveying information, such as requesting, promising, or commanding, used in dialogue systems to generate contextually appropriate responses based on communicative intent.

Structured Output: A language model capability that constrains generated responses to conform to predefined formats such as JSON schemas, enabling reliable extraction of both dialogue content and metadata necessary for game state management without post-processing heuristics.

Tokens Per Second (TPS): A performance metric measuring the throughput of language model inference, calculated as the number of text tokens processed or generated per unit time, critical for assessing real-time viability in interactive applications.

Validation Framework: A systematic approach to ensuring generated content adheres to specified constraints, typically involving rule-based filtering, self-reflective evaluation by the generating model, or separate classification systems that assess outputs for narrative consistency and appropriateness.

Vector Database: A specialized data storage system that organizes information as high-dimensional numerical representations (embeddings), enabling semantic similarity search to retrieve contextually relevant memories or knowledge based on meaning rather than keyword matching.

Chapter 6
From Trackers to AI:
Generative Music in Contemporary Game Design

Jörg Burbach
https://orcid.org/0000-0003-3100-8008
IU Internationale Hochschule, Germany

ABSTRACT

This chapter examines the evolving role of AI in video game music, from early tracker software to today's generative tools. AI-generated music raises questions of originality and authorship but also expands creative potential, especially for resource-limited or experimental teams. Using Margaret Boden's theory of combinatorial, exploratory, and transformational creativity, the chapter explores how AI operates within and beyond stylistic boundaries (Boden, 2004). A case study of an anonymized indie point-and-click game shows how human composers and AI can collaborate effectively. Ethical and practical issues—such as authorship, audience perception, and the risk of homogenization—are also discussed. The chapter analyzes how game genre influences the fit and acceptance of AI music and considers educational implications, calling for curricula that emphasize critical, not just technical, engagement. Rather than replacing human creativity, AI is framed as a co-creative tool that accelerates workflows, broadens stylistic range, and enables new forms of musical expression.

INTRODUCTION

Game audio has continually evolved alongside technological innovation. Early personal computers and consoles imposed strict limitations on sound, e.g. from the primitive beeps of 1980s home computers to the Commodore Amiga (1985) which

DOI: 10.4018/979-8-3373-4637-3.ch006

ght © 2026, IGI Global Scientific Publishing. Copying or distributing in print or electronic forms without written permission of IGI Global Scientific Publishing is prohibited. Use of this chapter to generative artificial intelligence (AI) technologies is expressly prohibited. The publisher reserves all rights to license its use for generative AI training and machine learning model development.

featured 4-channel stereo audio, a major step up at the time (Kotlinski, 2009). As hardware advanced, so did the tools and techniques for creating game music. The introduction of digital audio workstations (DAWs) in the 1990s and 2000s helped expanding the complexity and fidelity of game soundtracks. The next technological change is happening with generative artificial intelligence (AI) offering novel methods to design soundscapes, music tracks, and audio effects for games.

This chapter explores the historical, technical, and creative trajectory starting with early music *trackers,* programs like *Ultimate Soundtracker*, that pioneered sample-based music sequencing on microcomputers (Kotlinski, 2009). It concludes with cutting-edge AI-driven platforms such as *Soundful*, *Sona*, and modern DAWs like *FL Studio* with AI features (Soundful, 2024; Image-Line, 2024). We situate generative music within the broader evolution of game development workflows, highlighting how AI-generated audio is influencing prototyping, iteration cycles, and creative authorship across development teams. These technologies are examined not only as convenient tools for music production but as potential co-creative systems that influence level design, narrative pacing, ambient world-building, and player immersion. With generative AI's increasing accessibility, developers can now craft high-quality audio assets and dynamic soundscapes more rapidly, affordably, and flexibly than ever before. This is particularly relevant in cost-sensitive contexts like academic, indie, or experimental contexts.

By connecting technical innovation with design practice, the chapter offers not just a framework but a living map. One that reflects how generative audio tools are influencing game creation from the inside out. This chapter draws on real-world case studies and team-based project experience to illustrate the capabilities, the limitations and the ethic implications of current AI music tools.

Throughout this chapter, several terms describe the collaborative dynamic between humans and AI in creative processes. *Generative AI* refers to systems that autonomously produce content such as music or sound effects. *Co-creativity* and *human-in-the-loop* emphasize the human role in steering, curating, or refining AI output. *Prompt design* denotes the act of crafting inputs to influence the AI's results, while roles like *audio curator* or *AI assistant* reflect emerging creative workflows. These terms highlight the evolving interplay between authorship, control, and automation in game audio. This chapter addresses game developers, audio designers, educators, and researchers interested in the evolving role of AI in creative workflows. It combines historical analysis, practical case studies, and theoretical reflection to support both critical understanding and applied innovation in game audio.

HISTORICAL BACKGROUND: FROM MOD TRACKERS TO DAWS

Modern game music owes a considerable debt to the tracker scene of the late 1980s and 1990s. Tracker software introduced a new method of composing music using digital samples and pattern-based sequencing. In 1987, Karsten Obarski released Ultimate Soundtracker for the Commodore Amiga (Kotlinski, 2009; Borderie, 2021). It allowed musicians to arrange up to 15 sampled instruments across the Amiga's four audio channels using a grid-based interface. While not a commercial success due to its unorthodox layout, Soundtracker pioneered a technique that influenced game audio for years: it could export music as a standalone executable, allowing tracks to be shared and played independently of the software. The associated MOD format stored both sequencing data and instrument samples in a compact file, enabling rapid sharing even over floppy disks and slow BBS connections. This format cleverly distributed musical instructions and sound samples rather than bulky audio files, long before MP3s became viable.

The late 1980s and early 1990s saw the rise of the MOD scene, embraced by hobbyists and the demoscene, an underground computer art community focused on audiovisual demos (Collins, 2008). Trackers attracted a generation of users who, despite lacking formal training, were drawn to the creative potential of these tools. The demoscene valued how MOD music could be tightly integrated into programs, and iconic groups like Kefrens and Future Crew pushed hardware limits with dynamic soundtracks. This period laid the groundwork for a DIY ethos in game audio that would eventually influence mainstream development.

In the 1990s, tracker concepts migrated to the PC. Scream Tracker, developed by Future Crew for MS-DOS, expanded to 32 channels and introduced the S3M format. It was followed by FastTracker and Impulse Tracker, which became staples for PC game composers working with limited hardware. Despite their text-based interfaces, these programs featured advanced sample editing, effects, and MIDI support. Trackers enabled self-taught musicians to compose and share music widely, often accompanying freeware games and demos, without the need for professional equipment

By the late 1990s and early 2000s, the music software landscape transitioned toward graphical digital audio workstations (DAWs) like Cubase, Logic, and Cakewalk. These tools adopted piano-roll interfaces and multitrack capabilities, yet the influence of trackers endured. Their modular, pattern-based approach, breaking songs into reusable loops, remains integral to DAWs like FL Studio, whose early design was directly inspired by tracker workflows. Even today, many composers in electronic music and games rely on similar sequencing techniques.

This change from trackers to DAWs also reflected a broader cultural transformation. Early tracker communities were collaborative and non-commercial, often sharing full song source files for remixing. This culture prefigured today's remix and modding scenes in both music and games. Tracker formats also provided practical advantages to game studios (Collins, 2008). Due to their small file sizes, MODs were used in many Amiga, early PC, and handheld console titles to deliver rich soundtracks within tight memory budgets.

As DAWs evolved through the 2000s, they began incorporating intelligent features that hinted at AI integration. One milestone was Melodyne 2000, which enabled users to detect and edit individual notes within polyphonic recordings (Apple, 2020). Later versions could manipulate chord qualities or vocal melodies, offering new ways to transform audio. Similarly, Logic Pro X introduced features like Drummer and Smart Tempo, virtual musicians that used AI-like techniques to create realistic, style-specific performances (Apple, 2020). In the mid-2020s, Logic's Session Bassist and Keyboardist tools employed AI to generate accompaniment in real time, based on user input (Apple, 2020).

While these tools weren't fully generative, they demonstrated how music software could assist in composition, offering a glimpse of co-creativity. They laid the groundwork for current AI music tools by embedding intelligence into traditional workflows. The evolution from MOD trackers to modern DAWs established key foundations for today's AI-driven music tools. Trackers democratized music-making and introduced modular, software-based composition. Their legacy lives on in modern sequencing tools, while rising computational power in the 2010s enabled increasingly intelligent audio features. Together, these developments set the stage for today's generative systems that further automate, accelerate, and expand music creation in game development.

GENERATIVE AI IN MUSIC: TOOLS AND CAPABILITIES

Advancements in AI since the mid-2020s have led to powerful generative music platforms that can produce original compositions on demand (Mubert, 2023; McHenry, 2024). These range from web-based tools to AI features embedded within established audio software. For game developers, such tools offer a fast, accessible, and cost-effective way to create high-quality music and sound effects, particularly helpful for teams without in-house composers.

One class of tools includes online platforms like Soundful, AIVA, Boomy, and Sona (Soundful, 2024). These services generate full songs based on user-selected parameters such as genre, tempo, and mood. The results often sound professionally produced but may lack a distinctive creative voice due to their reliance on learned musical patterns.

Sona goes further by generating not only instrumental tracks but also lyrics and sung vocals. Given a simple text prompt, it creates complete vocal songs using AI voice synthesis. This allows even small teams to produce cinematic theme music without hiring vocalists or audio engineers.

These platforms typically operate via text or menu prompts, translating user input into musical outputs using deep learning, often transformer-based models trained on MIDI or audio data. While technical implementations vary, the primary appeal is usability: even non-musicians can generate competent results without needing to understand the underlying algorithms.

AI capabilities are also being embedded into **Digital Audio Workstations (DAWs)**. For instance, **FL Studio** includes a stem separation module that isolates vocals, drums, and instruments from mixed tracks (Image-Line, 2024). This allows developers to reuse, remix, or strip down music without requiring original session files or audio engineering skills.

Another tool, **automated mastering**, is now offered by services like **Mixea**, which adjust a track's loudness, EQ, and compression to professional standards (Mubert, 2023). While such mastering may trade dynamic nuance for loudness, it's typically more than sufficient for mobile games, prototypes, or casual titles.

A full AI-driven music workflow was tested as part of a research-oriented experiment: generating music with Soundful, cover art with MidJourney, mastering with Mixea, and publishing to Spotify, all in a single afternoon. A similar workflow could be used in game development to quickly generate background music, ambient loops, or even placeholder soundtracks during prototyping. These tools support rapid iteration. Developers can quickly regenerate tracks in different moods or split a composition into loops and layers for adaptive playback. This flexibility makes AI a strong companion for agile and iterative design processes (McHenry, 2024).

Generative AI has also entered **sound design**. Tools like **myedit.online** enable users to generate environmental sounds or UI effects from simple prompts (e.g., "gentle dog bark" or "metallic door click"). These outputs often require no further editing and can be used immediately in-game. DAWs and middleware increasingly include AI-based tools for noise reduction, reverb simulation, or generating subtle sound variations, key for avoiding repetition in interactive environments.

In sum, today's generative audio ecosystem spans from "one-click" song generators to embedded production features. Most tools offer royalty-free output and are designed with content creators in mind. They streamline workflows, reduce production costs, and give teams — especially indie developers — more control over their game's soundscape. AI is no longer just a futuristic novelty; it's becoming an essential part of the game audio toolbox.

CASE STUDY: *INDIE POINT & CLICK-GAME*

To ground the discussion in a real-world scenario, we presented "*Das Sanatorium*", an indie game project that extensively utilized generative music and audio tools. The game in German language is part of a broader research initiative called "AI-KI-DO" at IU Internationale Hochschule (Burbach, et al, 2024a). The resulting game, *Das Sanatorium*, was published as part of this study (Burbach et al, 2024b). The project explored the use of AI in creative practice and education. *Das Sanatorium* is a free point-and-click adventure game set in a mysterious hospital, and it provided an ideal testbed for AI-generated audio due to its limited budget and experimental nature [1].

From the outset, the goal for *Das Sanatorium*'s audio was to achieve a rich, atmospheric soundscape without the time and cost usually required. The development team opted to leverage AI tools at multiple levels: music soundtrack, ambient sound effects, and even UI sounds were largely generated rather than manually composed, created or recorded. This approach was born of necessity (a small team with no dedicated composer) but also of curiosity. It was an opportunity to evaluate how well current AI audio tools could meet the needs of a narrative-driven game.

Soundtrack with Sona: The most unexpected achievement was the creation of the game's title theme song using Sona (Soundful, 2024). With a single prompt describing the desired mood and theme, Sona was tasked to generate a piece of music complete with lyrics and vocals. The prompt was only a brief sentence, "a haunting, melodic theme about loneliness in a sanatorium,". Within a few minutes Sona returned several fully produced songs to choose from. The quality of these AI-produced songs was impressively high: one track had the appropriate melancholy tone, intelligible sung lyrics that loosely fit the game's story, and a clean mix. This track was adopted as the game's main theme without any additional editing, underscoring just how *game-changing* the technology can be. In a traditional workflow, creating a theme song with vocals would have required writing lyrics, composing music, recording a vocalist, and significant mixing/mastering effort, often a process taking days or weeks. By contrast, Sona delivered a usable result essentially on demand. By estimation, Sona saved roughly two full days of work and at least €1,000 in production costs compared to commissioning a custom song. While the team did sacrifice creative control by accepting the composition as-is, the time and budget savings can be crucial for projects like this.

Sound effects with Myedit.online (Mubert, 2023): In addition to music, *Das Sanatorium* needed a variety of sound effects to bring the environments to life (doors creaking, distant footsteps, medical equipment noises, etc.), as well as interface sounds (clicks, item pickups). Lacking a Foley artist and sound designer, the team turned to myedit.online, an AI-powered sound generation/editing tool. For instance, instead of searching through sound libraries for dog noises, they simply prompted the AI to generate a "dog barking" sound to use in an outdoor scene. The resulting bark audio was dropped into the game and provided convincing ambiance. Similarly, UI click sounds were generated by the AI to suit the game's aesthetic (soft, subtle clicks to match a tense, quiet atmosphere). These sounds were used with little or no post-processing, and importantly, players did not report anything noticeably "artificial" about them. This speaks to a key point: for *supporting audio* that doesn't take center stage like background noises or generic UI feedback sounds, AI-generated assets can work perfectly well and typically draw no attention to their origin. They fulfill their role of enhancing immersion without requiring the creative nuance that, say, a main character's voice acting or a leitmotif melody would need.

Integration and workflow: The workflow that emerged in *Das Sanatorium* can be seen as a template for small teams. The development process was roughly as follows: during early prototyping, the team identified places where music or sound would be needed to convey mood and feedback. Instead of leaving those blank or using placeholder assets, they immediately tried generating candidate audio with AI tools. For example, when blocking out the game's intro scene, they generated a moody background track via Soundful to test how music might influence the feel. This rapid *iteration* allowed them to gauge the game's audio atmosphere early and adjust it in tandem with game and graphics design. As production continued, they refined the audio choices and the use of AI audio became an iterative, interactive process.

Feedback from players and collaborators of *Das Sanatorium* was particularly enlightening. Many did not realize that the music and some sounds were AI-generated until told afterwards. In blind comparisons, some playtesters could not distinguish the AI-composed theme song from a conventionally produced indie game soundtrack. However, a few musically trained listeners did note that the game's older, pre-AI tracks (composed in earlier projects by team members) had a certain "human touch" that the new AI tracks lacked. This aligns with the observation that AI music, while technically competent, can sometimes feel generic or emotionally flatter. The acceptance of the AI music correlated with the players' demographic: younger players, who are accustomed to algorithmically generated playlists and stock music in content, were more likely to accept the AI music without question, whereas some older players or musicians themselves were more critical. But, the overall response was that the audio was effective and did not detract from the experience.

Lessons learned: Das Sanatorium's experiment revealed both the strengths and limitations of current generative audio. On the positive side, the speed and cost-efficiency are undeniable. What used to be a major production undertaking (e.g. scoring a game scene) can now be a quick AI query. This meant the team could *prototype with sound* very early, enhancing the development process; music and sound were no longer an afterthought or something waiting on an external contractor.

The AI often acted less like a tool and more like a strange, suggestive collaborator, one that could offer creative prompts the team might not have imagined on their own. A point we will revisit when discussing co-creativity.

On the other hand, the project also highlighted issues. Control and editing emerged as challenges: if the AI output was 90% good but needed small changes (say, removing a bar or changing a note that clashed with on-screen action), there was often no straightforward way to tweak it except to convert it to stems and manually edit. Or, even regenerate a whole new piece. This is a current limitation of many generative music services: they often lack fine-grained user controls for composition. Also, some AI outputs had to be discarded because they contained artifacts or stylistic choices that didn't fit (one Soundful track came out with an unexpected saxophone part that felt out of place for a horror game, for instance). So, human judgment and sometimes old-fashioned editing were still very much required to curate the final audio.

Das Sanatorium case study demonstrates that even complex, content-rich audio can be achieved with predominantly AI tools, a scenario that was considered highly speculative only a few years ago. The project's success (the game achieved its atmospheric audio goals and was completed on time) suggests that generative music can be a boon for indie developers and researchers. However, it also provides a grounded perspective on how these tools perform in practice: they work as rapid prototyping aids and fillers for non-critical audio content, but they are not "push-button" replacements for a composer's deliberate touch. More like rough sketches from a co-writer who knows a lot about trends, but little about nuance.

IMPLICATIONS FOR GAME DESIGN WORKFLOWS

Generative music tools have notable implications for how game developers may approach audio in the development process. As laid out before, creating or integrating music in a game can be time consuming and expensive, often involving external composers, licensing library tracks, or delaying sound design until late in production. AI-generated music alters this equation by making music readily available on-demand. This section examines where in the game development lifecycle AI music is most effective, how it influences design practices, and what limitations designers should remain aware of. We also propose a practical decision-making framework to help developers choose the right tool for the task at hand.

Music in Prototyping and Iteration: One clear benefit of AI music is in the *prototyping* phase of game development (McHenry, 2024). In early prototypes or game jams, teams rarely have original music. They either operate in silence or borrow some placeholder tracks, because commissioning music so early is impractical.

With AI-tools, teams can generate a background score, that loosely fits the mood of a prototype level within minutes. This can significantly improve the prototype's feel and the team's ability to evaluate the game's emotional tone. For instance, if you're prototyping a stealth game, you can instantly create a low-tempo, suspenseful ambient track to play while testing the mechanics. Such immediate availability of semi-custom audio encourages an **audio-inclusive design** process, where sound is considered as fundamental as visuals and gameplay from the start. Early access to music can also inspire changes in design. Developers might extend a gameplay sequence because a great music cue came up, or adjust the pacing of a level to sync with an intense musical moment.

Vertical Slice and Demos: Related to prototyping is the creation of a vertical slice, a polished demo of the game used for pitching to a publisher or milestone reviews. Vertical slices benefit enormously from high-quality audio to convey a finished feel. This can make the difference in impressing publishers or stakeholders. Moreover, AI music can be iterated upon quickly in response to feedback. If a reviewer says, "the demo's music is too repetitive or not matching the game's cultural setting," the developer can go back to the AI tool, adjust parameters or style prompts (e.g. "add traditional Japanese instruments"), and generate an updated track on short notice.

Interactive and Adaptive Music: One might wonder how generative music fits with *adaptive music* systems, where the music changes based on gameplay in real time (Collins, 2008). While most AI generators produce *static* tracks, designers can use those tracks as building blocks for interactive music. For example, a collection of AI-generated loops or stems in the same style can be triggered contextually (battle music vs. exploration music, etc.). There are also experimental AI systems that generate music on the fly during gameplay, but those are largely research prototypes at this stage (Elgammal, Liu, Elhoseiny, & Mazzone, 2017). In practice, teams can manually set up adaptive scores using AI-generated assets much as they would with conventional assets. The difference is that they can afford to generate a larger pool of variations, say 10 different tension loops, and thereby avoid players noticing repetition. In essence, AI tools can supercharge procedural audio approaches by supplying abundant variations.

Level Design and Narrative Rhythm: Music and sound have an important effect on a player's perception of pacing and intensity. With quick access to generative music, level designers can more readily experiment with different audio moods to see how they influence level flow. For instance, a designer might try a quiet, atmospheric track in one version of a level and a high-energy track in another, observing how each alters the player's behavior and feelings. This iterative pairing of level design and music selection used to be constrained by the limited music at hand; now a virtually unlimited palette is available. Narrative designers, too, can use AI music to set the rhythm of storytelling. If a certain scene in a game's story needs to evoke sadness, an appropriate piece can be generated to time with that scene. If later the story is rewritten to be more hopeful, a new piece can quickly be created to match. This tight integration of narrative development and music scoring is a compelling prospect: it makes music a more *fluid* part of the game's narrative prototyping, rather than a fixed asset developed after the script is locked.

Ambient Sound Design: Ambient audio (background environmental sound) sometimes is neglected in its importance, as it can be tedious work to create it. Generative tools can assist here as well. Need an eerie nighttime forest background? Instead of searching for one, a tool might generate a loop of rustling leaves and distant owl hoots tailored to your description. Some AI music generators can create pure ambient/noise tracks when prompted (e.g. "space station drone ambiance"). Using these, a level designer can quickly give each environment a unique sonic identity. In cases where generative output doesn't fit, AI can still accelerate the workflow: one could generate a base layer and then manually layer a few specific sounds over it. This way, designers don't need to from scratch.

Limitations and Quality Control: Despite the advantages, AI-generated music is not the solution for all musical needs (McCormack, Gifford, & Hutchings, 2019). A critical limitation is the risk of homogenization. If many developers use the same generative tools with similar prompts, the resulting music may sound formulaic or too similar across projects, even by different teams. Over-reliance on a particular AI's style could lead to a glut of games with indistinguishable soundtracks, reducing the uniqueness that a bespoke score can provide. Human composers often craft leitmotifs (recurring themes) or adapt music closely to game lore and character, something AI currently cannot currently do. And even if, it currently lacks contextual understanding beyond surface prompts.

Additionally, generative tools sometimes produce outputs with technical or musical flaws. While outright errors, like glitches in audio, are becoming rarer as models improve. But one still encounters occasional problems: a track might have an awkward looping, a misfit instrument choice, or sections that feel misplaced. Human oversight is needed to catch and address these issues. In a game context, that could mean editing the AI music in a DAW (trimming it, crossfading to make a clean loop, EQing to sit well under dialogue, etc.), or simply asking the AI for another attempt. This introduces some iteration overhead, and fast generation doesn't always equal fast finalization, especially if the team is picky about the result, or the generated music does not meet the creative expectations or quality.

Loss of Creative Authorship: An often-raised concern is the potential loss of creative authorship when using AI. From a workflow perspective, this means designers might default to what the AI provides rather than injecting their own creative ideas. If a team continuously picks from AI-generated options, the role of a *human* composer or sound designer changes towards a curator or prompt-tweaker rather than an originator of musical ideas. Some (not audio-)designers may find this liberating (focusing on high-level direction rather than low-level creation), while others feel it diminishes the artistry of the audio. In practice, a balance needs to be struck. For example, a designer could generate 5 different battle themes with an AI, then *manually* combine their favorite motifs from each into one track, thus exerting authorship over the final piece. The important point is that developers remain *critical* and *intentional* about audio choices, rather than using AI as an infallible oracle. The AI should serve the design vision, not define it.

Decision-Making Framework: Given the mix of pros and cons, how should game developers decide when and how to use generative music tools? The authors proposes a simplified decision framework:

- **Assess the Purpose of Music in Your Project:** Is the music central to the game's identity (as in a music-rhythm game or a story-driven epic), or is it primarily supportive/ambient? For core identity music, you may want the bespoke touch of a human composer, possibly using AI only for inspiration or as a filler. For supportive roles (e.g. ambient background tracks, generic tension music), AI-generated music is likely sufficient and efficient.
- **Consider Resources (Budget/Time/Skills):** If you cannot afford a composer or need a large quantity of music fast, AI is an obvious ally. If you have a skilled composer on the team, consider using AI to handle the less crucial pieces (like placeholder tracks during development, or bulk ambient sounds), freeing the human composer to focus on main themes and complex cues. As a rule of thumb, use AI to *augment* scarce human talent, not necessarily to replace it entirely.
- **Match Tool to Task:** Different generative tools have different strengths. For example, use *Sona* if you need vocals or lyrics, since not many AI tools provide full vocal songs. Use *Soundful* if you need instrumental music in specific genres and want a quick selection of options. Use integrated DAW features (like FL Studio's stem separation) if you already have some music material and want to expand or remix it. If you need adaptive music, consider generating multiple small pieces rather than one long track. Also, take advantage of trials. Many platforms allow some free generations, which you can experiment with to see if the style fits your game.
- **Iterate and Curate:** Don't settle for the first thing the AI gives if it's not right. Treat AI outputs as malleable. It's often effective to generate multiple versions and then maybe edit them together. For instance, one version might have a great intro and another a great climax. You can splice the two. Or use AI-generated stems to remix it. Keep the human in the loop by reviewing and

tweaking. Ensure the final music meets your quality standards and fits the game's timing and narrative. In other words, maintain *creative control.*

- o **Be Mindful of Limitations:** If your game requires very dynamic music that reacts bar-by-bar to player actions, pre-generated tracks might be limiting. In such cases, a combination of traditional adaptive music techniques (like layering and vertical remixing of stems) with AI provided content might be the way to go. Always test the audio in-game, because music that sounds fine in isolation may conflict with sound effects or become repetitive under gameplay loops.

By applying such a framework, developers can make informed choices. For example, an indie RPG developer might decide: "For overworld and town music (which must be memorable and thematic), hire a composer or compose ourselves, but for battle background music (which we need many variations of), use an AI to generate a pool of tracks, then pick the best." Another example: a VR meditation app could use an AI that generates endless ambient music in real-time to create a unique sound journey for each user, whereas a retro platformer might avoid AI music altogether to pursue a very specific chiptune style that existing AIs don't replicate well. The point is not that AI music should be used everywhere, but that it adds *new options* to the game audio toolkit. Savvy designers will deploy it where it adds value and refrain where it might detract from the experience.

THE ROLE OF GENRE IN AI MUSIC USE

The integration of AI-generated music into games is not genre-neutral. Different game genres present distinct aesthetic, structural, and emotional demands, which in turn influence how well AI-generated music fits, or falls short. In genres that favor systemic design or procedural generation, such as roguelikes, sandbox games, or strategy titles, AI music offers clear benefits. These genres often embrace replayability and dynamic content, where players engage with systems more than scripted narrative. Here, AI-generated or adaptive music can mirror gameplay variation, enhancing immersion through generative soundscapes that don't repeat in predictable loops.

Conversely, in genres that rely heavily on authored emotional arcs — such as story-driven RPGs, horror, or visual novels — music often functions as narrative glue. These games demand precise emotional control, pacing, and thematic coherence. While AI can assist with drafts or iteration, most teams still rely on human composers for key cues, leitmotifs, and emotional timing. In such contexts, AI might support early prototyping, but final scoring remains a handcrafted process.

Genre also shapes player expectations. A player of a cozy life sim may be more receptive to generative background music than someone expecting an epic orchestral fantasy score. Similarly, experimental or art games are often more open to AI-generated sound as a deliberate aesthetic choice, including embracing its "non-human" sonic character.

Recognizing genre-specific needs helps frame AI not as a universal replacement or one-size-fits-all tool, but as a flexible layer in the design toolbox. It also highlights where AI might expand possibilities — particularly in under-resourced genres — while underscoring where human authorship remains central to creative identity.

ETHICAL CONSIDERATIONS IN AI-GENERATED GAME MUSIC

As generative AI music moves from novelty to commonplace, it brings along a series of ethical and legal questions that game developers must grapple with. The convenience of pressing a button to get music belies the complexity behind the scenes: issues of copyright, training data provenance, ownership of generated content, and the broader cultural impact on music creators. This section examines these concerns and offers insight into how they might be navigated responsibly in the context of game development. This section however is not a legal advice.

Authorship and Copyright: Traditional notions of authorship credit a human composer as the creator of a piece of music (McCormack et al., 2019). AI-generated music complicates this: if an algorithm composes a track, who is the author? The user who prompted it, the company that made the AI, or the AI (which legally is not an entity that can hold copyright in most jurisdictions)? Currently, many jurisdictions (including the US and EU) hold that purely AI-created works *without human creative input* may not be eligible for copyright protection. In practical terms, this means that if a game developer obtains a track from an AI, they should carefully read the tool's terms of service. Most AI music platforms grant the user a license to use the output royalty-free, but they might not transfer an exclusive copyright. This could matter if another user generates an identical or very similar piece. There have already been cases of overlapping AI outputs given similar prompts. Developers should ensure they have clarity on whether the music is truly theirs to use, especially in commercial projects. Some companies are tackling this by incorporating a degree of human choice or tweaking in the generation process (which can strengthen the argument that the user is a creative contributor) (Wang, 2019). As a best practice, treating AI music as stock music for licensing purposes is wise: document where and how you got it and under what license, similar to how you would for a stock photo or sound library clip.

Training Data and Plagiarism: Generative music models are trained on vast datasets of existing music (Du Sautoy, 2019). This raises the question of whether the outputs are derivative of copyrighted works. While models like those behind Soundful or OpenAI's Jukebox attempt to create *novel* combinations, there have been instances where an AI output too closely resembled a known song (for example, generating a melody uncannily close to a Beatles tune). This is an ethical gray area: if an AI "learned" and applies parts of copyrighted music, using that output could infringe on rights. Developers using AI music need to be cautious of outputs that sound *too familiar*. In a commercial game, the last thing you want is a lawsuit because your background music inadvertently copies someone's hit song. To mitigate this, some AI platforms exclude known copyrighted songs from training or have internal checks for similarity. However, transparency is often lacking. AI providers rarely disclose exactly what data they trained on (McCormack et al., 2019). There is growing pressure for transparency in training data. Ethically, one might ask: was the model trained on artists' work without their consent? This parallels the debates in AI art and AI writing. A conservative approach helps to avoid and mimic very specific artists' styles, which could cross into appropriation.

Originality and Creative Integrity: Using AI-generated music can also pose the ethical question of *originality*. If a game's entire soundtrack is AI-composed, is it offering original artistic value or just a pastiche of existing music tropes? This ties into the notion of cultural impact: if many creators choose AI for expediency, human composers might have fewer opportunities, and the diversity of musical styles in games might shrink to what the mainstream-trained AI models can produce. Perhaps balancing AI use with commissioning unique pieces where possible helps. Or using AI to assist human musicians rather than replace them. Some developers approach this by treating AI output as a *draft* and then involving a human musician to refine or customize it, thereby ensuring a level of personal artistry remains. The concept of fair use and transformation also comes in: if a developer significantly edits or builds upon an AI track, they can arguably claim more ownership and creative input.

Licensing Clarity: Commercial game development demands clarity in licensing. AI music tools typically provide either an outright license for any generated piece (common in paid services) or a selection of license options. The ethical and practical risk is if those terms change or if the AI company goes out of business. Would the license still hold? Some services like *Mubert* offer a license certificate for generated music, a step toward formalizing licensing. Game developers should save those license documents and perhaps even consider generating all needed music at once under a known license version, to avoid future uncertainty. Moreover, if a developer uses an opensource model to generate music (like training their own AI or using community models), they should be aware of the model's license and dataset origins. There may be attribution requirements or usage restrictions.

Ethical Source of AI and Data: This case study was conducted as part of a broader research initiative focused on the application of generative AI in creative workflows. On one hand, AI allows a single developer to do the work of many, but on the other, if the AI's knowledge comes from uncredited musicians, there's a moral consideration of benefiting from others' work invisibly. This is part of a larger debate: should AI-generated content carry some form of acknowledgment of the creators whose styles influenced it? Perhaps future tools might provide metadata ("this piece was generated in the style of X, Y, Z influences"). For now, ethically-minded developers can make choices such as: not using AI to clone living artists' styles too closely, being transparent (when appropriate) about the use of AI in their game's credits, and participating in industry discussions about fair compensation (for example, if a company offered a model trained on indie musicians' works with their permission in exchange for a fee, using that might be more ethical than a completely opaque model).

Bias and Cultural Representation: Another ethical facet is bias in AI music generation (Manovich, 2013). If training data is skewed towards Western tonality and instrumentation (which it often is), then the AI might do a poor job generating music for a game set in a non-Western culture, or worse, it might produce stereotyped or inauthentic-sounding music. Developers should be cautious not to inadvertently propagate cultural insensitivity through generative tools. If a game requires a specific ethnic musical style, involving a cultural consultant or musician might be necessary, or at least carefully curating the AI output for authenticity. In the future, more region-specific or genre-specific models might emerge to address this.

Player Perceptions and Transparency: Do players have a right to know if music was AI-generated? This is more of an emerging ethical question. Some argue for transparency as a principle, e.g., disclosing in game credits that "Music was generated using X tool", while others say it's not materially different from using any digital tool with licensed samples and sequences. From a player's perspective, enjoyment is usually paramount, but there could be scenarios where it matters (for example, a game that markets itself on its soundtrack might face backlash if it was all AI-made without credit to any human). As a developer, being honest about AI usage, at least in postmortems or GDC talks, contributes to collective understanding and responsible norm-setting.

IMPACT ON CREATIVE ROLES AND THE EVOLVING SKILL SET

Generative AI music tools are prompting a reevaluation of roles within game audio and the broader creative team. Rather than outright replacing human composers and sound designers, AI is *changing* their roles and creating new hybrid positions.

How will roles like prompt designer and AI audio curator look like, and what skills will be important for game developers in this new landscape.

The Composer's New Role: Game composers traditionally craft music with a high degree of originality and intentionality, often in direct communication with the game directors and designers (McHenry, 2024). With AI able to handle the more routine or generic music tasks, composers might find their role becoming more *supervisory* or *curatorial*. The composer could act as a music director or quality controller, using their expertise to ensure coherence, emotional impact, and uniqueness in an AI-assisted score. They might focus their manual composition efforts on key themes or complex adaptive scores, whereas filler music and variations are delegated to AI. This requires composers to develop new skills: knowing how to get the best from AI (crafting effective prompts or training custom models), and the ability to creatively edit AI outputs. Far from making the composer obsolete, AI could make their job more efficient, like discussed before. However, it also means fewer junior composers might be needed for tasks like making 10 variations of the same theme. One senior composer with AI might handle it alone. Thus, the structure of audio teams could change, potentially reducing the number of hands-on music specialists and the creative diversity but increasing the need for a highly skilled lead who is adept with technology.

The "Prompt Designer": A new kind of role that is being discussed across industries is that of the prompt engineer or prompt designer (McHenry, 2024; Wang, 2019). Someone who specializes in communicating with AI systems to get the desired output. In game music, a prompt designer might be responsible for creating the textual or parametric prompts that yield music matching the game's needs. This role blends musical knowledge, linguistic skill, and familiarity with the AI's workings. For example, knowing that describing a scene in certain poetic terms yields a better lyrical song from an AI, or knowing how to tweak parameters to get a more suspenseful vs. more energetic result. In smaller teams, this might simply be a skill that designers or composers learn, rather than a distinct job title would describe. But it underscores, *semantic shaping* of music via descriptions becomes a part of the creative process.

Sound Designers and Audio Implementers: For those in charge of sound effects and integration, AI provides tools to speed up asset generation (as discussed earlier with myedit.online). This means a sound designer could also move more into a curation and integration role, focusing on how sounds fit in the game. They could supervise e.g. spatial audio mixing, or interactive logic, while spending less time on physically recording or synthesizing sounds from scratch. The creative energy may be selecting the right sounds from AI suggestions and balancing them, rather than the technical challenge of producing the raw sound. Additionally, a sound designer might take on some musical tasks if AI makes them easier. This flexibility could blur the lines between composer and sound designer roles, leading to hybrid audio practitioners.

Hybrid Human-AI Teams: We may see game studios explicitly planning their projects around a human/AI collaboration model (Wang, 2019). For instance, a studio might employ one composer who works with an AI system "partner." Some media companies have already experimented with AI in writers' rooms or art departments in a similar fashion. To make this work in audio, workflows will adapt by spending more time in generating and curating music rather than composing as well. Instead of collaborating with other musicians or a live orchestra, a composer might collaborate with data scientists or tool developers to improve their AI music pipeline. Interdisciplinary skills become valuable: an understanding of how AI "hears" and produces music can help the human guide it better.

Opportunities for Non-Musicians: A notable impact is empowering those without formal music training to create music (Mubert, 2023). Game designers or programmers who couldn't compose a tune can now use AI to get music for their prototypes. This democratization can lead to more people incorporating original music into their independent projects, but it might also reduce the reliance on contracting external composers for small projects. On the flip side, it could generate more appreciation for what composers do when non-musicians realize the limitations or iterations needed even with AI.

Job Displacement vs Transformation: The big question is whether AI will *displace* jobs in game music. In the short term, it appears more like transformation than wholesale replacement (McCormack et al., 2019). Just as photography did not eliminate painting. AI might not eliminate game composers but change what composing entails. Low-skill tasks might be automated, like transcribing MIDI, doing repetitive adjustments, producing lots of similar sound effects. But high-level tasks, like creating a unique memorable melody, designing a bespoke soundscape that emotionally resonates, remain in the human domain for now. However, entry-level positions may be reduced or scrapped altogether, as the lead composer with AI might handle it. The optimistic view is that this frees human composers to focus on higher-level creative challenges that AI cannot do, such as innovating new musical styles or deeply aligning music with nuanced storytelling. The pessimistic view is that fewer human composers will be commissioned, especially for mid- and low-budget projects, because AI is "good enough" for those needs. The actual impact will likely vary by market segment: big-budget AAA games may still value custom human scores for their branding and quality, whereas indie and mobile games might lean heavily on AI for cost reasons. Or, the other way around, producers of AAA games will go the "easy" way and try to save money with AI.

New Skill Requirements: The workforce must adapt. For composers and sound designers, familiarity with AI tools is increasingly expected. Some job postings in creative media are already asking for experience with AI content generation tools. This doesn't mean every composer must also be a machine learning expert, but having an open mindset to use AI as part of the toolkit will be important. It's analogous to how film editors had to learn to use digital editing software in the 1990s. Those who stuck purely to manual splicing lost out, although very few movies are still shot analogous because of the overall look and feel – which may be added by AI later on. In educational contexts, game design and audio programs are beginning to include modules on AI in the creative process. The research-project itself emphasizes integrating AI practice into creative education. Future audio specialists might need to learn how to "train" their own small models on specific sounds or how to fine-tune an AI to match a desired style, effectively merging programming skills with artistic ones.

Collaboration and Communication: With roles changing, communication in a team also changes. A game director might in the past have given a musical reference to a composer ("I want this level to sound like track X from composer Y"). Now, the director might directly attempt to generate something similar with AI as a proof of concept, or conversely, might expect the composer to generate multiple prototypes via AI for them to listen to. The turnaround expectations might become faster: instead of waiting weeks for demos, directors might ask, "can we have some AI-generated samples by tomorrow to review?" This can put pressure on audio teams to deliver more, more quickly. It also empowers other team members to be involved in music selection (for better or worse). For example, a creative director might on their own try some generative music tool and present it to the composer saying "I got this from an AI, can we use or tweak it?" The hierarchy of expertise becomes a bit more fluid, which can be collaborative but also potentially undermining if not managed well. Successful teams will likely establish workflows where the use of AI is coordinated and the expertise of the audio lead is respected in curating AI suggestions.

Likewise, generative AI is acting as a catalyst for the evolution of creative roles in game development. Possible and probably is a future with hybrid creative teams: human experts augmented by AI assistants. New roles like prompt design or technical composer will exist, and existing roles will change towards more oversight, curation, and integration tasks. The net impact on jobs will depend on the value we continue to place on human originality versus efficiency. Importantly, as roles change, the identity of what it means to be a "game composer" or "sound designer" may broaden.

CREATIVITY, ORIGINALITY, AND CO-CREATION IN AI-GENERATED MUSIC

AI excels at recombining learned musical patterns. A system might fuse a pop chord progression with a reggaeton rhythm and a K-pop-style melody contour, yielding a track that's novel but familiar. This is P-creativity (new to the user), but rarely H-creativity (new to culture). AI's brute-force permutation makes it a natural fit for combinatorial creativity. Style transfer or genre mashups are examples. While these outputs aren't truly original in the historical sense, they can still be useful or inspiring.

Exploratory Creativity: AI can effectively explore within stylistic constraints. Given the rules of Baroque chorales, it can produce countless plausible variations, pushing the boundaries of a style with a stamina humans lack. In game music, this might yield unexpected-yet-fitting phrases that expand the design palette. A slightly off-pattern melody could be just the variation that enriches a level. This exploration supports human creativity by covering more ground than a composer might have time or cognitive space for.

Transformational Creativity: Changing musical paradigms, like inventing new genres or compositional logics, is not something current AI does autonomously. It lacks meta-level insight and intentionality. Historical innovations in game music, like 8-bit loop tricks or adaptive audio systems, came from human ingenuity. AI can be used transformatively, but only when guided by humans — say, training it on non-musical data or using it out of context (e.g., a jazz model for dungeon ambience). These "creative misuses" require human vision.

Balancing Creativity Modes: Most AI-generated game music leans toward recombination. This risks homogenization unless developers actively push for more exploratory or transformational uses. A human-in-the-loop model is essential. Instead of taking AI output at face value, humans must evaluate and direct it — prompting alternative versions, tweaking parameters, and curating results. That's how AI becomes a creative tool, not a generator of tropes.

Human-in-the-Loop and Co-Creativity: Human-in-the-loop systems keep the composer engaged, guiding, editing, and selecting AI output. Tools that let composers adjust prompts, accept/reject variations, or fine-tune results foster a collaborative dynamic. For example, AI might extend a human-composed melody, or improvise harmony while someone plays. In these systems, the human retains authorship, and AI becomes a generative assistant.

In practical terms, a composer might generate themes with AI, then manually arrange them. A sound designer might generate 50 footstep sounds and pick the best 5. The human becomes a director/editor; the AI, an idea generator. Research shows that such setups often produce results neither could alone, like an AI suggesting a strange harmony the composer refines into something compelling (Wang, 2019).

The key is agency. If the AI is a black box and the user simply says yes/no to full tracks, co-authorship erodes. Better tools allow mid-generation influence, or accept custom loops for training, which helps composers embed their voice. Some systems even introduce randomness to provoke creative reactions, like a jam partner who throws in a surprising riff. These are early-stage, but align with how many artists want to work: not vending content, but sparking ideas.

Evaluating Originality in AI Music: Creativity often hinges on surprise and fit. AI may generate melodies that are technically "new," but often align closely with statistical norms, lacking true surprise. Yet, because AI doesn't follow human logic, it occasionally yields odd combinations, e.g. surprising chords or unlikely instrument pairings. Whether these are useful "happy accidents" or just errors depends on human interpretation, which itself becomes a creative act.

In games, originality matters when the music defines the game's identity. If an AI-generated track sounds like a dozen film scores, it might function well, but feel generic. Theories of remix culture (e.g., Manovich) suggest AI is an ultra-powerful remixer, blending known musical elements at scale. This might not be innovation in melody, but in how music is produced and integrated, for example dynamic soundtracks tailored to each player (Manovich, 2013).

Perception of Creativity: Audience perception plays a role too. If players think a track was composed by a human, they may ascribe emotion to it. If they know it's AI-generated, it might seem less expressive or authentic. Studies show bias against AI-made art is common. Some developers may choose not to disclose which tracks are AI-made, focusing instead on how well the music works. In practice, if the music enhances the player's emotional response, does its origin matter? Some say yes, citing emotional intent; others argue utility is enough, and the creativity lies in how it's used.

Agency and Authorship: AI challenges traditional notions of authorship. Is the composer the algorithm, the prompt designer, or the person who chose to include the output? Game teams can sidestep this by treating the game as the authored work and the AI output as one of many tools. The development team curates, arranges, and integrates content, that's authorship. Theoretical models like "posthumanist creativity" even embrace this blend, seeing creativity as a property of human-machine assemblages. Some propose the term "machine cocreativity" to reflect this shared input, reframing authorship as collaborative rather than singular (Dartnall, 1994).

Preserving Artistic Identity: To avoid sameness, composers can imprint their style by feeding AI custom motifs or mixing AI outputs with original compositions. The AI then amplifies a human idea rather than generating from scratch. A hybrid soundtrack can combine AI-generated filler content with key human-crafted themes, preserving a unique voice. This balances scale and speed with intentional artistry.

AI excels at expanding the possible, churning out variations and combinations, but it needs human curation to produce music that's fitting, surprising, and emotionally resonant. Used thoughtfully, AI becomes a creative amplifier, like a new kind of instrument. Without such direction, generative outputs risk sounding generic and forgettable. Game developers should treat AI suggestions not as answers, but as prompts: "Does this work? Why or why not?" That mindset enables richer, more original game music, and reframes AI as a creative partner rather than a shortcut.

CONCLUSION AND FUTURE OUTLOOK

AI-generated music is changing how game audio is produced and integrated, but it does not eliminate the role of human composers. Rather, it introduces a shift in workflow and decision-making. The progression from early trackers to current generative tools reflects a broader pattern: new technologies tend to expand, rather than replace, creative capabilities. Trackers gave more people access to music-making; today's AI tools similarly open up music production to developers without formal training. However, human oversight remains central to shaping meaningful outcomes.

For many game projects, especially smaller or early-stage ones, AI music tools offer practical advantages. They enable small teams to generate usable audio quickly, without hiring external specialists. A developer can create a score, test variations, and integrate the results within a short timeframe. This can support faster prototyping and help sound become part of early design discussions, rather than a late-stage addition. In educational contexts, AI tools may also serve as entry points for students learning about audio design.

At the same time, critical reflection is necessary. Developers using AI should regularly assess how the tools affect their creative process. Are they supporting exploration, or leading to formulaic outcomes? Are choices being made actively, or are defaults becoming design decisions? By maintaining awareness of these questions, teams can use AI tools in ways that add value without compromising distinctiveness or ethical standards.

Looking ahead, several directions and areas of development can be anticipated:

AI as Standard Toolset: AI-based music generators and plugins are likely to become regular features in game development environments, similar to physics engines or animation tools. Middleware like FMOD or Wwise may also incorporate adaptive AI music systems capable of generating context-sensitive audio during gameplay (Mubert, 2023).

Improved Co-Creative Interfaces: Future systems may allow finer control over AI-generated music. For example, composers might be able to adjust specific sections of a track or provide feedback mid-generation. Research into more transparent and flexible interfaces is ongoing.

Personalized Game Music: AI could enable games to generate music that adapts to player behavior or preferences. For instance, ambient styles for slower players, or more rhythmic tracks for faster ones. In narrative games, AI might generate motifs based on a player's choices, altering the soundtrack over time.

Quality and Uniqueness Trade-offs: As AI use grows, some developers may highlight manually composed scores as a differentiator. Meanwhile, AI tools are likely to improve in stylistic range, coherence, and long-form structure. Specialized models may emerge that are tailored to specific genres or aesthetics.

Regulatory and Ethical Considerations: Legal frameworks around AI-generated content will continue to develop. These may include rules for disclosing AI involvement, or licensing norms to ensure fair attribution when training data includes copyrighted works. Studios may establish internal guidelines, for example, restricting AI use to prototyping or requiring human review of final content.

Educational Shifts: As generative tools become part of the standard creative toolkit, educational programs in game design, music, and digital media will need to adapt. AI literacy is no longer a niche skill but increasingly a baseline expectation, particularly for students entering cross-disciplinary fields.

Curricula are already beginning to integrate modules on AI-assisted composition, generative sound design, and prompt engineering. However, the focus must extend beyond technical fluency. Students also need frameworks for evaluating AI outputs critically, asking not just whether something works, but whether it fits the desired tone, narrative, or gameplay context. Assignments that require remixing or editing AI-generated music can help cultivate this evaluative mindset (Wang, 2019).

Ethical awareness is another critical component. As students interact with tools trained on large-scale datasets, often of unclear origin, discussions about authorship, consent, and originality become central. Future education should not only teach how to use AI, but also when not to, emphasizing judgment and responsibility alongside creativity. There is also a pedagogical opportunity to emphasize hybrid workflows. For example, students might be tasked with composing a theme manually, then using AI to expand it into variations or adapt it to different game states. This mirrors real-world co-creative practices and helps students develop flexible, collaborative mindsets.

Ultimately, the goal is not to produce AI specialists, but well-rounded creators who see generative tools as part of a broader creative process. Programs that foster curiosity, criticality, and adaptability will better prepare graduates for an industry where human-machine collaboration is increasingly the norm.

New Game Formats: AI music may support new forms of interactive or procedural audio. Games might offer different music for each playthrough or use real-time generation to match player actions. These possibilities could lead to experiments in game mechanics and storytelling, with AI playing a more integral role in the audio system. In summary, AI represents a continuation of a broader trend in game audio: the use of tools to extend what creators can do under technical or time constraints. Just as trackers allowed musicians to create complex arrangements with limited hardware, AI allows developers to generate and test music quickly. The results depend not just on the tool, but on how it is used.

Developers should neither avoid AI entirely, nor rely on it uncritically. The most effective use lies in combining human intent with machine assistance, where AI helps generate possibilities, but human creators shape the outcome. As often noted, "AI won't replace you, but someone using AI might." This applies here: composers who learn to integrate these tools may gain an advantage, particularly in resource-limited settings (Boden, 2004). Incorporating generative music into game design introduces new questions around authorship, originality, and creative responsibility. But it also offers new methods and workflows. If used with care, balancing utility with critical reflection, it can contribute to a wider range of audio practices in games. The role of the composer or sound designer may evolve, but the need for thoughtful, context-aware decisions in audio design remains.

REFERENCES

Apple. (2020). *Logic Pro X user guide.* Apple Support. https://support.apple.com/de-de/guide/logicpro/welcome/mac

Boden, M. A. (2004). *The creative mind: Myths and mechanisms* (2nd ed.). Routledge. DOI: 10.4324/9780203508527

Borderie, X. (2021). Soundtracking sur Amiga: Passion, explications et exemples. https://xavier.borderie.net/blog/2021/07/11/soundtracking-sur-amiga-passion-explications-et-exemples/

Burbach, J., Meyer, A., Plank, M., & Trautzsch, N. (2024a). AI-KI-DO: Künstliche Intelligenz in Design und Online-Medien – A research initiative on AI in creative practice. IU Internationale Hochschule. https://www.iu.de/forschung/projekte/ai-ki-do/

Burbach, J., Meyer, A., Plank, M., & Trautzsch, N. (2024b). Das Sanatorium [Video game]. IU Game Design. https://iu-gamedesign.itch.io/das-sanatorium

Collins, K. (2008). *Game sound: An introduction to the history, theory, and practice of video game music and sound design. MIT Press.* https://mitpress.mit.edu/9780262033780

Dartnall, T. (Ed.). (1994). *Artificial intelligence and creativity*: An interdisciplinary approach (Studied in Cognitive Systems, Vol. 17). Springer. https://link.springer.com/book/10.1007/978-94-017-0793-0

Du Sautoy, M. (2019). *The creativity code.* The Science of Human Innovation.

Elgammal, A., Liu, B., Elhoseiny, M., & Mazzone, M. (2017). CAN: Creative adversarial networks, generating "creative" content [Preprint]. arXiv. https://arxiv.org/abs/1706.07068

Image-Line. (2024). *FL Studio online manual.* Documentation of FL Studio features including the stem separation tool. https://www.image-line.com/fl-studio-learning/fl-studio-online-manual

Kotlinski, J. (2009). *Amiga music programs* 1986–1995 – A historical overview of Amiga tracker software. https://goto80.com/chipflip/dox/kotlinski_(2009)_amiga_music_programs_89-95.pdf

Manovich, L. (2013). *Software takes command.* Bloomsbury. DOI: 10.5040/9781472544988

McCormack, J., Gifford, T., & Hutchings, P. (2019). *Autonomy, Authenticity, Authorship and Intention in computer generated art.* /arXiv.1903.02166DOI: 10.1007/978-3-030-16667-0_3

McHenry, D. (2024, August 8). *Mapping AI music tools across a spectrum of co-creativity*. Medium. https://medium.com/@dsm98/mapping-ai-music-tools-across-a-spectrum-of-co-creativity-c2a076af579a

Mubert. (2023). *A remarkably in-depth study of AI music: Creators, composers, adopters*. https://mubert.com/blog/an-in-depth-study-into-ai-music-its-creators-composers-and-adopters

Soundful. (2024). *The role of AI music generation for content creators*. Blog post. https://soundful.com/ai-music-generation-content-creators/

Wang, G. (2019). *Humans in the Loop: The Design of Interactive AI Systems*. Blog Post. https://hai.stanford.edu/news/humans-loop-design-interactive-ai-systems

ENDNOTE

1 *URL and project attribution withheld for double-blind review. Available upon acceptance*

Chapter 7
Innovative Procedural Content Generation (PCG) Using Generative AI:
A New Paradigm in Game Design

Monika Kumari
https://orcid.org/0000-0002-8468-3552
Poornima University, Jaipur, India

Sheena Tahira Khan
Poornima University, Jaipur, India

Kapil Gulati
Poornima University, Jaipur, India

Prarthana Sharma
https://orcid.org/0009-0001-2571-913X
Poornima University, Jaipur, India

Nikhil Kumar Goyal
https://orcid.org/0009-0007-4532-8033
Poornima University, Jaipur, India

Mohammed Firdos Alam Sheikh
https://orcid.org/0000-0002-8405-8482
Poornima University, Jaipur, India

ABSTRACT

Game design increasingly relies on automation to deliver dynamic, interactive, and immersive player experiences. Procedural Content Generation (PCG), traditionally driven by rule-based systems and stochastic methods, has enabled the scalable creation of game assets and environments with limited human input. Recent advancements in Generative Artificial Intelligence (AI) are redefining PCG by introducing intelligent, creative, and context-sensitive content generation capabilities. This chapter presents an in-depth analysis of state-of-the-art generative AI models—including Generative Adversarial Networks (GANs), Transformers, Diffusion Models, and Reinforcement Learning—and their applications across various PCG domains such as terrain and environment generation, narrative design, character development, and

DOI: 10.4018/979-8-3373-4637-3.ch007

;ht © 2026, IGI Global Scientific Publishing. Copying or distributing in print or electronic forms without written permission of IGI Global Scientific Publishing is prohibited. Use of this chapter to generative artificial intelligence (AI) technologies is expressly prohibited. The publisher reserves all rights to license its use for generative AI training and machine learning model development.

adaptive gameplay. The chapter further examines the architecture of AI-based PCG systems, integration with real-time engines and toolkits, and evaluates generated content using criteria like creativity, diversity, coherence, and player engagement.

1. INTRODUCTION

1.1 The Evolution of Game Design and PCG

Game design has been radically changed in the last 20 years, with the shift between the static, hand-created content to the dynamic, algorithmically driven worlds. Procedural Content Generation (PCG), the algorithmic generation of game content, has played a key role in allowing Game environments to be expansive, games to have replay ability and allowing cost-effective development pipelines. PCG is Indiana dungeon crawler games such as Rogue and Elite, whose dungeon layouts or galaxy maps were procedurally generated with deterministic algorithms and seed-based randomness. Although revolutionary at the time, these methods were mostly based on hard-coded rules, tile-based reasoning and pre-determined templates that constrained the complexity and variety of the output content (Goodfellow et al., 2014).

With the maturity of the gaming industry, PCG has become an essential element of games that wanted to offer open-world exploration, infinite levels, or content customization. Games like Minecraft, Spelunky, and No Man Sky have shown that procedural generation can be applied to generate virtually unlimited content without taxing development teams to the point of breaking. But the rule-based systems behind such games still must be manually tuned, and may not have the creative flexibility, situational awareness, and learning or adaptation capabilities. This makes way to a new era, an era of artificial intelligence, in which machines not only create content but perceive, learn and invent with human designers.

Figure 1. Historical Evolution Of PCG Techniques

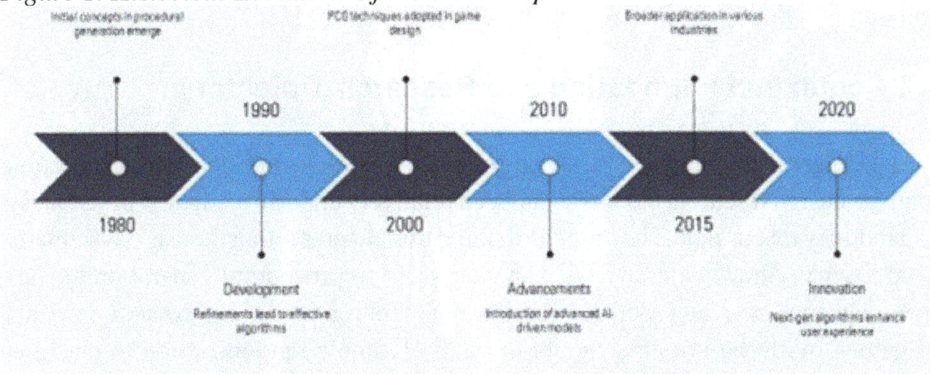

1.2 Role of Generative AI in Next-Gen Game Development

Generative AI promises to enable entirely new possibilities in PCG, since it allows machines to independently acquire creative patterns in the data and generate original, consistent content in a variety of modalities: text, images, 3D models, audio, and more. Generative models, in particular Generative Adversarial Networks (GANs), Variational Autoencoders (VAEs), Transformers, and Diffusion Models, unlike more traditional procedural approaches that most closely resemble handcrafted rules and templates, can resemble human creativity, learn deep semantic relationships, and adjust to novel player behaviors or design restrictions (Radford et al., 2019).

To game developers, this implies they can now create highly detailed game levels, sophisticated NPC conversations, quest chains that depend on context, dynamically driven soundscapes or stylized art that can be created in real-time and that are tied to the narrative and aesthetic of a game. Generative AI can not only decrease the overhead of development but also increase creativity through providing design ideas, allowing the diversity of content and creating custom experiences between various players. Beyond that, however, and using tools such as ChatGPT to generate dialogue, Stable Diffusion to synthesize art, and the ML-Agents repository within Unity to train adaptive agents, developers now possess a set of powerful and scaleable technologies which can be inserted directly into game development pipelines.

Generative AI is not just automating repeatable parts of the design process, it is transforming the creative process itself as it further develops. Game designers no longer have to be constrained by pre-determined logic or even static assets, but are now working with intelligent systems that can begin to comprehend design intent, generate content variations, and even create content that is surprising even to its creators. This paradigm shift provides the possibility of the new generation of games that are not only larger and more sophisticated, but also more responsive, immersive and emotion grabbing (Risi & Togelius, 2020).

1.3 Contextual Foundation and Research Trajectory

The intersection between PCG and generative AI looks like an exciting direction of game design research, but has so far been relatively underinvestigated in scholarly and industry discussion. The rationale behind this chapter is that there is a systematic need to survey how generative AI can be applied to procedural generation to augment, enhance or even redefine procedural generation in various content domains of games. With the possible sleight of hand of simple randomization to machine creativity this integration will enable developers with the tools they need to create high quality, believable, and player specific content with very little manual curation (Summerville et al., 2018).

This chapter has a scope that covers the technological basis, architectural incorporation, area of application, and future of AI-based PCG. It will cover important generative models and how they can be adapted to game content types, terrain and architecture to narrative and behavior. A particular emphasis is made on the way these models are trained and evaluated as well as integrated into real-time game engines. Moreover, the chapter considers the issues of ethics, content regulation, bias, and IP considerations, as well as outlines the new research avenues like explainable AI, collaborative creativity, or regulatory compliance in generative systems.

In the end, the chapter is supposed to become a universal guide that can be used by researchers, developers, and designers who need to learn more about the transformative power of generative AI in the field of procedural content generation. It does not only focus on the how, but the why- why this fusion is an important leap towards making game worlds more interactive, personal and empathic to the players worldwide.

2. FOUNDATIONS OF PROCEDURAL CONTENT GENERATION (PCG)

2.1 Definition and Historical Context

Procedural Content Generation (PCG) is the algorithmic generation of game content with minimial or indirect human feedback. Such content may be game levels, game environments, game quests, game characters, game dialogue, game items or game worlds. The procedural label derives out of the fact that computational procedures such as rules, scripts or algorithms are used to generate content either automatically or semi-automatically. PCG is not about automation only but about making games more creative, lowering the manual burden, and adding variation and replayability to games (Johnson, Yannakakis, & Togelius, 2010).

PCG in historical context was brought on by the hardware constraints. Early 1980s Memory and storage limits required developers to produce content algorithmically instead of storing suitable volumes of pre-generated data. One of the first uses of procedural generation to enable "massive" game experiences with only minimal resources was in Rogue (1980) and Elite (1984). Gradually, PCG turned into a design ideology, allowing infinite variety and non-linear gameplay. Early systems, however, were deterministic, based upon pseudo-randomness and hand-written rules, with little adaptability or semantic richness (Yang et al., 2023).

2.2 Traditional PCG Techniques

Traditional PCG uses a couple of well-developed methods, such as random generation, noise functions (such as Perlin or Simplex noise), grammar-based systems, tile-based generation, and constraint satisfaction algorithms. As an illustration, cellular automata, BSP (Binary Space Partitioning) or random walk algorithms are frequently employed to generate the interconnected rooms and corridors in a dungeon. Fractals or layered noise are often used in terrain generation to approximate the appearance of natural topography, and grammar-based systems have been applied to the generation of narrative and quests (Silver et al., 2017).

These are light and deterministic techniques which provide control and predictability to the designers. They can quickly create content to fit in a particular structural or gameplay need. They are however, usually boring, uninspired and fail to respond to player actions or plot developments. Rule-based systems require a exhaustive codification and although they guarantee coherence, they restrict the expressivity of procedural content. Consequently, despite the effectiveness of traditional PCG when it comes to creating structural frameworks, it fails at creating content that is semantically rich or emotionally evocative.

2.3 Types of Procedurally Generated Content

The different types of procedural content may fall into a number of categories each presenting its own design and computational needs. Level or environment generation (also one of the most common) is a type in which game maps, dungeons or terrains are generated by algorithms. Games such as Spelunky, Terraria and No Man s Sky have used PCG to create dynamic worlds that vary each playthrough, creating more replay value and surprise. The content of this kind frequently deals with spatial reasoning, navigational restrictions and esthetic consistency.

Figure 2. **Procedural Content Generation**

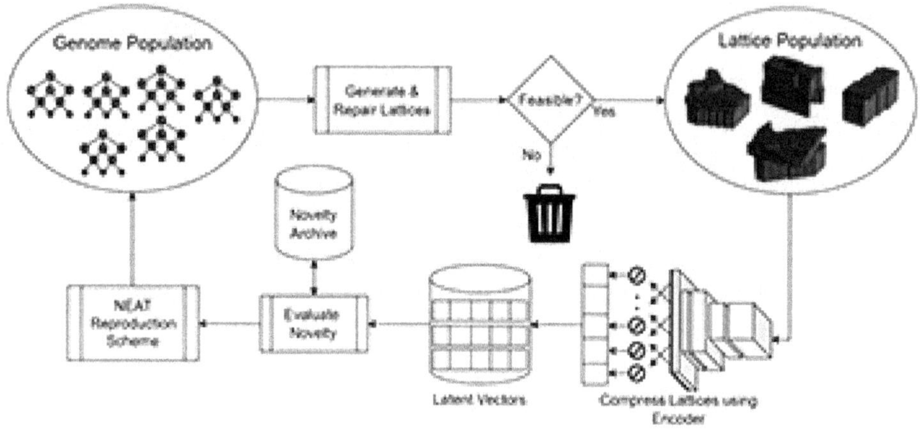

Character and item generation is another important category. Information Games such as Diablo and Borderlands employ PCG to generate random weapons, armor, and powers with custom statistics and appearances to make loot systems more complex. Equally, narrative and dialogue generation is becoming more prominent, where quests, plot lines, and character interactions are procedurally generated through grammar rules or through AI language models. AI Dungeon is a prominent example of such evolution, proposing interactive fiction, which is modified in accordance with the player input in real-time. Finally, the aesthetic elements, such as music, textures, and lighting patterns, can as well be procedurally created in order to offer immersive and diverse audio-visual experiences (Guzdial & Riedl, 2016).

The variety of these contents outlines the flexibility and the range of PCG in contemporary games development. But they also highlight its drawbacks, especially the challenge of balancing randomness and design intent, keeping a narrative consistent, and making a gameplay fair. Here, generative AI holds a lot of promise, allowing PCG systems to improve with data and become context-aware, generating content that has the feel of hand crafting, but is generated by a machine.

3. GENERATIVE AI TECHNOLOGIES FOR PCG

3.1 Generative Adversarial Networks (GANs) in Game Content Creation

Generative Adversarial Networks (GANs) have already become a potent means of creating very realistic and imaginative content. GANs are neural networks composed of two networks namely generator and discriminator, which are trained in a competitive mode. The generator produces content (an image or a level etc.), and the discriminator determines whether this content looks real or fake. This adversarial process enhances the capability of the generator to create outputs that appear genuine with time (Lucas, Liu, Kendall, & Togelius, 2021).

GANs have found application in game development to generate textures, terrains, and character sprites and even entire level layouts. As an example, pixel art or 3D models generated by GAN can be styled to fit a certain visual style without requiring manual drawing. Since GANs can be used to generate levels in 2D platformers such as Super Mario Bros., researchers have also shown that new levels can be learned based on real ones and that they can be generated with similar intricacy. GANs excel at creating visually stunning assets but the functionality and playability of that content is not easily controlled, frequently needing post-processing or other rule-based restrictions (Compton & Mateas, 2006).

3.2 Transformers and Language Models for Narrative Generation

The workhorse of current natural language processing Transformers have revealed a new horizon in procedural storytelling and dialogue generation. Language models like GPT-3 and GPT-4 have the ability to create coherent and contextually aware text depending on player input, which can be used to real-time branching of stories, generation of quests and dynamic NPC interactions. These models are based on the self-attention mechanism to capture the relationships between the words and produce text that makes sense with the user intent or the story direction.

Games such as AI Dungeon and Latent Space are built on transformer-based models to generate limitless, player-penned narratives whose plot points naturally adjust to actions and choices. Such interactivity provides a level of agency never before seen, and as such, every time one plays the game, it is an entirely different experience. Outside of dialogue, transformers may be used to create items descriptions, backstories, lore, and even procedural quest logic. Nevertheless, narrative coherence, prevention of contradictions, and the filtration of inappropriate content remains a current issue that demands the adjustment of models and human monitoring.

3.3 Diffusion Models and Stable Generation for Visual Content

A current advancement in image generation is diffusion models, which are behind Stable Diffusion or DALL·E 2. Such models begin with pure noise and progressively refine it to create high-fidelity images, textures or ideas based on text prompts. Their advantage consists in the possibility to produce high-resolution and semantically regulated visuals that can be adjusted to exact instructions or thematic objectives.

Within PCG, diffusion models could be employed to create concept art, mood boards, game worlds or even modular asset packs. These models can be iteratively asked by the designers to generate variations on an idea, narrowing visual direction quickly. Also, these models can be trained or fine-tuned on particular art styles, which will be consistent throughout the game world. Nevertheless, embedding them into real-time pipelines is a computationally expensive task, which frequently necessitates pre-generation and asset management (Sarkar, Momennejad, & Lake, 2023).

3.4 Autoencoders and Reinforcement Learning for Environment Design

Autoencoders (especially Variational Autoencoders, VAEs) can be trained on a compact representation of content (e.g. level layouts or character designs) and then used to generate new variations by sampling the latent space. They can be thought of as particularly useful in interpolation between styles or combination of design patterns to allow the creation of new content with a sense of continuity.

Instead, Reinforcement Learning (RL) enables agents to optimize over the content generation strategies based on reward signal. Adaptive level design In PCG, RL has been applied to adapt environments to player skill or engagement rates. As an example, a level generator could be taught to adapt the difficulty or pacing, based on player behaviour in earlier levels. RL agents may also be used to co-create content when iteratively testing and improving layouts with respect to player feedback or completion rates (Roohi & Bidarra, 2021).

4. ARCHITECTURE OF GENERATIVE AI-BASED PCG SYSTEMS

Figure 3. **Generative AI Architecture**

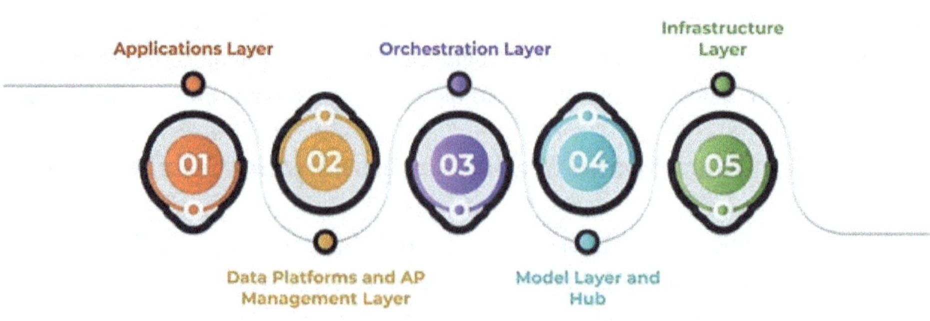

4.1 Content Pipeline: Input, Generation, Validation

An effective procedure content generation system relies considerably on an organized architecture that describes the information stream as raw input into useful game content. Generally, the pipeline in this architecture is four-phased, including data acquisition, model training, content generation, and content validation. All the stages are important in order to make sure the end product is creative and functionally correct.

At the first stage, developers need to prepare superior quality datasets, which can be level blueprints, environmental assets, character dialogue, quests, and labeled gameplay logs. Such dataset serve as the training corpus over which the AI model learns underlying distributional regularities and design heuristics. By way of example, training a GAN on dungeon layouts, the model picks up on structural motifs, like how rooms cluster together, or how wide corridors are, or how frequently particular enemies appear. A common step to improve model generalization is preprocessing: normalization, tokenization (of text), or augmentation (of visual data) (Gisselbrecht, Bontrager, Togelius, & Hoover, 2019).

Generation stage commences once training commences. In this case, the model generates novel content following learnt representations or input prompts. Outputs may be single-text prompts (e.g. "generate a sci-fi city level") depending on the model architecture: GAN, VAE, transformer or diffusion. The outputs can be plausible at face value, but in most cases they need to be examined in a validation loop, where functional and aesthetic accuracy can be verified.

The most important, but also complicated step is validation. The content that is generated should not just be according to the design intent, but it also needs to conform to the game mechanics as well as the player expectations. As an example, a mountain range created by AI can look beautiful and yet be utterly inpassable by player characters. In the same way, dialogue trees can be grammatically correct, but can disrupt narrative flow, or otherwise disregard player choice. In opposition to that, validation layers can involve heuristic rule-checkers, constraint solvers, AI playtesting agents, and even human-in-the-loop testing. The generation and validation can be repeated to enable the models to be updated according to the rejection rules resulting in more dependable and better-quality results (Karth & Smith, 2017).

The key idea of this content pipeline is the criticality of balance in AI-assisted PCG- using the creative power of generative models but inserting sufficient control structures to make the result usable and coherent. The pipeline does not remain unchanged, player feedbacks, and runtime learning, and model updates close a continuous circle of content enhancement.

4.2 Integration with Game Engines (Unity, Unreal Engine)

To be practical in use, generative AI needs to work well with game engines, which are the development and runtime environments. The two most popular engines, Unity and Unreal Engine, have also developed the ability to work with machine learning frameworks and provide solid interoperability with Python, C++, and external APIs, which in turn makes them the best engines to embed generative AI workflow.

E.g., the ML-Agents Toolkit of Unity allows developers to bridge the gap between Unity environments and reinforcement learning algorithms. Agents can be trained to create or exercise procedural levels, emulate player behaviours or learn ideal enemy positions. Offered in the toolkit is not only an interface, but reward functions, behavior trees, sensory inputs that can all be utilized in the generation of the dynamic content. Equally, Unity offers Barracuda inference engine-based runtime importation of external ML models at runtime, enabling the streaming or triggering of AI-generated assets at runtime (Short, Cook, & Smith, 2020).

Unreal Engine, which is a high-fidelity renderer, has plugins such as UnrealCV and direct access to C++ APIs which can call AI services in real time. As an example, a dialogue model executed on a Python backend can be used to drive NPC dialogue in Unreal via event-driven triggers, allowing fully dynamic and context-sensitive dialogue. Unreal blueprint system also enables level designers and writers to connect AI outputs to gameplay events using visual scripting, requiring no coding knowledge.

Some applications of AI in both engines include serving as a co-author, whereby it can generate terrain when the player has arrived at an unexplored area, scale the level difficulty depending on player actions, or generate dialogue choices depending on narrative conditions. Such integrations help in transforming the stagnant game world into a reactive ecosystem, whereby the content changes alongside the actions of the players. With the falling latency and hardware pinch, this sort of real-time generation will be even more prevalent in both AAA and indie game development.

The ongoing effort to standardize APIs, model-serving systems (such as TensorRT and ONNX) and cloud-hosted AI-services (such as Azure Cognitive Services or Google Vertex AI) also increase the scalability and availability of AI integration in game engines. Such technologies are not only rendering AI-driven PCG technically possible but experimentally effective.

4.3 Tools and Frameworks

In recent years, the space of tools and frameworks supporting generative AI in PCG has grown tremendously, providing developers with a broad choice of possibilities to initialise, train, serve and query generative models. They are tools that lie on a spectrum of simplicity to complex machine learning libraries and game design-specific systems that allow creators of all levels of experience and aspirations to achieve their creative ambitions.

On the base level, TensorFlow, PyTorch, and JAX are the main platforms to train and construct generative models. These libraries offer high-level abstractions over building and training neural networks, GPU computation, and distributed training - allowing developers to build GANs, transformers, and diffusion models with low-level control. Combined with libraries such as Hugging Face Transformers or Diffusers, developers can quickly prototype with already trained models, or train them on their own gamespecific domains, like fantasy story generation or environment texture synthesis (Yannakakis & Togelius, 2011).

To achieve integration and quick deployment, platforms such as RunwayML and Replicate offer low-code settings in which artists and designers may access generative models through user-friendly interfaces or by making API calls. These tools allow multimodal creation (text, image, audio) and especially will come in handy during prototyping stages. Developers are able to test various models, apply real time tests on their outputs and export assets to be used in Unity or unreal.

Another major innovation is Promethean AI - it is aimed specifically at 3D environment creation. It allows designers to create lifelike and thematically coherent sets with the help of AI-suggested recommendations of what can be asked by the narrative context or by user request. Promethean AI is an artificially intelligent creative assistant that can analyse scene composition and suggest elements such as furniture, lighting and architectural details within seconds, alleviating labor-intensive world-building processes (Touvron et al., 2023).

Charisma AI is a dialogue system, allowing writers to author branching or reactive dialogues with emotional context, memory, and motivation. It fills the gap between interactive storytelling and natural language processing and enables fluid character-driven experiences. Such tools as Inworld AI and Altered Studio are also entering the field, providing voice-driven AI NPCs capable of unscripted dialogue with the player.

Also in the category of enterprise tools, NVIDIA Omniverse provides collaborative AI-assisted pipelines to bigger studios. Omniverse enables AI to be incorporated into the game production scale with huge size and multiple users with support of USD (Universal Scene Description) and real-time physics simulation.

These tools create a growing ecosystem which is reducing the barrier of entry into AI-assisted game development. It could be a single developer applying RunwayML to generate concept art, or it could be a AAA studio with GANs deployed in Unreal generating levels, but the availability, customizability, and power of generative AI tools are only increasing - changing the very nature of game design and development (Liao, Liu, & Smed, 2021).

5. APPLICATIONS IN MODERN GAMES

5.1 Real-World Use Cases (Minecraft, No Man's Sky, AI Dungeon)

Procedural content generation has been used in many commercial games, indie games and experimental prototypes as an element of design that defines the player experience and challenges the limitations of what can be achieved with automated systems. Minecraft is probably one of the most well-known cases of procedural world generation. Terrain and structure generation systems are largely rule-based and deterministic, but because of the scale and diversity this allows, a huge modding community has arisen. These community made mods have also implemented generative adversarial networks (GANs) to accomplish things such as biome generation, custom textures, and terrain variance. Such attempts demonstrate that AI can also improve already known PCG systems by adding more elaborate patterns and different aesthetics (Kolve et al., 2017).

No Man s Sky is a game created by Hello Games, and it is a breakthrough in the world of procedural generation games, as its advanced algorithms create more than 18 quintillion planets. The planets differ largely, as each of them has a climate, topography, flora and fauna, and civilizations. The generation system of the game is less AI-generated and more rule-based and mathematical, but it proves the scalability and immersion potential of automated content generation. Procedural logic is the key to shaping the way the player feels when exploring, discovering, and never knowing what to expect next, which is a core part of the gameplay loop in many roguelikes and Metroidvanias, and it can do so with little to no handcrafted content per world.

AI Dungeon shifts the dialogue into the realm of generative AI in particular. The game is based on OpenAI GPT-2 and subsequently GPT-3, and players can type any action, thought, or dialogue, to which the system will generate coherent narrative progressions, reactions of the characters, and plot twists. Such interaction on this level is enabled by transformer-based models pretrained on big datasets. AI Dungeon is the first text-based RPG to feature emergent narrative construction, or an experience that is continuously evolving and player-driven, where no two stories are ever alike as they were in the older, fixed-branch text-based RPGs. It is an example of how AI can scale storytelling systems well beyond pre-scripted experiences, providing Creative freedom and emotional engagement that was cumbersome to achieve at scale earlier (Brown et al., 2020).

Collectively these games demonstrate the extent to which procedural and generative AI systems can be used, even in the generation of infinitely lived worlds, the generation of story environments, or the enabling of profound player agency. Another factor they encompass is the growing amalgamation of the difference between procedural approach and machine learning models so that they became the foundation of modern game development.

5.2 Story Generation and Dynamic Dialogue Systems

One of the important areas where generative AI made a radical shift in strokes is narrative. Conventionally, in-game narrations are based on manually-written texts and branching dialogue-tree style which are effective, but as a premise lacks general large-scale and flexibility. Because games are increasingly complex and involve player decision making, these fixed structures may limit immersion especially in open world and role playing games where the expectation is that the player can have varying consequences and play through their own story lines.

Since the emergence of generative models trained on transformers, such as GPT, BERT, and their fine-tuned versions, it has been possible to build conversations that are semantically rich, more contextual, and adaptive to what happens in the game. Such systems are able to change dialogues in real-time on the basis of past decision and character progression of a player as well as their moral orientation. As an example, an NPC may mention the player betraying his earlier kindness, mention previous kindness, or even have mood swings such as anger, gratitude or suspicions all without explicit scripting by a writer. Such responsiveness adds depth in a story and makes a game more natural and living when the player interact with each other (Harikrishna & Pandey, 2023).

High-end systems even support nonlinear quest generation: missions can be generated procedurally with regard to the current world situation, faction activity, or the individual objectives of the player. AI-generated lore, descriptions of the environment, and character motivation can be put into the quests, and they stay the same at multiple sessions. These types of models do not merely generate text, they model emergent narrative structure that changes and becomes more complete with time, creating the sense of a persistent and intelligent game world.

The models have persisted in receiving upgrades and as they do, they are increasingly getting used in applications by authors and narrative designers. AI can help to write quests, propose dialog options, or even check the affective appeal on the simulated player. Such characteristics do not only enhance productivity but also opens new creative opportunities, with storytelling a collaborative effort between human imagination and machine intelligence.

5.3 Adaptive Level Design and User-Centric Experiences

One more radical-impactful use of generative AI in contemporary games is the adaptive level design that creates environments and in-game attributes by means of the responses to the specification of the players. In contrast with a fixed level structure, AI-enhanced systems can adapt in real-time to information like player skill/playstyle/emotional reaction or history. This adaptive ability will make sure that players will never feel overwhelmed or bored and will always feel challenged.

People may customize game environments on the fly using various methods like reinforcement learning and player modeling. To take an example, in a roguelike dungeon crawler game, the setting and difficulty of the enemies would be modified in real time depending upon the amount of time it takes a player to clear previous areas or the number of times he or she has died. Likewise, in a first-person shooter, the AI could take note of the fact that the player will prefer staying unnoticed rather than to be offensive and control future maps in such a way on supporting sneaky paths and less noisy scenes (Tatar & Ali, 2018).

Such adaptation systems are not mechanical changes. AI could scan trends in the preferences of the players, their emotional reactions (through biometrics or behavior analytics), and choices about the story to tailor e.g. thematically or emotionally driven parts. In horse games, e.g. horror games, the system could pick up cues to stress (e.g. hesitation, erratic movement), and increase jump scaring, the intensity of the background music, or even lower lighting levels to increase the tension. On the other hand, when the system notices that a player is losing focus, it may resort to dramatic twists, plot hooks or visual information in order to draw players back to attention.

The outcome is an approach to design that is player-centric with everyone having a unique journey. Such systems will allow the introduction of individual storytelling, variable tempo, emotionally intelligent reaction AI with experience and responsive to human behavior. This type of interactivity is a departure of the one-size-fits-all design and represents the future where games are more of a responsive ecology than a pre-authored activity.

6. EVALUATION OF GENERATED GAME CONTENT

6.1 Metrics: Playability, Coherence, Diversity, Aesthetic Quality

The procedurally generated content is a special problem to evaluate, particularly the one generated by generative AI because it is non-deterministic and entirely dependent on the player. In contrast to the content created by hands, which can be reliably tested at least once, and then be fairly evaluated, the AI-created content can vary across sessions or respond to user input, or develop over time. Hence, its analysis should not focus only on its being right, but follows various levels of quality.

Playability is the most basic measure. No matter how new or eye-catchy the material is, it should be playable on the game engine and does not paralyze the game, on the contrary, it should not impede the matter of the game or impede control. In platformers, e.g. it might imply testing the accessibility of inaccessible platforms, dead-ends, or too-punishing enemy placement. Playability in narrative-based games implies that the resulting plot chains are logical and that the challenges are realizable without any doubts or misunderstandings. An automated check can be done such as simulated agents, or heuristic validators or test cases (Chen & Koltun, 2017).

Coherence is a reference to the structure of the created items in terms of the inner logic, theme, and tone of the game. A game taking place in a medieval world should not add in modern slang or cyberpunk technology out of nowhere without the game universe being a genre breaker in the first place. Coherence in the environment or levels implies architectural consistency, biome uniformity or style consistency in assets. The immersion can be described as a key element of emotional appeal in the games; this is made possible by coherence.

Another essential sign of content value is diversity in generative systems. Among the more general risks/dangers of neural models, especially those experiencing mode collapse (in GANs) or overfitting, is generating redundant or super-close outputs. Variety brings fun and selection so that there is no repetition of topics in one session. It plays a key role in a game that encourages replayability (e.g. roguelikes or sandbox games), instead of providing experiences that are overwhelmingly similar to previously played ones. The diversity of feature vectors may be quantified individually by comparing across outputs or determining a redundancy of patterns by clustering algorithms.

Lastly, aesthetic quality deals with the aesthetic on the looks, the sound and the fashioning attractiveness of content. The aesthetic quality is highly subjective, but it can be quantified in part by human judgment (e.g. preference testing), style classifier, or distance to known ground truth art styles. Generative models in music and sound design can be tested in terms of psychoacoustic characteristics or analysing rhythm. In case of visual components, the quality of images and the adherence to style can be evaluated using metrics like Fr 20018 researcher analysis of a variety of metrics to evaluate visual elements, such as Fr 20018 researcher analysis of a variety of metrics to evaluate visual elements, such as Fr Frechet Inception Distance (FID). Finally, both kind of algorithmic evaluation and human subjectivity should be in balance to obtain aesthetic performance entirely.

6.2 User-Centric Testing and Feedback Loops

Although automated testing proves to be priceless, it is not able to offer the colorful intuitiveness of a human-based assessment. To be sure that generated content meets the expectations of the real world, evokes emotional responses, developers should perform the structured user play tests where data must be collected both in quantitative and qualitative frames. During such tests, individuals play with the AI generated content in controlled environments and their actions, tastes as well as frustration are keenly monitored.

Such measures of engagement as average playing time, current level restart status, story progression completion stats and drop-off placements may be considered significant predictors of efficacy in the content. As an example, when people leave the same level at a particular point and regularly, there is a possibility of increased difficulty or an error in the layout design. To supplement these behavioral measures, surveys, interviews, and usability sessions can be used in order to get further indicators of how the players assess the creativity, believability, and emotional force of the generated materials. The responses will assist the designers in understanding the human element in the appreciation of enjoyment like the novelty, challenge, satisfaction, or immersion (Liapis, Yannakakis, & Togelius, 2013).

As a method of closing the loop of evaluation, some have been integrating learning on the basis of feedback; player preferences and ratings are used directly when generating future content. In reinforcement learning or user model systems the AI is optimized continuously on player reactions, and gets closer to target engagement rates with each iteration. This may be through direct voting systems, as in the case of AI Dungeon in which the user upvotes or downvotes sections of a story, or learning indirectly through behavioral monitoring. This type of models enables games to grow with their consumers, remaining fresh and up to speed over time. User feedback not only increases the quality but also develops a feeling of player agency, where the player feels he helps create the game world.

6.3 Benchmarking Against Human-Created Content

Perhaps the most illuminating test of AI-produced game content can be by testing it against that produced by the human designers. Such a benchmarking exercise may come in various forms including blind preference test where players are presented with two levels or story lines, one generated by an AI agent and another by a human agent and then asked to guess which one was done by whom. Their decisions and responses are essential information on the comparison between generative systems and conventional craftsmanship. A/B testing is another technique, in which some users will be randomly selected and will continue their way by seeing the human or the AI content and their engagement will be measured collectively.

The success of AI generated content or beating human-designed content ensures that AI is creatively viable. It shows, too, how these models can scale creativity, generating thousands of variations or environments or quests in the same time it would take humans to make a few. But it is not to make duplicates of the human products. Instead, the benchmarking should be around the unique powers of generative models, including variating at scale, flexing to the play style of the player, and the capacity to combine disparate things in new ways.

It is also crucial to see the complementary nature of AI in gaming development. A human creative mind should regard generative models not as the substitutes but as the enhancements of creativity. Although the number of iterations that AI may create is endless, humans are most likely to develop game vision, emotional conFigureuration, and Rafkin depth. It is not the ability of AI to produce results that rival human performance that is the real value of benchmarking; it is the demonstration of how AI can expand the possibilities of the creatively and operationally imaginable. Through such a paradigm, AI would be used as a force enhancer bringing teams to achieve more, discover more and invent quicker than ever before (Lucas & Runge, 2022).

7. CHALLENGES AND LIMITATIONS

7.1 Creativity vs. Randomness: Balancing Control

Balancing unlimited creativity and design control is one of the oldest issues in Procedural Content Generation (PCG) driven by AI. Generative models have the power to produce rich and surprising results, but exactly this aspect can produce text that is not structurally watertight, narratively fragmented, or even unplayable. When it comes to game design, when content has to fit within tight restrictions of player interaction, physics, game play and player progress, the more freedom you give the creators the more likely it is that the game will hurt itself.

To reduce such problems, programmers also put into practice hybrid approaches that integrate deep learning-based AI with the rule-based rule approach. The generative element leads to the generation of new or diverse content, whereas the rule-based layer applies logical, aesthetic and gameplay restrictions. This enables the system to be innovative without killing the main gameplay loop. Moreover, they can be used to condition modern generative models (based on thematic prompts, information about the behavior of players, or latent vector constraints) to generate outputs within certain parameters. As an example, when training on maps with level layout, they can be taught to create exclusively "_easy forest-themed maps_" or "_desert zones for real players_." Yet, the process of manually tuning those systems to the best possible balance of control and automation is a complicated, never-ending issue in aids to design (Oberlander & Salge, 2019).

7.2 Computational Constraints and Model Size

The clipping of generative AI into games does however involve having technical impediments. Among the prohibitive limitations, the computer requirement of state-of-the-art models, in particular those founded on deep neural networks such as transformers or diffusion models, must be mentioned. The models are very huge and demand high memory and processing to train and to be used during the inference. Although this might not be as problematic in the development context alongside high-end cloud infrastructure, bringing such models into the real-time gaming, it is particularly a problem on the consumer platform, in particular, Scalepedias on consoles, smartphones, or VR headsets.

Model optimization strategies are being increasingly resorted to by developers making real-time integration a possibility. Limits are imposed on memory and compute requirements using techniques such as lowering the precision of models used, less complex network designs, content being pre- computed during uncritical stages of game play etc. Generative AI in practice is currently mostly applied at a "design-time": Assets, stories or even levels are generated offline and imported into the game as static entities to be tested after the process. This reduces flexibility at the expense of performance. Although creating lightweight models and on-device inference continue becoming a research topic, generative AI constitutes a considerable hardware overhead that might constrain its use in smaller or mobile games.

7.3 Bias in Generated Content

One more issue of immediate importance is the ethical nature of AI-generated content. As these models are trained on thousands of corpora containing extant human-generated information, they learn and can output biases inherent in it. The forms in which such biases might be enacted in a game situation include roles of characters, Dialogue, procedural naming schemes and even Cultural expression. Without control, this will amount to an unconscious offending or exclusionary experience, particularly in games where storyline is important and games dispersed across different regions over the world.

There is a need to tackle these obstacles with some intention. The developers will have to spend resources on moral AI applications that extend beyond simply being correct. The proficiency points to curate training datasets, enforce content moderation filters, and create reinforcement learning loops with a penalty on biased or harmful outputs, all of which is crucial in terms of achieving fairness and inclusivity. Alongside, ethical review proceedings and cross-cultural testing have of lately played a bigger role in the validation of the generated content. The neglect of these issues poses a threat of reputation excepts, bans, and breach with player communities. Thus, ethical AI-generated content cannot be considered an optional layer of protection anymore but an essential design constituent of AI-enhanced games.

7.4 Intellectual Property and Ownership Issues

The issue of intellectual property (IP) about the content of AI has not been solved in most jurisdictions and is a possible threat to both developers and players. When the music or a character design or a story arc was generated by a model, there is confusion as to ownership of the content. This gets even more complicated when the generative model was already trained using copyrighted data- there is even a chance that some of its outputs might be deemed derivative works.

Practically, licences and terms of service that come with the model or platform tend to determine the rights of authors to AI-generated content. Different developers prefer to hold all rights over outputs designed based on their own training data, whereas others depend on the platforms-specific license that can limit redistribution and commercial use. What is also in question in the case of community-driven games, in which the players are co-creating content using embedded AI-tools, is who the creator is, the player or the publisher? The lack of legal criteria imposes on the studios the duty of defining ownership policies on a contractual basis, which is frequently the end-user license agreement or license to a development tool (Peng, Ma, & Zhang, 2022).

These IP questions will only be increasingly urgent as generative models become closer to the way content pipelines are run and especially in tools that enable procedural storytelling, music composition, or 3D asset generation. It will be essential to introduce established, transparent, fair, and enforceable IP frameworks to close the viability of AI-generated game content within such commercial environments as long as possible.

8. Future Directions and Research Opportunities

8.1 Explainable AI for Game Designers

The inner dynamics of generative models can look more like a black box as they grow more complicated; generating terrific outcomes but providing no insight into how and why specific choices were made. The uninterpretability may present an enormous challenge to the game designers as they should strike a balance between a lack of poured cement game and a lack of creativity in the game. Explainable AI (XAI) is a concept that tries to solve this problem, trying to supply some interpretable information on behavior of AI models, so that the developers get an idea and are then able to understand, analyze and do a better job at tuning generative output.

Regarding PCG, explainability makes it so that designers are able to understand the influence of different inputs, which could be prompts, parameters, or training data, on the output generated. As an example, in the transformer-based dialogue system, the attention heatmaps can be used to show that some part of the user input prompt triggered a specific response of a character and enable the writer to tighten up dialogue flows or tone. A comparable facility in the context of the visual generation with GANs or diffusion models would let the navigation of the latent space map how 2-D input vectors relate to the stylistic or structural variation indicated in the output. This freedom allows creators and game designers to change their content generation model with creative certainty and shifts the AI tool out of the black box to the open collaborator.

In addition, XAI can help in the ethics of its development because it shows possible biases or incoherence in the model. In the situation where designers could trace the source of an unwanted or inappropriate output they are in a better position to put in place safeguards or change the training data. Potential areas of future explainable PCG development might be real-time feedback subsystems, or visual dashboards that depict model behavior, and natural language interfaces where designers can ask models questions about their outputs, and have the model explain why it reached its conclusion. It is probable that explainability will be needed to allow high-level human oversight as the creative agency of AI increases.

8.2 Co-Creation Tools: Human-AI Collaboration in Game Design

Artificial intelligence is not something that will replace game developers but rather something that will collaborate with them in the future. Co-creation tools join the paradigm of collaboration between human designers and AI systems to perform creative tasks in iterative processes. The tools are not independent content generators, rather they are intelligent aids that may suggest, elaborate or refine content, dependent upon input by the designer. Their cooperation is dialogical: a designer could draw the map of a dungeon, and the AI would place in it the necessary rooms, enemies, and puzzles, according to the mechanics of the game or plot situations.

These tools essentially change how one creates. Their use facilitates quick brainstorming and testing of various design solutions and makes prototyping at high speed possible without requiring pain-staking construction of all the items. To look at an example, world-builder may create a core biome, and the AI offer variations that meet mood or genre requirements. The process is more fluid and flexible, as designers can approve a suggestion or disapprove it or simply go back to the previous iteration. Co-creation tools also enable a developer to think at a macro level by diminishing the amount of tedious work on scenes and assets, placing, balancing characters, or tiling terrain so that they may concentrate on the art, narrative, and affect.

Notably, these are democratizing game creation since they reduce the technicality of game creation to non-programmers or independent designers. Development tools can be approached by writers, artists, teachers, and even players in a more natural way. In future, co-creation interfaces can become a multimodal environment integrating voice control, sketching-based input and natural language feedback loops, making it possible to perfectly synchronize the human imagination and functionality with the machine aid. As the systems grow of age, the distinction between the tool and member of the team will persist to dissolve.

8.3 Towards Fully Autonomous Game Development

The idea of absentee game development (where game development is handled entirely by an autonomous system) remains somewhat theoretical, but artificial intelligences making their way into the multi-modal revolution are making it a more realistic possibility. The ability to process and generate in text, pictures, sound, and code suggests that end-to-end game generation could be possible, too, through AI. The thesis would be that with a relatively straightforward prompt (a type of game, a topic, or a one-sentence idea), a game would be created, with not only assets, rules, user interface design, sonic design, and even promotional content created by the AI.

This future may already be signalled by early tools, such as Natural-language-to-code translators such as OpenAI Codex, and tools such as DreamFusion that generate 3D assets based on just a text prompt. Connected to generative level design tools, character modelers, audio synthesis tools, and LLMs to dialogue or quest scripts, however, these technologies may become part of a pipeline capable of writing and publishing wholly playable games with a minimum of direct involvement by humans. It would transform the game development process to hobbyists, teachers, and small-scale developers so that they can build their games inexpensively in a short time.

Nevertheless with the move to independent development there is a possible gross miscalculation of quality control, originality, ethics checks, and artist motive. Games are not systems, they are experience, stories, and cultural artifacts. Total delegation of their design to machines can potentially represent a threat to emotional subtlety, theme, or societal responsibility. Thus, although AI has come to a stage where it can be automated, human entries in the form of curating, testing, and refinement should continue being part of the process.

8.4 AI Agents That Play and Design Games

The future frontier is the creation of AI agents not just generating content, but also playing with it and performing user experience evaluations to achieve a feedback loop of content generation and optimizing of user experience. Such agents are able to approximate player behavior, evaluate the challenging intensity of the levels and give real time experiences as to how play-friendly, interesting or frustrating particular aspects of the games are. As an example, an AI agent could notice that players are failing in one particular aspect and propose certain changes in level design or difficulty balancing.

They can be especially helpful in games which are extremely large, and/or open-ended games, where it is not efficient to perform the testing of all the possibilities by hand. The AI playtesters can quickly test thousands of variations of content, allowing the designers to dedicate their time to the most promising one. Other works look at meta-learning agents--AIs that not only play games but learn how to make better generators--itself. Based on retention data, behavioural models and trends, these agents evolve an iteration of PCG algorithms, giving rise to games that update and refine themselves with time.

In live-service or multiplayer games, such functionality may be expanded into real-time adaptation, with the AI agents observing live player data and rectifying or adding content in real-time -- proposing new quests, to re-balancing loot systems, or in some cases changing AI behaviours to remain challenging and fun. The addition of these agents symbolizes a change towards dynamic game design, as opposed to more game design in the form of reactive growing worlds that learn and evolve with its users.

9. CASE STUDIES

9.1 Case Study: Narrative Generation in AI Dungeon

AI Dungeon is a paradigm-shift interaction story as it relies on transformer-based generative models and especially OpenAI GPT-2 and GPT-3. Its story development can be effectively compared to the choice-based format of traditional RPGs or visual novels, where storylines are pre-scripted and dialogue accessed via trees, as opposed to having potentially limitless story development due to the natural language generation component of AI Dungeon. Players start with a cue to act and exploit the game world by typing commands on the background of which the AI compiles the dynamic sceneries, events, and conversations in real time.

The most stunning aspect of AI Dungeon is that it is able to not only respond to the input by the player, but actually produce responses that have the elements of creativity, world-building, and contextual memory. system provides a feeling of group learning, whereby the player as well as the AI model create the story together. It encourages genre versatility, including fantasy and sci-fi, horror, and mystery, and it can transform freely in terms of tonality and speed in accordance with the choices of the player (RunwayML, 2023).

Nevertheless, there are also major issues of generative AI in games revealed by AI Dungeon. The system may in certain instances produce logically inappropriate or inconsistent contents especially where the prompt content is vague or adversarial. This has been addressed by developers through safety filters, moderation mechanisms and precise models but it demonstrates the need of ethical safeguards and model constraints in storytelling models relying on AI. Nevertheless, AI Dungeon remains a milestone in the demonstration of how it is possible to incorporate language models into interactive systems in the development of emergent storytelling interactions which are not limited in advance.

9.2 Case Study: Visual Level Generation with GANs

Generative Adversarial Networks (GANs), procedural level generation has become the area of interest in academic and independent game development circles alike. One of the most prominent ones is the use of GANs in Super Mario Bros-style level generation. Datasets of already created Mario levels were accumulated, and GAN models were trained to obtain the spatial location of tiles, structure of enemy placements, and platforms. After being trained, the GAN potentially would be able to create completely original levels, yet ones that would be able to coincide with the design philosophy and difficulty of the originals.

Among the innovations in the study is the fact that the generated levels were not just tested on the basis of visual similarity but also on the parameter of playability based on the use of simulation based agents or player path validation. The agents made sure that the levels were achievable, had the right pace and did not present insurmountable challenges. Refinement of the generated output was done using post-processing operations, namely: constraint enforcement or rule-based editing when they are required (Unity Technologies, 2022).

The case indicates the GANs to be able to speed up the cycle of content developments, but with respect to the gameplay logic. It also suggests that data quality of the training should matter - what GAN has learned to date, is also the limit of its creating, so the diversity of training data has a direct impact on creativity. Besides, the utility of the system is more congruent with the utilization of interpretability tools or manipulation of latent space, so the designers can dynamically explore variations and tune difficulty. The future possibilities in GANs in the generation of procedural levels grows as GANs grow, and when combined with reinforcement learning or semantic tagging.

9.3 Case Study: Co-Design Tools for Indie Game Developers

Co-design tools run by generative AI have greatly contributed to democratizing game development. Such tools as Promethean AI or RunwayML can provide designers with smart support by automating repetitive creation processes and making context-specific recommendations. An example would be Promethean AI, an assistant to building worlds in a virtual world, assisting artists use realistic 3D designs. It breaks down the geographical design of scene and proposes props, architecture style and positioning of objects from the prompt of designers and frees them the time and concentration of primitive balance of story and aesthetics.

However, RunwayML becomes a general AI toolkit dedicated to creative people. It offers a simple interface to pre-trained generative models (GANs, LLMs, diffusion) to use image synthesis, video editing, voice cloning, and many other tasks. As applied in the case of indie game development, these tools can be utilized in creating concept art, prototyping character animation, or even trying out how various art styles would appear when it is applied to the various game assets. RunwayML removed the technical boundary to allow smaller studios or individual software developers who lack extensive knowledge of machine learning to find a technical advantage (Promethean AI, 2023).

This means a new epoch in the domain of AI-assisted creativity, when the role of the developer switches to functions of oversight and overarching creative guidance. They enable leaner, iterative, exploratory, and agile design processes. Moreover the AI co-design tools will support inclusivity in designing the games as users will not have to be multidisciplinary or work in technical backgrounds to design games, and will instead be able to perform the work with minimal learning experience (writers, artists or educators can develop their games through that).

Going forward, these tools will be succeeded, in due time, by full-blown systems of collaboration (augmenting explainable AI and multi-modal) interaction in which developers converse with AI collaborators by means of sketches or speech or realtime feedback loops. The co-design systems do not only act as a productivity tool, however, they constitute a transformation in the process of creation itself, an introduction of machine intelligence to human intent.

10. CONCLUSION

The future use of generative AI in Procedural Content Generation promises to be one of the milestones in the history of game design. A way to circumvent technical constraints has evolved into a complex design process that can revolutionise the way games are conceived, constructed and played. Due to the introduction of formulations such as GANs, transformers and diffusion-based models, PCG has become not only more algorithmic but highly data-driven and creative. Such systems do not simply automate the content but generate new artistic, narrative and structural possibilities that adapt to and anticipate both the behavior of the players and the intention of the designer.

In this chapter, we have covered the technology basis, architecture of the work of generative AI as well as the application in PCG in the real world. We have studied how it can be used to create cohering narratives, adaptive environments and responsive systems and how it has been integrated with contemporary game engines and development pipelines. Meanwhile, we also critically evaluated such shortcomings as the control aspect, the cost in computational terms, ethical considerations and legal systems and advised restraint and careful application.

In future, then, the use of AI in game creation may evolve further, as it morphs into a co-worker of its creators--a co-author of their work. The future fields of explainable AI, federated design systems and autonomous game generation seem to point towards a direction of creativity that would no longer solely be based in human minds, but instead are co-created by intelligent systems. It is an exciting new paradigm, both in terms of more variable ways to play games as well as democratizing the process of game creation as well. It is not only a matter of the near future, but the era of generative games is already dawning.

REFERENCES

Brown, T., Mann, B., & Ryder, N.. (2020). Language Models are Few-Shot Learners. *Advances in Neural Information Processing Systems*, *33*, 1877–1901.

Chen, X., & Koltun, V. (2017). Photographic Image Synthesis with Cascaded Refinement Networks. *Proceedings of the IEEE International Conference on Computer Vision*. DOI: 10.1109/ICCV.2017.168

Compton, K., & Mateas, M. (2006). Procedural Level Design for Platform Games. *Proceedings of the 2nd AIIDE Conference*.

Gisselbrecht, T., Bontrager, P., Togelius, J., & Hoover, A. K. (2019). Learning Level Design with Generative Adversarial Networks. *IEEE Conference on Games (CoG)*.

Goodfellow, I., Pouget-Abadie, J., Mirza, M., Xu, B., Warde-Farley, D., Ozair, S., & Bengio, Y. (2014). Generative Adversarial Nets. *Advances in Neural Information Processing Systems*, ●●●, 27.

Guzdial, M., & Riedl, M. (2016). Game Engine Learning from Video. *Proceedings of the 2016 International Conference on the Foundations of Digital Games*.

Harikrishna, R., & Pandey, S. (2023). Game Level Design Automation Using Deep Reinforcement Learning. *Expert Systems with Applications*, *213*, 119157.

Johnson, L., Yannakakis, G. N., & Togelius, J. (2010). Cellular Automata for Real-Time Generation of Infinite Cave Levels. *Proceedings of the 2010 Workshop on Procedural Content Generation in Games*. DOI: 10.1145/1814256.1814266

Karth, I., & Smith, A. M. (2017). Addressing the Fundamental Tension of PCGML with Discriminative Learning. *Proceedings of the 12th International Conference on the Foundations of Digital Games*.

Kolve, E., Mottaghi, R., Gordon, D., Zhu, Y., Gupta, A., & Farhadi, A. (2017). AI2-THOR: An Interactive 3D Environment for Visual AI. arXiv preprint arXiv:1712.05474.

Liao, K., Liu, L., & Smed, J. (2021). GAN-based Procedural Content Generation: A Survey. *Multimedia Tools and Applications*, *80*, 24185–24221.

Liapis, A., Yannakakis, G. N., & Togelius, J. (2013). Sentient Sketchbook: Computer-Aided Game Level Authoring. *Proceedings of the 8th International Conference on the Foundations of Digital Games*.

Lucas, M., & Runge, J. (2022). Ethical Risks of AI-Generated Game Content: Bias, Appropriation, and Moderation. *Games and Culture*, *17*(5), 652–670.

Lucas, S. M., Liu, J., Kendall, G., & Togelius, J. (2021). *AI and Games: A Handbook for Practitioners*. Springer.

Oberlander, J., & Salge, C. (2019). Evolutionary Algorithms for Procedural Story Generation. *IEEE Transactions on Games*, *11*(2), 157–166.

Peng, Y., Ma, Y., & Zhang, J. (2022). A Review of Transformer-Based Models for Procedural Narrative Generation. *Artificial Intelligence Review*, *55*(6), 4937–4971. PMID: 35002010

Promethean, A. I. (2023). The AI Assistant for 3D World Building. [Online]. Available: https://prometheanai.com

Radford, A., Wu, J., Child, R., Luan, D., Amodei, D., & Sutskever, I. (2019). Language Models are Unsupervised Multitask Learners. *OpenAI Blog*, *1*(8), 9.

Risi, S., & Togelius, J. (2020). Increasing Generality in Machine Learning through Procedural Content Generation. *Nature Machine Intelligence*, *2*(8), 428–436. DOI: 10.1038/s42256-020-0208-z

Roohi, N., & Bidarra, R. (2021). Explainable AI for Game Design: A Review. *Entertainment Computing*, *37*, 100414.

Runway, M. L. (2023). AI for Creatives: Tools and Use Cases. [Online]. Available: https://runwayml.com

Sarkar, A., Momennejad, I., & Lake, B. M. (2023). Generative Agents: Interactive Simulacra of Human Behavior. arXiv preprint arXiv:2304.03442.

Short, E., Cook, M., & Smith, A. M. (2020). Procedural Generation of Video Game Levels Using Evolutionary Algorithms. *ACM Transactions on Multimedia Computing Communications and Applications*, *16*(1s), 1–20.

Silver, D., Schrittwieser, J., Simonyan, K., Antonoglou, I., Huang, A., Guez, A., Hubert, T., Baker, L., Lai, M., Bolton, A., Chen, Y., Lillicrap, T., Hui, F., Sifre, L., van den Driessche, G., Graepel, T., & Hassabis, D. (2017). Mastering the Game of Go without Human Knowledge. *Nature*, *550*(7676), 354–359. DOI: 10.1038/nature24270 PMID: 29052630

Summerville, A., Snodgrass, S., Guzdial, M., Holmgård, C., Hoover, A. K., Isaksen, A., Nealen, A., & Togelius, J. (2018). Procedural Content Generation via Machine Learning (PCGML). *IEEE Transactions on Games*, *10*(3), 257–270. DOI: 10.1109/TG.2018.2846639

Tatar, S., & Ali, A. (2018). Evaluating Procedural Generation Systems for Game Design. *Entertainment Computing*, *26*, 56–64.

Touvron, H., Lavril, T., Izacard, G., ... (2023). LLaMA: Open and Efficient Foundation Language Models. arXiv preprint arXiv:2302.13971.

Unity Technologies. (2022). ML-Agents Toolkit: Using Reinforcement Learning in Unity Games. [Online]. Available: https://github.com/Unity-Technologies/ml-agents

Yang, G., Wang, J., Zhang, Y., Tang, Y., & Cui, S. (2023). A Survey of Diffusion Models in Generative AI. arXiv preprint arXiv:2307.09004.

Yannakakis, G. N., & Togelius, J. (2011). Experience-Driven Procedural Content Generation. *IEEE Transactions on Affective Computing*, *2*(3), 147–161. DOI: 10.1109/T-AFFC.2011.6

Chapter 8
Procedural Generation and Adaptive Gameplay:
The Role of AI and Generative AI in Contemporary Game Development

Aparajita Biswal
https://orcid.org/0000-0002-4598-3691
Parul Institute of Engineering & Technology, Parul University, Vadodara, India

Khyati Zalawadia
https://orcid.org/0000-0002-7033-1740
Parul Institute of Engineering & Technology, Parul University, Vadodara, India

Kush Bhushanwar
https://orcid.org/0009-0008-4868-5703
Parul Institute of Engineering & Technology, Parul University, Vadodara, India

Prangya Parimita Pradhan
Centurion University of Technology and Management, India

Parag Gurdharbhai Paija
B.H. Gardi College of Engineering and Technology, India

Syed Ibad Ali
https://orcid.org/0000-0001-6312-6768
Parul Institute of Engineering and Technology, Parul University, Vadodara, India

ABSTRACT

Artificial intelligence (AI) and generative artificial intelligence (GI) are revolutionizing contemporary game development through the facilitation of adaptive gameplay, procedural content production, and intricate narrative structures. AI-driven solutions provide real-time responses to player inputs, hence fostering dynamic and evolving gaming experiences, in contrast to traditional game design, which relies on prescripted procedures and static environments. These technologies equip developers

DOI: 10.4018/979-8-3373-4637-3.ch008

ht © 2026, IGI Global Scientific Publishing. Copying or distributing in print or electronic forms without written permission of IGI Global Scientific Publishing is prohibited. Use of this chapter to generative artificial intelligence (AI) technologies is expressly prohibited. The publisher reserves all rights to license its use for generative AI training and machine learning model development.

with innovative tools to create immersive, tailored, and intelligent gaming environments, ultimately revolutionizing the processes of game development, gameplay, and user experience. Procedural content generation, which enables developers to produce extensive, dynamic environments with no human involvement, is one of the most potent applications of artificial intelligence in gaming.

INTRODUCTION

The emergence of generative artificial intelligence in game creation is one of the most intriguing and contentious technological breakthroughs of recent years. This powerful technology has the potential to revolutionize several aspects of game creation, from coding to graphics and beyond. This paper will examine the impact of generative artificial intelligence on game creation, the associated challenges, and how creators could utilize automation tools to navigate this emerging landscape. Artificial Intelligence-Driven Procedural Content Generation Procedural content creation (PCG) in game development currently offers novel potential due to generative artificial intelligence. Generative artificial intelligence systems are advancing towards the creation of realistic environments, 3D models, landscapes, novel quests and levels, and stunning visual effects, although currently excelling in text and static 2D picture production. While Large Language Models (LLMs) are now prominent, not all generative artificial intelligence systems are powered by LLMs. Contemporary PCG employs several artificial intelligence techniques, including alternative machine learning approaches and deep neural networks, among others. These technologies enable the creation of creative and diverse content applicable in gaming, art, music, and other domains. PCG techniques, primarily founded on the analysis of extensive text data to generate novel content, depend on LLMs. Nonetheless, these technologies remain very nascent and cannot supplant human brain and creativity. While technology undoubtedly enhances and assists the creative process, it is ultimately individuals that determine the course of action and actualize the content. Artificial intelligence-driven PCG should be seen as a tool rather than a substitute for human producers. Automating Redundant Programming Tasks Generative artificial intelligence is also facilitating the automation of monotonous programming tasks, in addition to visual and content production. Artificial intelligence-driven code generation tools are accelerating development by managing mundane and time-intensive coding tasks. Some predictive code generation systems may propose entire lines or blocks of code, while others provide automatic bug detection and remediation, so not only identifying potential issues but also recommending appropriate fixes, significantly expediting the coding process. This enables designers to focus on more artistic and complex aspects of game development, hence generating increasingly innovative and captivating gaming experiences. Nevertheless, it appears that these tools are increasingly beneficial with the frequency of adherence to a certain coding methodology. In other words, they are proficient for the programming issues that several developers have previously faced and disseminated online. The efficacy of the LLM-driven code generation approach diminishes as the originality of the work increases.

Quality Assurance Automation in the Era of Artificial Intelligence

Generative artificial intelligence offers significant opportunities for quality assurance (QA) while also introducing new challenges. Due to the proliferation of AI-generated code and content, traditional quality assurance methods are no longer applicable. A generative artificial intelligence system may provide either generic or potentially erroneous and unplayable output. From little Match-3 puzzle games to extensive multiplayer games, automating key QA chores has become essential for thoroughly testing all feasible scenarios and validating AI outputs when modifications are made to code and content. Two primary domains of functional testing increasingly emphasize the automation of gaming testing. Commencing with quality assurance, they assess functionality. The second pertains especially to game design. They want amusement and equilibrium. In other words, "how does it function?" or "does it operate as desired?" ensures engaging and fair player experiences.

Fostering confidence via transparency and regulation Developers must trust both the source material and intellectual property rights, as well as the direct outputs produced by generative artificial intelligence, to ensure it provides genuine value without infringing on others' intellectual property. Concerning the safeguarding of intellectual property—such as images or narratives generated wholly or predominantly by generative artificial intelligence—numerous unsolved questions persist about their potentialities. Ensuring creative control and aligning artificial intelligence with the game's objectives need transparency and oversight. The integration of human judgment with automated support in a hybrid model mitigates risks and optimizes outcomes. Industry Benchmark: Valve's New Policy and Strategic Direction Forward Recognizing the necessity for transparency, Valve has revised its disclosure standards for AI-driven games. This move creates a benchmark for the sector and underscores the significance of collaboration between developers and platform holders to formulate standards for openness and quality. The establishment of best practices will facilitate collaboration and ensure that games employing artificial intelligence meet regulatory requirements and player expectations. Developing for Generative Games: Future Prospects While generative artificial intelligence holds significant potential for game development, optimization is imperative. Developers must strive for efficient, player-centric programming that maximizes the benefits of generative artificial intelligence while mitigating any risks. Artificial intelligence provides a dimension of creative freedom by generating substantial content that individuals may not have conceived themselves. Although certain aspects are commendable and others are abysmal, divergent perspectives may yield innovative and imaginative designs and narratives that contest established norms. Developers may cultivate a future in which generative artificial intelligence enhances creativity for a new generation of exceptional gaming experiences by adopting automation technologies, promoting transparency, and collaborating with industry stakeholders. Generative AI will increasingly gain significance as the landscape of game development evolves. Developers may unlock new realms of creativity and efficiency through the utilization of artificial intelligence and the implementation of effective strategies, therefore facilitating the provision of highly inventive games to players globally. Generative artificial intelligence is revolutionizing gaming and fostering innovation and creativity inside the industry. Whether via procedurally generated content, AI-generated narratives, or the reimagining of game design and user experience, it heralds a transformation unprecedented in the industry. This article examines the transformative potential of generative artificial intelligence in gaming, focusing on its impact on game mechanics, ethical considerations, and future prospects, to explore how game developers may leverage this technology for the next generation of gaming.

What is generative artificial intelligence in gaming? Generative artificial intelligence is designed specifically for creativity and content generation, rather than strictly adhering to established protocols. Generative artificial intelligence automates several aspects of game design, including environment, character, story, and music creation, therefore augmenting the immersive and interactive qualities of games.

The Impact of Generative AI on Gaming

The gaming industry has been significantly transformed by generative artificial intelligence mostly for the following reasons: Generative artificial intelligence can rapidly create diverse gaming environments and scenarios, therefore providing a dynamic gameplay experience that adapts to players' actions and preferences. Analyzing player activity enables generative artificial intelligence to produce unique experiences tailored to individual preferences, encompassing varying levels of difficulty and information suited to their style. This increased personalization leads to more engagement and satisfaction.

LITERATURE SURVEY

The integration of generative artificial intelligence (GAI) with creative industries, particularly in game development, has revolutionized digital environment design, story creation, and interactive systems. Through deep learning, subject modeling, and natural language processing, GAI significantly alters procedural production, automation, and human-machine creative collaboration.

The advancement of distributed semantic representations and contextual embeddings has propelled the growth of generative artificial intelligence. Top2Vec, created by Angelov (2020), employs unsupervised document embedding for topic modeling, effectively encapsulating the semantic structure of material in alignment with the objectives of generative storytelling in games. Bianchi, Terragni, and Hovy (2021) demonstrated that pre-training with contextualized embeddings significantly enhances coherence in generated material, an essential capability for good gaming narratives and conversational systems.

Bahroun et al. (2023) emphasized the capacity of Generative Artificial Intelligence (GAI) to automate and customize content in educational settings, a finding that is equally relevant to gaming, as game environments, missions, and settings are dynamically generated to meet user requirements. The applications of GAI demonstrate its role not just as a content creation tool but also as an ally in experience design.

The utilization of GAI in code generation has significantly reduced the human effort needed for repetitive programming tasks. ProcessGPT, created by Beheshti et al. (2023), use generative models to tackle business process management. Comparable artificial intelligence methodologies propose code completions, game loop optimization, and automated debugging in gaming, so allowing developers to focus on more sophisticated innovation.

Pattanaik et al. (2023) noted that these systems operate optimally when executed according to deliberate strategies or established methodologies. This constraint is critical in game development, as innovative gameplay approaches and experimental logic may diverge from the datasets employed to train these models, so diminishing their efficacy. The proliferation of GAI in creative domains raises significant ethical and legal concerns. Andrews et al. (2023) articulated ethical considerations about the utilization of human-centric data, underscoring the necessity of consent, fairness, and responsibility—principles pertinent to character and environment creation in games. Alsharhan, Al-Emran, and Shaalan (2023) emphasized the need of transparency and intellectual property (IP) management in artificial intelligence systems, hence advocating for regulation in the development of AI-generated game content. The responses of the gaming industry to these concerns reflect them. For instance, Valve's policy alteration requiring developers to disclose AI-generated content aligns with broader demands for ethical AI implementation. Moreover, generative artificial intelligence is increasingly contributing to the automation of Quality Assurance (QA) operations. As the intricacy of AI-generated content increases, traditional quality assurance methods have become inadequate. Liu (2021) emphasized the necessity of intelligent feedback loops in education—a notion that parallels quality assurance in gaming, where user interaction data can be utilized to identify deficiencies and enhance user experience.

The automation of functional and experiential assessment mirrors tactics employed in other domains. Atzeni, Bacciu, Mazzei, and Prencipe (2022) investigated the integration of machine learning with network systems, demonstrating how topic modeling and anomaly detection approaches may be used for software quality assurance and game testing procedures. Analyzing player feedback and conduct enables GAI to customize content. Kumar, Singh, and Bhardwaj (2022) utilized natural language processing to extract emotion and actionable feedback from educational settings, hence highlighting its potential applications in games to align with player preferences.

Kwon and Kim (2021) demonstrated the implementation of predictive analytics in retention strategies by advocating for proactive systems grounded in behavioral data. When applied to game design, these approaches enable artificial intelligence to generate levels, obstacles, and narratives tailored to each player's style and skill level, therefore enhancing engagement and pleasure.

Generative models are increasingly regarded as collaborative instruments rather than replacements for human creativity. Aziz and Dowling (2019) assert that artificial intelligence enhances creativity by automating monotonous jobs, hence liberating artists to explore more abstract or innovative avenues. Kraft and Papay (2014) present data supporting the notion that professional environments conducive to experimentation and feedback yield superior outcomes—an insight pertinent to game development firms where hybrid human–AI methodologies may thrive. Kraft, Marinell, and Yee (2018) emphasized the importance of organizational context in promoting innovation and suggested that well-structured, supportive workplaces enhance the benefits of artificial intelligence. Despite its significant promise, GAI remains an emerging field with several unresolved issues. Alsharhan et al. (2023) have established a multi-faceted research agenda encompassing stakeholder collaboration, transparency, and trust. In gaming, the intersection of AI-driven development, user-generated content, platform limitations, and creative direction presents critical difficulties. The future likely entails hybrid intelligence systems in which artificial intelligence serves as a creative and technical aid under human supervision. To ensure responsible innovation, these platforms will require robust review processes, intellectual property legislation, and ethical standards (Andrews et al., 2023; Bahroun et al., 2023). The literature indicates that generative artificial intelligence is poised to revolutionize the technological and creative benchmarks of game creation. GAI is enhancing methods and re-evaluating the conceptualization and development of digital games, encompassing procedural content generation, programming automation, quality assurance, personalization, and ethics. Its efficacy, however, relies on diligent implementation, transparency, and collaborative engagement between intelligent systems and human creators.

RESEARCH METHODOLOGY

Generative artificial intelligence optimizes content development, enabling developers to concentrate on more inventive elements. The ability of AI to automatically produce assets and facilitate game testing leads to expedited development and decreased costs. Progression of Innovation and Gaming The gaming business has progressed from rudimentary 2D games to vast, immersive 3D settings. The shift to 3D graphics and virtual reality represented a substantial progression, allowing realistic landscapes and enhanced interactions. Mobile gaming has significantly broadened the industry by allowing millions of users globally to access games. The evolution of game development is set to revolutionize creativity and improve user engagement as artificial intelligence and augmented reality advance. These technology breakthroughs are broadening the boundaries of practicality and generating new prospects for more customized, interactive, and immersive gaming experiences. The gaming industry is transforming owing to innovative innovations that influence its future.

Principles of Generative AI Generative artificial intelligence creates sophisticated techniques and models that yield innovative representations of existing data. It has revolutionized several domains, particularly in gaming, where varied experiences may be generated. Generative artificial intelligence functions via algorithms, models, and data.

Thorough data analysis enables the development of generative artificial intelligence models via pattern detection and association establishment. These models are often taught by unsupervised or semi-supervised learning methods, enabling them to derive information from unlabeled data. The models utilize a loss function that quantifies the difference between predicted and actual outcomes, therefore minimizing the discrepancy and yielding more accurate findings. Deep learning architectures modeled after human brain synapses enable neural networks to identify intricate patterns in data. Training sets may include text, graphics, audio, and video, among other types. The model's output is profoundly influenced by the variety and caliber of these sources. Common architectures comprise autoregressive models, Generative Adversarial Networks (GANs), and Variational Autoencoders (VAEs). Each has unique advantages and disadvantages depending on its use. Utilizations of

Generative AI in the Gaming Industry Generative artificial intelligence (Generative AI) may captivate a player and augment creativity through advanced algorithms. A few of common variants include: Text-to-Image Generation is an artificial intelligence model that converts textual descriptions into visual representations. Employed in the game business, it produces dynamic assets, character designs, environments, and conceptual visuals. By rapidly conceptualizing and refining ideas, this aids game creators in expediting creative processes, hence producing more immersive game worlds and experiences for players.

Procedural Content Generation (PCG) is the method by which content, whether levels, maps, or graphics, is generated autonomously without human involvement. Generative artificial intelligence creates dynamic and varied gaming worlds and experiences. Producing diverse content allows developers to provide players personalized experiences, hence enhancing engagement and retention. Generative artificial intelligence creates dynamic narratives that alter in real-time based on player decisions. This fosters a more immersive experience wherein each run is unique and significant.

Figure 1. The incorporation of generative artificial intelligence (AI) into the game development process

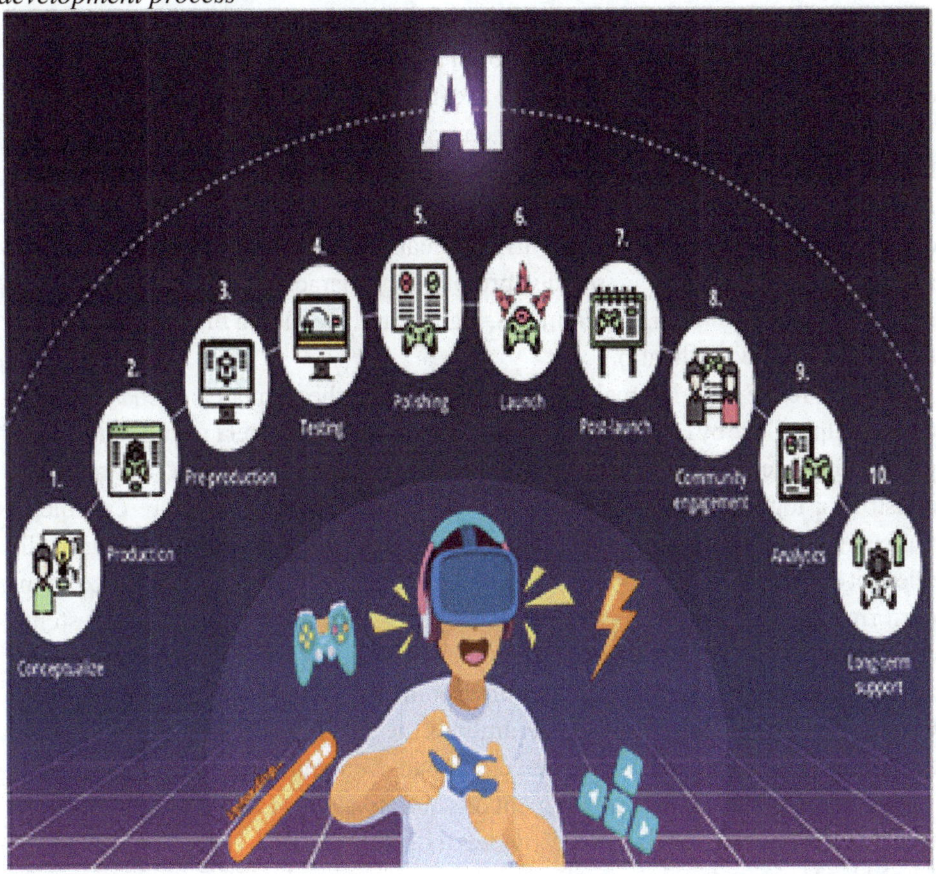

The integration of generative artificial intelligence (AI) into the game development pipeline represents one of the most profound and transformative evolutions in the digital entertainment industry. The block diagram provided encapsulates this paradigm shift with remarkable clarity, offering a systematic view of how cutting-edge AI models are now embedded into various stages of the game creation lifecycle. At its foundation, the process begins with the conceptualization phase, where human-centric design principles and creative ideation play a pivotal role. Game design requirements—articulated through high-level constructs such as narrative architecture, gameplay mechanics, thematic motifs, environmental aesthetics, and level progression logic—serve as the initial inputs into the generative system. These requirements are often supplemented with structured or unstructured prompts, derived from either natural language input or domain-specific scripting, enabling AI models to interpret, infer, and generate multimodal content aligned with the intended artistic and gameplay vision.

At the core of this transformative pipeline lies an ensemble of specialized generative AI architectures that are each tailored to address different modalities of game content. Among these, diffusion-based text-to-image models such as Stable Diffusion, MidJourney, and DALL·E 3 have emerged as powerful tools for synthesizing high-resolution, stylistically coherent visual assets from descriptive prompts. These models employ latent space denoising processes to iteratively construct images that capture the semantic richness and artistic nuance of the input text. Such models are particularly valuable in rapidly prototyping character designs, environment concepts, props, and interface elements, significantly reducing the turnaround time from ideation to visualization.

Parallel to the visual domain, generative code synthesis models such as OpenAI Codex, AlphaCode by DeepMind, and Amazon's CodeWhisperer leverage large-scale pretraining on code repositories to facilitate automated generation of programming constructs, logic sequences, and gameplay scripts. These models are capable of translating natural language instructions into syntactically correct and semantically relevant code, enabling developers to automate mundane coding tasks, optimize game performance routines, or implement game mechanics such as inventory systems, combat logic, and AI behaviors without manual scripting. The integration of these models into integrated development environments (IDEs) such as Visual Studio Code and JetBrains Rider further streamlines the development process by offering real-time code suggestions, error detection, and even unit test generation.

Equally pivotal is the deployment of narrative generation models built on transformer-based large language models (LLMs) such as GPT-4, Claude, and LLaMA. These systems have demonstrated exceptional proficiency in crafting interactive narratives, dynamic dialogues, and contextual storytelling that adapt to player choices and game states. By modeling long-range dependencies in text, these LLMs enable the creation of non-linear story arcs, richly characterized NPCs (non-player characters), and procedurally generated quests that contribute to heightened player immersion. The contextual awareness and adaptive capabilities of these models mean that game narratives are no longer static or pre-scripted but evolve dynamically in response to user interactions, thereby personalizing the gameplay experience at scale.

Complementing the visual, code, and narrative modalities is the integration of neural audio synthesis systems such as Jukebox by OpenAI, Google's AudioLM, and Meta's AudioCraft. These models are capable of generating ambient soundscapes, background music, and even character voiceovers that are stylistically and contextually aligned with the game environment. Leveraging techniques from generative adversarial networks (GANs), variational autoencoders (VAEs), and transformer-based models, these tools produce high-fidelity audio that enhances the sensory and emotional depth of digital games. Whether it is simulating the rustling of leaves in a procedurally generated forest, the crescendo of battle music during combat, or the nuanced inflection of a character's voice during dialogue, AI-generated audio adds a layer of realism and responsiveness that traditional methods struggle to achieve.

Once generated, the multimodal outputs—be it images, scripts, narratives, or audio assets—are seamlessly integrated into real-time development environments such as Unity, Unreal Engine, or Godot. These engines, which serve as the backbone of game execution, are increasingly augmented with plugins and extensions that support AI-generated content ingestion, asset management, and real-time rendering. This interoperability between generative models and game engines accelerates the iterative development cycle, allowing developers to preview, test, and deploy AI-generated elements with minimal friction. Moreover, AI can assist in optimizing asset performance across platforms by automatically adjusting textures, mesh densities, and sound formats to suit target device capabilities.

A critical phase that follows the initial content generation is human review and curation—a human-in-the-loop mechanism that ensures creative direction, quality control, and ethical compliance. Despite the capabilities of generative AI, the subjective dimensions of artistic judgment, emotional resonance, and cultural sensitivity require human oversight. Designers and developers evaluate the coherence, originality, and narrative alignment of AI outputs, making refinements or discarding elements that do not meet the production standards. This collaborative interface between human creativity and machine intelligence exemplifies the principle of co-creation, where AI serves as a powerful tool to amplify rather than replace human ingenuity.

The diagram further illustrates the testing and deployment phase, where compiled game builds are subjected to rigorous quality assurance (QA) processes. Here too, AI plays a critical role. Reinforcement learning agents and simulation-based models can emulate player behavior to test edge cases, uncover hidden bugs, and assess gameplay balance. For example, AI agents can be trained to navigate through levels, identify collision errors, or detect exploitative strategies that could undermine game integrity. Additionally, AI can assist in A/B testing by analyzing player feedback and telemetry data to refine game mechanics, user interfaces, and monetization strategies post-launch.

What distinguishes this AI-driven pipeline is its iterative nature, represented by feedback loops that inform and refine subsequent rounds of generation. For instance, if AI-generated assets fail to align with the intended emotional tone or gameplay mechanics, designers can fine-tune their prompts or retrain models using reinforced datasets. This continuous feedback mechanism supports an agile development approach where prototyping, testing, and deployment are harmonized in near real-time. Advanced prompt engineering techniques, such as few-shot or chain-of-thought prompting, can be employed to guide model behavior more precisely, ensuring outputs that are not only syntactically accurate but contextually rich and gameplay-appropriate.

Beyond the technical integration, the diagram also draws attention to the multifaceted ethical, legal, and operational considerations that arise from the adoption of generative AI in game development. Data provenance and intellectual property (IP) rights pose significant challenges, especially when models are trained on copyrighted datasets. Developers must navigate the grey areas of creative ownership—determining whether AI-generated content is eligible for copyright protection, and who holds the rights: the tool creator, the prompt engineer, or the end-user. Algorithmic bias is another concern, particularly in narrative and character generation, where unchecked models may propagate harmful stereotypes or culturally insensitive tropes. Transparency in AI decision-making, responsible data sourcing, and inclusive model training are essential to mitigating such risks.

From an operational standpoint, the deployment of generative AI introduces questions around workforce displacement and role redefinition. Traditional roles such as concept artists, level designers, and sound engineers may see a shift in responsibilities from content creation to content supervision and curation. Conversely, new roles emerge, including AI ethicists, prompt engineers, and machine learning content supervisors, signaling a reconfiguration of the game development workforce. Companies that embrace this transition strategically can leverage AI not as a cost-cutting measure but as a catalyst for creative innovation and productivity enhancement.

Economically, the benefits of generative AI are substantial. By automating repetitive tasks and accelerating asset creation, development timelines are shortened, and resource allocation becomes more efficient. Indie developers, who previously lacked the resources to produce high-quality games, now have access to tools that democratize content creation, leveling the playing field against large studios. Personalization at scale is another key advantage. With generative models, developers can create tailored game experiences for individual players, adjusting narratives, difficulty levels, or aesthetic elements based on user preferences and behavioral data.

In summation, the block diagram offers a sophisticated visualization of the convergence between generative AI technologies and interactive digital media, portraying a future where human creativity is exponentially amplified by machine intelligence. This fusion redefines traditional game development workflows, replacing linear, labor-intensive pipelines with dynamic, responsive, and collaborative ecosystems. By leveraging the strengths of multimodal generative models—spanning visual, textual, auditory, and behavioral domains—developers can craft richer, more immersive, and personalized gaming experiences than ever before. While challenges related to ethics, ownership, and human agency persist, the trajectory clearly points toward a future where generative AI is not merely a tool but a creative partner in the evolving art of game creation. This marks a tectonic shift not only in how games are developed but in how interactive digital storytelling is conceived, executed, and experienced on a global scale.

The application of artificial intelligence in game design has experienced significant advancements in design, development, and gameplay. This transition is characterized by three principal elements: personalized gaming experiences, procedural generation, and AI-assisted game development.

AI-Assisted Game Development By automating laborious and repetitive tasks, artificial intelligence enhances creativity. Machine learning enables non-player characters to exhibit dynamic behavior, so allowing personal experiences to vary based on player interactions. Automated testing methods that identify issues and imbalances have accelerated growth via the use of artificial intelligence. Furthermore, AI-driven content generation facilitates the creation of expansive immersive virtual environments with compelling narratives. This often yields a more comprehensive gaming experience and a superior game design experience particularly.

PROCEDURAL GENERATION TO ENHANCE GAMING REALISM

Expansive, dynamic gaming worlds generated by various generative approaches evolve and fluctuate based on player activities. AI-driven procedural content generation creates unique settings and levels, ensuring that no two experiences are identical. This type of study is perpetual, since environments evolve in response to player activities.

Furthermore, advancements in NPC interactions facilitated by machine learning and reinforcement learning are enhancing artificial intelligence capabilities. These strategies instruct NPCs to behave in a more human-like manner, hence enhancing immersion and realism. The dynamic interplay between NPC activities and player decisions enhances the overall experience.

Tailored Gaming Experiences With NPC Encounters and Dynamic Storylines

Contemporary game development is becoming tailored, with AI facilitating content alterations based on user choices. Dynamic storytelling systems alter narratives in real time, hence enhancing immersion. Furthermore, NLP artificial intelligence has facilitated more substantive responses and enhanced, personalized interactions that characterize each gameplay experience by enabling seamless, context-aware discussions with NPCs.

Artificial Intelligence-Driven Originality in Gaming Environments

It pertains to rapid transformations in visual narratives, music, and imaginative storytelling. This enhances the vibrancy and engagement of games significantly. This transition is delineated by three primary divisions: picture creation, crafting engaging game narratives, and enhancing audio production.

Developing Dynamic Narrative Structures for Games

Dynamic, player-driven storylines in video games have enhanced storytelling overall. Essential components include emergent storytelling, wherein player choices alter plotlines and yield unique experiences. Non-player characters powered by artificial intelligence retain previous encounters, reply suitably, and enhance engagement. Procedural narrative generation allows artificial intelligence to create limitless storytelling possibilities, hence keeping gaming experiences novel and enhancing user control.

Images Generated by Artificial Intelligence

A significant domain is graphic design in gaming. Generative design, with its visually realistic environments, enables artificial intelligence to create intricate resources, such as individuals and locales, at a much accelerated pace compared to human capabilities. Through each player's investigation, procedural content generation yields expansive, dynamic terrains that provide unique experiences. Moreover, artificial intelligence may alter visual designs to align with user preferences or gameplay, so enriching the narrative and personalizing the aesthetic experience. This fosters a deeper connection with both game themes and player choices.

Musical Compositions, Acoustic Environments, and Vocal Performance

The use of adaptable soundtracks that modify according to gameplay dynamics has revolutionized audio in video games. AI-generated music adapts to emotional tones, while advancements in voice acting allow realistic, dynamic speech. AI creates sound effects based on player actions, ensuring that audio consistently aligns with gameplay and provides a seamless, engaging experience.

Innovative Gameplay Strategies

The integration of artificial intelligence (AI) into games has established virtual ecosystems and enhanced player experiences through dynamic difficulty adjustments, hence unlocking new gaming opportunities. Significant domains in which artificial intelligence is exerting considerable effect are enumerated here.

Novel Recreational Opportunities Propelled by Artificial Intelligence

Artificial intelligence is transforming gaming by exhibiting flexibility and allowing games to respond to user behavior. Procedural Content Generation (PCG) is a primary technique utilized in which artificial intelligence generates various game environments, levels, and objectives. This approach ensures high reproducibility and reduces development costs. Dynamic Event Generation creates events triggered by player actions through customized scenarios, hence enriching the immersive experience.

Personalizing Player Experience: Adaptive Difficulty Adjustments

Dynamic Difficulty Adjustment (DDA) use artificial intelligence to create obstacles that correspond to the player's skill level. The artificial intelligence monitors real-time performance and adjusts game parameters to maintain balance. A player's performance will influence the strength of adversaries or the complexity of the puzzles.

Artificial Intelligence-Driven Virtual Ecosystems: Non-Player Character Behavior

Artificial intelligence may enhance the behavior of Non-Playable Characters (NPCs), hence augmenting the attractiveness of virtual settings. Through player interactions, NPCs acquire knowledge and modify their behavior based on experience; for instance, they form alliances or exhibit emotional responses. Non-player characters may promptly adjust their methods using machine learning, so generating dynamic obstacles that maintain player engagement and provide unpredictability into games.

Challenges in Creativity and Ethics in AI-Generated Games

The advent of artificial intelligence in game production raises ethical and creative concerns around ownership and authorship, limitations of AI creativity, potential bias, and fairness.

Authorship and Proprietorship

The ownership of AI-generated work presents complex legal challenges, as copyright protection typically relies on human authorship. This situation has ignited debates on whether ownership should reside with the programmer or the user, hence highlighting the necessity for amendments to copyright regulations that clearly delineate ownership in the context of AI-generated creations.

Constraints of AI Creativity

The debate over robots' capacity for genuine creativity centers on the traditional definition encompassing originality, intention, and passion. While artificial intelligence may generate novel concepts, critics argue that AI lacks genuine creativity due to its absence of consciousness. Frequently, the most consequential results arise from human-AI collaboration, wherein AI enhances human creativity.

AI-Created Games: Equity and Prejudice

Given that artificial intelligence derives knowledge from historical data, which may encompass societal biases, the presence of bias in AI-generated content becomes a significant ethical concern. This can affect character representations and narrative arcs, perhaps perpetuating unfavorable preconceptions. To ensure an equitable gaming experience for all players, producers must utilize various datasets and engage in continuous monitoring.

THE FUTURE OF ARTIFICIAL INTELLIGENCE IN GAMING

The future of artificial intelligence in gaming is exceptionally promising, facilitating the creation of customized, dynamic, and entertaining user experiences. The emergence of next-generation artificial intelligence with adaptive gameplay represents a significant advancement. This method adjusts difficulty levels and gaming components in real-time based on a player's performance.

Moreover, generative artificial intelligence will enable the creation of procedurally generated environments that evolve over time, offering distinct experiences for each player. AI-driven non-playable characters (NPCs) will demonstrate more realistic and responsive actions, hence enhancing their engaging and challenging nature for interaction.

Furthermore, artificial intelligence will be crucial in developing the metaverse, crafting immersive, interactive environments that respond to player actions. Customized experiences enable AI to modify content according to player decisions, hence fostering more engagement. Furthermore, the integration of artificial intelligence with virtual and augmented reality will enhance immersion by personalizing experiences in real-time, hence broadening the accessibility of these technologies to a wider range of users.

CONCLUSION

Generative artificial intelligence is profoundly impacting the game industry by facilitating the creation of dynamic, immersive experiences. Procedural content generation enables the creation of locations, narratives, and NPC behaviors that adapt based on player actions. This ensures a unique experience with each play. This technology accelerates development and provides tailored, personalized gameplay that enhances user engagement. The advent of artificial intelligence in gaming introduces ethical and artistic challenges about ownership, authorship, and bias. Addressing these challenges will be essential as artificial intelligence evolves to ensure proper integration and advance a fair and inclusive gaming environment. Blockchain technology is spearheading a transformation in gaming. Contemporary games offer players genuine digital ownership, financial engagement, and community governance, in addition to just entertainment value. This white paper examines the impact of blockchain on gaming, economics, and creativity, facilitating immersive, player-focused experiences that seamlessly integrate technology, culture, and finance to shape the future of interactive digital environments.

The New Era of Gaming Commences

Over the decades, the gaming industry has evolved into a cultural and economic behemoth. Blockchain signifies a new age in which digital ownership, creator-centric economies, and decentralized communities revolutionize gaming into an immersive, participatory, and financially empowered Gameverse.

The Advancement of Digital Engagement

Initially rooted in fundamental laboratory assessments, gaming has transformed into a global entertainment powerhouse valued at over $100 billion. The evolution encompasses arcade classics, three-dimensional visuals, online multiplayer experiences, and digital distribution platforms, spanning decades of technological advancements. Each advancement expanded the reach and cultural significance of gaming, establishing it as the predominant form of entertainment available to billions globally.

The Potential of Blockchain in the Gaming Industry

Since the advent of internet connectivity, blockchain technology represents the most significant paradigm shift in the gaming industry. Blockchain provides players with genuine ownership of their virtual assets, in contrast to traditional games where digital commodities are confined within proprietary systems. This fundamental alteration transforms the relationship between the player and creator from dependence to collaboration, hence facilitating new economic models in which gaming serves as a mechanism for generating real-world value.

The Convergence of Technology and Culture

Currently positioned at the intersection of culture and technology, gaming serves as a primary platform for creative expression and exerts impact on music, fashion, and social media. Blockchain accelerates this convergence and creates a "Gameverse" that integrates shared digital environments, merging entertainment with decentralized finance and community governance, therefore intertwining play, creativity, and economic opportunity.

Blockchain Reconfigured Game Mechanics

The authentic ownership of assets via blockchain, player-driven economies, and algorithmic equity are transforming fundamental gaming concepts. The emergence of smart contracts, NFTs, and tokenized incentives revolutionizes gaming operations, providing players with more transparency, control, and tangible economic value.

Playable Digital Assets in the Form of NFTs

Non-fungible tokens have revolutionized in-game goods by converting virtual real estate, armament, and personas into distinct, verifiable assets that players genuinely own. NFTs exist independently on the blockchain, in contrast to traditional digital assets confined to certain games, hence facilitating cross-platform utility and unrestricted marketplace transactions. This confirmed ownership facilitates new prospects for asset interoperability and substantial player investment outside individual games.

Tokens and the Generation of Real-World Value

Tokenized economics facilitated by blockchain gaming enables the transformation of virtual achievements into tangible advantages. Play-to-earn models enable gamers to monetize their skills and time, transforming gaming from a mere amusement expense into a potential source of income. These tokenized systems facilitate internal game mechanics and external market dynamics by creating sustainable economic opportunities and robust foundations that maintain value over time.

Self-executing smart contracts establish game rules, transactions, and prizes autonomously, so functioning as the game's logic. These systems mitigate the risk of manipulation by ensuring transparent rule enforcement, verifiable outcomes, and seamless asset transfers. Smart contracts facilitate distributed governance through open, automated mechanisms that promote trust and enhance community engagement, allowing participants to actively influence decisions on game development.

Addressing Issues of Fairness, Ownership, and Fraud Among Players

Blockchain addresses fundamental gaming issues through genuine asset ownership, fraud prevention, and transparent operations. Although blockchain's immutable records render counterfeiting nearly infeasible, participants disengage from restricted settings where investments may disappear. The technology's intrinsic transparency, by enabling all transactions and procedures to be publicly observable, promotes fairness and establishes reliable circumstances that allow participants to invest with assurance.

Economies of Play: Value Generation Within Digital Realms

Blockchain is revolutionizing the in-game economy by converting gameplay into active involvement and ownership. Through income models, user-generated content, and asset interoperability, players are empowered as producers, investors, and stakeholders, therefore creating value across virtual realms and fostering the expansion of decentralized digital economies.

Play-to-Earn Compared to Play-and-Own Models

NFTs for achieving or exceeding objectives enable certain players—regrettably—to see gaming as their profession. Play-to-earn models must be properly and intentionally designed; otherwise, they may foster unsustainable economic dynamics. By valuing behavior (interaction and curation) above exploitative practices, Play-and-

Own models prioritize long-term asset ownership and foster improved economic dynamics through a cycle of creation.

User-Generated Content and Producer Incentives

Blockchain enables parties to create, mint, and get benefit from digital assets, hence facilitating content production. User-generated material, including unique skins or whole levels, may provide as a significant revenue stream for blockchain gaming, facilitated by NFT ownership and automatic royalty payments. This reverses common knowledge, enabling grassroots innovation and allowing producers to profit from their successful assets in markets, so transforming individuals from passive consumers into active participants in the ecosystem.

Interoperability: Objects Across Gaming Realms

One of the most revolutionary features of blockchain gaming is the capacity to transfer assets between many "worlds". Items acquired in one game can be utilized in another, traded in most open markets, combined with another game, and so on. It creates a unified digital economy in which participants own a digital identity and a consistent inventory across several experiences, so providing the foundation for an interconnected metaverse.

Empowerment of Players Through Decentralized Governance

Blockchain empowers participants to act as decision-makers and financial agents, rather than only consumers. Gaming evolves into a community-driven ecosystem where influence, incentives, and trust are collectively managed through decentralized governance, player-operated guilds, and verified digital ownership.

Decentralized Autonomous Organizations transfer authority from corporate executives to player communities inside gaming ecosystems. Through their votes on game development, economic policies, and community standards, token holders contribute to aligning the game's evolution with user interests rather than solely commercial objectives. Smart contracts eradicate bias by autonomously executing predetermined decisions, hence enhancing player commitment to the success of the game.

Guilds as Economic Intermediaries

Contemporary gaming guilds are intricate economic entities that consolidate resources, coordinate strategies, and enhance collective advantages. These groups function as social hubs that enhance community connections and amplify individual player influence through collaborative networks, hence facilitating more participation via scholarships, asset loans, and training opportunities.

Digital Fright and Authentic Provenance

Blockchain generates unique assets and immutable ownership records, hence facilitating genuine digital scarcity. The complete history of each object is rendered publicly auditable, so preventing fraud and establishing clear value propositions grounded in verifiable rarity and authenticity. This transparency cultivates trust in virtual economies and produces substantial collecting events that surpass mere games.

Technological Framework: Infrastructure Facilitating Innovation

An robust technological framework will influence the future of blockchain gaming. This infrastructure facilitates immersive, secure, and seamless experiences through scalable Layer 2 solutions, high-performance platforms, artificial intelligence, and extended reality integration, therefore transforming interactive entertainment and ownership.

Applications of Blockchain Technology in Gaming

The platform utilized significantly impacts game performance and accessibility. Despite its scalability challenges, Ethereum possesses the most advanced ecosystem, equipped with comprehensive development tools. Polygon provides Ethereum compatibility with improved performance and reduced costs, whereas Solana facilitates rapid gameplay with high-speed processing. Each platform provides distinct advantages for various game objectives.

Layer 2 and Scalability Solutions

Layer 2 solutions address scalability limitations by executing transactions off-chain while maintaining security through settlement on the main chain. Blockchain gaming is more accessible to mainstream audiences seeking seamless experiences, since these technologies provide rapid, cost-effective interactions that allow real-time gaming and high-volume transactions.

Incorporating XR and AI into Blockchain Gaming

The integration of blockchain, augmented reality, and artificial intelligence offers unprecedented opportunities for immersive experiences. Blockchain ensures secure asset ownership; artificial intelligence personalizes gaming experiences and enhances virtual economies. Extended reality refers to gaming experiences that merge virtual and physical realities, allowing fully immersive scenarios where blockchain-secured assets gain enhanced interactive aspects.

Challenges and Limitations

Blockchain gaming has significant challenges in scalability, user onboarding, and maintaining economic sustainability. Addressing these obstacles and achieving sustainable success while ensuring player inclusion in the creation of decentralized gaming ecosystems will rely on technological innovation, meticulous design, and ethical considerations.

Efficiency and Expandability

Blockchain gaming has significant scaling challenges despite advancements. Peak demand may induce network congestion, resulting in process delays and increased costs. The blockchain trilemma of decentralization, security, and scalability is a challenging issue that necessitates innovative Layer 2 solutions and specialized gaming blockchains to achieve optimal performance at scale.

Challenges in User Experience and Onboarding

The equilibrium between player incentives to engage in a game and the preservation of value, the integration of new users vs the depreciation of token and currency value inside in-game economies, among other factors, will ascertain the long-term viability of virtual economies in blockchain gaming.

Numerous early blockchain games faltered because growth stagnated, resulting in a depreciation of digital assets and time for the participants. Numerous hours of innovative design and contemplation will be required in sustainable design for economic systems that attract individuals to engage, invest time or wealth, encourage their peers to remain active participants, and preserve the enduring value of their assets.

Economic Resilience and Ethics

Ethics and morality pose more risks as many individuals are often unaware of concepts related to digital ownership rights, environmental impacts of ownership, or the speculation that designers and developers may engage in, either consciously or unknowingly.

The sector must address and reassess collateral incursions regarding ethical practices, particularly concerning stakeholders in moral theory, while fostering sustainable economies that prioritize user welfare over ephemeral and intangible profits derived from transient engagements.

Blockchain Gaming: The Future

Blockchain gaming is transitioning from a prototype phase to a fully fledged, mainstream-ready market. The adoption of blockchain, gaming, and player ownership is increasing as technology advances, platforms become more scalable, and global regulations become clearer. Traditional gaming corporations are aligning with gamers through sustainable player-owned tokenomics, cross-chain interoperability, and emerging institutional interest, all of which contribute to enhanced stability and scalability within the gaming ecosystem.

The implementation of artificial intelligence produces dynamic player-performance-reactive settings, generally referred to as virtual environments (VI). AI collaboratively builds games and promptly alters the economy, therefore personalizing experiences and immersing participants in the narrative. This alteration fortifies the realm of blockchain gaming and presents more opportunities for gamers. The player transitions from a spectator in games to a co-owner of a digital environment, where the design incorporates creators, users, and user investment for community ownership.

Ultimately, blockchain gaming is transforming our interactions with one other and with games. Blockchain gaming empowers players by providing a secure ownership framework for digital assets, granting communities greater control over game development and evolution, and recognizing the time invested in gameplay. Gaming is seen as an interactive pastime in which participants can strive for constructive objectives.

The integration of blockchain with artificial intelligence and immersive technology to create captivating, interactive spaces appears to illuminate the future. Gamers, producers, brands, and investors each have a role to fulfill. This new era must be founded on fairness, openness, and collective accountability to thrive. Each individual contributes to the evolving gameverse.

REFERENCES

Alsharhan, A., Al-Emran, M., & Shaalan, K. (2023). Chatbot adoption: A multi-perspective systematic review and future research agenda. *IEEE Transactions on Engineering Management*, 1–13. DOI: 10.1109/TEM.2023.3298360

Andrews, J. T., ... (2023). Ethical considerations for collecting human-centric image datasets. arXiv preprint arXiv:2302.03629. https://arxiv.org/abs/2302.03629

Angelov, D. (2020). Top2Vec: Distributed representations of topics. arXiv preprint arXiv:2008.09470. https://doi.org//arXiv.2008.09470DOI: 10.48550

Atzeni, D., Bacciu, D., Mazzei, D., & Prencipe, G. (2022). A systematic review of Wi-Fi and machine learning integration with topic modeling techniques. *Sensors (Basel)*, *22*(13), 4925. DOI: 10.3390/s22134925 PMID: 35808430

Aziz, S., & Dowling, M. (2019). Machine learning and AI for risk management. In Disrupting finance: FinTech and strategy in the 21st century (pp. 33–50). DOI: 10.1007/978-3-030-02330-0_3

Bahroun, Z., Anane, C., Ahmed, V., & Zacca, A. (2023). Transforming education: A comprehensive review of generative artificial intelligence in educational settings through bibliometric and content analysis. *Sustainability (Basel)*, *15*(17), 12983. Advance online publication. DOI: 10.3390/su151712983

Beheshti, A., ... (2023). ProcessGPT: Transforming business process management with generative artificial intelligence. arXiv preprint arXiv:2306.01771. https://arxiv.org/abs/2306.01771 DOI: 10.1109/ICWS60048.2023.00099

Bianchi, F., Terragni, S., & Hovy, D. (2021). Pre-training is a hot topic: Contextualized document embeddings improve topic coherence. In *Proceedings of the 59th Annual Meeting of the Association for Computational Linguistics and the 11th International Joint Conference on Natural Language Processing (ACL-IJCNLP 2021)* (pp. 759–766). Association for Computational Linguistics. DOI: 10.18653/v1/2021.acl-short.96

Kraft, M. A., Marinell, W. H., & Yee, D. S. W. (2018). School organizational contexts, teacher turnover, and student achievement: Evidence from panel data. *American Educational Research Journal*, *53*(5), 1411–1449. DOI: 10.3102/0002831216667478

Kraft, M. A., Marinell, W. H., & Yee, D. S. W. (2018). School organizational contexts, teacher turnover, and student achievement: Evidence from panel data. *American Educational Research Journal*, *53*(5), 1411–1449. DOI: 10.3102/0002831216667478

Kraft, M. A., & Papay, J. P. (2014). Can professional environments in schools promote teacher development? Explaining heterogeneity in returns to teaching experience. *Educational Evaluation and Policy Analysis*, *36*(4), 476–500. DOI: 10.3102/0162373713519496 PMID: 25866426

Kraft, M. A., & Papay, J. P. (2014). Can professional environments in schools promote teacher development? Explaining heterogeneity in returns to teaching experience. *Educational Evaluation and Policy Analysis*, *36*(4), 476–500. DOI: 10.3102/0162373713519496 PMID: 25866426

Kumar, A., Singh, R., & Bhardwaj, V. (2022). Sentiment analysis of student and teacher feedback using natural language processing. *Journal of Computer Assisted Learning*, *38*(4), 517–529.

Kumar, A., Singh, R., & Bhardwaj, V. (2022). Sentiment analysis of student and teacher feedback using natural language processing. *Journal of Computer Assisted Learning*, *38*(4), 517–529.

Kwon, H., & Kim, H. (2021). Predictive analytics in teacher retention: Leveraging AI for proactive HR management. *International Journal of Educational Technology in Higher Education*, *18*(1), 112–130. PMID: 34977335

Kwon, H., & Kim, H. (2021). Predictive analytics in teacher retention: Leveraging AI for proactive HR management. *International Journal of Educational Technology in Higher Education*, *18*(1), 112–130. PMID: 34977335

Liu, M. (2021). Artificial intelligence in education: Challenges and opportunities. *Journal of Educational Technology Development and Exchange*, *14*(1), 47–60.

Liu, M. (2021). Artificial intelligence in education: Challenges and opportunities. *Journal of Educational Technology Development and Exchange*, *14*(1), 47–60.

Chapter 9
The Evolution of Artificial Intelligence in Shaping the Future of Interactive Entertainment

Mohamed Elgazar
Faculty of Engineering, Mansoura National University, Egypt

Mohamed Elafifi
Faculty of Engineering, Mansoura National University, Egypt

Majed Elshenawy
Faculty of Engineering, Mansoura National University, Egypt

Mohamed Ebrahim
Faculty of Engineering, Mansoura National University, Egypt

Mohamed Setate
Mansoura National University, Egypt

Mohamed Fayed
Mansoura National University, Egypt

Mohamed Ramadan
Faculty of Engineering, Mansoura National University, Egypt

Abdelrahman Mansour
Faculty of Engineering, Mansoura National University, Egypt

Sarah M. Ayyad
https://orcid.org/0000-0001-8356-1644
Computers and Control Systems Department, Faculty of Engineering, Mansoura University, Egypt

Abstract

Dive into the captivating evolution of Artificial Intelligence (AI) and discover its profound impact on the gaming universe. This comprehensive chapter unravels AI's journey from its earliest philosophical stirrings to its current status as a technological cornerstone. It asks: How did the abstract concept of "thinking machines" transform

DOI: 10.4018/979-8-3373-4637-3.ch009

ght © 2026, IGI Global Scientific Publishing. Copying or distributing in print or electronic forms without written permission of IGI Global Scientific Publishing is prohibited. Use of this chapter to generative artificial intelligence (AI) technologies is expressly prohibited. The publisher reserves all rights to license its use for generative AI training and machine learning model development.

into the dynamic force shaping our digital realities? The chapter illuminates AI's pivotal role in revolutionizing game design, from crafting infinitely expansive worlds and intelligent non-player characters to weaving adaptive narratives that respond to your every choice. Furthermore, the chapter explores how AI streamlines game development, optimizes performance, and even redefines economic models within the industry. Finally, the cutting-edge hardware innovations that power this revolution are discussed, posing a critical question: As AI continues to push the boundaries of virtual experiences, what uncharted territories of immersion and interaction await us, and what complex debates will define its future?

1. INTRODUCTION

Artificial Intelligence (AI) is a pivotal branch of computer science dedicated to engineering systems capable of executing tasks that traditionally necessitate human cognitive abilities, such as comprehension, logical reasoning, decision-making, and complex problem-solving (Fetzer, 1990). A defining characteristic of this field is its focus on designing mechanisms that empower machines to learn autonomously and iteratively refine their performance over time, independent of direct human intervention. The core objective of AI extends beyond mere process automation. It aims to augment human capabilities and simplify daily life through intelligent technologies that interact effectively with their environments. This aspiration is manifested in AI systems' increasing adeptness at reducing human error, automating repetitive tasks, operating with exceptional speed and accuracy, and offering continuous availability, thereby accelerating research and development across diverse domains (Ayyad et al., 2021)(Elsayed, Hasoon, Zidan, & Ayyad, 2024) (Qadir et al., 2025). The shift in AI's primary objective, moving beyond simple automation to explicitly enhancing human capabilities, represents a fundamental re-evaluation of its perceived value and application. This progression indicates that AI is increasingly viewed not as a replacement for human labor, but as a powerful tool for augmentation, efficiency, and innovation across diverse sectors, ultimately freeing human capital to focus on higher-impact challenges.

Although the widespread adoption of AI is a relatively recent phenomenon, its conceptual underpinnings can be traced back to the mid-20th century, a period when pioneering researchers began to explore fundamental questions regarding the feasibility of replicating human cognition through mechanical means (van Assen, Muscogiuri, Tessarin, & De Cecco, 2022). Today, AI has evolved from a specialized academic pursuit into a cornerstone of modern technology, seamlessly integrated into daily life, from social media interactions to complex business operations, with its influence continuing to expand. Contemporary AI tools are notable for their capacity to operate at speeds far surpassing human processing, concurrently generating a diverse array of creative outputs, including textual content, visual imagery, and video productions. The early mention of AI's ability to generate creative outputs, even in an introductory context, subtly foreshadows the significant rise of generative AI, suggesting a future trajectory where AI's role extends beyond analytical tasks to active co-creation. This indicates that the foundational aspirations of AI, while initially focused on mimicking human reasoning, have expanded to encompass human creativity, setting an expectation for AI's evolving role as a generative force.

This chapter offers a comprehensive historical analysis of artificial intelligence, meticulously tracing its conceptual origins, detailing its developmental timeline, acknowledging the significant contributions of key scientists, and identifying the pivotal roles played by various companies and institutions. The information presented is rigorously compiled from academic and research-based sources to ensure an accurate and profound understanding of AI's intricate evolution.

2. FROM ANCIENT LOGIC TO DIGITAL PLAYGROUNDS: A HISTORICAL CONVERGENCE OF GAMING AND ARTIFICIAL INTELLIGENCE

The intertwined histories of gaming and AI reveal a profound and enduring human fascination with replicating and augmenting cognitive abilities through machines. From the earliest philosophical inquiries into the nature of thought to the complex digital environments of today, games have consistently served as both a crucible and a canvas for the development of artificial intelligence. This chapter delves into the historical convergence of these two fields, tracing their shared lineage and highlighting pivotal moments that shaped their symbiotic evolution.

2.1. The Deep Roots of Machine Intelligence and Play

How did ancient philosophical inquiries into logic and early mechanical marvels lay the groundwork for intelligent machines and interactive experiences? The journey begins not with circuits and code but with the very structure of human thought.

2.1.1. Ancient Foundations of Logic and Reasoning

The conceptual underpinnings of AI, particularly the idea of formal logic, can be traced back to ancient Greece. Aristotle (384–322 BCE), a towering figure in philosophy, systematically formulated the concept of the syllogism, a cornerstone of deductive reasoning. This argument structure, exemplified by "All humans are mortal; Socrates is human; Therefore, Socrates is mortal," provided the first formal expression of reasoning from premises to a conclusion (Fetzer, 1990). Aristotle's work, meticulously detailed in his six-part book *The Organon*, held an unparalleled position in scholarly thought for over two millennia, with many believing he had exhausted the topic of logic. His articulation of basic axioms, such as the Law of Identity, the Law of Non-contradiction, and the Law of the Excluded Middle, further defined his comprehensive logical system (van Assen, Muscogiuri, Tessarin, & De Cecco, 2022).

This formalization of deductive reasoning by Aristotle is more than a philosophical curiosity; it represents the earliest conceptual blueprint for rule-based systems, a fundamental component of early AI. The syllogism defines a structure where, if premises are accepted as true, the conclusion must logically follow, based purely on its logical form. This mirrors the fundamental operation of early symbolic AI and rule-based systems, where explicit rules (analogous to premises) are applied to symbols to derive new information (conclusions). In its earliest form, the idea of a machine "thinking" or "reasoning" was an attempt to mechanize this Aristotelian deductive process. This highlights a deep, enduring human fascination with automating thought, a conceptual foundation for AI that predates any physical computing device by millennia.

2.1.2. Medieval and Renaissance Visions of Automated Knowledge

Centuries after Aristotle, the Catalan mystic and philosopher Ramon Llull (born 1232/33, died 1315/16) made a significant conceptual leap with his Ars Magna (1305–08), or "The Great Art" (Castella-Martinez & Saiz-Raimundo, 2024). This elaborate system of logic and language was conceived as a universal method for discovering truth, primarily intended to support the Roman Catholic faith and unify all branches of knowledge. Llull's method involved the use of symbolic notation and combinatory diagrams, employing complex mechanical techniques to relate theology, philosophy, and the natural sciences as interconnected manifestations of a divine order.

Llull's *Ars Magna* was not merely an abstract logical system; it represented an early, systematic, and almost mechanical approach to knowledge generation, foreshadowing computational methods (Fidora, 2011). His use of "logic and complex mechanical techniques involving symbolic notation and combinatory diagrams" to relate knowledge moved beyond simple deduction to the idea of automating the process of deriving truth or new information. This vision directly prefigures the concept of a machine processing symbols to generate new knowledge, a core aspect of AI's pursuit of knowledge representation and reasoning. The ambitious goal of *Ars Magna* to unify all knowledge and "find truth" through a systematic process aligns directly with AI's long-term aspiration of creating general intelligence capable of synthesizing vast amounts of information and solving complex problems. This demonstrates an early human desire not just to calculate, but to *reason* and *discover* through automated means.

2.1.3. The Rise of Automata: Mimicking Life and Intelligence

The 17th and 18th centuries marked a period of remarkable innovation in mechanical engineering, witnessing the flourishing of intricate automata—mechanical devices designed to mimic human and animal actions. These marvels captivated audiences and pushed the boundaries of engineering, serving as early attempts to embody intelligence. The Dutch mathematician Christiaan Huygens (1600s) created a notable mechanical army for the King of France. More famously, the French inventor Jacques de Vaucanson developed "The Digesting Duck" in 1739, a copper mechanical marvel with over 400 moving parts per wing (Marshall, 2022). This ingenious creation appeared to eat, digest, and excrete food. However, it was later revealed to store consumed grain in one compartment and release pre-fabricated pellets from another. Vaucanson also constructed a five-and-a-half-foot mechanical flute player capable of playing twelve different tunes, a remarkable achievement given the instrument's complexity.

Later in the 18th century, the Swiss watchmaker Pierre Jaquet-Droz and his son created three renowned mechanical dolls: "The Musician," "The Draughtsman," and "The Writer" (Bedini, 1964). "The Writer," considered the most complex, contained over 6,000 parts and could dip its pen in ink to write up to forty different letters, which could be customized by the user (Bedini, 1964). Similarly, Henri Maillardet's "Draughtsman Writer" (early 19th century) demonstrated an impressive mechanical memory, capable of drawing four different pictures and writing three poems. These automata, including the "Silver Swan" (1773) by James Cox and John Joseph Merlin, were widely regarded as early ancestors of modern computers.

These sophisticated automata were more than mere entertainment; they represented early attempts at *embodied intelligence*, showcasing complex sequences of actions and even apparent "memory" and "creativity" through mechanical programming (Bedini, 1964). The intricate designs and thousands of moving parts in creations like Jaquet-Droz's Writer or Vaucanson's Duck embodied the concept of pre-programmed, intricate behaviors that mimicked human capabilities. The "Writer" even demonstrated a form of "programmability" by allowing the user to change the letters it wrote. This directly relates to the AI goal of replicating human-like abilities. The public fascination with and the engineering challenges overcome in creating these automata highlight a long-standing human desire to build machines that *act* intelligently, even if the underlying mechanism was purely mechanical. This historical thread feeds directly into the later development of AI, where the focus shifted from mechanical complexity to computational algorithms to achieve similar, but far more flexible, forms of "intelligent" behavior.

2.2. The Dawn of Programmable Thought: Babbage, Lovelace, and the Analytical Engine

What visionary insights from the 19th century foreshadowed the symbiotic relationship between computation and creative expression? The transition from mechanical mimicry to programmable machines marked a pivotal moment.

2.2.1. The Jacquard Loom: A Blueprint for Programmability

The 19th century introduced a revolutionary innovation in automation that would profoundly influence the trajectory of computing: the Jacquard loom. Invented by Frenchman Joseph Marie Jacquard (Davis & Davis, 2005) and first demonstrated in 1801, this mechanism transformed textile weaving by employing thousands of punch cards laced together. Each row of punched holes on these cards corresponded to a specific row of a textile pattern, enabling the creation of complex and detailed designs with unprecedented efficiency, even by unskilled workers. This system represented a profound shift in human-machine interaction, effectively utilizing a form of binary code (a punched hole representing one state, no hole another) to instruct a machine in an automated process.

The Jacquard loom's success in automating complex patterns through programmable cards directly inspired the architecture of the first theoretical general-purpose computer (Davis & Davis, 2005). The loom demonstrated that complex, varied tasks could be encoded and executed by a machine, moving beyond fixed-function devices. This concept of "programmable automation" was a direct inspiration for Charles Babbage's Analytical Engine. The principle of flexible, re-programmable machinery is fundamental to modern computing and, by extension, to AI, which relies on algorithms to adapt and generate diverse behaviors. The Jacquard loom's impact illustrates how industrial needs, specifically in textile production, inadvertently laid a critical conceptual foundation for information technology.

2.2.2. Charles Babbage's Analytical Engine: The Dawn of the Computer Concept

The innovative use of punch cards in the Jacquard loom profoundly influenced British mathematician Charles Babbage. He envisioned the Analytical Engine, widely regarded as the first design for a modern general-purpose computer (Hyman, 1985).

Babbage's ambitious plan detailed a machine that would receive instructions and numerical data from punch cards to execute complex mathematical calculations. Although the Analytical Engine was never fully constructed during his lifetime, its theoretical design laid the conceptual groundwork for universal computation, proposing a machine capable of far more than simple arithmetic.

Babbage's design, directly inspired by the Jacquard loom, represented a significant conceptual leap beyond mere calculation to a vision of a machine capable of executing any algorithmic function. This concept of a machine that could be *programmed* to perform a vast array of operations, rather than being hard-wired for a single task, is the essence of a general-purpose computer (Abdelkhabir et al., 2025) (Ayyad et al., 2022) (Sasse et al., 2025). This universality is a prerequisite for any intelligent machine, as intelligence inherently implies adaptability across various problems and domains. The theoretical existence of the Analytical Engine marked the point where the idea of a machine capable of more than fixed arithmetic became tangible. It sets the stage for the abstract notion of computation that would later underpin AI, where intelligence is often framed as the ability to execute complex algorithms.

2.2.3. Ada Lovelace: The First Programmer and a Visionary of Machine Creativity

Ada Lovelace (born 1815, died 1852 at age 36), daughter of the poet Lord Byron, was a gifted mathematician and a pivotal collaborator with Charles Babbage. In 1843, she translated an Italian article on Babbage's Analytical Engine by Luigi Menabrea, augmenting it with extensive annotations that were three times the length of the original paper. Within these "Translator's Notes," published under her initials "A.A.L." to conceal her identity, Lovelace described a step-by-step process for the Analytical Engine to compute Bernoulli numbers. This detailed exposition is regarded as the first computer algorithm, establishing her as the world's first computer programmer. She utilized a recursive equation for this calculation, deliberately choosing an elaborate method to demonstrate the engine's advanced capabilities.

Crucially, Lovelace's visionary understanding extended far beyond numerical calculation. She was the first to articulate the groundbreaking realization that the Analytical Engine could manipulate numbers and symbols and that these symbols could represent entities beyond mere quantities, such as musical notes. This insight marked a fundamental transition in the understanding of computing, suggesting that machines could potentially compose music or generate graphics, thereby laying the conceptual groundwork for universal computation. Her recognition that machines could manipulate *symbols* beyond just numbers was a profound conceptual leap, giving birth to the idea of general-purpose programming. Lovelace explicitly stated the Analytical Engine could "act upon other things besides number" and could compose music if musical relations could be expressed symbolically. This moves beyond Babbage's focus on calculation to the abstract manipulation of information, a core aspect of AI, which is fundamentally about processing and generating symbolic representations of knowledge, language, or actions. This understanding is the genesis of modern computer programming and the very foundation of AI, implying that intelligence, in a computational sense, is not just about crunching numbers but about processing and transforming *any* form of information that can be formalized into symbols. Her algorithm for Bernoulli numbers served as a concrete demonstration of this abstract power.

In her "Translator's Note G," Lovelace also articulated what later became known as "Lovelace's Objection" (or "Lady Lovelace's Objection"), famously stating that "The Analytical Engine has no pretensions whatever to originate anything. It can do whatever we know how to order it to perform.". This assertion implied that computers could not be truly intelligent or creative without direct human input, a philosophical debate that continues to resonate in contemporary AI discussions. However, some modern scholars argue that this interpretation is a misreading of her original intent, suggesting Lovelace's statement was more concerned with human perception and the machine's potential capacity for originality. In response to this ongoing discussion, the concept of the "Lovelace Effect" has been proposed. This describes situations where users *perceive* computing systems' behavior as original and creative, shifting the focus from inherent machine capability to human attribution and the cultural constructions of creativity. The "Lovelace Objection" and the subsequent "Lovelace Effect" demonstrate that the definition of "intelligence" and "creativity" in machines is not purely technical but also deeply philosophical and perceptual. This debate has shaped, and continues to shape, the goals and criticisms of AI research, particularly in generative AI and artistic applications.

2.3. Post-War Computing and the Genesis of AI: A New Era of Games

How did the post-World War II technological boom and the formalization of AI immediately intertwine with the nascent world of digital games? The mid-20th century saw theoretical breakthroughs rapidly manifest in early computing devices and interactive experiences.

2.3.1 The Biological Inspiration: McCulloch-Pitts Neuron

In 1943, a pivotal theoretical development occurred with the publication of "A logical calculus of ideas immanent in nervous activity" by neurophysiologist Warren McCulloch and logician Walter Pitts (Arbib, 2000). This paper introduced the first artificial neuron, known as the McCulloch-Pitts (MCP) neuron. Inspired by biological neural circuitry, their model represented a neuron as a Threshold Logic Unit (TLU) with binary inputs and outputs. It would "fire" (produce an output) if the sum of its excitatory inputs met a certain threshold, provided no inhibitory inputs were active. This foundational work provided a computational model for the "nerve net" in the brain, laying theoretical groundwork for artificial neural networks.

The McCulloch-Pitts neuron marked a critical pivot from purely symbolic, rule-based logic to models inspired by biological neural structures, paving the way for machine learning. The MCP neuron was explicitly designed as a "computational model of the 'nerve net' in the brain" (Arbib, 2000), with its inputs, weights, and outputs analogous to biological neurons. While early AI often focused on symbolic logic, the MCP neuron introduced the idea of distributed processing and learning through connections, a fundamental concept for neural networks and deep learning. This departed from the "computer as symbol manipulator" paradigm that had dominated earlier thought (Fetzer, 1990). This theoretical breakthrough provided a mathematical basis for machines to "learn" from data by adjusting connection strengths (weights), rather than being explicitly programmed with explicit rules. This shift was crucial for AI's evolution beyond the limitations of purely symbolic systems, and its eventual success in complex pattern recognition and game strategies.

2.3.2 Alan Turing: Defining Machine Intelligence and the Game Testbed

British mathematician Alan Turing, a seminal figure in modern computing, profoundly influenced the nascent field of AI. In a 1947 lecture in London, he delivered what is widely considered the earliest public discussion of computer intelligence, stating, "What we want is a machine that can learn from experience" and that the "possibility of letting the machine alter its instructions provides the mechanism for this" (LaCurts, 2011). This vision of machines adapting and improving their programs was remarkably prescient for a time when the first electronic computers were still in their infancy.

In his highly influential 1950 paper, "Computing Machinery and Intelligence," published in the philosophical journal *Mind*, Turing introduced the concept of the Turing Test, which he originally called the "Imitation Game". This test proposed a pragmatic alternative to the ill-defined question "Can machines think?" Instead, it asked whether a machine could act indistinguishably from a human in a natural language conversation conducted via text, such that a human interrogator could not reliably tell them apart. Turing also recognized the utility of games, specifically chess, as a testbed for machine intelligence, acknowledging their challenging yet clearly defined problems.

Turing's focus on games (specifically chess) and his "Imitation Game" established a paradigm where well-defined challenges could serve as measurable benchmarks for machine intelligence, moving AI from abstract theory to practical demonstration. By framing intelligence as a performance in a game (whether chess or the linguistic Imitation Game), Turing provided a concrete, albeit controversial, metric for AI progress. This allowed researchers to build and test systems against human performance, a critical driver for early AI. This approach established games as fundamental "micro-worlds" for AI research, offering controlled environments where complex problems could be simplified and solved and where AI performance could be objectively evaluated. This causal link explains why games became, and remain, central to AI development and benchmarking.

The Turing Test has, however, faced various philosophical criticisms over the decades. Arguments have been raised that it is "too easy," suggesting that even "brute force" machines, like Ned Block's hypothetical "Blockhead" or early programs such as ELIZA, could potentially pass without possessing genuine intelligence (Shrager, 2024). Conversely, some argue it is "too narrow," as it primarily tests linguistic ability and might not capture the full spectrum of intelligence. A prominent criticism is John Searle's Chinese Room argument (1980), which posits that symbol manipulation alone, even if it produces seemingly intelligent responses, does not constitute true understanding or consciousness. These philosophical debates, sparked by Turing's work, continue to shape the understanding and evaluation of artificial intelligence.

2.3.3. The Formal Birth of AI and Early Game Demonstrations

The formal genesis of the field of AI occurred at the Dartmouth Summer Research Project on Artificial Intelligence, commonly known as the Dartmouth Conference. This pivotal gathering commenced on June 18, 1956, and ran for approximately eight weeks. Organized by four visionary American computer scientists—John McCarthy (who is credited with coining the term "artificial intelligence"), Marvin Minsky, Nathaniel Rochester, and Claude Shannon—the conference brought together some of the brightest minds in computer science, mathematics, and cognitive psychology (McCarthy, Minsky, Rochester, & Shannon, 2006). Their ambitious proposal stated a belief that "every aspect of learning or any other feature of intelligence can in principle be so precisely described that a machine can be made to simulate it," with the goal of finding out "how to make machines use language, form abstractions and concepts, solve kinds of problems now reserved for humans". This conference coalesced AI into a distinct field of study, laying the foundational concepts for machine learning and neural networks.

In parallel with this formalization of AI, the very first computer games began to emerge, often serving as compelling public demonstrations of nascent computing capabilities:

- Bertie the Brain (1950): Built by Josef Kates for the Canadian National Exhibition in Toronto, this imposing 4-meter (13-foot) tall computer allowed exhibition attendees to play tic-tac-toe against an artificial intelligence (Kates, 1950). It featured an adjustable difficulty level and was designed to be unbeatable at its highest setting. Although disassembled after just two weeks on display, it is considered potentially the first computer game to feature any visual display, albeit using light bulbs rather than a screen (Kates, 1950).
- Nimrod (1951): Constructed by British engineering firm Ferranti for the Festival of Britain, this substantial 12x9x5-foot (3.7x2.7x1.5-meter) machine was custom-built to play the ancient mathematical game of Nim against an AI (Sumner, 2014). Advertised as "faster than thought" and an "electronic brain," Nimrod's primary purpose was to illustrate the principles of the digital computer to the public (Sumner, 2014). It famously drew large crowds, including West Germany's economics minister, Ludwig Erhard, whom it defeated three times in a row at the Berlin Industrial Show in October 1951.
- OXO (1952): Developed by A.S. Douglas, a PhD candidate at Cambridge University, OXO is one of the earliest graphical computer games. Played on Cambridge's EDSAC computer, this version of tic-tac-toe displayed the game board on a 35x15 dot cathode ray tube, with moves entered by the player using a rotary telephone dial. Few outside of Cambridge ever played OXO (Aarseth & Hammar, n.d.).
- Tennis for Two (1958): Created by physicist William Higinbotham at Brookhaven National Laboratory, this electronic tennis game was first introduced on October 18, 1958, during one of the Lab's annual visitors' days (Higinbotham, 1958). It utilized an analog computer (initially designed for ballistic missile trajectory calculations) and an oscilloscope as a screen, allowing two players to control the ball's trajectory with separate controllers. Hundreds of visitors lined up to play this pioneering interactive experience.

Table 1. reports a brief comparison between role of AI in old computer games. These early computer games provided an immediate, tangible, and engaging way to demonstrate the abstract concepts of computing and AI to a skeptical or uninitiated public. Despite their simplicity, games like Bertie the Brain and Nimrod explicitly showcased the "electronic brain" concept and the ability of machines to perform tasks that seemed to require intelligence, such as playing games. This helped demystify computing and build public interest. Games served as crucial early marketing and educational tools for the nascent fields of computer science and AI. This early public engagement, driven by games' interactive and competitive nature, fostered an environment where AI research could gain traction and funding, establishing a symbiotic relationship from the very beginning.

Table 1. A brief comparison between role of AI in old computer games

Period	Event/Development	Authors	Significance to AI	Significance to Gaming
Ancient Greece	Aristotle's Logic (Syllogism)	Aristotle	Foundations of formal logic, deductive reasoning, proto-algorithm.	Conceptual basis for game logic and rule systems
13th-14th Century	Llull's Ars Magna	Ramon Llull	Early symbolic reasoning, mechanical knowledge generation	Conceptual basis for automated systems and complex interactions
17th-18th Century	Automata (e.g., Digesting Duck, The Writer)	Christiaan Huygens, Jacques de Vaucanson, Pierre Jaquet-Droz, Henri Maillardet	Mimicry of intelligent behavior, pre-programmed complexity, embodied intelligence.	Early interactive mechanical devices, complex animated figures
1801	Jacquard Loom	Joseph Marie Jacquard	Blueprint for programmability, binary code concept.	Precursor to digital control and pattern generation in interactive systems
1843	Analytical Engine (concept) & Lovelace's Algorithm	Charles Babbage, Ada Lovelace	First computer design, first algorithm, symbolic manipulation, universal computation, debate on machine creativity.	Theoretical basis for complex game logic and creative generation
1943	McCulloch-Pitts Neuron	Warren McCulloch, Walter Pitts	First artificial neuron, theoretical basis for neural networks, connectionist AI.	Foundation for adaptive game AI and learning agents
1947	Alan Turing's Lecture on Learning	Alan Turing	Earliest public mention of computer intelligence, machine learning concept.	Conceptual basis for adaptable game opponents
1950	Turing's "Computing Machinery and Intelligence"	Alan Turing	Introduced the Turing Test, games as intelligence benchmarks.	Established games as a valid testbed for AI performance
1950	Bertie the Brain	Josef Kates	First computer game AI, public demonstration of computing.	One of the first computer games with a visual display (light bulbs)
1951	Nimrod	Ferranti, John Makepeace Bennett, Raymond Stuart-Williams	Early AI opponent, public education on computing principles.	Custom-built game machine, "electronic brain" demonstration
1952	OXO	A.S. Douglas	Early graphical computer game.	First graphical display of a game on a CRT
1956	Dartmouth Conference	John McCarthy, Marvin Minsky, Nathaniel Rochester, Claude Shannon	Coined "Artificial Intelligence," formalized the field.	Catalyzed research into machine learning and robotics for game development
1958	Tennis for Two	William Higinbotham	Analog computer simulation, real-time physics.	One of the first interactive electronic games with real-time physics simulation

2.4 Games as Intellectual Arenas: The Symbolic AI Era (1960s)

Why did classic board games become the "Drosophila" of early AI research, and what fundamental AI principles emerged from these digital contests? The 1960s cemented games' role as crucial proving grounds for nascent AI.

2.4.1. The Drosophila of AI: Why Games Mattered

During the 1950s and 1960s, classic board games such as chess, checkers, and Go became critically important testbeds for AI research. They were frequently referred to as the "Drosophila of artificial intelligence" (Ensmenger, 2012), an analogy to the fruit fly's role in genetics. This comparison arose from their inherent convenience for AI development: games are relatively simple to model in code, can be simulated extremely fast (allowing for millions of moves per second on modern computers, though much slower on early machines), and provide a clear, objective means to compare computer performance with human intelligence. They offered "micro-worlds" with well-defined rules and boundaries, simplifying the complexities of the real world for early computers and enabling rapid progress in algorithm development.

The structured, rule-bound nature of games provided an ideal, low-cost, and measurable environment for developing and testing complex AI algorithms, particularly when computational resources were severely limited. Early computers possessed constrained memory and processing power. Games offered a contained environment where the "state space" (the vast number of possible moves and positions) could be managed, allowing researchers to focus on algorithmic efficiency, such as search strategies and heuristics, rather than grappling with the complexities of real-world data. This "laboratory" function of games was crucial for AI's early development. It allowed researchers to iterate rapidly, observe the effects of different algorithms, and demonstrate incremental progress, fostering the growth of the field even before the advent of powerful general-purpose computers (Will, 2012). This causal relationship explains why games were not merely a recreational pursuit, but a strategic choice for advancing AI research.

2.4.2. Pioneering AI Research Hubs and Game Programs

The 1960s witnessed the concentration of AI research in key institutions, including Carnegie Mellon University (CMU), the Massachusetts Institute of Technology (MIT), and Stanford University, alongside the University of Edinburgh (Monnens &

Goldberg, 2015). While each institution cultivated its distinct research style, game-playing programs emerged as a common and significant area of focus.

Several pioneering game programs from this era showcased fundamental AI concepts:

- Arthur Samuel's Checkers Program (IBM): A seminal achievement in early AI, Arthur Samuel, an IBM engineer, began work on his checkers-playing program in 1952.[40] This program, developed on the IBM 701, was revolutionary for its ability to learn from experience (Will, 2012). Samuel, who is credited with coining the term "machine learning," designed the program to record game positions and whether those positions ultimately led to wins or losses. By incorporating these learned values into its subsequent decision-making, the program consistently improved its play the more games it engaged in (Will, 2012). In 1962, after playing thousands of games against itself to refine its skills, Samuel's program famously defeated Robert Nealey, a self-described "checkers master" and former Connecticut champion (Will, 2012). Samuel's Checkers program was not just a game-playing AI; it was a foundational experiment in self-improving algorithms, directly giving rise to the field of machine learning. Instead of explicitly programming every rule or strategy, Samuel enabled the machine to *discover* optimal strategies through iterative experience. This is the core principle of modern machine learning, particularly reinforcement learning. Games provided the perfect environment for this breakthrough because they offer clear feedback (win/loss) and a vast number of repeatable scenarios, demonstrating how the pursuit of game mastery led to a fundamental paradigm shift in AI, moving beyond purely symbolic rule-following to adaptive, data-driven learning.
- Logic Theorist (Newell, Simon, Shaw): Developed by Allen Newell, Herbert Simon, and Cliff Shaw between 1955 and 1956, this program was a significant early success in symbolic AI. It demonstrated sophisticated problem-solving capabilities by successfully proving elementary theorems from Whitehead and Russell's *Principia Mathematica* (Monnens & Goldberg, 2015). While not a game in the recreational sense, its ability to perform formal reasoning and theorem-proving was crucial for the development of rule-based AI systems applicable to game logic.
- Kotok-McCarthy Chess Program (MIT/Stanford): Between 1959 and 1962, a group of MIT students, under the guidance of John McCarthy, developed one of the earliest chess programs capable of playing competently against amateur human players (Newborn, 2014). This program notably employed alpha-beta pruning, a key heuristic search algorithm that significantly reduced the number of possible moves the AI needed to evaluate. In 1966, an improved

version of this program, utilized by John McCarthy at Stanford, participated in the first-ever machine-versus-machine chess match, conducted via telegraph against a Soviet program. The Soviet program ultimately won the four-game match 3-1 over a period of nine months.

- Spacewar! (MIT): Created in 1962 by Steve Russell and a group of "hackers" at MIT, *Spacewar!* was developed for the newly installed DEC PDP-1 minicomputer (Russell, Graetz, & Witaenem, 1962). This two-player space combat game featured torpedo-firing spaceships, simulated gravity, limited fuel, and a "hyperspace" feature for emergency escapes. *Spacewar!* was instrumental in establishing video games' interactive and visual aspects, directly inspiring the first commercial arcade games, *Computer Space* and *Galaxy Game*, both released in 1971.
- Mac Hack (MIT): In 1967, Richard Greenblatt at MIT developed Mac Hack, a chess program that achieved a significant milestone by becoming the first chess program to be officially ranked and to win against a human in a tournament setting (Greenblatt, Eastlake III, & Crocker, 1967).
- Robert Dupchak's Penny-Matcher (CMU): Around 1964, Robert Dupchak, a graduate student at CMU, constructed a small machine designed to play the game of "penny matching" (Parnas, 2017). This machine consistently defeated its human opponents. Dupchak's creation demonstrated that a computer could *appear* intelligent by simply remembering past opponent moves and identifying patterns, without necessarily possessing genuine understanding or complex reasoning. This highlights the distinction between apparent and genuine intelligence. This echoes criticisms of the Turing Test, where a "brute force" machine could pass without true intelligence. This distinction is crucial in AI philosophy, questioning whether successful performance in a game (behavioral intelligence) equates to true understanding or consciousness (cognitive intelligence). Games, by providing clear behavioral outputs, inadvertently became the arena for these deeper questions about what constitutes "intelligence" in a machine, influencing how AI is evaluated and understood. Table 2. Summarizes the pioneering AI research hubs and its outcomes

Table 2. A brief comparison of Pioneering AI Research Hubs and its Outcomes

Year	Game/Program Name	Developer	AI Concepts	Key Outcomes
1950	Bertie the Brain	Josef Kates	Early AI opponent, adjustable difficulty	First computer game with a visual display (light bulbs)
1951	Nimrod	Ferranti, J.M. Bennett, R. Stuart-Williams	Game-playing AI, public education on computing	First digital computer designed specifically to play a game, beat human opponents
1952	OXO	A.S. Douglas	Early graphical AI opponent	First graphical computer game on a CRT
1952 (began)	Samuel's Checkers Program	Arthur Samuel / IBM	Machine learning, learning from experience, alpha-beta pruning	Coined "machine learning," defeated human master in 1962
1955-56	Logic Theorist	Newell, Simon, Shaw	Symbolic reasoning, theorem proving, general problem solving	Proved 38 elementary theorems, foundational for rule-based AI
1958	Tennis for Two	William Higinbotham	Analog computation for physics simulation	Early interactive electronic game, used oscilloscope for display
1959-62	Kotok-McCarthy Chess Program	MIT / John McCarthy	Heuristic search (alpha-beta pruning), early competitive chess AI	First machine-vs-machine chess match (lost 3-1 in 1966)
1962	Spacewar!	Steve Russell / MIT	Interactive game mechanics, real-time physics	Influenced first commercial arcade games (Computer Space, Galaxy Game)
1964 (approx.)	Penny-Matcher	Robert Dupchak / CMU	Apparent intelligence through pattern recognition	Demonstrated distinction between apparent and genuine intelligence
1967	Mac Hack	Richard Greenblatt / MIT	Advanced chess AI	First chess program to be ranked and win against a human in a tournament

2.5 The Evolution of AI in Gaming: From Heuristics to Deep Learning

As AI evolved beyond symbolic reasoning, how did games continue to push the boundaries of machine learning and intelligent behavior? The limitations of early approaches spurred new paradigms, with games remaining at the forefront.

2.5.1. From Symbolic Limitations to Neural Network Breakthroughs

While symbolic AI achieved notable early successes in structured environments like games and theorem-proving during the 1960s, it encountered significant drawbacks that limited its scalability and adaptability. These limitations included its inherent inability to handle ambiguity, the immense complexity of encoding real-world knowledge into explicit rules, and a general lack of adaptability to unforeseen situations. These challenges spurred a critical shift towards alternative approaches, notably machine learning and neural networks (Justesen, Bontrager, Togelius, & Risi, 2019) (Balaha et al., 2023).

The 1990s marked a period of significant breakthroughs, often driven by game-playing AI:

- TD-Gammon (IBM): In the 1990s, IBM's TD-Gammon, a neural network specifically designed for backgammon, powerfully demonstrated the efficacy of learning through trial and error (Will, 2012). Equipped with 30,000 artificial synapses, this program significantly improved its play by engaging in thousands of games against itself, mirroring the iterative learning process observed in human cognition (Will, 2012). This program was a crucial precursor to the later successes of deep learning.
- Deep Blue (IBM, 1997): A landmark event in AI history occurred in 1997 when IBM's Deep Blue computer defeated Garry Kasparov, the reigning world chess champion, in a six-game series. This marked the first instance of a machine defeating a world chess champion in a match, showcasing the immense power of computational brute force combined with sophisticated heuristic search algorithms (Will, 2012).
- IBM Watson (2011): Extending AI's game-playing capabilities beyond traditional board games, IBM's Watson famously triumphed over two of the most successful *Jeopardy!* champions in 2011. This achievement demonstrated advanced natural language processing, knowledge representation, and complex reasoning capabilities within an open-domain question-answering game.
- AlphaGo (DeepMind, 2016): The mastery of the ancient strategy game Go by DeepMind's AlphaGo in 2016 (defeating world champion Lee Sedol) represented a profound leap for AI. Go, long considered more abstract and intuitive than chess with an astronomically larger search space, was thought to be beyond AI's reach. AlphaGo's success, driven by deep neural networks and reinforcement learning that learned strategies from scratch by playing against itself, demonstrated AI's ability to develop human-like intuition and creativity in highly complex domains.

The limitations encountered by symbolic AI in games, such as encoding complex knowledge, directly spurred the development and adoption of data-driven machine learning and neural network approaches. Symbolic AI struggled with "ambiguity and the complexity of encoding real-world knowledge". The successes of TD-Gammon and Deep Blue relied on learning from vast amounts of data and powerful search, not just explicit rules (Will, 2012). Games, with their vast amounts of structured data (game states, moves, outcomes), provided the perfect training ground for these new data-driven AI paradigms. The imperative to surpass human performance in games like chess and Go pushed AI beyond its symbolic "AI Winter" limitations. This highlights a crucial causal relationship: the challenges posed by games forced AI researchers to innovate beyond initial conceptual frameworks, leading to the development of techniques like reinforcement learning and deep learning that now power much of modern AI across diverse applications.

2.5.2. AI's Pervasive Role in Modern Gaming and Beyond

Today, AI is an indispensable component of the gaming industry, fundamentally revolutionizing player experiences and game development processes. AI's role in gaming has expanded significantly beyond simply creating intelligent opponents (Non-Player Characters or NPCs) that exhibit lifelike behavior and respond intelligently to player actions. It now encompasses a broader spectrum of applications:

- AI-driven content generation: AI is employed for procedural storytelling and dynamic world-building, enabling the creation of more immersive and adaptive gaming environments that can surprise and engage players (Nong, Sun, & Wang, 2025) (Gulsoy, Kokach, Kocaçınar, & Akbulut, 2024).
- Automated testing and quality assurance: AI algorithms are used to simulate thousands of player scenarios, efficiently identify bugs and glitches, and optimize game performance. This significantly reduces development time and enhances game stability, ensuring a smoother experience for users (Ranjitha, Nathan, & Joseph, 2020).
- Personalized gaming: AI can analyze player preferences and historical gameplay data to recommend games, tailor in-game experiences, and dynamically adjust difficulty, creating a highly personalized gaming journey (Brisson et al., 2012).

Beyond commercial gaming, complex game environments continue to serve as vital training grounds for developing AI with applications far beyond gameplay. Examples include the RoboCup tournament (Kitano, Asada, Kuniyoshi, Noda, & Osawa, 1997), where robots are trained to compete in soccer, pushing the boundaries of real-time perception, decision-making, and physical interaction.

Modern gaming is not just a consumer of AI but an active contributor to AI research, pushing the boundaries of generative AI, simulation, and complex decision-making. AI is now used for "AI-driven content generation, procedural storytelling, and dynamic world-building" and "automated testing" in games (Nong, Sun, & Wang, 2025). Games like StarCraft and Angry Birds are used in AI competitions, demonstrating their utility as complex, dynamic environments for AI development. This shows that AI in gaming has matured beyond just opponent AI. Games are now complex ecosystems where AI is used to *create* content, *test* systems, and *personalize* experiences, requiring advanced AI techniques like generative models and sophisticated simulation (Nong, Sun, & Wang, 2025) (Brisson et al., 2012). The relationship has evolved into a continuous feedback loop. As AI advances, it enables more complex and immersive games. In turn, the challenges posed by these increasingly sophisticated games (e.g., real-time strategy, open-world environments) drive further AI research and innovation, creating a virtuous cycle that benefits both fields and pushes the frontiers of what AI can achieve.

2.6 Conclusion: The Enduring Interplay and Future Horizons

What profound lessons do the intertwined history of gaming and AI offer for understanding intelligence itself, and what frontiers lie ahead? The long journey of this convergence reveals a continuous quest to understand and replicate cognition.

2.6.1. Synthesizing the Historical Narrative

The historical convergence of gaming and artificial intelligence is a rich tapestry woven from ancient philosophical inquiries into logic, medieval attempts at mechanical reasoning, and the intricate automata of the Enlightenment era. These early threads laid the conceptual and mechanical groundwork for the digital age. Aristotle's systematic formulation of the syllogism provided the foundational concept of formal logic, which underpins rule-based AI (Fetzer, 1990). Ramon Llull's *Ars Magna* demonstrated early attempts at mechanical knowledge generation through symbolic manipulation. The sophisticated automata of de Vaucanson and Jaquet-Droz showcased the human desire to mimic intelligent behavior through complex engineering.

The 19th century brought the blueprint for programmability with the Jacquard loom and the visionary theoretical computing of Charles Babbage and Ada Lovelace (Albaugh, McCann, Yao, & Hudson, 2021). Lovelace's "first algorithm" foresaw machines manipulating symbols beyond numbers, a crucial step towards general-purpose computing and machine creativity. The post-World War II era formalized AI with the McCulloch-Pitts neuron, providing a biological inspiration for neural networks, and the Dartmouth Conference, which officially coined the term "artificial intelligence." Simultaneously, the first interactive computer games emerged, including Bertie the Brain, Nimrod (Sumner, 2014), OXO (Aarseth & Hammar, n.d.), and Tennis for Two (Reddy, 2005). These games served as crucial public demonstrations of computing capabilities and early testbeds for AI.

The 1960s solidified games as the "Drosophila of AI", driving breakthroughs in machine learning, exemplified by Arthur Samuel's Checkers program, and competitive AI, seen in the Kotok-McCarthy chess program and Mac Hack. The subsequent decades witnessed AI in games evolve from heuristic-driven systems to the profound successes of deep learning, culminating in triumphs like IBM's Deep Blue and DeepMind's AlphaGo, continually pushing the boundaries of machine intelligence (Will, 2012).

The continuous thread throughout this history is humanity's persistent desire to understand, replicate, and augment its own cognitive processes through machines. Games provide a unique, controlled environment to explore this. From Aristotle's logic to Llull's knowledge machine, to automata mimicking human actions, and then to digital computers playing chess and Go, the underlying motivation has consistently been to formalize, mechanize, and ultimately *replicate* aspects of human thought and behavior. Games, with their inherent challenges and clear objectives, offer a simplified yet sufficiently complex proxy for real-world cognitive tasks. They allow researchers to isolate and test specific aspects of intelligence, such as strategy, learning, perception, and decision-making, in a quantifiable manner. This historical continuity suggests that the convergence of gaming and AI is not accidental but fundamental to the human endeavor of understanding intelligence itself. Games act as a mirror, reflecting our current understanding of cognition and providing a safe, iterative space to push its boundaries.

2.6.2. Philosophical Questions Revisited

The philosophical debates ignited by Ada Lovelace's Objection and Alan Turing's Test remain highly relevant in the contemporary landscape of AI. While modern AI, particularly advanced deep learning models like GPT-4, can generate human-like text and perform complex tasks that once seemed exclusive to human intellect, the core question of whether they truly "think," "understand," or "originate" remains a subject of intense academic scrutiny. The concept of the "Lovelace Effect" emphasizes that the perception of AI's creativity and originality is often a human attribution, highlighting the inherently subjective nature of evaluating artificial intelligence.

The definition of intelligence in machines is fluid, constantly being redefined by AI's increasing capabilities, with games often serving as the proving ground for these new definitions. Lovelace's Objection (machines cannot originate) and Turing's Test (can machines act indistinguishably from humans) set early benchmarks for machine intelligence. However, as AI achieves these milestones, such as Deep Blue defeating Kasparov or AlphaGo mastering Go, the criteria for "true" intelligence often shift to more complex, less defined domains. This dynamic is evident in the progression from simple game AIs to systems capable of natural language processing (Watson) and intuitive strategy (AlphaGo). Each success in a game prompts new questions about the nature of intelligence. The history of AI in games reveals that "intelligence" is not a static target but a moving one, constantly being re-evaluated as machines become more capable [37]. This dynamic interplay means games will likely continue to be at the forefront of AI research, not just as testbeds, but as arenas where the very philosophical boundaries of artificial intelligence are explored and redefined.

2.6.3. Future Horizons

The convergence of gaming and AI is poised for even greater integration and mutual influence. Future developments will likely include increasingly sophisticated applications of AI in game design, such as generative AI creating entire game worlds, dynamic narratives, and adaptive challenges in real-time. This will lead to highly personalized player experiences, where games evolve and respond uniquely to individual players' styles and preferences. Furthermore, complex game environments will continue to serve as invaluable training grounds for general AI agents, enabling them to learn to navigate and solve problems in diverse, unpredictable scenarios that mirror real-world complexities. As AI becomes more deeply embedded in interactive systems, ethical considerations surrounding its impact on human behavior, the nature of human-AI interaction, and questions of agency and creativity will become increasingly paramount, requiring ongoing interdisciplinary dialogue and research.

3. HOW HARDWARE EVOLUTION PAINTED NEW WORLDS

3.1 Introduction: The Unseen Architects of Digital Realms

Have you ever paused mid-game, or witnessed an AI's astounding feat, and wondered about the invisible scaffolding beneath the digital spectacle? What unseen architects laid the groundwork for these immersive experiences, and how did their silicon blueprints paint new worlds into existence? This section embarks on a historical odyssey, charting the profound and often symbiotic relationship between the relentless evolution of computing hardware and the burgeoning capabilities of artificial intelligence within the realm of interactive digital experiences. From the earliest philosophical musings on automated thought to the intricate neural networks powering today's virtual realities, this journey reveals that the digital worlds we inhabit are not just products of ingenious code, but deeply intertwined with the physical constraints and liberating advancements of the silicon itself. Each leap in processing power and memory capacity has not merely facilitated, but fundamentally reshaped, the very canvas upon which digital realms are rendered and intelligent behaviors are enacted.

3.2 The Dawn of Calculation: From Philosophical Blueprints to Mechanical Dreams

3.2.1 Early Conceptualizations: The Logic Before the Machine

Before the whir of gears or the glow of vacuum tubes, the very notion of automated reasoning was a philosophical pursuit. Centuries ago, Ramon Llull, a Catalan mystic and poet, conceived of the *Ars Magna* (Latin for "The Great Art") between 1305 and 1308. This complex system of logic and language, involving symbolic notation and combinatory diagrams, aimed to unify all branches of knowledge and prove Christian doctrine through rational discussion. While far from a physical computer, Llull's work is recognized as a significant precursor to combinatorial logic and the idea of formalizing reasoning, laying a conceptual groundwork for later computational thought.

Llull's *Ars Magna* predates electronic computers by over six centuries, yet it embodies a fundamental human desire: to systematize knowledge and automate reasoning. This is not merely a historical curiosity; it suggests that the drive for artificial intelligence is deeply rooted in philosophical inquiry into logic and knowledge representation, long before the technical means existed. The very idea of a "calculus" of thought, as later pursued by mathematicians like George Boole and Gottlob Frege, and ultimately foundational to computer science, has its origins in this early, abstract quest. This historical perspective highlights that hardware evolution, while undeniably critical, is often a direct response to pre-existing intellectual and philosophical aspirations. The conceptual canvas for automated intelligence was envisioned long before the physical silicon paintbrushes were forged.

3.2.2 Mechanical Precursors: Automata and the Illusion of Life

The 17th and 18th centuries saw the rise of intricate automata—self-operating mechanical devices designed to mimic living beings. Notable examples include Jacques de Vaucanson's "The Digesting Duck" (1739), a copper mechanical duck capable of seemingly eating, digesting, and excreting food, with each wing featuring over 400 moving parts [8]. Later, in the early 19th century, Henri Maillardet's "Draughtsman Writer" could draw four different pictures and write three poems, demonstrating a sophisticated form of mechanical memory. These devices, while not programmable in the modern sense, captivated audiences by creating a compelling illusion of intelligence and life, pushing the boundaries of mechanical engineering.

Moving into the 20th century, Leonardo Torres Quevedo, a Spanish engineer, created *El Ajedrecista* (The Chess Player) in 1912, publicly demonstrated in Paris in 1914. This automaton could play a modified chess endgame (king and rook vs. lone king) and always deliver checkmate, showcasing early mechanical decision-making. In Japan, Makoto Nishimura built *Gakutensoku* in 1929, considered the first robot built in the East, capable of changing facial expressions and moving its head and hands via air pressure mechanisms.[8] These creations, though specialized, were tangible steps towards machines performing complex tasks, hinting at the potential for computational thought. The automata of these centuries were engineering marvels that simulated intelligent behavior. Their popularity stemmed from the compelling illusion of life and thought they presented. This pre-digital era established a public fascination with "thinking machines" and set a precedent for judging machine intelligence by its outward behavior, a theme that would resonate strongly with the later Turing Test. The ingenuity of these early designs lay in creating complex mechanical sequences that *appeared* intelligent, rather than truly *reasoning*. This historical context suggests that human perception and the "performance" of intelligence have always been central to the development and acceptance of AI. The canvas was not just about raw computation, but about crafting believable experiences.

3.2.2 The Analytical Engine and Ada Lovelace: The First Algorithm

The true conceptual leap towards modern computing arrived with Charles Babbage's designs for the Analytical Engine in the 1830s (Essinger, 2014). Inspired by the punched cards used in Joseph-Marie Jacquard's loom (patented 1804), which automated complex weaving patterns, Babbage envisioned a machine that could receive instructions and data via similar punch cards to perform mathematical calculations. However, it was Ada Lovelace, daughter of Lord Byron and a gifted mathematician, who truly grasped the Analytical Engine's universal potential. In her extensive "Translator's Notes" (published under the initials "A.A.L.") (Reddy, 2005), which were three times longer than the original Italian article she translated, Lovelace articulated concepts foundational to modern computing. She was the first to distinguish between numbers and symbolic operations, realizing that the machine could manipulate not just quantities, but any symbols according to rules, extending its utility beyond mere arithmetic to realms like music and graphics. Crucially, she wrote what is widely regarded as the first computer algorithm: a step-by-step description for the Analytical Engine to compute Bernoulli numbers (Fillebrown, 1992). This recursive algorithm, though for a machine never fully built, demonstrated the power of automated computation.

Lovelace's profound contribution was not just about programming a machine to calculate Bernoulli numbers. Her "Translator's Notes" explicitly stated the Analytical Engine's potential to manipulate *symbols* beyond numbers, suggesting applications in music and graphics. This was a critical conceptual development: it framed computation not merely as a tool for arithmetic, but as a medium for *creative expression* and *pattern generation*. This vision, nearly a century before the first programmable computers, laid the conceptual groundwork for fields like generative art and music, and even the procedural content generation seen in modern games. The conceptual canvas was expanding from numerical tables to abstract symbolic patterns.

Lovelace also famously posited what Alan Turing later dubbed "Lady Lovelace's Objection" in his 1950 paper, "Computing Machinery and Intelligence" (Turing, 1980). She argued that the Analytical Engine "has no pretensions whatever to originate anything. It can do whatever we know how to order to perform. It has no power of anticipating any relations or truths" (Turing, 1980). This objection, often misinterpreted as a blanket denial of machine intelligence, is now seen by some scholars not as skepticism but as an invitation to define the human's role in this new field and to develop machines capable of originality. This reinterpretation has led to the concept of the "Lovelace Effect," describing situations where users perceive creativity in computational outputs. Lovelace's work established that the power of computing lay in its *programmability* and *symbolic manipulation*, not just raw calculation. This foreshadowed the entire trajectory of AI, from game-playing algorithms to large language models, all of which operate by manipulating symbols according to rules. Her "objection" itself sparked a central philosophical debate about machine creativity that continues today.

3.2.3 The Theoretical Foundations of AI: From Neurons to Thinking Machines

The mid-20th century marked a pivotal shift from mechanical dreams to the theoretical bedrock of artificial intelligence. In 1943, Warren McCulloch and Walter Pitts published "A Logical Calculus of the Ideas Immanent in Nervous Activity," introducing the McCulloch-Pitts artificial neuron (Arbib, 2000). This foundational model, inspired by biological neural circuitry, represented a neuron as a binary logical element, firing or not firing based on weighted inputs and a threshold. This abstract mathematical model provided a blueprint for neural networks, a cornerstone of modern AI.

Alan Turing, a towering figure in computer science, further propelled the field. In a 1947 lecture in London, he articulated a radical vision: "What we want is a machine that can learn from experience," suggesting that the mechanism for this would be the machine's ability to "alter its own instructions". This is arguably the earliest public mention of computer intelligence and the concept of machine learning. Three years later, his seminal 1950 paper, "Computing Machinery and Intelligence," introduced the "Imitation Game," now famously known as the Turing Test (Turing, 1980). This behavioral test proposed that if an interrogator could not reliably distinguish a machine from a human through text-based conversation, the machine could be said to “think”. The paper also addressed various objections, including Lovelace's, and highlighted the “universal” nature of digital machinery—that any sufficiently powerful digital computer could simulate any other.

The Turing Test, despite its profound influence, has faced significant philosophical criticisms. Ned Block's “Blockhead” thought experiment, for instance, proposes a machine that passes the test via a massive lookup table of pre-programmed responses, questioning whether such “brute force” behavior constitutes genuine intelligence. John Searle's “Chinese Room Argument” (1980) similarly argues that symbol manipulation according to rules does not equate to understanding or consciousness, challenging the idea that “appropriately programmed computers literally have cognitive states”. These debates underscore the enduring complexity in defining and measuring true machine intelligence. The McCulloch-Pitts neuron provided a theoretical *hardware-inspired* model for computation, while Turing's work focused on the *software's* ability to mimic human intelligence. The critiques of the Turing Test reveal a fundamental tension: can intelligence be purely behavioral, or does it require an underlying *conscious* mechanism? This is not just a philosophical debate; it directly impacts how AI is designed and evaluated. If a machine simply processes symbols without “understanding,” is it truly intelligent, or merely a sophisticated automaton? This question forces a deeper look at the *internal architecture* (both hardware and software) required for genuine intelligence, moving beyond mere external performance. The conceptualization of AI was intrinsically linked to the underlying hardware model, even when hypothetical. The limitations of early hardware meant that AI research was largely confined to philosophy and theory, but these theoretical blueprints, like the McCulloch-Pitts neuron, would later guide the development of the physical “silicon canvas” needed to realize them.

3.2.4 The Birth of a Field: Dartmouth and the AI Winter

The term Artificial Intelligence itself was coined at a landmark academic gathering: the Dartmouth Summer Research Project on Artificial Intelligence. Held in the summer of 1956 at Dartmouth College in Hanover, New Hampshire, this two-month workshop was organized by John McCarthy, Marvin Minsky, Nathaniel Rochester, and Claude Shannon (McCarthy, Minsky, Rochester, & Shannon, 2006). Their ambitious proposal stated that “every aspect of learning or any other feature of intelligence can in principle be so precisely described that a machine can be made to simulate it”. The conference brought together leading thinkers in computer science, mathematics, and cognitive psychology, sparking widespread interest and laying the foundational goals for AI research.

This initial optimism, however, was followed by what became known as the “AI Winter” in the 1980s. Early AI systems, while successful in specific tasks, struggled with broader challenges, leading to waning funding and interest. This period highlighted the gap between ambitious theoretical goals and the practical limitations of the hardware and algorithms available at the time. The "AI Winter" of the 1980s was not merely a failure of imagination or algorithms; it was significantly influenced by hardware limitations. Early computers lacked the processing power and memory to bring ambitious AI ideas to life. The grand visions articulated at Dartmouth in 1956 simply outstripped the available "silicon canvas." This causal relationship is crucial: hardware constraints directly dictated the pace and scope of AI advancement, forcing researchers to confront the practical realities of their theoretical constructs. The "winter" was a period of necessary maturation, awaiting the hardware spring. This cycle of ambitious theoretical leaps followed by practical hardware limitations and subsequent "winters" is a recurring pattern in technological history. It underscores that progress in AI is not solely an algorithmic endeavor but is deeply tethered to the underlying computational infrastructure.

Could these early mechanical dreams truly foresee the digital canvas they were preparing, or were their visions merely *shadows on the cave wall* of what was to come? The seeds of universal computation were sown, yet the vibrant hues of interactive worlds remained beyond their wildest *byte*-mares. Their foresight was profound, but the *pixelated reality* of their distant future was a landscape they could only *compute* in theory.

3.3 Pixels and Patterns: The Rise of Interactive Worlds (1950s-1990s)

3.3.1 The First Digital Playgrounds: Beyond Calculation to Interaction

The mid-20th century saw the emergence of the first true digital games, transforming computers from mere calculators into interactive canvases. One of the earliest examples was the computerized game of *Nim*, demonstrated in 1951 at the Festival of Britain by the Ferranti-built NIMROD computer (Reddy, 2005). This 12-foot wide, 5-foot tall, 9-foot deep machine allowed attendees to play the ancient mathematical strategy game against an artificial intelligence, regularly winning even against skilled human players (Reddy, 2005).

In 1950, Josef Kates developed *Bertie the Brain* for the Canadian National Exhibition, a 13-foot tall computer that played tic-tac-toe against an AI with adjustable difficulty. A.S. Douglas, a Cambridge University PhD candidate, created *OXO* in 1952, a tic-tac-toe game played on the EDSAC computer, displaying the board on a cathode-ray tube. A significant leap in interactive graphics came with William Higinbotham's *Tennis for Two*, introduced on October 18, 1958, at Brookhaven National Laboratory (Monnens & Goldberg, 2015). This game, built using an analog computer and an oscilloscope, allowed two players to control rackets and hit a ball over a net, displaying the action as a moving dot on a screen. These early games, though simplistic by modern standards, were groundbreaking demonstrations of computers engaging humans in real-time interaction, laying the groundwork for the burgeoning video game industry (Monnens & Goldberg, 2015).

These early computer games were primarily *demonstrations* of computing power, designed to impress and explain the new technology to a skeptical public. However, their very nature as *interactive experiences* quickly revealed a deeper potential: to engage and entertain. This shift from "proof of concept" to "player engagement" was critical. The hardware, initially built for complex calculations and even military ballistics, found a new "canvas" in simulating simple physical interactions, paving the way for the entertainment industry. The "magic" of the electronic brain was less about its raw computational power and more about its ability to *play*. This illustrates how technological advancements often find their most impactful applications in unforeseen domains [27]. The initial purpose of the hardware was quickly transcended by its capacity to create compelling interactive experiences, highlighting the emergent properties of new technologies.

3.3.2 The Arcade and Home Console Boom: Miniaturization and Mass Appeal

The 1970s and 1980s witnessed an explosion in arcade games and the birth of home consoles, driven by increasing miniaturization and affordability of hardware. Table 3 illustrates the rapid growth in processing power and memory over two decades, directly correlating with the increasing complexity of game AI and graphics.

Table 3. Historical Trends in Computational Hardware (CPU/GPU Power, Memory) and Their Impact on Game AI

Console	Release Date (NA)	CPU	RAM	VRAM
Atari 2600 (VCS)	October/November 1977	MOS 6507 @ 1.19 MHz	128 bytes	(Integrated with CPU)
NES (Famicom)	July 15, 1983 (JP) / June 1985 (NA)	Ricoh 2A03 8-bit (MOS 6502 core) @ 1.79 MHz (NTSC)	2 KB work RAM, 256 bytes sprite RAM	2 KB video RAM
Sega Genesis (Mega Drive)	August 1989 (NA)	Motorola 68000 16/32-bit @ 7.6 MHz; Zilog Z80 8-bit @ 3.58 MHz	64 KB RAM, 8 KB audio RAM	64 KB video RAM

continued on following page

Table 3. Continued

Console	Release Date (NA)	CPU	RAM	VRAM
PlayStation (PS1)	September 9, 1995 (NA)	R3000A 32-bit RISC @ 33.87 MHz	2 MB main EDO DRAM	1 MB Video RAM
Nintendo 64	September 29, 1996 (NA)	NEC VR4300 64-bit @ 93.75 MHz	4 MB RDRAM (expandable to 8 MB)	(Unified Memory Architecture)

3.3.3 Early Game AI Techniques: The Art of Illusion

Despite the significant hardware constraints evident in Table 3, early game developers crafted ingenious AI to create compelling challenges.

Pac-Man (1980): The Ghosts with Personalities

Namco's arcade hit *Pac-Man* is a prime example of early, effective game AI. The four iconic ghosts—Blinky (red), Pinky (pink), Inky (cyan), and Clyde (orange)—each possessed distinct, deterministic "personalities" or behaviors, despite being governed by simple mathematical rules. In "Chase Mode," Blinky directly targets Pac-Man's current tile, making him the most aggressive. Pinky aims for a tile four spaces ahead of Pac-Man, attempting to ambush. Inky's target is more complex, depending on both Pac-Man's and Blinky's positions, allowing him to flank. Clyde, uniquely, targets Pac-Man when far away but reverts to "Scatter Mode" (targeting his home corner) if he gets within eight tiles, creating unpredictable "cowardly" behavior.[51] These distinct movement patterns, combined with "Scatter Mode" where each ghost retreats to a specific maze corner, created the illusion of intelligent, coordinated opponents.

The Legend of Zelda (1986) and Metroid (1986): Patterned Adversaries

On early home consoles like the NES, games like *The Legend of Zelda* (released August 1986 in Japan) and *Metroid* (released August 1986 in Japan) featured enemies with simple, predictable movement patterns (Cuddy, 2008). Enemies often moved along grid-based paths, changing direction only at specific intersections or when colliding with obstacles. For instance, in *Zelda*, dynamic objects (enemies, projectiles) were allocated memory and their AI tracked states and handled collisions. Their movement was often tied to subpixel speeds and grid offsets, ensuring consistent, albeit simple, behavior. Reverse engineering efforts have revealed the underlying logic, often based on finite state machines (FSMs). The widespread adoption of Finite State Machines (FSMs) became a core AI model for Non-Player

Characters (NPCs) during this era (Reddy, 2005). An FSM defines a fixed set of states (e.g., patrolling, chasing, attacking) and transitions between them based on specific rules or events (e.g., "player in sight"). This structured approach allowed developers to manage character behavior effectively even with limited memory and processing power (Reddy, 2005).

The limited hardware of the 8-bit and 16-bit eras (e.g., Atari 2600's 128 bytes of RAM, NES's 2KB work RAM) forced developers to become masters of "constraint-driven innovation." Instead of complex simulations, they relied on deterministic patterns and finite state machines (FSMs) to create the *illusion* of intelligence. The distinct "personalities" of Pac-Man's ghosts are a prime example: simple rules yielding complex-seeming emergent behavior. This was not about simulating human thought, but about crafting exploitable, yet challenging, *patterns*. This approach also facilitated easier debugging and predictability, crucial for the nascent industry. This period demonstrates that innovation is not solely about raw power; it is often about ingenious problem-solving within severe limitations. The canvas was small, but the artists learned to paint with *pixels of perception*, making every byte count. The predictable patterns, while simple, became a core part of the gameplay loop, encouraging players to learn and master the AI's "tells."

How did these seemingly simple digital adversaries, constrained by nascent hardware, lay the groundwork for worlds far more complex than their pixelated origins suggested? Through the art of *pattern recognition*, both humans and machines, proved that even basic rules could create compelling *play-scapes*, hinting at the *ghosts in the machine* to come. The *sparse data* of early memory banks forced a focus on *elegant algorithms*, which, like a master painter's limited palette, yielded surprisingly rich *digital tapestries*.

3.4. The Third Dimension and Beyond: Hardware Fuels AI Sophistication (Late 1990s-2000s)

3.4.1. Leap to 3D and Enhanced AI: Spatial Reasoning Comes Alive

The late 1990s marked a dramatic shift in gaming with the widespread adoption of 3D graphics, demanding a new level of sophistication from AI. Games like *Half-Life* (released November 1998 by Valve Corporation) became a landmark for their pioneering AI. Unlike many contemporary first-person shooters that relied on simplistic "bullet sponge" enemies, *Half-Life*'s Human Grunts and other adversaries exhibited advanced behaviors such as squad tactics, flanking maneuvers, and dynamic reactions to the player and environment. This was achieved by leveraging a heavily modified Quake engine using C++, allowing for more complex AI programming techniques. The AI was designed to make enemies feel like living, thinking creatures, reacting to sound, seeking cover, and even retreating when injured. Valve's design process, often described as building the game "one room at a time" with constant playtesting, allowed for highly polished and intelligent encounters.

3.4.2 Navigation Meshes (NavMeshes): The AI's GPS

As game worlds transitioned from 2D grids to complex 3D environments, traditional pathfinding methods became computationally expensive. The solution arrived with Navigation Meshes (NavMeshes) [44], abstract data structures popularized in video game AI around 2000. A NavMesh is a collection of 2D convex polygons that define traversable areas in a 3D environment, allowing AI agents to efficiently find paths while avoiding obstacles like trees or walls. Pathfinding within a single polygon is trivial (a straight line), and pathfinding between polygons utilizes graph search algorithms like A* [45]. This approach significantly simplified calculations that would otherwise need to be done in the "true" 3D space, enabling more realistic and fluid movement for NPCs.

The shift to 3D gaming (e.g., *Half-Life*) was not just a graphical upgrade; it necessitated a fundamental rethinking of AI. Simple grid-based movement was insufficient for complex 3D environments [46]. This directly led to the popularization of Navigation Meshes around 2000. NavMeshes are a crucial architectural solution to a hardware-imposed problem: how to efficiently enable AI spatial understanding and navigation in computationally intensive 3D worlds. Without this abstraction layer, the complex AI behaviors seen in games like *Half-Life* would have been far more difficult, if not impossible, to implement effectively on the hardware of the time. The canvas gained depth, and the paint needed a new way to flow across it. This demonstrates a recurring theme: as hardware enables new dimensions of realism (e.g., 3D graphics), it simultaneously creates new computational challenges that AI must solve, often leading to novel algorithmic solutions like NavMeshes. This continuous feedback loop drives innovation in both domains.

3.4.3 The GPU Revolution: Unleashing the AI Engine

A monumental shift in hardware architecture occurred with the introduction of the Graphics Processing Unit (GPU). NVIDIA's GeForce 256, launched on October 11, 1999, is widely recognized as the "world's first GPU". Its revolutionary feature was the integration of a hardware Transform and Lighting (T&L) engine. This meant that complex 3D graphics calculations, previously handled by the CPU, were offloaded to the specialized GPU (Lyu, Madanapalli, Vishwanath, & Sivaraman, 2024).

This crucial shift had a profound ripple effect on AI development. By freeing the CPU from intensive graphics rendering tasks, significant processing power became available for more complex AI behaviors, sophisticated physics simulations, and richer game logic. GPUs, with their highly parallel processing capabilities, proved exceptionally well-suited for accelerating machine learning and deep learning operations. This parallel processing power, initially designed for rendering pixels, became the backbone for training large neural networks and enabling advanced AI functionalities like spatial understanding and navigation in increasingly complex 3D environments (Lyu, Madanapalli, Vishwanath, & Sivaraman, 2024).

The GeForce 256's introduction of hardware T&L was primarily aimed at improving graphics rendering (Peddie, 2023). However, a critical development is that this innovation *unintentionally* laid the groundwork for the modern AI revolution. By offloading graphics computations from the CPU, it created a *new computational resource* (the GPU's parallel processing cores) that was later discovered to be incredibly effective for machine learning and deep learning. This is a prime example of a hardware advancement creating an entirely new "canvas" for AI, far beyond its original design intent. The "silicon canvas" was not just painted *on*, but became a *painter* itself. This illustrates how technological convergence and serendipitous discoveries can profoundly alter the trajectory of related fields. The GPU, initially a graphics specialist, became a general-purpose AI accelerator, fundamentally changing the scale and complexity of AI that could be deployed in games and beyond.

As hardware rendered worlds with unprecedented realism, did the AI within them truly think, or merely simulate intelligence with greater finesse, blurring the lines between code and consciousness? The line blurred, as algorithms, now accelerated by silicon, learned to dance with deception, making the canvas of reality ever more convincingly alive. The pixelated puppets of yesteryear gained digital souls, their movements guided by geometric grace and parallel processing power.

3.5 The Algorithmic Alchemists: Procedural Generation and Generative AI (2000s-Present)

3.5.1 Procedural Content Generation (PCG): Infinite Worlds from Finite Rules

Procedural Content Generation (PCG) has transformed game development by enabling the creation of vast, unique game worlds and elements using algorithms, rather than manual design (Sarkar et al., 2023). This technique, rooted in earlier examples like *Elite* (1984), which generated 8 galaxies with 256 star systems each on limited hardware, has scaled dramatically.

Modern titans such as *No Man's Sky* (2016) exemplify the sheer scale achievable, boasting over 18 quintillion procedurally generated planets, each with unique flora, fauna, and geology. Other notable examples include *Minecraft* (2009) (Duncan,

2011), which creates limitless 3D worlds from forests to caves, and *Dwarf Fortress* (2006) (Adams, 2019), known for generating entire histories, creatures, and narratives. PCG relies on pseudorandomness and deterministic principles, often using "seeds" to ensure reproducibility while appearing random. Table 4 illustrates the increasing scale of procedural content generation, directly correlating with the increasing computational power available.

Table 4. The increasing scale of procedural content generation

Game Title	Year of Release	Procedural Content	Scale / Quantity
Elite	1984	Galaxies, Star Systems	8 galaxies, 256 star systems each (approx. 2,000 planets)
Minecraft	2009	3D World (terrain, biomes)	Effectively infinite
No Man's Sky	2016	Planets, flora, fauna, geology	Over 18 quintillion unique planets
Dwarf Fortress	2006	World history, creatures, narratives	Vast, complex, multi-layered

3.5.2 Generative AI in Game Development: The Digital Alchemists

The latest evolution in AI, particularly generative AI, is profoundly reshaping game development.

Automated Content Creation: Generative AI automates traditionally time-consuming tasks such as concept art, 3D modeling, texturing, and even voice acting. This significantly speeds up development cycles and reduces costs, allowing developers to focus on creative aspects rather than manual labor (Nong, Sun, & Wang, 2025).

Intelligent NPCs and Dynamic Dialogue: AI-powered NPCs, leveraging technologies like Inworld AI and large language models (LLMs) such as ChatGPT, offer unprecedented depth in contextual understanding and dynamic dialogue (Gallotta et al., 2024). This allows NPCs to respond uniquely and emotionally to player input, creating more immersive and personalized interactions that can even influence narrative progression.

Dynamic Difficulty Adjustment (DDA): AI systems now analyze player performance in real-time to dynamically adjust game difficulty, ensuring an optimal balance between challenge and enjoyment. For instance, *Left 4 Dead*'s AI Director tracks player performance and adjusts enemy numbers, item drops, and combat intensity to maintain engagement (Zohaib, 2018).

Testing and Balancing: AI-powered playtesting revolutionizes quality assurance. AI algorithms can simulate millions of gameplay scenarios, identify bugs, glitches, and pinpoint gameplay imbalances (e.g., overpowered characters or unfair advantages) with unprecedented efficiency, saving significant time and resources compared to human testers (Ranjitha, Nathan, & Joseph, 2020).

The evolution from early game AI (e.g., Pac-Man ghosts) *within* the game to modern generative AI *assisting game development* is a crucial shift. It is no longer just about AI as an opponent or NPC, but AI as a *co-creator* and *optimizer*. This is enabled by the sheer computational power of modern GPUs and cloud-based AI supercomputers, which can train massive models for tasks like content generation, testing, and balancing. The "canvas" is no longer just the game world, but the *entire development pipeline*. This represents a fundamental change in economics and creative processes of game development. It promises faster iterations, higher quality, and unprecedented scale, but also raises questions about the future role of human artists and designers.

3.5.3. Challenges and Ethical Considerations: The Shadow Side of Progress

Despite the immense potential, the integration of advanced AI in game creation presents significant challenges and ethical dilemmas.

"AI Hallucinations" and Unintended Outputs: A prominent issue is "AI hallucination," where AI models generate inaccurate, misleading, or entirely fabricated content (Bracken, 1977). This can manifest as illogical reasoning, nonsensical responses in dialogue, or visually unappealing or unplayable elements in procedurally generated levels. These "glitches" often arise from overfitting to training data or limited contextual understanding, leading the AI to "make things up" when faced with unfamiliar inputs.

Ethical Dilemmas: The increasing sophistication of AI in games raises critical ethical concerns:

- Data Privacy: AI systems often require access to vast amounts of player data (behaviors, preferences) for personalization and optimization, necessitating strict adherence to data privacy regulations like GDPR.
- Player Autonomy and Manipulation: Dynamic adjustments to difficulty or narrative elements, while enhancing engagement, could potentially manipulate player behavior or create addictive experiences, undermining player agency (Bowey, Birk, & Mandryk, 2015). The illusion of freedom might be constrained by underlying algorithmic control.

- Bias and Fairness: If AI models are trained on biased data, they may perpetuate stereotypes or produce unfair outcomes, particularly in systems like matchmaking or in-game economies (Balaha et al., 2024).
- Copyright Infringement: Generative AI tools trained on copyrighted material risk legal issues and penalties for developers.
- Over-automation and Human Touch: Over-reliance on AI could lead to sterile or formulaic games, potentially diminishing the unique human creativity that defines compelling experiences.

As AI becomes more “creative” through procedural generation and generative models, the concept of “AI hallucinations” emerges as a critical challenge. This is not just a bug; it is a philosophical artifact. It highlights the difference between *generating plausible output* and *understanding truth or context*. These “glitches” reveal the limitations of current AI in truly “thinking” or “creating” in a human sense, often leading to “nonsensical” or “illogical” results. This creates an “uncanny valley” for AI-generated content, where it is almost, but not quite, right. The presence of hallucinations and the ethical concerns about player manipulation force a re-evaluation of AI's role. It is a reminder that while hardware enables incredible feats, the *quality* and *integrity* of the digital world still demand human oversight and ethical frameworks. The “canvas” can be painted rapidly, but ensuring the “art” is meaningful and responsible requires human discernment.

As AI paints with broader strokes, generating entire worlds and narratives, where does human creativity end and algorithmic artistry begin, and what unexpected *artifacts* might emerge from this digital alchemy? In the *digital brushstrokes* of procedural generation, the artist's hand becomes the *seed*, guiding a universe of possibilities, yet sometimes, the canvas reveals unexpected *glitches*—a testament to the unpredictable beauty of emergent complexity. The *algorithmic muse* may compose symphonies, but the *human conductor* remains essential to ensure the *harmony* of experience.

3.6 Conclusions

From Llull's abstract logical systems and the intricate gears of 18th-century automata to Ada Lovelace's foundational algorithm for the Analytical Engine, the journey of AI and gaming has been a testament to human ingenuity and the relentless pursuit of computational power. The theoretical blueprints of McCulloch-Pitts neurons and Turing's “thinking machines” laid the groundwork for the digital age, even as early hardware limitations led to an “AI Winter.” Yet, with each successive generation of silicon—from the humble 128 bytes of the Atari 2600 to the multigigabyte GPUs of today—the canvas for digital worlds has expanded exponentially.

This hardware evolution has not only enabled the leap from pixelated patterns to immersive 3D environments with complex AI behaviors like *Half-Life*'s squad tactics and NavMesh navigation but has also ushered in an era of algorithmic alchemy through procedural generation and generative AI, capable of crafting entire universes and dynamic narratives. The symbiotic relationship between hardware and AI is undeniable: one constantly pushes the boundaries of the other, painting ever more intricate and interactive digital realms.

The trajectory suggests a continued, deeper convergence of hardware and AI. Dedicated AI accelerators and neuromorphic computing promise to further blur the lines between traditional processing and intelligent computation, potentially enabling AI to not just simulate, but perhaps even *originate* truly novel experiences. We may see AI designing its own hardware, or creating games that adapt in ways currently unimaginable, learning from player emotions and even generating new game genres on the fly. The "canvas" will become increasingly adaptive, responsive, and perhaps, self-aware.

The silicon canvas is far from complete. Each brushstroke of hardware innovation adds new dimensions, new colors, and new depths to the digital worlds we explore and the intelligent entities we interact with. The ongoing interplay between the physical substrate and the algorithmic spirit promises a future where the distinction between the real and the rendered becomes ever more artfully obscured, inviting us to ponder: what new worlds, indeed, will the silicon paint next?

4. THE EVOLUTION OF AI IN GAME CREATION: TOWARDS FULLY AI-BUILT GAMES

4.1. A Transformative Shift in Game Design Driven by AI

The field of Artificial Intelligence is undergoing an unprecedented evolution, opening new horizons for the gaming industry. AI is no longer merely a tool to enhance Non-Player Character (NPC) behavior or adjust game difficulty; it is progressing towards the capability of creating entire games, from designing worlds and characters to crafting complex narratives and dynamically adapting the experience. This transformative shift promises a revolution in how games are developed and experienced.

Artificial Intelligence, defined in 1955 as "the science and engineering of making intelligent machines," encompasses a suite of technologies that enable computers to perform advanced functions typically requiring human intelligence, such as language comprehension, data analysis, and recommendation generation. In game development, this evolution manifests in AI's ability to automate workflow tasks, refine character behavior, and contribute to procedural world-building. This expansion of capabilities indicates a gradual yet accelerating transition from AI being merely an assistive tool for human developers to becoming an independent, creative entity. For instance, Google DeepMind's SIMA (Scalable Instructable Multiworld Agent) project aims to develop generalist AI agents capable of understanding and executing natural language instructions across diverse 3D environments, including commercial video games. This ambition to develop agents that can "accomplish anything a human can do in any simulated 3D environment" underscores the trajectory towards more autonomous and comprehensive roles for AI in game creation, fundamentally redefining the nature of the game development process itself.

The economic implications of this AI-driven transformation are profound and rapidly expanding. The global AI in gaming market, valued at approximately $1.2 billion in 2022, is projected to reach a staggering $7.1 billion by 2028. This represents a fivefold increase in just six years, with a robust Compound Annual Growth Rate (CAGR) of around 30% from 2022 to 2028, signifying heavy investment by developers and publishers in AI-powered features. By 2029, the market is estimated to grow by an additional $27.47 billion, driven by the increasing adoption of augmented reality (AR) and virtual reality (VR) games, alongside the emergence of cloud gaming. This rapid expansion positions AI as a core component of gaming, not just a fleeting trend, making it a necessity for studios to remain competitive and profitable in an increasingly dynamic market.

4.2. Adaptive AI: Gaming Experiences That React and Learn

Adaptive AI moves beyond pre-programmed behaviors, offering gaming experiences that react to and learn from player actions in real-time (Ram, Ontañón, & Mehta, 2007). This type of AI continuously analyzes player performance, choices, and even emotional states, adjusting gameplay elements such as difficulty, enemy behavior, and even story progression to ensure a continuous and uniquely personalized challenge. This dynamic adaptation is crucial for maintaining player engagement and preventing frustration or boredom, thereby creating a "just right" level of challenge for each individual. Table 5 shows examples for adaptive AI in games.

Table 5. Notable Examples of Adaptive AI in Games

Game	Adaptive AI Feature	Impact on Player Experience
Resident Evil 4	Dynamic Difficulty Adjustment	Balanced challenge, avoids boredom or frustration [7]
The Last of Us Part II	Reactive and Realistic Enemy Behavior	Increased immersion and realism, constant strategy adaptation
Middle-Earth: Shadow of Mordor	Nemesis System (Evolving Enemies)	Personalized rivalries and customization, increased reliability
Left 4 Dead	AI Director (Pacing Management)	Unpredictable gameplay, continuously adapting challenge
Red Dead Redemption 2	Realistic NPC Daily Routines	Living, independent world, enhanced immersion [20]

4.2.1. Dynamic Difficulty Adjustment (DDA)

Dynamic Difficulty Adjustment (DDA) is a prime example of adaptive AI in action (Zohaib, 2018). In games like *Resident Evil 4*, the AI subtly adjusts the game's difficulty based on player performance. This can influence factors such as the rate of ammunition drops, the strength of enemies, and the amount of damage they inflict. If a player is struggling, the game might become slightly easier, providing more resources or reducing enemy health. Conversely, if a player is performing exceptionally well, the AI might increase the challenge, making enemies tougher or resources scarcer. This real-time fine-tuning eliminates the need for manual difficulty settings, offering a smoother and more satisfying gameplay experience that keeps players consistently engaged.

4.2.2. Intelligent Non-Player Character (NPC) Behaviors

Modern AI techniques empower NPCs to make decisions based on complex models that factor in player behavior, environmental variables, and social dynamics (Zhu, 2019). Titles such as *The Last of Us Part II* and *F.E.A.R.* showcase significant advancements in NPC behavior. Enemies in these games do not merely follow predetermined paths; they adapt to situations in real-time, communicating with each other, attempting to flank the player, and making strategic decisions based on what is happening around them. They can even exhibit emotional reactions to fallen comrades, expressing fear or mourning, which creates a more dynamic and immersive world. This interactive behavior enhances the realism of encounters and compels players to constantly adapt their strategies.

Innovative systems that create unique and memorable interactions include:

- The Nemesis System in *Middle-Earth: Shadow of Mordor*: This groundbreaking system generates unique enemies with distinct personalities, strengths, and weaknesses. If a player is defeated by an enemy, that enemy gains power, remembers the encounter, and may return with a personalized vendetta, fostering a dynamic rivalry that evolves throughout the game. This adds an unprecedented layer of customization and replayability, making each playthrough feel distinct and impactful (Kroon, 2016).
- The AI Director in *Left 4 Dead*: This sophisticated system controls the game's pacing and intensity, dynamically adjusting enemy spawns, resource distribution, and even environmental events based on player performance and emotional state. This ensures an unpredictable and thrilling experience every time, with the challenge continuously adapting to keep players engaged and on edge.
- NPCs with Detailed Daily Routines in *Red Dead Redemption 2*: This game showcases an exceptional level of realism in NPC behavior, with characters following intricate daily routines that include working, interacting with the environment, and sleeping. This makes the game world feel incredibly alive and independent of player actions, significantly enhancing overall immersion.

Open-ended question for the reader: How might adaptive AI redefine the concept of "fair challenge" in games, and will it reach a point where its behaviors become truly unpredictable to human designers?

Adaptive AI meticulously balances challenge and reward to ensure a continuously enjoyable experience, aiming for a "just right" difficulty for each player, neither too easy nor too hard. As algorithms become increasingly complex and are trained on vast amounts of player data and interactions, predicting AI behaviors becomes progressively more difficult. Current systems, despite their sophistication, still operate within defined rules or patterns. However, continuous learning and real-time adaptation mean that the behaviors emerging from these systems can become highly non-linear and challenging for humans to fully anticipate. This evolution pushes the boundaries of what is "scripted" versus "organic" in gameplay, making the game world feel more alive and less static. In the future, we might witness systems that adapt in ways unforeseen even by their creators, leading to truly unique experiences that transcend programmed human expectations and potentially blur the lines between artificial and emergent intelligence.

4.3. Generative AI: From World-Building to Narrative Crafting

Generative AI represents a significant leap in the gaming industry, capable of automatically creating vast and diverse content, thereby reducing manual development workload and expanding creative scope. This technology is transforming how game worlds are conceived, and narratives are woven, offering unprecedented possibilities for scale and personalization. Table 6 shows some of applications of generative AI in game design.

Table 6. Applications of Generative AI in Game Design

Game Aspect	AI Technology	Game/Project Examples	Value Added
World Generation	Procedural Generation	*Minecraft, No Man's Sky*	Infinite worlds, unprecedented diversity, reduced developer effort
Narrative/Story Generation	Large Language Models (LLMs)	*AI Dungeon, Detroit: Become Human, The Witcher 3*	Interactive stories, personalized experiences, multiple paths
Generalist AI Agents	Reinforcement Learning, Neural Networks	SIMA (Google DeepMind)	Simulates general human intelligence, interacts with any virtual environment

4.3.1. Procedural Content Generation (PCG)

Procedural Content Generation (PCG) is a cornerstone in building expansive and dynamic worlds. Games like *Minecraft* and *No Man's Sky* utilize complex algorithms to generate nearly infinite worlds, including terrain, biomes, creatures, and even star systems (Hendrikx, Meijer, Van Der Velden, & Iosup, 2013). This allows players to explore unique environments in every playthrough, as the world is not stored as static 3D data but dynamically generated based on the player's position and other inputs. This technique offers immense savings in storage and memory, as details are randomized using a predetermined "seed" that ensures consistent results each time, allowing for truly massive game universes that would be impossible to create manually.

4.3.2. Interactive Narratives and Branching Storylines

AI is also revolutionizing narrative design by enabling interactive narratives and complex branching storylines. Platforms like *AI Dungeon* leverage large language models (LLMs) to create dynamic, interactive text-based adventures that respond to user input, offering limitless narrative possibilities. These models are trained on massive datasets to predict and generate coherent text sequences, allowing the narrative to evolve dynamically based on player choices. Games such as *Detroit: Become Human* and *The Witcher 3* demonstrate how AI can manage complex branching storylines, where player decisions influence the plot and character fates, leading to multiple endings and outcomes. This grants players a profound sense of agency and impact on the game world, making each playthrough a unique and personal journey.

4.3.3. The Rise of Generalist AI Agents

The development of generalist AI agents capable of understanding and interacting with diverse virtual environments marks a pivotal step towards fully AI-built games. Google DeepMind's SIMA (Scalable Instructable Multiworld Agent) is a prime example, aiming to achieve Artificial General Intelligence (AGI) in virtual settings (de la Torre, Aragón-Jurado, Crespo-Álvarez, & Bárcena-González, 2024). SIMA can interpret natural language instructions and execute tasks across a variety of 3D video game environments, interacting with any virtual environment as a human would, without needing access to the game's source code or bespoke APIs. This initiative is not merely about achieving high scores in specific games but about developing more broadly useful AI agents for any environment, paving the way for AI agents that can "play" games generally, and potentially "build" them too, by learning from diverse gaming worlds.

Open-ended question for the reader: Can AI truly create gaming experiences that transcend human imagination, or will it always be constrained by the data it is trained upon?

AI possesses the capacity to explore unexpected design spaces and generate unprecedented content diversity. While generative AI fundamentally relies on its training data, its ability to combine elements in novel and unforeseen ways can lead to "creations" that human developers might not have directly conceived. Although AI can produce vast worlds and dynamic narratives, the quality and coherence of this content, especially in terms of meaningful gameplay and compelling storytelling, still heavily depend on human-designed algorithms, parameters, and the curation of training data. AI's "creativity" often emerges as a property of sophisticated algorithms and massive datasets, rather than independent conceptualization. However, human imagination continues to guide the initial framework, setting the rules and constraints within which AI operates, making it more of a co-creative partner than a fully autonomous entity at present. The future challenge lies in enabling AI to move beyond statistical prediction to genuine conceptual understanding and original creative thought, which will truly test the limits of human imagination and redefine the boundaries of digital artistry.

4.4. Challenges and Future Outlook: Towards Fully Self-Generating Games

Despite remarkable progress and transformative potential, the prospect of fully AI-built games presents significant challenges that require innovative solutions across technical, ethical, and economic domains.

4.4.1. Technical Challenges

Designing AI algorithms capable of generating all aspects of a game, including intricate graphics, realistic physics, compelling narratives, and nuanced character behavior—in a cohesive and high-quality manner is an immense undertaking. These algorithms demand advanced machine learning and neural network techniques, such as Convolutional Neural Networks (CNNs) for image processing and Recurrent Neural Networks (RNNs) for sequential data like text and audio. Furthermore, the training and operation of the necessary AI models for comprehensive game creation require immense computational power, vast storage capacities, and ultra-fast data processing capabilities. The quality of generative AI outputs is highly dependent on the quality and quantity of its training data; thus, collecting, curating, and organizing such massive and diverse datasets for complex games represents a substantial logistical and technical hurdle. Ensuring that AI-generated content maintains artistic vision, narrative consistency, and bug-free functionality across a vast, dynamically created world remains a complex engineering feat.

4.4.2. Ethical Challenges

The integration of AI into gaming raises a complex array of ethical considerations. AI algorithms can inadvertently reflect and amplify biases present in their training data, potentially leading to unvaried content, perpetuating harmful stereotypes, or even affecting matchmaking systems in multiplayer games. This amplification means that any inherent bias in the data can rapidly propagate throughout an entire game world or its narrative, extending beyond a single biased character to impact the entire gameplay experience. Adaptive and personalized games that rely on extensive collection of player data also raise serious concerns regarding user privacy and how this sensitive data is utilized. There is also the risk of manipulative design, where AI could be used to subtly adjust game difficulty or reward systems in ways that encourage players to spend more on microtransactions or play for extended periods, raising profound ethical questions about exploiting player behavior. When AI generates content, questions arise about who owns the intellectual property rights to this content, and whether machine creativity can be considered "original" in the human sense. The industry faces a critical juncture: embracing AI's transformative power while simultaneously developing robust ethical frameworks and regulatory guidelines to prevent unintended societal harms and ensure responsible innovation.

4.4.3. Economic Implications: Reshaping the Business of Gaming

The integration of AI into game development is not merely a technological shift but a significant economic disruption, fundamentally reshaping how games are produced, monetized, and consumed.

4.4.3.1. Market Growth and Investment Trends

As previously noted, the global AI in gaming market is experiencing explosive growth, projected to reach $7.1 billion by 2028 from $1.2 billion in 2022, with a CAGR of approximately 30%. This rapid expansion is fueled by heavy investment from developers and publishers who recognize AI as a critical competitive advantage. The market's trajectory is further boosted by the increasing adoption of AR and VR games, alongside the emergence of cloud gaming platforms, which rely heavily on AI for their functionality and immersive experiences. This positions AI as an indispensable component for studios aiming to remain competitive and profitable in the evolving gaming landscape.

4.4.3.2. Efficiency and Cost Reduction in Development

AI is delivering tangible efficiency gains in game development. While 73% of studios are already using AI, and 88% plan to in the future, nearly 40% report productivity gains of over 20%. Although direct cost savings are trailing slightly behind, with 25% reporting a similar reduction, this is largely because current AI tools often function as "co-pilots" rather than full automation. They assist teams in working faster and refining workflows, rather than entirely replacing human labor. For instance, AI can significantly reduce repetitive work by assisting with dialogue writing, generating concept art, creating 3D assets, and automating debugging and testing processes. This efficiency can lead to a 20-30% reduction in overall production costs, enabling smaller studios to compete more effectively by lowering the need for massive manual asset creation teams. AI allows developers to focus on higher-level creative tasks, accelerating game production cycles.

4.4.3.3. Evolving Monetization Strategies

AI is fundamentally reshaping game monetization strategies, moving beyond traditional models to create hyper-personalized and dynamic revenue streams. The global gaming industry is projected to reach $280.65 billion by 2029, with mobile gaming accounting for approximately 50% of revenues. AI plays a significant role in driving this growth by enhancing game realism and optimizing player engagement.

- Hyper-Personalized Ads: AI optimizes ad campaigns by analyzing vast datasets in real-time, enabling developers to deliver ads that resonate deeply with individual players. Unlike traditional static campaigns, AI dynamically adjusts strategies based on user behavior, demographics, and contextual cues, ensuring ads feel less intrusive and more relevant. AI algorithms can segment users into "micro-segments" (e.g., "competitive spenders" or "casual explorers") to tailor strategies for high-value groups, optimizing ad campaigns and in-game offers for maximum impact.
- Dynamic In-Game Purchases: AI transforms in-game stores into adaptive marketplaces, where offers evolve based on individual player preferences and past spending habits. By analyzing gameplay data, AI identifies what players value most, whether it's power-ups, cosmetics, or time-saving boosts. Developers can use AI to track player engagement and adjust pricing, offer bundles, or special deals accordingly, leading to increased purchase rates and user satisfaction.
- Predictive Analytics for Retention: Player retention is critical for sustainable monetization in live-service games. AI-driven predictive analytics offer invaluable insights into player retention by identifying at-risk users and devising proactive strategies to keep them engaged. By analyzing patterns such as session duration, frequency, and in-game achievements, AI can forecast when players might disengage and proactively offer personalized incentives to retain them, which is critical for long-term revenue generation.

4.4.3.4. Workforce Transformation and Competitive Dynamics

The economic landscape of AI integration in gaming is not without its challenges, particularly concerning the workforce. While AI promises efficiency, there are concerns about job displacement, with reports indicating that game studios collectively cut 10% of their workforces in the past year, and 30% of developers view AI-powered tools as doing "more harm than good." This highlights a tension between the perceived benefits of AI by executives (who often see its potential for cost savings and efficiency) and the concerns of individual developers.

However, AI is also driving a transformation in human roles, shifting the focus from manual, repetitive tasks to more strategic and creative oversight. Developers may evolve into "prompt engineers" or "AI curators," working in partnership with AI systems to guide their creative outputs. The competitive nature of the market means that AI investment often becomes a strategic necessity rather than a direct path to higher profitability. As competitors rapidly adopt similar AI improvements, companies are compelled to invest merely to stay competitive, with benefits often passed on to consumers through better products and lower prices (Monnens & Goldberg, 2015). This competitive pressure can lead to a scenario where AI investment becomes a strategic imperative, with its primary value being market survival and differentiation rather than immediate, direct profit maximization. Table 6 shows some of applications of generative AI in game design.

Future-Oriented Questions

With AI's rapid advancement, fundamental questions arise regarding the future of the gaming industry and the role of humans within it:

- What are the long-term economic and societal implications of fully AI-built games on traditional developer roles, and will this lead to the emergence of entirely new creative professions for humans, such as "experience architects" or "AI ethicists" who guide and refine AI-generated content?
- How will the roles of players and communities transform in a world dominated by self-generating games, and will this lead to more isolated or more interconnected experiences? What psychological challenges might arise from interacting with infinite, constantly adapting content, and how will players form meaningful connections within such fluid virtual spaces?
- Could AI develop its own form of "consciousness" or genuine agency within game worlds, and what would that mean for the future of human-machine interaction? If AI entities become indistinguishable from human players in their behavior and emotional responses, will we reach a point where these entities demand rights or special ethical considerations, and how would society grapple with such a paradigm shift?

5. DISCUSSION: NAVIGATING THE UNCHARTED TERRITORIES OF AI IN GAMING

The transformative power of AI in gaming is undeniable, yet its ultimate trajectory remains a subject of intense debate and speculation. As we stand at the precipice of a new era, critical questions emerge regarding AI's creative autonomy, its symbiotic relationship with hardware, and the very essence of human involvement in game creation.

One of the most compelling discussions revolves around the feasibility of AI fully building games from a simple human prompt. Is it an inevitable future where a developer merely types "create a sprawling fantasy RPG with a morally ambiguous protagonist and dynamic political factions," and an AI generates a complete, playable experience? Proponents argue that with the rapid advancements in generative AI, particularly LLMs and multimodal AI, this vision is increasingly within reach. Tools like Google DeepMind's SIMA, which can understand natural language instructions and operate across diverse 3D environments, hint at a future where AI can interpret complex creative directives and translate them into game logic and assets. This perspective suggests that human creativity will shift from direct asset creation to high-level conceptualization and curation, acting as "AI orchestrators" who guide the generative process. However, skeptics contend that while AI excels at pattern recognition and content generation based on existing data, it lacks genuine understanding, original artistic intent, or the nuanced human intuition required for truly compelling game design. The ability to generate vast worlds is one thing, but ensuring narrative coherence, emotional resonance, and truly innovative gameplay mechanics that surprise and delight players might remain a uniquely human domain. They argue that AI's "creativity" is fundamentally statistical, a sophisticated remix of its training data, and that the spark of true originality—the ability to conceive something entirely new and meaningful—is beyond its current capabilities.

Another pivotal debate concerns the future balance of power between hardware and software in driving gaming innovation. Will specialized AI hardware, like NVIDIA's Tensor Cores, AMD's MI300 series, or Intel's Gaudi accelerators, become the dominant force, dictating the ultimate gaming experience? Or will increasingly sophisticated AI software, capable of optimizing performance across diverse hardware, maintain its supremacy? The trend towards dedicated AI processing units within GPUs and CPUs suggests a future where hardware is explicitly designed to accelerate AI workloads, leading to unprecedented visual fidelity and complex in-game AI. Technologies like neuromorphic computing, which mimics the human brain's architecture for ultra-low latency and power consumption, or photonic-electronic chips that process data at the speed of light, could fundamentally redefine what's possible in real-time game environments within the next two decades. This could lead to a scenario where only games optimized for specific AI chips can deliver the ultimate experience, creating a fragmented market. Conversely, advancements in AI software, such as universal upscaling technologies like FSR and XeSS, aim to democratize access to cutting-edge visuals across a wider range of hardware. The economic implications are immense: if hardware dictates performance, companies will invest heavily in chip design; if software can bridge the gap, the focus shifts to algorithmic innovation. Ultimately, the future likely lies in a symbiotic relationship, where groundbreaking AI software pushes the limits of what's possible, while specialized hardware provides the raw computational power needed to bring these ambitious visions to life. The question isn't just about who holds the power, but how this evolving partnership will redefine the very essence of interactive entertainment.

6. CONCLUSION AND FUTURE TRAJECTORY OF AI IN GAMING

Artificial intelligence has fundamentally transformed the gaming landscape, evolving from a supplementary tool to an integral, co-creative force that reshapes every aspect of game design, development, and player interaction. From enabling the generation of infinitely vast worlds and crafting NPCs with lifelike behaviors and emotional depth, to streamlining development processes through automated testing and dynamic difficulty adjustments, AI has consistently pushed the boundaries of what is possible in interactive entertainment. The continuous evolution of AI within gameplay, culminating in advanced models like transformers and generalist agents, promises even more immersive, personalized, and dynamic experiences. As AI continues to blur the lines between virtual and reality, what new frontiers will it unlock for player agency and narrative depth in the games of tomorrow, and how will the ongoing dialogue between human creativity and artificial intelligence redefine the very essence of play itself?

REFERENCES

[] AARSETH, E., & HAMMAR, E. L. (n.d.) No Worries? Game Research in Denmark.

Abdelkhabir, S. G., Ezz-eldeen, S. S., Gabr, A. E., Eldakrory, A. M., Ali, A. M., Elkhameesy, O. K., . . . Ali, Z. H. (2025). Enhancing Antimicrobial Activity Predictors Based on Machine Learning Approaches. In Navigating Innovations and Challenges in Travel Medicine and Digital Health (pp. 257-276). IGI Global Scientific Publishing. DOI: 10.4018/979-8-3693-8774-0.ch013

Adams, T. (2019). Emergent narrative in dwarf fortress. In *Procedural storytelling in game design* (pp. 149–158). AK Peters/CRC Press. DOI: 10.1201/9780429488337-15

Albaugh, L., McCann, J., Yao, L., & Hudson, S. E. (2021, May). Enabling personal computational handweaving with a low-cost jacquard loom. In *Proceedings of the 2021 CHI Conference on Human Factors in Computing Systems* (pp. 1-10). DOI: 10.1145/3411764.3445750

Arbib, M. A. (2000). Warren McCulloch's search for the logic of the nervous system. *Perspectives in Biology and Medicine, 43*(2), 193–216. DOI: 10.1353/pbm.2000.0001 PMID: 10804585

Ayyad, S. M., Badawy, M. A., Shehata, M., Alksas, A., Mahmoud, A., Abou El-Ghar, M., Ghazal, M., El-Melegy, M., Abdel-Hamid, N. B., Labib, L. M., Ali, H. A., & El-Baz, A. (2022). A new framework for precise identification of prostatic adenocarcinoma. *Sensors (Basel), 22*(5), 1848. DOI: 10.3390/s22051848 PMID: 35270995

Ayyad, S. M., Shehata, M., Shalaby, A., Abou El-Ghar, M., Ghazal, M., El-Melegy, M., Abdel-Hamid, N. B., Labib, L. M., Ali, H. A., & El-Baz, A. (2021). Role of AI and histopathological images in detecting prostate cancer: A survey. *Sensors (Basel), 21*(8), 2586. DOI: 10.3390/s21082586 PMID: 33917035

Balaha, H. M., Ayyad, S. M., Alksas, A., Elsorougy, A., Badawy, M. A., Shehata, M., & El-Baz, A. (2023, October). Early diagnosis of prostate cancer using parametric estimation of ivim from dw-mri. In *2023 IEEE International Conference on Image Processing (ICIP)* (pp. 2910-2914). IEEE. DOI: 10.1109/ICIP49359.2023.10222716

Balaha, H. M., Ayyad, S. M., Alksas, A., Shehata, M., Elsorougy, A., Badawy, M. A., Abou El-Ghar, M., Mahmoud, A., Alghamdi, N. S., Ghazal, M., Contractor, S., & El-Baz, A. (2024). Precise Prostate Cancer Assessment Using IVIM-Based Parametric Estimation of Blood Diffusion from DW-MRI. *Bioengineering (Basel, Switzerland), 11*(6), 629. DOI: 10.3390/bioengineering11060629 PMID: 38927865

Bedini, S. A. (1964). The role of automata in the history of technology. *Technology and Culture*, *5*(1), 24–42. DOI: 10.2307/3101120

Bowey, J. T., Birk, M. V., & Mandryk, R. L. (2015, October). Manipulating leaderboards to induce player experience. In *Proceedings of the 2015 annual symposium on computer-human interaction in play* (pp. 115-120). DOI: 10.1145/2793107.2793138

Bracken, P. (1977). Unintended consequences of strategic gaming. *Simulation & Games*, *8*(3), 283–318. DOI: 10.1177/003755007783001

Brisson, A., Pereira, G., Prada, R., Paiva, A., Louchart, S., Suttie, N., & Oliveira, M. (2012). Artificial intelligence and personalization opportunities for serious games. In *Proceedings of the AAAI Conference on Artificial Intelligence and Interactive Digital Entertainment* (Vol. 8, No. 5, pp. 51-57).

Castella-Martinez, S., & Saiz-Raimundo, M. (2024). Ramon Llull and the Communicating Vessels Between Catholicism and Occultism in Early Twentieth-Century France. *Romance Quarterly*, *71*(4), 277–291. DOI: 10.1080/08831157.2024.2399009

Cuddy, L. (2008). *The Legend of Zelda and Philosophy: I link therefore I am* (Vol. 36). Open Court.

Davis, M., & Davis, V. (2005). Mistaken ancestry: The jacquard and the computer. *Textile (Oxford)*, *3*(1), 76–87. DOI: 10.2752/147597505778052594

de la Torre, J. C., Aragón-Jurado, J. M., Crespo-Álvarez, A., & Bárcena-González, G. (2024). GAGI: Game engine for Artificial General Intelligence experimentation. *SoftwareX*, *26*, 101665. DOI: 10.1016/j.softx.2024.101665

[] Duncan, S. C. (2011). Minecraft, beyond construction and survival.

Elsayed, M. Z., Hasoon, A., Zidan, M. K., & Ayyad, S. M. (2024, July). Role of AI for plant disease detection and pest detection. In *2024 International Telecommunications Conference (ITC-Egypt)* (pp. 824-829). IEEE. DOI: 10.1109/ITC-Egypt61547.2024.10620496

Ensmenger, N. (2012). Is chess the drosophila of artificial intelligence? A social history of an algorithm. *Social Studies of Science*, *42*(1), 5–30. DOI: 10.1177/0306312711424596 PMID: 22530382

Essinger, J. (2014). *Ada's algorithm: How Lord Byron's daughter Ada Lovelace launched the digital age*. Melville House.

Fetzer, J. H. (1990). What is artificial intelligence? In *Artificial intelligence: Its scope and limits* (pp. 3–27). Springer Netherlands. DOI: 10.1007/978-94-009-1900-6_1

Fidora, A. (2011). *Ramon Llull, from the Ars Magna to artificial intelligence* (Sierra, C., Ed.). Artificial Intelligence Research Institute.

Fillebrown, S. (1992). Faster computation of Bernoulli numbers. *Journal of Algorithms, 13*(3), 431–445. DOI: 10.1016/0196-6774(92)90048-H

Gallotta, R., Todd, G., Zammit, M., Earle, S., Liapis, A., Togelius, J., & Yannakakis, G. N. (2024). Large language models and games: A survey and roadmap. *IEEE Transactions on Games*, 1–18. DOI: 10.1109/TG.2024.3461510

Greenblatt, R. D., Eastlake, D. E., III, & Crocker, S. D. (1967, November). The Greenblatt chess program. In Proceedings of the November 14-16, 1967, fall joint computer conference (pp. 801-810).

Gulsoy, M., Kokach, V., Kocaçınar, B., & Akbulut, F. P. (2024, October). AI-Driven Contextual Story Creation with Integrated Text and Visual Generation. In 2024 Innovations in Intelligent Systems and Applications Conference (ASYU) (pp. 1-6). IEEE.

Hendrikx, M., Meijer, S., Van Der Velden, J., & Iosup, A. (2013). Procedural content generation for games: A survey. [TOMM]. *ACM Transactions on Multimedia Computing Communications and Applications, 9*(1), 1–22. DOI: 10.1145/2422956.2422957

Higinbotham, W. (1958). *Tennis for two. Brookhaven National Laboratory.* Oscilloscope.

Hyman, A. (1985). *Charles Babbage: Pioneer of the computer.* Princeton University Press.

Justesen, N., Bontrager, P., Togelius, J., & Risi, S. (2019). Deep learning for video game playing. *IEEE Transactions on Games, 12*(1), 1–20. DOI: 10.1109/TG.2019.2896986

Kates, J. (1950). *Bertie the brain.* Canadian National Exhibition.

Kitano, H., Asada, M., Kuniyoshi, Y., Noda, I., & Osawa, E. (1997, February). Robocup: The robot world cup initiative. In *Proceedings of the first international conference on Autonomous agents* (pp. 340-347). DOI: 10.1145/267658.267738

Kroon, J. C. (2016). Nemesis Narratives: The relationship between embedded and emergent narrative in Middle Earth: Shadow of Mordor (Master's thesis).

[] LaCurts, K. (2011). Criticisms of the turing test and why you should ignore (most of) them. Official blog of MIT's course: Philosophy and theoretical computer science.

Lyu, M., Madanapalli, S. C., Vishwanath, A., & Sivaraman, V. (2024, March). Network Anatomy and Real-Time Measurement of Nvidia GeForce NOW Cloud Gaming. In International Conference on Passive and Active Network Measurement (pp. 61-91). Cham: Springer Nature Switzerland. DOI: 10.1007/978-3-031-56249-5_3

Marshall, S. J. (2022). *The Story of the Robot: A Short History of Automation and Robotics*. Stephen J Marshall.

McCarthy, J., Minsky, M. L., Rochester, N., & Shannon, C. E. (2006). A proposal for the dartmouth summer research project on artificial intelligence, august 31, 1955. *AI Magazine*, *27*(4), 12–12.

Monnens, D., & Goldberg, M. (2015). Space Odyssey: The long journey of Spacewar! from MIT to computer labs around the world. Kinephanos. Revue d'études des médias et de culture populaire, 124-147.

Newborn, M. (2014). *Computer chess*. Academic Press.

Nong, Y., Sun, J. Q., & Wang, K. (2025). AI-Driven Procedural Content Generation for VR/AR Environments. *Authorea Preprints*. DOI: 10.36227/techrxiv.173747345.50267117/v1

Parnas, D. L. (2017). The real risks of artificial intelligence. *Communications of the ACM*, *60*(10), 27–31. DOI: 10.1145/3132724

Peddie, J. (2023). The first era of GPUs. In *The history of the GPU-eras and environment* (pp. 105–150). Springer International Publishing.

Qadir, H. M., Suleman, M. T., Khan, R. A., Sohaib, M., Hasan, M. J., & Hussain, S. A. (2025). Optimizing learning outcomes: A deep dive into hybrid AI models for adaptive educational feedback. *Journal of Big Data*, *12*(1), 1–26. DOI: 10.1186/s40537-025-01187-6

Ram, A., Ontañón, S., & Mehta, M. (2007, May). Artificial Intelligence for Adaptive Computer Games. In *FLAIRS* (pp. 22-29).

Ranjitha, M., Nathan, K., & Joseph, L. (2020). Artificial intelligence algorithms and techniques in the computation of player-adaptive games. [). IOP Publishing.]. *Journal of Physics: Conference Series*, *1427*(1), 012006. DOI: 10.1088/1742-6596/1427/1/012006

Reddy, R. (2005). The Origins of the American Association for Artificial Intelligence (AAAI). AI Magazine, 26(4), 5-12.

[] Russell, S., Graetz, M., & Witaenem, W. (1962). Spacewar. Computer software.

Sarkar, A., Guzdial, M., Snodgrass, S., Summerville, A., Machado, T., & Smith, G. (2023). Procedural content generation via knowledge transformation (PCG-KT). *IEEE Transactions on Games*, *16*(1), 36–50. DOI: 10.1109/TG.2023.3270422

Sasse, L., Nicolaisen-Sobesky, E., Dukart, J., Eickhoff, S. B., Götz, M., Hamdan, S., Komeyer, V., Kulkarni, A., Lahnakoski, J. M., Love, B. C., Raimondo, F., & Patil, K. R. (2025). Overview of leakage scenarios in supervised machine learning. *Journal of Big Data*, *12*(1), 1–23. DOI: 10.1186/s40537-025-01193-8

Shrager, J. (2024). ELIZA Reinterpreted: The world's first chatbot was not intended as a chatbot at all. arXiv preprint arXiv:2406.17650.

Sumner, J. (2014). Defiance to compliance: Visions of the computer in postwar Britain. *History and Technology*, *30*(4), 309–333. DOI: 10.1080/07341512.2015.1008962

Turing, A. M. (1980). Computing machinery and intelligence. Creative Computing, 6(1), 44-53.

van Assen, M., Muscogiuri, E., Tessarin, G., & De Cecco, C. N. (2022). Artificial intelligence: A century-old story. In *Artificial Intelligence in Cardiothoracic Imaging* (pp. 3–13). Springer International Publishing. DOI: 10.1007/978-3-030-92087-6_1

Will, A. I. (2012). The Manifest Destiny of Artificial Intelligence.

Zhu, X. (2019). Behavior tree design of intelligent behavior of non-player character (NPC) based on Unity3D. *Journal of Intelligent & Fuzzy Systems*, *37*(5), 6071–6079. DOI: 10.3233/JIFS-179190

Zohaib, M. (2018). Dynamic difficulty adjustment (DDA) in computer games: A review. *Advances in Human-Computer Interaction*, *2018*(1), 5681652. DOI: 10.1155/2018/5681652

Zohaib, M. (2018). Dynamic difficulty adjustment (DDA) in computer games: A review. *Advances in Human-Computer Interaction*, *2018*(1), 5681652. DOI: 10.1155/2018/5681652

Chapter 10
The Future of AI and Generative AI in Virtual Worlds and the Metaverse:
Transforming Gaming Experiences

Ayush Shekhar
Marwadi University, India

T. Premavathi
https://orcid.org/0009-0003-0172-2021
Marwadi University, India

Damodharan Palaniappan
https://orcid.org/0009-0003-0721-3068
Marwadi University, India

ABSTRACT

As virtual worlds and the Metaverse improve, AI and GenAI have a major impact on the evolution of video games. These technologies enable non-player characters (NPCs) to be more intelligent, surroundings to change, gameplay to be personalized, and levels to be created with ease. Generative AI and its components, such as large language models, diffusion models, and neural rendering, assist in the automatic creation of dialogues, storylines, game items, and world elements. In this chapter, real-life stories from key game developers and Metaverse services are included to demonstrate how the use of AI/GenAI boosts the creativity, growth, and busywork of users. Moreover, it closely examines issues such as protecting people's personal data, managing online content, safeguarding legal rights for content, and

DOI: 10.4018/979-8-3373-4637-3.ch010

ght © 2026, IGI Global Scientific Publishing. Copying or distributing in print or electronic forms without written permission of IGI Global Scientific Publishing is prohibited. Use of this chapter to generative artificial intelligence (AI) technologies is expressly prohibited. The publisher reserves all rights to license its use for generative AI training and machine learning model development.

supporting ethical conduct in VR and AR. Overall, this chapter discusses how AI and Generative AI are building fresh paths for game development and how users interact in virtual worlds.

1. INTRODUCTION

Games on the video have been technological pioneers. The evolution of the arcade machines, which were primitive in the past, to the highly detailed digital worlds is undisputable. Artificial intelligence is now fundamentally transforming this landscape, not only in how visually faithful the games can be and how their mechanics work, but also the actual creation and dynamic progression of games. This is also quite visible in the new metaverse, where the environments are not fixed but actively react to the actions of players and even to their emotional conditions.

The control of development of traditional games was strict. Before a game was released, designers carefully wrote out all of the narrative beats and non-player character paths in advance. This method produced iconic titles, but usually resulted in low replayability and insignificant decisions. In comparison, the current AI-driven characters have the ability to recite the previous interactions, which adds some unexpected challenges based on the individual playstyle. On the same note, game worlds may procedurally change as they are traversed, so two players in the same server instance may find two completely different quests.

The integration of AI and the metaverse does not just lie in the more realistic graphics or even more refined performance. It radically reinvents the roles in experience creation. The players have become co-creators and they can now create worlds with the assistance of developers using sophisticated AI tools. Schools are trying virtual classrooms in which the setting is adjusted to the varying learning styles. More so, there are also vibrant economies that are developing around the business of trading digital assets among users. The following section will explore the technologies that make this change possible specifically neural networks that can be used to generate terrain dynamically and behavior algorithms that can learn by analyzing player data, and the changing collaborative models between studios and their communities. We are actually experiencing a mutation of the DNA of gaming in real time. It has led to the creation of AI-driven solutions that assist in all types of manufacturing, but it has also spread to other scientific domains, including gaming (Ortiz et al., 2025), and accelerated by powerful AI frameworks such as TensorFlow and PyTorch, which have become publicly available since 2017. The development of AI in the game industry has turned into more than the mere decision-making algorithms but rather the highly sophisticated systems that adapt to the gameplay in real-time, making it more immersive and enjoyable to the players.

2. TECHNOLOGICAL INNOVATIONS

2.1 Foundations of Virtual Worlds & the Metaverse

Virtual worlds and the Metaverse have their foundations in the realms of virtual worlds and virtual reality. Virtual worlds and virtual reality are the foundations of Virtual Worlds and the Metaverse.

Virtual reality is totally immersive. By putting on a headset, you are instantly transported to a completely different plane, where the real world is blocked out and the digital world is substituted. This is also further improved by spatial audio, which makes the sounds seem to be coming in certain direction. Haptics is provided by controllers or gloves that fool your hands into feeling a texture and weight. This complete immersion is essential to the AI systems as they need vast amounts of data, including how the players turn their heads, on which objects they first touch, and how long they stare at a particular object. All this data is being processed to dynamically correct experiences without interrupting the flow.

AR works in a different manner. It does not replace reality, but rather superimposes digital components on what you already know using your phone or glasses. A classic example is Pokemon GO, which uses the information regarding your real location, local weather conditions, time of day, etc. to decide which virtual creatures appear. The similarity between the two technologies lies in the fact that they are both based on solid backend AI. VR requires AI in order to change the environment to your behavior without apparent latency, whereas AR relies on machine learning to convincingly combine digital materials with live camera images or environmental data. Both technologies keep on advancing because processing power is becoming cheaper and algorithms are becoming better in their ability to predict human behavioral patterns in real-time. AR in the Metaverse enables users to engage with the game objects in the physical, virtual and mixed reality with AI customizing the interaction.

The other important factor is endurance. In contrast to the traditional game sessions where the in-game world is cleared each time a player goes offline, in persistent virtual worlds the world still exists and moves forward even when the individual is not playing. Cloud computing and server-side design typically support such persistence, allowing the creation of massive shared worlds in which the actions of one player can make a permanent difference to other players. Persistence in AI also pertains to the ever-expanding set of interactions, and can be exploited to enhance the behavior of NPCs, modify the state of the environment, and give a story continuity across time.

The fourth pillar is the decentralization which is usually facilitated by blockchain technology. This enables player-owned assets, such as skins, weapons, or virtual land, to be saved in the form of personal digital token, which can be resold, bought or utilised in other applications. Peer-to-peer economies are also made possible by decentralization, in which AI agents can freely exchange, negotiate, or manage assets on behalf of players.

It is these foundations that AI and Generative AI stand a chance to flourish. The immersive canvas provided by AR and VR, continuity through persistence, value and ownership through decentralization, and AI giving life, intelligence, and creativity to these worlds make these worlds a reality. The adaptive, player-led experiences that the AI-powered Metaverse designs are based on could not exist without these technological underpinnings. In particular, content creation, personalization, and intelligent dialogue in the Metaverse are impossible without artificial intelligence, based on such functions as the digital twin, 3D reconstruction, and real-time rendering (Xu et al., 2023) (Chamola et al., 2023).

2.2. Role of AI in the Metaverse

AI brings the virtual worlds to life and makes them intelligent, versatile, and realistic as the cognitive engine of the Metaverse. One of the main uses in the gaming world is the transformation of NPC characters. In the past, NPCs had specific behaviors and followed predetermined routes, repeated words, and responded to a few preset stimuli. Conversely, the NPCs in the Metaverse powered by AI feature context-sensitive behavior, recollection of previous encounters, and the ability to adapt their tone according to the reputation of the player and even changing their level of skill to that of a player. This renders them as real-life characters and not paper-written obstacles (Yan et al., 2023). Procedural content generation is another important use, in which AI algorithms generate content in a game (e.g. landscapes, quests, puzzles, or dungeons) autonomously. This frees developers of the tedious content creation work and guarantees variety of player experience. PCG based on AI may also be customized to a specific player preference; as an example, when a player prefers stealth, missions will be designed with more chances of disguise and infiltration. AI is also essential to real-time decision-making systems. Such systems observe the movement patterns of players, their interaction decisions, reaction, and predictive analytics to dynamically change the difficulty of the game, its pacing, and the plot. AI may also be used in multiplayer games as an auxiliary game master, to even out matches by allocating roles or resources, or to dynamically adjust the difficulty. This will give everyone an equal and exciting experience. Adaptive storytelling is one of the most imaginative AI implementations in the Metaverse. Unlike other games that have one storyline, AI-created stories are developed naturally depending on the decisions of players. AI combines past events, morality of players and in-game relationships and creates a narrative of events that unfold (Buongiorno et al., 2024). Basically, AI makes the Metaverse more of a living ecosystem than a stage. Each interaction between the players adds to the richness of the information the AI employs to make the world more lifelike, predictable, and engaging.

2.3. Game Development AI

Generative AI does not just analyze and alter the existing situations; it actually creates new ones. It generates graphics, audio, writing and even gameplay, which is a stark contrast to archaic procedures and experiences in game design. Non-Player Characters can now talk as the real people with Large Language Models. Gone are the times when players had only a choice of pre-recorded lines when talking to NPCs, having to choose it on response menu. Players have the ability to ask questions on the spur of the moment, joke with their characters or engage in unusual discussions (Hu et al., 2024). Such GenAI-driven NPCs will be able to respond with contextualized information, humor, and even remember the previous interaction. This produces an impression of communicating with real personalities not just script characters. GenAI also speeds up asset's creation.

Whereas in the past, artists took months to sculpt or create a landscape or character, diffusion models and neural rendering can now create environments and models in a fraction of the time. The developers are able to feed in prompts such as "an ancient temple covered with vines at sunset" which then generates an entire usable textured environment. Tedious work is done by GenAI, but artists still do not lose their input, which gives them more liberty to fine-tune and innovate. GenAI can be used to improve adaptive game music by making it more intense in case of fighting and less intense in case of exploration. (Gnatyuk et al., 2025) GenAI has the capability to create sound effects procedurally, and modify them dynamically, to bridge audio-visual effects smooth.

The outcome is a logical, immersive and extremely personalized experience. The democratizing effect of GenAI on the development of games is even greater. Software based on models gives indie developers, whose output is usually end-user oriented, the ability to create assets, quests, or even full levels that cannot be distinguished visually or functionally with those of larger studios. This radically changes the production of content which used to be dominated by mega studios (Jacobides et al., 2023). GenAI also removes any technical barriers, bringing in a wider range of voices within the gaming ecosystem. Although these have advantages, there are also threats posed by GenAI. Stereotypes or cultural insensitivity can be unintentionally spread in the created characters and tales through model biases.

Moreover, the widespread adoption of AI tools could also cause homogenization of creative expression, as artists focus on the results provided by algorithms rather than on original human art. In order to overcome these obstacles, it is necessary to pay attention to the careful curation, a wide range of training data, and constant human control of the creative cycle. Of course, there are the problems of originality, rights and quality management with democratization. But the possibilities are also enormous: the development cycle is reduced, the worlds are more effective, and each player can create an experience that can be shaped individually. Simply put, GenAI is not replacing human ingenuity; it just gives it a lot of power so that those who want to carve their imagination at a rate and magnitude never seen before can do that. This generative ability of GAI reinvents the skill set of content generation, in which primary creators are replaced by more specialized editors, who enhance AI-generated content (Kanbach et al., 2023). Such a change allows developers to attend to more creative processes, including conceptualization and narrative consistency, and use AI to produce content elements through an iterative process.

3. USER EXPERIENCE & CO-CREATION

3.1. Co-Creation amongst Developers and Players

Culturally, the most important change is co-creation, which has been introduced by AI and Generative AI. Games are no longer just products created by developers, but are participatory platforms in which gamers actively add to content development. This method focuses on the engagement of players, which is made easier through AI-related applications to simplify the creative process. Players are able to merely explain their ideas using common words, and the system will turn them into assets, quests, or characters in the game. An example is that a user can talk about an arena in the desert full of running sand beasts, and in a few minutes, an artificial environment created by an AI will be ready to play. This development changes the developer-player dynamic, where developers create the platform and establish the quality norms, and players share ideas, assets and stories through interactive experiences, thus adding to the game world. AI is the key that will turn these ideas into real game elements that create a self-sustaining, self-managed community ecosystem, founded upon the collective imagination of its members.

This would develop AI further to generate more and more user-generated content that would be easier to make. Consequently, it is a real opportunity since it does not require coding or designing since players become real participants and directly affect their gameplay experience. This level of democratization makes participation more active because players are not only consumers, but also co-creators of the worlds they live in.

Co-creation surely possesses its strong points, such as variety of content, more robust ties of the community, and ever-changing game worlds. But this also has thorny problems. What are the ways of splitting the revenues of assets and creations with players? Who is the true owner of the AI-supported asset or creation: the player, developer or both? And, how are inappropriate material to be avoided? These issues should be addressed in order to have a healthy ecosystem. Another risk factor has to do with the psychology of engagement. The personalization caused by AI may be so free that it results in compulsive gaming or even addiction especially among the younger users. Despite the fact that co-creation assists in promoting empowerment, there is a need to engage in responsible design choices so that creativity is not realized at the expense of health.

It has its challenges, however, to go through in order to achieve these benefits. Co-creation is a paradigm shift, a shift to non-static games to games as living and evolving collaborative art forms. The game and the creation are merged in these spaces and the Metaverse is a place to explore and place to make. This participatory development model, especially through the incorporation of generative AI, requires the involvement of creative professionals to make sure that AI tools are not isolated technological delights but rather ingrained in the creative processes to the largest possible extent to harness its potential to generate innovative game designs in order to democratize the expression of creativity in the development of games (Inie et al., 2023). (Linares-Pellicer et al., 2025). This is crucial so that human intuition and moral judgment determine the application of the other creative abilities of generative AI, to create unparalleled innovation and democratize creative expression in various domains.

4. ETHICAL ISSUES AND PROBLEMS

4.1. Artificial Intelligence-based Avatars and Self-Scheduling Agents

In the Metaverse, avatars become more than just digital entities and become smart extensions of a player. These intelligent AI avatars evolve, both in the short term with impulsive choices, and in the long term with habitual behavior. The system is very attentive to play styles, favorite choices and even social communication preferences. As an example, an avatar may always wear the clothes chosen by the user, or its body language may reflect the interaction of the player with other players in the game. This high-tech intertwining poses serious questions about the identity formation and social interaction in virtual reality, including the possibility of the subtle impact of AI-driven actions on a user on his/her self-image and attitude in the real world. Moreover, the growing autonomy of such avatars, especially when generative AI is included to create dynamic interactions and subtle expressions, makes the boundary between those behaviors that user's control and those that are created by AI more complicated, creating tricky accountability and authorship problems in virtual communication.

The Proteus effect, in which the look of an avatar affects the attitudes and behaviors of a user in real-life, is even more salient in cases where avatars are given AI-controlled autonomy, which may affect self-identity and social biases in the potentially immersive metaverse. It requires a close attention to the psychological effects of AI-enhanced virtual identities and the younger demographic of users that is still forming its own sense of self. The use of generative AI with non-playable characters adds a layer of dynamic nature to the relationships between players and non-playable characters, which adds additional complexity to the moral dimension of AI-driven virtual worlds.

The risk of identity fragmentation and mental health problems because of the large and broad representation of identities in the metaverse also demand a strong technological and regulatory response. Creating sophisticated technological means to verify identities and authenticity of content, as well as clear regulatory systems that establish legal limits of virtual avatars and computer-generated content, is essential to the solution of these issues. Other important questions that these frameworks should answer are how to provide privacy and prevent misuse, as well as to provide a balanced approach to governance that replicates the rules of the real world into the virtual world and promote the expression of identity flexibly. Besides, the digital beings of the metaverse, even extremely autonomous ones, are in demand of new legal frameworks to resolve the problem of identity recognition, behavior assessment, and responsibility.

4.2. Ethical, Legal and Privacy

The ethical and legal aspects of AI usage are crucially important and cannot be overlooked because of the scale of the planned integration of AI into the Metaverse. One of the main issues is the privacy of data. Contrary to the old-fashioned web interactions, which track such simple actions as mouse clicks, the immersive VR and AR technologies can capture incredibly sensitive biometric data, such as eye and facial expressions, speech patterns, and overall body movements. Should this granular information fall into the wrong hands, it could reveal the intimate information about the emotional condition, health, or behavioral tendencies of a user, leaving people highly vulnerable. The companies that deal with such data have a heavy burden of responsibility to guarantee that it is kept secure and used in an ethical manner that does not involve using it to engage in intrusive advertising or even illegal surveillance. With the possibility of an almost any person making assets, narratives, or characters through the power of AI and Generative AI, there is a constant threat of harmful, offensive, or inappropriate content infiltrating mainstream virtual spaces.

In order to create and sustain safe and inclusive communities, developers should quickly introduce powerful moderation frameworks that preferably incorporate advanced AI filtering with much-needed human intervention. The absence of these essential protection measures may cause harmful effects on the players, taking into account that younger age groups constitute a significant share of the gamers. The issue of intellectual property rights also makes things more complicated. When a player develops an AI utility to create special in-game weapons or other creations, then who belongs to such rights? Is it the developer who was the provider of the platform or the company that trained the AI model? Without clear rules, the issue of ownership will always be a controversial one, especially when digital objects have a real economic value in an NFT-based or tokenized economy. These are complicated legal dilemmas that are applied to virtual crime, in which behaviors that would be criminal in the real world, including harassment or theft, must be enforced using new legal structures in the metaverse (Yang et al., 2024). Such a complex environment requires the creation of new legal frameworks that will help to balance innovation and protection to have a safe and fair virtual environment (Jung et al., 2023). Moreover, AI models generate synthetic data, which poses even more risks such as the possibility of breaking the privacy laws, enabling new vectors of cyberattacks, and raising complicated questions around consent, anonymization, and data ownership (Verma et al., 2025).

Ethics of generative AI is a complicated issue, which involves concerns about data security and privacy, copyright infringement, misinformation, and the promotion of biases, and this problem can only be solved through an interdisciplinary approach to tackle the multidimensional problem. That is why, it is essential to develop a set of comprehensive ethical standards and regulatory principles to reduce the risks related to biased AI systems and possible misuse of generative AI technologies (Kanbach et al., 2023). Thus, ethical training procedures and the need to mitigate existing prejudices in AI models should be revealed and implemented through a multi-stakeholder approach that requires the involvement of developers, regulators, and end-users.

4.3. Challenges & Limitations

Another ethical issue that makes the AI models more problematic is the possibility of them hallucinating or creating false information, which can misguide the users and make them question the responsibility and the truth of virtual experiences. Biases, misinformation, and intellectual property concerns are also among the most important issues brought about by the deployment of generative AI, which require the creation of strong ethical frameworks and regulation (Das et al., 2024). Also, the potential privacy, bias, and ethical issues that may arise due to the ability of large language models to produce dynamic and personalized experiences in the metaverse should be considered carefully and mitigated.

In particular, the use of the big language models such as GPT in metaverse applications to facilitate learning, entertainment, and personalization, and provide dynamic user experiences, by definition, raises valid concerns about privacy, the presence of implicit biases, and overall ethical considerations. To overcome these issues, it is important to create a balance between the need to drive innovation in AI and building the overall regulatory frameworks that safeguard the rights of individuals and intellectual property, especially when the AI models are trained on large amounts of data that can potentially contain copyrighted content (Das et al., 2024).

Additionally, the practicality of machine learning algorithms to recognize their users with high precision using the least amount of VR movement data highlights the fact that the metaverse requires improved privacy settings and effective identity management systems (Yang et al., 2024). This requires a multi-dimensional solution, such as technical protection such as differential privacy and homomorphic encryption, and explicit policy statements regarding the collection, use, and storage of data. These are essential to avoid the abuse of sensitive user data and to make sure the abundance of opportunities that the metaverse offers does not occur at the cost of personal privacy. Moreover, the nature of certain advanced AI models, especially large language models, is very opaque which is a major obstacle in comprehending how they make their decisions in order to address biases or inaccuracies (Sheth et al., 2024).

5. AI AND GENAI IN THE METAVERSE FUTURE

The further improvement of semiconductor technology and new computing architectures and the emergence of AI-optimized hardware such as GPUs and TPUs will enable considerable computational power, making the process of the large-scale implementation of GenAI and digital twins more viable and more affordable in the framework of the metaverse (Xu et al., 2024). This increased computing power will be able to make more advanced and detailed virtual worlds that will push the limits of immersiveness (Chamola et al., 2024). The development of these technologies will also enable the implementation of hyper-realistic simulations, digital beings, and spaces, which will enable more emotionally powerful interactions between users and digital avatars. On the same note, new studies in facial expression, motion capture and behavioral modeling have enhanced the degree of interactivity and realism of avatars and digital beings.

Moreover, these technological developments will enable the real-time processing of multifaceted AI models, which will result in more interactive and reactive interactions between users and AI-based virtual actors. The swift development of AI (and, in this case, generative AI) has already made it much easier to produce very realistic digital content, which only contributes to the immersive experience of the metaverse. The same simplification can be applied to the automated creation of virtual worlds, characters, and plots, which makes development more affordable and fast-tracks innovation in these digital worlds.

Nevertheless, the given technological development also comes with a number of serious security concerns, including the possibility of producing deepfakes or writing untraceable identities, which is a serious security issue. These security issues require more complex authentication systems and stronger cryptographic keys to protect the user identity and data integrity in the virtual worlds that are becoming more realistic. Furthermore, the widespread use of AI-Extended Reality in metaverses, despite the fact that it offers full immersion and customized experience, inevitably creates new vulnerabilities, which require safe and reliable AI applications (Qayyum et al., 2023). To overcome them, AI security and privacy-sensitive AI methods, including federated learning and differential privacy, will play a significant role in making sure that user data is protected and avoiding the malicious use of AI in the metaverse. The future of the metaverse is inherently connected with the ongoing development of AI, especially generative AI, that is likely to automate the content creation process and customize the user experience on a scale never seen before.

REFERENCES

Buongiorno, S., Klinkert, L. J., Chawla, T., Zhuang, Z., & Clark, C. (2024). PANGeA: Procedural Artificial Narrative using Generative AI for Turn-Based Video Games. https://doi.org/DOI: 10.48550/ARXIV.2404.19721

Chamola, V., Bansal, G., Das, T. K., Hassija, V., Reddy, N. S. S., Wang, J., Zeadally, S., Hussain, A., Yu, F. R., Guizani, M., & Niyato, D. (2023). Beyond Reality: The Pivotal Role of Generative AI in the Metaverse. arXiv (Cornell University). https://doi.org//arxiv.2308.06272DOI: 10.48550

Chamola, V., Bansal, G., Das, T. K., Hassija, V., Sai, S., Wang, J., Zeadally, S., Hussain, A., Yu, F. R., Guizani, M., & Niyato, D. (2024). Beyond Reality: The Pivotal Role of Generative AI in the Metaverse. *IEEE Internet of Things Magazine*, *7*(4), 126–135. DOI: 10.1109/IOTM.001.2300174

Das, A., Jha, D., Sanjotra, J., Susladkar, O., Sarkar, S., Rauniyar, A., Tomar, N. K., Sharma, V., & Bagci, U. (2024). Ethical Framework for Responsible Foundational Models in Medical Imaging. *arXiv (Cornell University)*. https://doi.org//arxiv.2406.11868DOI: 10.48550

Gnatyuk, V., Koriukina, V., Levoshevich, I., Nurminskiy, P., & Wallner, G. (2025). In the Blink of an Eye: Instant Game Map Editing using a Generative-AI Smart Brush. DOI: 10.48550/ARXIV.2503.19793

Hu, C., Zhao, Y., Wang, Z., Du, H., & Liu, J. (2024). Games for Artificial Intelligence Research: A Review and Perspectives [Review of Games for Artificial Intelligence Research: A Review and Perspectives]. IEEE Transactions on Artificial Intelligence, 1. Institute of Electrical and Electronics Engineers. DOI: 10.1109/TAI.2024.3410935

Inie, N., Falk, J., & Tanimoto, S. L. (2023). Designing Participatory AI: Creative Professionals' Worries and Expectations about Generative AI. *arXiv (Cornell University)*. https://doi.org//arXiv.2303.08931DOI: 10.1145/3544549.3585657

Inie, N., Falk, J., & Tanimoto, S. L. (2023). Designing Participatory AI: Creative Professionals' Worries and Expectations about Generative AI. *arXiv (Cornell University)*. https://doi.org//arXiv.2303.08931DOI: 10.1145/3544549.3585657

Jacobides, M. G., Candelon, F., Krayer, L., Round, K., & Chen, W. S. (2023). Building synthetic worlds: Lessons from the excessive infatuation and oversold disillusionment with the metaverse. *Industry and Innovation*, *31*(1), 105–129. DOI: 10.1080/13662716.2023.2279051

Jung, T., Cho, J., Han, D. D., Ahn, S. J., Gupta, M., Das, G., Heo, C. Y., Loureiro, S. M. C., Σιγάλα, M., Trunfio, M., Taylor, A., & tom Dieck, M. C. (2023). Metaverse for service industries: Future applications, opportunities, challenges and research directions. *Computers in Human Behavior*, *151*, 108039. DOI: 10.1016/j.chb.2023.108039

Kanbach, D. K., Heiduk, L., Blueher, G., Schreiter, M., & Lahmann, A. (2023). The GenAI is out of the bottle: Generative artificial intelligence from a business model innovation perspective. *Review of Managerial Science*, *18*(4), 1189–1220. DOI: 10.1007/s11846-023-00696-z

Kanbach, D. K., Heiduk, L., Blueher, G., Schreiter, M., & Lahmann, A. (2023). The GenAI is out of the bottle: Generative artificial intelligence from a business model innovation perspective. *Review of Managerial Science*, *18*(4), 1189–1220. DOI: 10.1007/s11846-023-00696-z

Linares-Pellicer, J., Izquierdo-Domenech, J., Ferri-Molla, I., & Aliaga-Torro, C. (2025). *We Are All Creators: Generative AI, Collective Knowledge, and the Path Towards Human-AI Synergy*. https://doi.org/DOI: 10.48550/ARXIV.2504.07936

Linares-Pellicer, J., Izquierdo-Domenech, J., Ferri-Molla, I., & Aliaga-Torro, C. (2025). *We Are All Creators: Generative AI, Collective Knowledge, and the Path Towards Human-AI Synergy*. https://doi.org/DOI: 10.48550/ARXIV.2504.07936

Ortiz, A., Santiago, R. R., Hernández, D. E., & Lopez-Montiel, M. (2025). Multiclass Evaluation of Vision Transformers for Industrial Welding Defect Detection. *Mathematical & Computational Applications*, *30*(2), 24. DOI: 10.3390/mca30020024

Qayyum, A., Butt, M. A., Ali, H., Usman, M., Halabi, O., Al-Fuqaha, A., Abbasi, Q. H., Imran, M. A., & Qadir, J. (2023). Secure and Trustworthy Artificial Intelligence-extended Reality (AI-XR) for Metaverses [Review of *Secure and Trustworthy Artificial Intelligence-extended Reality (AI-XR) for Metaverses*]. *ACM Computing Surveys, 56*(7), 1. Association for Computing Machinery. https://doi.org/DOI: 10.1145/3614426

Sheth, S., Baker, H. P., Prescher, H., & Strelzow, J. (2024). Ethical Considerations of Artificial Intelligence in Health Care: Examining the Role of Generative Pretrained Transformer-4. *The Journal of the American Academy of Orthopaedic Surgeons*, *32*(5), 205–210. DOI: 10.5435/JAAOS-D-23-00787 PMID: 38175996

Verma, A., Sankhyayan, S., Jawanda, K., & Tandon, S. N. (2025). Generative Artificial Intelligence and Cybersecurity Risks: Issues and Challenges. In *Lecture notes in networks and systems* (p. 321). Springer International Publishing. https://doi.org/DOI: 10.1007/978-981-97-8602-2_29

Xu, H., Omitaomu, O. A., Sabri, S., Li, X., & Song, Y. (2024). Leveraging Generative AI for Smart City Digital Twins: A Survey on the Autonomous Generation of Data, Scenarios, 3D City Models, and Urban Designs. *arXiv (Cornell University).* https://doi.org//arxiv.2405.19464DOI: 10.48550

Xu, Y., Feng, D., Zhao, M., Sun, Y., & Xia, X. (2023). Edge Intelligence Empowered Metaverse: Architecture, Technologies, and Open Issues. *IEEE Network, 37*(6), 92–100. DOI: 10.1109/MNET.2023.3317477

Yan, M., Li, R., Zhang, H., Wang, H., Yang, Z., & Yan, J. (2023). LARP: Language-Agent Role Play for Open-World Games. arXiv (Cornell University). https://doi.org//arxiv.2312.17653DOI: 10.48550

Yang, L., Yan, X., & Pan, H. (2024). Metaverse Identity: Core Principles and Critical Challenges. *arXiv (Cornell University).* https://doi.org//arxiv.2406.08029DOI: 10.48550

Chapter 11
The Role of AI in Preserving and Remastering Classic Games

P. Selvakumar
https://orcid.org/0000-0002-3650-4548
Department of Science and Humanities, Nehru Institute of Technology, Coimbatore, India

Pallavi Jaggi
https://orcid.org/0000-0002-7003-7576
Chandigarh School of Business, Chandigarh Group of Colleges, Jhanjeri, India

S. Poorani
https://orcid.org/0000-0001-7179-431X
Kongu Engineering College, India

Mohit Sharma
https://orcid.org/0009-0007-2280-8077
Maharshi Dayanand University, Rohtak, India

Vinod Waiker
https://orcid.org/0000-0003-4960-318X
Datta Meghe Institute of Management Studies, India

Manjunath T. C.
https://orcid.org/0000-0003-2545-9160
Rajarajeswari College of Engineering, India

Satheesh Kumar D.
https://orcid.org/0000-0002-3808-9595
Hindusthan College of Engineering and Technology, India

ABSTRACT

Video games, once considered mere entertainment for children or niche enthusiasts, have grown into a global cultural and artistic force. They are no longer simply digital pastimes but complex narratives, technological achievements, and reflections

DOI: 10.4018/979-8-3373-4637-3.ch011

ght © 2026, IGI Global Scientific Publishing. Copying or distributing in print or electronic forms without written permission of IGI Global Scientific Publishing is prohibited. Use of this chapter to generative artificial intelligence (AI) technologies is expressly prohibited. The publisher reserves all rights to license its use for generative AI training and machine learning model development.

of society's values and creativity at particular moments in time. From the pixelated adventures of the early 1980s to the immersive open-world epics of the present day, video games have evolved into a unique medium that bridges art, storytelling, technology, and interactivity. However, as the medium has evolved, so too has the threat of loss. Just as film historians fight to preserve silent movies or archivists work to protect classic literature, there is a growing and urgent need to preserve classic video games. These early and foundational titles are disappearing at an alarming rate due to technological obsolescence, hardware degradation, and legal challenges that prevent access and emulation. Classic games offer a lens into the past.

INTRODUCTION TO GAME PRESERVATION

Video games, once considered mere entertainment for children or niche enthusiasts, have grown into a global cultural and artistic force. They are no longer simply digital pastimes but complex narratives, technological achievements, and reflections of society's values and creativity at particular moments in time. From the pixelated adventures of the early 1980s to the immersive open-world epics of the present day, video games have evolved into a unique medium that bridges art, storytelling, technology, and interactivity. However, as the medium has evolved, so too has the threat of loss. Just as film historians fight to preserve silent movies or archivists work to protect classic literature, there is a growing and urgent need to preserve classic video games. These early and foundational titles are disappearing at an alarming rate due to technological obsolescence, hardware degradation, and legal challenges that prevent access and emulation. Classic games offer a lens into the past. They capture the aesthetics, mechanics, and design philosophies of their time, reflecting the hardware limitations and innovations that defined different gaming eras. They also reveal how developers overcame constraints with creativity, leading to game mechanics and genres that continue to influence modern titles. As gaming hardware becomes obsolete and physical media degrade, many older games become unplayable without significant technical effort. Cartridges, floppy disks, and early CD-ROMs suffer from decay, while the consoles needed to play them are increasingly rare or non-functional. Even digital games released in the early 2000s face disappearance due to expired online services or incompatible operating systems. Unlike books or vinyl records, video games are dependent on complex hardware and software ecosystems, making their preservation especially challenging. Emulation, software preservation, and hardware maintenance are all essential strategies, but each comes with technical, legal, and ethical complexities. One of the most controversial aspects of game preservation is legality.

Many efforts to archive or emulate classic games are hindered by copyright laws that do not adequately account for digital preservation. While developers and publishers have a right to protect their intellectual property, the rigidity of current copyright structures often leaves preservationists in a difficult position, particularly when games are no longer commercially available. For example, many games are considered "abandonware" because their creators are no longer in business, or the rights have lapsed into unclear ownership. In such cases, legal emulation or archival becomes nearly impossible without legislative reforms or cooperation from rights holders. Without a clear legal framework that balances intellectual property rights with cultural preservation, many classic games risk being lost forever. Institutions and grassroots organizations alike have begun taking steps to combat this growing crisis. The Video Game History Foundation, Internet Archive, and various museum initiatives have all worked to archive, document, and preserve classic games and their associated materials, such as manuals, source code, advertisements, and even developer interviews. These supplementary materials are vital for historical accuracy and context, much like behind-the-scenes content for film or literature. Academic institutions are also beginning to offer game studies programs that emphasize preservation and analysis, further legitimizing games as subjects of scholarly interest and cultural value. However, these efforts remain fragmented and under-resourced compared to the scale of the challenge.

THE CHALLENGES OF PRESERVING CLASSIC GAMES

Preserving classic video games is a multifaceted endeavor fraught with significant challenges—technical, legal, financial, and cultural. While the importance of safeguarding video games as part of our digital heritage is increasingly recognized, the road to achieving effective and lasting preservation is anything but straightforward. At its core, the act of conservation must ensure that future generations can access, play, and understand classic games in their original or intended forms. Yet doing so is extraordinarily complex. Unlike books, paintings, or even films, video games are interactive experiences dependent on an intricate web of software, hardware, and often proprietary ecosystems that are rapidly becoming obsolete (Usha S G A., et al, 2025). From deteriorating physical media and aging hardware to the restrictive frameworks of copyright law and the lack of institutional support, the challenges are numerous and deeply interwoven. The consequences of inaction are clear: as technology progresses and original materials disappear, many classic titles may become inaccessible, lost not only as entertainment but as cultural artifacts. One of the most pressing technical challenges in preserving classic games is hardware obsolescence. Early video game systems such as the Atari 2600, the NES, or the Sega Genesis were designed for specific hardware configurations that are no longer produced. Over time, these physical components degrade. Capacitors leak, circuit boards corrode, magnetic storage media like floppy disks lose their data integrity, and optical discs suffer from "disc rot." Even if an original console remains in working condition, finding functioning peripherals, such as controllers, light guns, memory cards, or the display equipment required to play these games, can be an insurmountable task. CRT televisions, once ubiquitous, are now rare, yet many older games were designed with the quirks and resolutions of CRTs in mind. Playing a light gun game like *Duck Hunt* or an arcade classic like *Time Crisis* is nearly impossible on modern LCD or OLED displays without significant modification or emulation (Dodiya K R., et al, 2025). Preserving games, therefore, isn't just about preserving software but about recreating or emulating the full gameplay environment. Legal and copyright issues present another formidable barrier to game preservation. Video games are protected under intellectual property laws that were not designed with digital preservation in mind. In many jurisdictions, even making a personal backup of a legally purchased game can exist in a legal gray area, let alone the mass archiving or distribution of games for preservation purposes. Many classic games are still under copyright, even if they are no longer commercially available, and copyright holders are not always willing to cooperate with preservation efforts. This is especially problematic in cases of "abandonware," where the original developers or publishers have gone out of business or no longer support the title.

The lack of clarity surrounding ownership in such cases means that preservationists often risk legal action by attempting to archive or share these games. Furthermore, many publishers actively oppose emulation or fan preservation projects, issuing takedown notices or lawsuits against archivists and developers who are, in many cases, the only reason certain games still exist in any playable form. Without significant reform in copyright law, such as exemptions for non-commercial preservation or fair use, the legal landscape remains hostile to many of the grassroots efforts essential to game preservation. The financial cost of preserving classic games is also a significant obstacle. Proper preservation is resource-intensive. It involves not only archiving the game itself but also documenting source code, creating detailed metadata, preserving related media like instruction manuals, box art, and advertisements, and maintaining or recreating the original hardware environment. For museums, libraries, and private collectors, these tasks demand time, expertise, and equipment that often exceeds available budgets (Aker O., 2025). Institutions that do engage in game preservation, such as The Strong National Museum of Play, the Library of Congress, or the Video Game History Foundation, often operate with limited funding and must prioritize select titles or systems, leaving much of gaming history undocumented or vulnerable to loss. Moreover, unlike film or literature, the commercial market for classic games is fragmented, making it difficult to generate sustained funding from consumer interest alone. Crowdfunding and community support can help, but they are rarely enough to sustain long-term archival efforts at scale. Cultural challenges also play a role in the difficulty of game preservation. Despite growing academic and artistic recognition, video games have not always been treated as legitimate cultural artifacts worthy of preservation. For decades, games were viewed as transient commercial products rather than historical works, and this perception contributed to widespread neglect. Developers and publishers frequently failed to archive their materials, and many early titles were simply lost due to a lack of foresight. Additionally, the gaming community's attitudes toward preservation can be inconsistent. While there is strong grassroots support for emulation and archiving, there are also segments of the community that view unauthorized access to old games as piracy rather than preservation. Bridging this cultural divide requires education, advocacy, and a shift in how society views the value of games as part of our collective history.

THE ROLE OF AI IN GAME PRESERVATION AND REMASTERING

Artificial Intelligence (AI) has rapidly emerged as a transformative force across numerous industries, and the realm of video game preservation and remastering is no exception. As the challenges of safeguarding and revitalizing classic games grow more complex, AI offers innovative tools that can help overcome the technical, logistical, and creative barriers that traditional methods struggle to address. Whether through enhancing visuals, reconstructing lost assets, enabling intelligent emulation, translating old games, or automating the reconstruction of source code, AI stands at the forefront of a new era in digital preservation. While not a panacea, the integration of AI technologies into the preservation toolkit represents a paradigm shift—one that brings both immense promise and profound ethical questions (Anantrasirichai N., et al, 2025). The expanding capabilities of AI make it possible to not only keep older games playable but also to restore and reimagine them in ways that preserve their original spirit while making them accessible to new generations of players. One of the most visible ways AI is contributing to game preservation is through graphical enhancement and remastering. Classic games, especially those from the early 3D era, often feature low-resolution textures, jagged polygonal models, and animation limitations due to the hardware constraints of their time. Using AI-driven upscaling techniques such as deep learning-based super-resolution, neural networks can intelligently enhance these assets by filling in missing details and sharpening imagery in a way that is far more natural and accurate than traditional filtering techniques. Tools like ESRGAN (Enhanced Super Resolution Generative Adversarial Networks) and Topaz Gigapixel AI can analyze and upscale textures to 4K or higher while maintaining aesthetic consistency with the original art direction. These models are trained on vast datasets and learn to predict high-resolution textures based on low-resolution input, allowing for dramatic improvements without needing the original high-quality source files. This process has already been used in unofficial fan remasters of games like *Final Fantasy VII*, *Resident Evil 4*, and *The Elder Scrolls III: Morrowind*, breathing new life into classic titles while preserving their original visual charm. Beyond visuals, AI is being employed to address one of the thorniest problems in game preservation: the loss or inaccessibility of source code (Ma Y P., 2021). In many cases, especially for games developed in the 1980s and 1990s, the original code has been lost or was never properly archived. Without it, remastering or porting games to new platforms becomes an enormous challenge. AI, particularly models designed for code reconstruction and decompilation, can assist by reverse-engineering compiled binaries back into usable code. These AI models use pattern recognition and probabilistic analysis to infer high-level logic from machine code, enabling developers to rebuild functionality, patch bugs, or optimize performance for modern systems. While this process is not flawless and often requires human oversight, it drastically reduces the time and expertise needed to make old software usable again. It also opens the door for partial or full remasters of games that were once considered impossible to revive.

AI's role in documentation and metadata generation is equally important for archiving purposes. A significant part of game preservation involves cataloging games, manuals, promotional materials, development notes, and more. AI can automate much of this process by scanning and categorizing large volumes of documents, identifying game mechanics, parsing source code, and extracting gameplay footage for analysis. Optical character recognition (OCR) and natural language processing (NLP) tools can transcribe and organize printed materials such as box art, developer diaries, or strategy guides. Furthermore, AI can create playable timelines, annotate development milestones, or even simulate developer intent based on surviving interviews and documentation. Ethical concerns abound, particularly around the use of AI to replicate voice performances or reconstruct source code without the original developers' consent. There are also questions about authenticity: when AI enhances or alters a game, is the result still "original"? Some preservationists argue that AI remasters may distort or erase the creative limitations that defined a game's character (Fu Y., et al, 2025). Others counter that modern players should be able to enjoy classic games in a form that is accessible and aesthetically pleasing by today's standards. Striking a balance between preservation and modernization is crucial, and it requires thoughtful input from developers, historians, and the gaming community.

In conclusion, AI is rapidly becoming an indispensable ally in the fight to preserve, restore, and revitalize classic video games. Its capabilities extend beyond what was previously possible with manual methods, allowing for the intelligent upscaling of graphics, reconstruction of lost code, enhancement of sound and voice, emulation of legacy systems, and translation of games into new languages. At the same time, its use raises important ethical, legal, and philosophical questions about authorship, authenticity, and equitable access. The role of AI in game preservation is not simply technical; it is deeply human. It is about using our most advanced tools to protect, celebrate, and pass down the stories, artistry, and innovations that have defined generations of digital play. As AI continues to evolve, it offers a powerful but nuanced path forward—one that, if navigated thoughtfully, could ensure that the legacy of classic games remains vibrant and accessible for centuries to come.

AI-ASSISTED EMULATION: PRESERVING CLASSIC GAME ENVIRONMENTS

As the preservation of classic video games becomes an increasingly urgent concern in digital heritage, emulation has emerged as one of the most powerful and practical tools for ensuring continued access to aging software. Emulators replicate the behavior of older gaming hardware, such as the NES, Sega Genesis, PlayStation, or arcade boards—allowing classic games to be played on modern devices. Traditionally, emulation has been a painstaking process that requires developers to reverse-engineer the intricacies of legacy systems, manually simulate chipsets, and mimic hardware behavior through software. However, the limitations of traditional emulation methods—ranging from imperfect hardware simulation and incompatibility issues to inefficient performance—have spurred interest in using artificial intelligence (AI) to enhance and streamline the emulation process (Nimo & Ravishankar, 2024). AI-assisted emulation represents a technological leap forward, offering innovative ways to not only recreate classic gaming environments more accurately but to improve them with minimal deviation from their original feel. By analyzing gameplay behavior, interpreting graphical output, and predicting hardware-level functions, AI is helping to preserve the interactive experience of older games in ways previously thought impossible. One of the most compelling uses of AI in emulation is in learning-based system modeling. Rather than hand-coding every instruction, AI can observe and learn the operational patterns of original hardware through machine learning techniques. For instance, a neural network can be trained on data gathered from the input/output behavior of a real console, allowing it to develop a functional approximation of the hardware's internal logic. This method not only accelerates emulator development but can also lead to more accurate results in systems where timing, sound processing, and visual rendering are tightly coupled with obscure hardware operations. AI models can interpolate missing hardware behavior and predict system states that were previously undocumented, creating more faithful reproductions of the original gameplay environment (Wang Y., 2023). Another groundbreaking contribution of AI in emulation lies in graphical restoration and frame interpolation. Many classic games run at 30 frames per second (FPS) or lower, and their native resolutions are a far cry from today's high-definition displays. AI-enhanced emulators can integrate technologies like machine learning-based frame interpolation to generate smoother animations and create the illusion of higher frame rates without altering game mechanics. Additionally, deep learning upscaling techniques such as ESRGAN (Enhanced Super Resolution Generative Adversarial Networks) have been incorporated into emulation platforms to upscale textures and environments in real time. This makes games visually palatable on modern screens while staying true to their artistic intent. Importantly, these enhancements are often non-destructive, meaning players can toggle them on or off, ensuring purists and modern gamers alike can experience the game according to their preferences.

One of the subtler, yet equally significant contributions of AI to emulation is in preserving peripheral support and input ecosystems. Many classic games relied on specialized hardware—light guns, arcade sticks, dance pads, steering wheels, or even obscure accessories like the Power Glove. These peripherals were designed with specific physical interactions in mind and are rarely compatible with modern systems. AI-driven motion mapping and input simulation techniques can emulate these controls using modern hardware, such as webcams, VR controllers, or haptic devices. For example, AI can translate hand gestures into input commands for a light gun game or convert dance pad sequences to touchscreen taps or motion-sensing devices. This not only keeps these games playable but preserves the full experience, including the physicality that was often central to gameplay. However, as with all AI-powered preservation efforts, emulation raises important ethical and legal questions (Antony & Huang, 2025). One core issue is fidelity: when AI improves or interprets aspects of a game, such as smoothing out frame rates or upscaling visuals, is it still the same game? Some preservationists argue that altering a game's original performance or appearance, even slightly, risks undermining historical accuracy. Others maintain that as long as the original experience remains accessible, enhancements should be considered part of a preservation continuum that makes classic games more approachable for contemporary audiences. Most AI-assisted emulators now offer configuration options that allow users to toggle enhancements on or off, striking a balance between fidelity and accessibility. Another concern is the legal ambiguity surrounding emulation, particularly when AI is used to simulate proprietary systems or run games still under copyright. While some countries recognize fair use exceptions for preservation and research, others impose strict controls, leaving emulator developers vulnerable to legal action, even when their work serves cultural preservation. In conclusion, AI-assisted emulation represents a vital evolution in the effort to preserve classic game environments (Kaur M., et al, 2025). By intelligently replicating hardware behaviors, enhancing graphics and audio, maintaining authentic control systems, and enabling smarter performance optimization, AI makes it possible to keep the spirit and functionality of classic games alive in a rapidly changing technological landscape. It addresses the core issue of access, not just in terms of playability, but in preserving the feeling and context of the original gaming experience. As AI continues to mature, its role in emulation will likely expand from a tool of enhancement to a cornerstone of digital heritage. Yet the success of AI in this space depends not just on its technical capabilities, but on how thoughtfully it is integrated, balancing authenticity, legality, accessibility, and respect for the games and creators that built the foundation of interactive entertainment. In this delicate balance, AI-assisted emulation offers a powerful vision of the future—one where the games of the past remain vivid, playable, and meaningful for generations to come.

AI-POWERED GRAPHICS ENHANCEMENT: UPSCALING AND TEXTURE RECONSTRUCTION

The visual appeal of video games plays a pivotal role in their cultural impact and player engagement. Classic games, especially those from the 8-bit, 16-bit, and early 3D eras, often suffer from pixelation, low-resolution textures, and limited color palettes due to hardware constraints at the time of their development. As display technology has dramatically advanced, with ultra-high-definition (4K and beyond) screens becoming the norm, these legacy visuals can appear blurry, blocky, or outdated, detracting from the original artistic vision and accessibility to modern audiences. Traditional methods of improving game graphics, such as manual redrawing or hand-crafted remasters, are labor-intensive, expensive, and often subjective, risking alteration of the game's authentic aesthetic (Samal A., et al, 2025). In recent years, AI-powered graphics enhancement, particularly through sophisticated upscaling algorithms and texture reconstruction techniques, has emerged as a revolutionary approach that balances fidelity to the original art with significant visual improvement. These technologies enable preservationists, developers, and enthusiasts to restore and modernize classic game visuals efficiently, unlocking new possibilities for experiencing and preserving gaming history. At the heart of AI-powered graphics enhancement lies image upscaling, which involves increasing the resolution of low-resolution textures and sprites to match the display capabilities of modern hardware. Unlike traditional interpolation methods such as nearest neighbor, bilinear, or bicubic scaling, which simply enlarge images by averaging pixel values and often produce blurry or artifact-prone results, AI-driven upscaling uses deep learning models trained on vast datasets of high- and low-resolution image pairs. Convolutional neural networks (CNNs), generative adversarial networks (GANs), and other neural architectures learn to predict and synthesize missing pixel details, preserving edges, textures, and patterns with remarkable accuracy (Jessen T D., et al, 2022). These models can infer fine details that were not originally present but are consistent with the visual style of the source image, thus providing a sharp, clean, and natural-looking enhancement. For classic games, this means that pixel art sprites, UI elements, and background assets can be enlarged dramatically while maintaining the crispness and charm characteristic of the original designs. One of the most widely known applications of this technology in gaming is the upscaling of sprite sheets and 2D textures. Many retro titles rely on a limited set of pixel art assets repeatedly used across various game scenes. AI-based upscalers analyze these sprites holistically, understanding their shapes, shading, and artistic intent, then generate higher-resolution versions that can be applied seamlessly in emulators or remastered editions. This avoids the need for artists to painstakingly redraw each sprite by hand, saving time while preserving authenticity. Furthermore, AI models can adapt to different pixel art styles—whether the sharp outlines and limited palettes of early platformers or the more detailed and colorful sprites of late 16-bit RPGs—making the technology versatile across game genres and eras.

In addition to upscaling, texture reconstruction plays a critical role in enhancing 3D games and environments. Early 3D games used heavily compressed, low-resolution textures due to limited memory and storage. These textures often appear blocky or blurry when rendered on modern displays, detracting from immersion. AI-powered texture reconstruction involves analyzing these coarse textures and generating refined, high-resolution replacements that respect the original color schemes, patterns, and material properties. Techniques like neural style transfer and texture synthesis enable the generation of visually coherent textures that maintain the artistic integrity of the original while improving clarity and detail. By incorporating spatial context and patterns learned from similar textures in large datasets, AI can fill in missing details or remove compression artifacts, resulting in cleaner and more realistic surfaces in classic game worlds (Malenfant S., et al, 2022). One notable advancement is the use of super-resolution GANs (SRGANs) that specialize in enhancing textures and images by generating highly detailed, photo-realistic results. These models have been applied successfully to reconstruct complex textures such as foliage, fabric, stone, and metal surfaces in remastered versions of classic games. The ability of GANs to hallucinate plausible details beyond what is explicitly present enables the recreation of textures that are not only higher in resolution but also richer in visual complexity, which can greatly enhance the player's sense of realism and immersion without compromising the game's stylistic coherence. AI-powered graphics enhancement also addresses the challenge of color palette limitations and dithering, common techniques used in older games to simulate color depth. Classic games often used dithering patterns or limited palettes due to hardware constraints, resulting in visual noise or color banding on modern displays. ML algorithms can analyze these patterns and reconstruct smoother gradients and more natural color transitions while preserving the original artistic style. This enhances the overall visual quality and makes classic games more visually appealing to contemporary audiences accustomed to richer color depth (Gill S S., et al, 2022). Moreover, AI techniques facilitate dynamic and real-time graphics enhancement, which can be integrated into emulators or game launchers. Real-time AI upscaling algorithms process frames on the fly, allowing players to experience classic games with enhanced visuals without modifying the original game files. This approach preserves the authenticity of the original software while leveraging modern hardware capabilities to improve display quality. Projects like NVIDIA's DLSS (Deep Learning Super Sampling) and similar real-time super-resolution technologies demonstrate how AI can boost frame rates and resolution simultaneously, which could be adapted to classic game preservation contexts.

AI-DRIVEN SOUNDTRACK REMASTERING: AUDIO QUALITY IMPROVEMENT

Audio is a foundational element of video games that deeply influences player immersion, emotional resonance, and overall experience. Classic video games, particularly those from the 8-bit, 16-bit, and early CD-ROM eras, often feature iconic soundtracks and sound effects that have become ingrained in gaming culture and nostalgia. However, the audio quality of these soundtracks is often limited by the technological constraints of their time—low bitrates, limited frequency ranges, compressed data formats, and hardware-specific synthesis. As technology advances, the preservation and restoration of these classic soundtracks have become a critical focus within game preservation efforts. In recent years, the emergence of AI-driven soundtrack remastering has revolutionized the way audio quality improvement is approached, enabling the restoration, enhancement, and even creative reimagination of classic game audio with unprecedented fidelity and efficiency. One of the key capabilities of AI in soundtrack remastering is audio super-resolution, which involves enhancing the quality and bandwidth of low-fidelity audio (Brown L., 2024). Classic game audio is often constrained to low sampling rates (e.g., 22 kHz or less) and limited bit depth, resulting in muffled, tinny, or flat sound profiles. Using neural networks designed for super-resolution, such as convolutional or recurrent architectures, audio can be upsampled to higher sampling rates with the reconstruction of missing frequency components. These models infer plausible high-frequency harmonics and subtle nuances that were absent or heavily compressed in the original, thereby enriching timbre, brightness, and spatial presence. The result is a more vibrant and natural sound that better suits modern listening environments and playback equipment, such as high-quality headphones and surround sound systems. AI-powered remastering also excels in dynamic range expansion and equalization correction, which help restore the emotional impact and tonal balance of classic soundtracks. Early game audio was often heavily compressed to fit hardware limitations, which flattened the dynamic range and diminished the distinction between quiet and loud passages. Neural models can intelligently expand the dynamic range by analyzing contextual audio cues and restoring the original loudness contrasts. Simultaneously, AI-driven equalization algorithms adjust frequency balances to correct muddiness or excessive brightness, all while preserving the original artistic intent. These enhancements bring clarity to complex compositions, allowing listeners to appreciate orchestral nuances, layered synthesizers, and percussive elements that were previously obscured.

Figure 1. AI-based privacy-preserving techniques

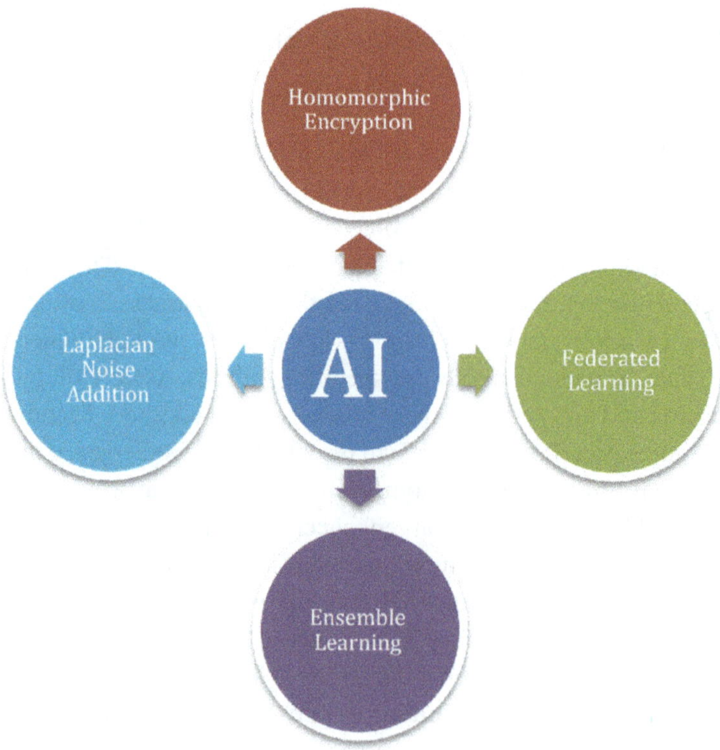

Beyond restoration, AI technologies enable instrument separation and remixing of classic game music, which is invaluable for both preservation and creative reinterpretation. Using source separation models, individual instruments and melodic lines can be extracted from stereo or mono mixes, enabling archivists to isolate, analyze, or remaster specific tracks independently. This capability opens doors for rebalancing mixes, enhancing particular instruments, or creating surround sound versions. For fans and musicians, it facilitates the creation of remixes, covers, and adaptive soundtracks that respond dynamically to gameplay. Additionally, AI can reconstruct missing or damaged audio components by learning stylistic patterns from intact sections or related compositions, allowing the faithful recreation of incomplete soundtracks (Dahiya R., et al, 2025). Generative AI models also play an innovative role in soundtrack enhancement by recreating or augmenting audio based on stylistic learning. Using architectures such as WaveNet, Jukebox, or other neural music generation models, AI can synthesize missing instrumental tracks, harmonize melodies, or generate new arrangements that complement the original compositions. Classic game audio was often generated by dedicated sound chips, each with unique characteristics and limitations, such as aliasing, sample rate conversion noise, and channel crosstalk. While these artifacts contribute to the nostalgic sound palette, they can also degrade audio quality or become distracting on modern systems. AI models can learn to identify and selectively suppress these hardware-induced noises without compromising the authenticity of the audio signal. This allows for a cleaner listening experience while retaining the character and charm associated with vintage sound chips like the Yamaha YM2612 or the SID chip from the Commodore 64 (Bobel M C., et al, 2022). In summary, AI-driven soundtrack remastering represents a powerful and versatile approach to audio quality improvement in classic video games. Through noise reduction, super-resolution, dynamic range restoration, instrument separation, and generative augmentation, AI technologies breathe new life into aging soundtracks, preserving their emotional and cultural significance while adapting them for modern listening environments. As these tools continue to advance and integrate into preservation initiatives, they promise to safeguard the rich auditory legacy of video games, ensuring that iconic soundscapes remain vibrant, accessible, and inspiring for generations to come.

AI-Generated Content: Level Design, Characters, and Storylines

The advent of artificial intelligence (AI) in the realm of video game development has catalyzed a profound shift in how game content is conceived, created, and evolved. Among the most groundbreaking applications of AI is its capacity to autonomously generate core gameplay elements such as level design, characters, and storylines. This revolution in content creation is not only transforming the production pipelines of modern games but also offering new possibilities for preserving and expanding the legacy of classic games. AI-generated content leverages machine learning, procedural generation, natural language processing, and neural network architectures to craft diverse, dynamic, and often surprising gameplay experiences with unprecedented efficiency and scalability. This synthesis explores the multifaceted role of AI in generating game content, emphasizing the creative, technical, and preservationist implications of AI-assisted design in levels, characters, and narratives (Connor A., 2025). Starting with level design, AI-driven procedural generation has long been used to algorithmically create game environments ranging from simple mazes to vast open worlds. Traditionally, procedural generation relies on predefined rules and randomization techniques to produce variable but controlled outputs. However, recent advances in AI have introduced more sophisticated approaches utilizing deep learning models such as generative adversarial networks (GANs), variational autoencoders (VAEs), and reinforcement learning agents that can learn design principles from vast datasets of existing levels and player interactions. These AI models analyze patterns in layout, pacing, challenge distribution, aesthetic coherence, and player flow, enabling them to generate levels that not only meet technical requirements but also embody design styles and thematic elements consistent with specific games or genres. For example, AI can create platforming levels that balance difficulty curves, exploration opportunities, and visual appeal in ways that mimic or innovate upon human-designed stages (Chib S., et al, 2025). This is particularly valuable for classic games preservation, where AI can recreate or extend original level designs that may have been lost, corrupted, or deemed too resource-intensive to reproduce manually. Moreover, AI-generated level design facilitates dynamic and adaptive environments that respond in real time to player actions and preferences. By integrating player data and reinforcement learning, AI can tweak level elements such as enemy placement, item distribution, and environmental hazards on the fly, tailoring difficulty and pacing to individual skill levels. This personalization enhances player engagement and accessibility, making classic game experiences more inclusive and varied for contemporary audiences. Additionally, AI-driven level generators support rapid prototyping and iteration for developers, dramatically reducing development times and costs while fostering creative experimentation and procedural storytelling.

Dialogue and narrative interaction are also profoundly impacted by AI's capabilities in natural language processing (NLP) and text generation. Language models, such as transformers and GPT architectures, can generate contextually relevant, stylistically consistent dialogue for characters, supporting richer storytelling and player immersion. AI-driven dialogue systems can create branching conversations, adaptive responses, and lore expansion that evolve based on player decisions, enhancing narrative depth without requiring extensive scripting by human writers. For classic games with sparse or repetitive dialogue, AI can augment storylines with new content that respects original themes and tone, preserving narrative integrity while increasing replayability (Kanerva S K., 2024). At the narrative level, AI is increasingly capable of generating complex storylines, quests, and lore through a combination of procedural content generation and natural language generation. By training on large corpora of story data—including classic game scripts, novels, and mythology—AI models can construct plot structures, character arcs, and thematic motifs that integrate seamlessly with existing game worlds. This capacity allows developers and preservationists to expand upon classic narratives with side quests, alternative endings, or entirely new campaigns generated procedurally but guided by human oversight to maintain coherence and style. Such AI-generated narratives foster emergent storytelling, where player choices and AI-generated content interact to create personalized and unpredictable experiences. The advantages of AI-generated content extend beyond creativity into scalability and efficiency. Manual content creation is laborious, costly, and often bottlenecked by human creativity and resources. AI-assisted generation can produce vast amounts of content rapidly, making it feasible to release expanded versions of classic games, modifiable game environments, and continuous content updates that keep player communities engaged. Furthermore, AI can aid in content localization and accessibility by adapting generated assets for different languages, cultural contexts, or accessibility needs, broadening the reach and inclusivity of classic games (Kavitha L., 2023). However, the rise of AI-generated content raises important ethical, artistic, and practical considerations. Questions of authorship and creative ownership emerge when AI models produce content derived from existing works, potentially leading to disputes over intellectual property and creative credit. Maintaining the authenticity and original artistic vision of classic games is crucial; overreliance on AI-generated content risks diluting the unique charm and handcrafted qualities that define many beloved titles. Moreover, AI outputs may sometimes generate incoherent, inappropriate, or culturally insensitive content, necessitating rigorous human oversight and curation. Balancing automation with human creativity, editorial control, and community involvement is essential to harness the full potential of AI-generated content responsibly.

CHALLENGES AND LIMITATIONS OF AI IN GAME PRESERVATION AND REMASTERING

Artificial intelligence (AI) has emerged as a transformative force in the preservation and remastering of classic video games, offering innovative solutions for restoring, enhancing, and extending the life of cherished titles. However, despite its remarkable capabilities, AI-driven approaches face significant challenges and limitations that must be carefully addressed to ensure that preservation efforts are effective, ethical, and respectful of original artistic intent. This analysis explores the multifaceted obstacles inherent in applying AI to game preservation and remastering, focusing on technical, artistic, legal, and cultural issues that constrain the current and future potential of AI technologies in this domain. One of the foremost challenges is the technical complexity and variability of legacy game assets and codebases (Ling P., 2023). Classic games were developed across a vast spectrum of hardware platforms, software environments, and proprietary file formats, many of which are poorly documented or no longer supported. This heterogeneity complicates the training and application of AI models, which often require large, high-quality, and well-labeled datasets to learn effectively. . In cases where assets are heavily corrupted, incomplete, or completely missing, AI must rely on extrapolation or creative generation, which risks introducing inaccuracies or anachronisms. Additionally, legacy codebases may contain undocumented behavior, quirks, or intentional "bugs" that contribute to a game's unique feel and balance; replicating these faithfully with AI-assisted tools requires deep reverse engineering and domain expertise, which are labor-intensive and error-prone. Another technical limitation lies in the inherent unpredictability and lack of transparency of AI-generated content. Many AI models, especially deep learning systems such as generative adversarial networks (GANs) or large language models (LLMs), operate as "black boxes," producing outputs without clear, interpretable decision-making processes (Limbore N V., et al, 2025). This opacity poses significant risks in preservation and remastering contexts, where authenticity and fidelity to the original work are paramount. AI-generated enhancements—whether upscaled textures, reconstructed animations, or remastered audio—may inadvertently alter or distort the artistic vision, leading to "over-restoration" that smooths away characteristic imperfections or stylistic details intrinsic to the original. This can alienate fans and scholars who value the historical and cultural accuracy of preserved games. The challenge is compounded by the difficulty in systematically evaluating AI-generated restorations, as subjective assessments of artistic quality and "faithfulness" often vary widely among stakeholders.

Another significant limitation is the computational and resource-intensive nature of advanced AI methods. High-quality restoration and remastering often require training and running large neural networks on powerful hardware, which can be prohibitively expensive and environmentally taxing. Smaller preservation teams, independent developers, or community-driven initiatives may lack the financial and technical resources necessary to implement cutting-edge AI techniques. This disparity risks creating a preservation ecosystem where only well-funded projects can access advanced AI tools, potentially leaving many classic titles and niche games underserved or neglected (Rane N., et al, 2024). The challenge of contextual and cultural understanding represents another critical barrier for AI in preservation. Games are complex cultural artifacts embedded with narratives, symbolism, and player experiences that extend beyond their technical components. AI systems, while adept at pattern recognition and content generation, struggle to fully grasp the cultural significance, humor, historical context, or subtle design philosophies underlying classic games. This limits their ability to make nuanced decisions during restoration or remastering that respect the original's spirit and social meaning. For example, an AI might misinterpret culturally sensitive content or fail to preserve gameplay mechanics that were intentionally designed to evoke specific emotional responses or player behaviors.. Skepticism towards AI can slow adoption and limit collaborative efforts between developers, archivists, and fans. Building transparent workflows, openly documenting AI's role, and involving community stakeholders in restoration decisions are crucial steps toward fostering acceptance and collaborative stewardship. In conclusion, while AI offers transformative potential in game preservation and remastering—providing tools for restoration, enhancement, content generation, and analysis—it also faces substantial technical, artistic, legal, ethical, and cultural challenges (Ray P P., 2023). The opacity of AI models, data limitations, intellectual property concerns, computational costs, and the need for cultural contextualization all restrict the scope and efficacy of AI interventions. Building effective AI-assisted preservation frameworks requires careful collaboration among technologists, artists, legal experts, and community stakeholders to balance innovation with respect for authenticity and heritage. Human expertise and oversight remain indispensable in guiding AI's application, ensuring that classic games are preserved not only as functional software artifacts but as vibrant cultural legacies that continue to inspire and engage players across generations.

FUTURE DIRECTIONS: EMERGING AI TECHNIQUES AND APPLICATIONS

As artificial intelligence (AI) continues its rapid evolution, the future of game preservation, remastering, and development promises to be deeply transformed by emerging AI techniques and novel applications. While current AI tools have demonstrated impressive capabilities in restoring damaged assets, generating new content, and enhancing gameplay experiences, the ongoing advancements in machine learning architectures, multimodal understanding, generative models, and human-AI collaboration are poised to unlock even more profound possibilities. This forward-looking discussion explores the emerging directions in AI research and technology that could reshape how classic games are preserved, revitalized, and expanded upon, highlighting innovations that address existing limitations and create new paradigms for interactive entertainment (Saboury B., et al, 2021). One of the most promising future directions lies in the integration of multimodal AI systems that combine visual, auditory, textual, and behavioral data to achieve a holistic understanding and generation of game content. Unlike current AI models that often specialize in a single modality, such as image super-resolution or audio enhancement, multimodal AI can simultaneously analyze graphics, sound, dialogue, player inputs, and game mechanics to better capture the complex interdependencies within classic games. For example, a multimodal model could learn to reconstruct a missing game level by synthesizing its visual design, ambient sounds, enemy behaviors, and narrative context in concert, producing a restoration that feels cohesive and authentic. These systems leverage transformer architectures and cross-modal attention mechanisms to fuse diverse data streams, enabling richer and more context-aware AI outputs. As research in multimodal learning advances, game preservationists and developers will gain tools capable of recreating immersive, multidimensional experiences from fragmented or incomplete source materials. In parallel, the maturation of foundation models and large pre-trained neural networks, trained on massive, diverse datasets encompassing not only gaming content but also art, music, literature, and human interaction, will profoundly impact AI-assisted game work (She R., et al, 2021). These models can serve as versatile "base layers" that can be fine-tuned or prompted for highly specialized tasks such as texture reconstruction, procedural level generation, or dialogue writing in styles reminiscent of classic games. For instance, a foundation model trained on a wide corpus of pixel art, chiptunes, and retro narratives could be adapted to generate new assets or stories that harmonize seamlessly with vintage aesthetics. This approach lowers the barrier to entry for developers and preservationists by providing powerful, general-purpose AI engines that can be customized without requiring extensive retraining from scratch.

The future also holds promise for AI-enhanced tools that facilitate more nuanced human-AI collaboration in game creation and preservation. Advances in explainable AI and interactive machine learning will empower developers and archivists to guide AI processes more intuitively, providing feedback, constraints, and creative direction in real time. For instance, a preservationist could iteratively refine an AI-generated restoration by highlighting areas needing correction or stylistic adjustment, with the AI adapting its outputs accordingly. This synergy allows the strengths of AI—speed, pattern recognition, and generative capacity—to be balanced with human creativity, cultural insight, and ethical judgment. It also fosters accessibility, enabling non-experts or fan communities to participate meaningfully in preservation and content creation (Stahl & Eke, 2024). Another future trajectory involves the development of standardized AI-based preservation frameworks and protocols. As AI becomes more embedded in preservation workflows, establishing shared datasets, benchmarking tools, metadata schemas, and evaluation metrics will be essential to ensure transparency, reproducibility, and quality control. International collaboration among gaming companies, museums, archivists, and researchers can create repositories of AI models, training data, and restoration guidelines to support sustainable preservation efforts. Open-source AI tools tailored for game preservation will democratize access and foster innovation, reducing dependency on proprietary solutions. Looking further ahead, the convergence of AI with emerging technologies such as virtual reality (VR), augmented reality (AR), and cloud gaming will redefine how classic games are experienced and preserved. AI-generated content may be integrated into immersive VR reconstructions of classic game worlds, allowing players to explore these environments in entirely new ways while preserving historical accuracy. AR applications could overlay restored game elements onto physical spaces, blending nostalgia with real-world exploration. Cloud-based AI engines will enable real-time, scalable enhancement and adaptation of classic games on diverse devices, making preservation more accessible and dynamic (Tamilarasi C., et al, 2025). In summary, the future of AI in game preservation and remastering is poised to be shaped by advances in multimodal learning, foundation models, reinforcement learning, neural rendering, and human-AI collaboration. These emerging techniques promise richer, more authentic, and more accessible restorations and new content that honor the legacy of classic games while pushing creative boundaries. The convergence of AI with legal frameworks, community participation, and immersive technologies will foster sustainable preservation ecosystems and dynamic gameplay experiences that bridge past and future. By navigating technical, ethical, and cultural challenges thoughtfully, the gaming community can harness the full potential of AI to safeguard and celebrate video games as vital cultural artifacts for generations to come.

ETHICAL CONSIDERATIONS: OWNERSHIP, AUTHORSHIP, AND CULTURAL SENSITIVITY

The integration of artificial intelligence (AI) into the preservation and remastering of classic video games brings to the forefront a complex array of ethical considerations centered around ownership, authorship, and cultural sensitivity. While AI offers powerful tools to restore and enhance games that hold deep cultural and nostalgic value, it simultaneously raises challenging questions about who holds the rights to the original and newly generated content, how credit is attributed to creators and contributors, and how cultural contexts and values are respected throughout the preservation process. These issues demand careful reflection and responsible governance to ensure that the use of AI in game preservation supports not only technological advancement but also fairness, respect, and inclusivity within the broader gaming community and society at large (Kommineni M., et al, 2025). Should AI be recognized as a co-creator? To what extent do the original human creators retain authorship over AI-modified works? And how should the developers of AI tools be credited for their role in enabling content generation? Ethically, transparency in disclosing AI's involvement is crucial to honor the contributions of all parties and maintain trust within the gaming community. Failure to do so risks diminishing the legacy of original creators or obscuring the provenance of restored content. Moreover, clear attribution helps address concerns about appropriation, plagiarism, or misrepresentation, fostering respect for the creative process even amid technological mediation. Cultural sensitivity and contextual understanding constitute another critical ethical dimension. Video games are cultural artifacts embedded with the values, norms, and social contexts of their time and place of creation. Classic games often reflect specific cultural narratives, humor, symbolism, and social attitudes that may be unfamiliar or problematic when viewed through contemporary lenses. AI-driven preservation and remastering efforts must handle such content with nuance and care (Zhong T., et al, 2024). Automated processes risk unintentionally altering or sanitizing culturally significant elements, erasing marginalized perspectives, or perpetuating stereotypes if not guided by informed human judgment. For example, restoring dialogue or character representations in games containing racially insensitive language or imagery demands thoughtful consideration to balance historical accuracy with modern ethical standards. Moreover, the cultural heritage embodied in games from diverse regions and communities requires sensitivity to local values and traditions to avoid homogenization or cultural appropriation. Inclusive collaboration with cultural experts, historians, and community members is essential to ensure AI-assisted preservation honors the multifaceted identities and legacies embedded in gaming history.

The ethical deployment of AI in game preservation also involves issues of accessibility and equity. AI tools have the potential to democratize preservation by lowering technical barriers and enabling smaller teams, indie developers, or fan communities to contribute to restoring and expanding classic games. However, disparities in access to AI technologies, computational resources, and expertise can exacerbate inequalities, privileging well-funded organizations while marginalizing under-resourced groups and less mainstream game titles. This raises ethical questions about whose games are preserved and how cultural diversity within gaming history is maintained (Sreekanthaswamy N., et al, 2025). Ensuring equitable access to AI tools, open data, and collaborative platforms is vital to fostering inclusive preservation ecosystems that reflect a broad spectrum of gaming cultures and histories. Another ethical aspect relates to transparency, accountability, and consent. Stakeholders involved in preservation projects—including original creators, rights holders, developers, players, and communities—should be informed about how AI is employed and what changes are made to classic games. Transparent documentation of AI processes, decision-making criteria, and the provenance of restored or generated content supports accountability and enables critical evaluation by scholars and fans alike. Involving the community in restoration decisions promotes democratic stewardship and helps avoid unilateral actions that might be perceived as disrespectful or exploitative. In conclusion, the ethical considerations surrounding ownership, authorship, and cultural sensitivity in AI-assisted game preservation and remastering are multifaceted and profound (Zhang & Aslan, 2021). Addressing these challenges requires a concerted effort to develop legal frameworks, attribution standards, cultural consultation practices, and inclusive collaboration models that respect the rights and legacies of creators, protect cultural diversity, and foster equitable access. Transparency, accountability, and sustainability must underpin AI's role in safeguarding gaming heritage, ensuring that technological innovation complements rather than compromises ethical values. By engaging thoughtfully with these issues, the gaming community can harness AI not only as a tool for technical enhancement but as a means to honor, preserve, and celebrate the rich cultural tapestry embodied in classic video games for present and future generations.

CONCLUSION

The future of classic video games is increasingly intertwined with the rapid advances in artificial intelligence (AI), heralding a transformative era where preservation efforts and creative innovation converge to both safeguard gaming heritage and reimagine timeless experiences. As AI technologies continue to evolve, they offer unprecedented opportunities to revitalize classic titles, making them accessible, engaging, and relevant to contemporary and future audiences while honoring their original spirit. This convergence of AI-driven preservation and innovation will shape the trajectory of how classic games are archived, experienced, and expanded upon, heralding a future where the boundary between restoration and creation becomes fluid, and the legacy of early digital culture thrives within a dynamically evolving digital ecosystem. Simultaneously, AI will empower innovative reimagining and remasters of classic games that appeal to modern sensibilities without compromising their foundational design philosophies. Advanced generative models and neural rendering techniques will allow developers to enhance visual fidelity, audio quality, and user interfaces in ways that respect the original aesthetic while leveraging contemporary graphical and sound technologies. This blend of preservation and innovation fosters a living heritage where classic games are not static relics but evolving works that continue to inspire and engage diverse audiences across generations. Another exciting prospect is the rise of AI-driven content generation inspired by classic games, enabling entirely new titles that capture the essence, mechanics, and storytelling styles of vintage games while introducing novel twists. Moreover, AI can be a co-creative partner, working interactively with human designers to brainstorm ideas, refine mechanics, or generate alternative narrative paths, fostering a collaborative creative process that amplifies human ingenuity. The integration of AI with immersive technologies such as virtual reality (VR) and augmented reality (AR) will further redefine how classic games are experienced and preserved. AI can reconstruct 3D game worlds with enhanced spatial audio and graphical detail suitable for VR exploration, allowing players to immerse themselves in classic titles in ways previously unimaginable. AR applications can overlay elements of classic games onto real-world environments, creating hybrid experiences that blend nostalgia with contemporary interactive storytelling. These immersive renditions will not only preserve the games but expand their experiential dimensions, making them accessible to new audiences and contexts, such as museums, educational settings, and cultural exhibitions, thus bridging entertainment with cultural heritage. Ethical considerations will remain central as AI shapes the future of classic games. Balancing the rights of original creators and current rights holders with community interests will require ongoing dialogue and innovative legal frameworks that recognize AI's role in generating derivative works. Transparent attribution practices and consent mechanisms will ensure respect for authorship and cultural provenance. By fostering inclusive, ethical, and sustainable practices, AI can help ensure that classic games remain culturally relevant and widely accessible, serving as a bridge between generations and a source of inspiration for the ever-evolving landscape of interactive entertainment. The fusion of preservation and innovation heralds a future where classic games are not merely preserved as artifacts but celebrated as living, evolving cultural treasures that continue to captivate and inspire in the digital age.

REFERENCES

Aker, O. (2025). "AI-Assisted Music Mastering: An Exploration of Human and AI Practices in Contemporary Music Production." Understanding Generative AI in a Cultural Context, pp. 34. DOI: DOI: 10.4018/979-8-3693-7235-7.ch002

Anantrasirichai, N., Zhang, F., & Bull, D. (2025). "Artificial Intelligence in Creative Industries: Advances Prior to 2025." arXiv preprint, arXiv:2501.02725. DOI: /arXiv.2501.02725DOI: 10.48550

Antony, V. N., & Huang, C. M. (2025). ID. 8: Co-Creating Visual Stories with Generative AI. *ACM Transactions on Interactive Intelligent Systems*. Advance online publication. arXiv2309.14228. DOI: 10.48550/arXiv.2309.14228

Bobel, M. C., Al Hinai, A., & Roslani, A. C. (2022). Cultural Sensitivity and Ethical Considerations. *Clinics in Colon and Rectal Surgery*, *35*(5), 371–375. DOI: 10.1055/s-0042-1746186 PMID: 36111081

Brown, L. (2024). Rethinking Remakes: Value and Culture in Video Game Temporalization. *Games and Culture*, *0*(0), 1–20. DOI: 10.1177/15554120231163655

Chib, S., Mehta, A. K., Selvakumar, P., Saravanan, A., Mishra, B. R., & Manjunath, T. C. (2025). Mental Health Challenges and Solutions in High-Pressure Work Environments. In Harriott, S. (Ed.), *Innovative Approaches to Managing Conflict and Change in Diverse Work Environments* (pp. 247–272). IGI Global Scientific Publishing., DOI: 10.4018/979-8-3693-9556-1.ch011

Connor, A. (2025). In Real Life: Gaming Community Engagement in Museums. *Curator (New York, N.Y.)*, *00*(1), 1–14. DOI: 10.1111/cura.12622

Dahiya, R., & Selvakumar, P. Vidyadhara & Manjunath T C. (2025). Design and Aerodynamics: Principles and Advances. In M. Mellal (Ed.), *Innovations and Developments in Unmanned Aerial Vehicles* (pp. 145-170). IGI Global Scientific Publishing. https://doi.org/DOI: 10.4018/979-8-3693-8462-6.ch007

Dodiya, K. R., Kumar, K., Thakar, A., & Pithiya, G. (2025). *Unleashing the Power of AI: Exploring the Transformative Landscape of Image Analysis*. Utilizing AI and Machine Learning in Financial Analysis., DOI: 10.4018/979-8-3693-8507-4.ch022

Fu, Y., Newman, M., Going, L., Feng, Q., & Lee, J. H. (2025). "Exploring the Collaborative Co-Creation Process with AI: A Case Study in Novice Music Production." arXiv preprint, arXiv:2501.15276. DOI: /arXiv.2501.15276DOI: 10.1145/3715336.3735829

Gill, S. S., Xu, M., Ottaviani, C., Patros, P., Bahsoon, R., Shaghaghi, A., Golec, M., Stankovski, V., Wu, H., Abraham, A., Singh, M., Mehta, H., Ghosh, S. K., Baker, T., Parlikad, A. K., Lutfiyya, H., Kanhere, S. S., Sakellariou, R., Dustdar, S., & Uhlig, S. (2022). AI for Next Generation Computing: Emerging Trends and Future Directions. *Internet of Things : Engineering Cyber Physical Human Systems*, *15*(3), 567–589. DOI: 10.1016/j.iot.2022.100514

Jessen, T. D., Ban, N. C., Claxton, N. X., & Darimont, C. T. (2022). Contributions of Indigenous Knowledge to Ecological and Evolutionary Understanding. *Frontiers in Ecology and the Environment*, *20*(2), 93–101. DOI: 10.1002/fee.2435

Kanerva, S. K. (2024). "Utilising Artificial Intelligence in a 3D Video Game Environment Design and Creation Process." *Theseus.fi*, Bachelor's Thesis, pp. 1–58. DOI: URN:NBN:fi:amk-2024052817219.

Kaur, M., Selvakumar, P., & Dinesh, N. Mohit, Chandel P S, & Manjunath T C. (2025). Reconstruction and Preservation Strategies for Cultural Heritage. In S. Oflazoğlu & M. Dora (Eds.), *Preserving Cultural Heritage in Post-Disaster Urban Renewal* (pp. 385-412). IGI Global Scientific Publishing. https://doi.org/DOI: 10.4018/979-8-3693-9097-9.ch016

Kavitha, L. (2023). Copyright Challenges in the Artificial Intelligence Revolution: Transforming the Film Industry from Script to Screen. *Trinity Law Review*, *4*(1), 1–15. DOI: 10.48165/tlr.2024.4.1.1

Kommineni, M., Chundru, S., Maroju, P. K., & Selvakumar, P. (2025). Ethical Implications of AI in Sustainable Development Pedagogy. In Chinedu, C., Mafarja, N., Hussein, M., & Saleem, A. (Eds.), *Rethinking the Pedagogy of Sustainable Development in the AI Era* (pp. 17–36). IGI Global Scientific Publishing., DOI: 10.4018/979-8-3693-9062-7.ch002

Limbore, N. V., Anute, N., Ahluwalia, G. K., Chordiya, P. B., Kalshetti, P., & Selvakumar, P. (2025). Ethical Leadership and Corporate Responsibility. In Harriott, S. (Ed.), *Innovative Approaches to Managing Conflict and Change in Diverse Work Environments* (pp. 193–218). IGI Global Scientific Publishing., DOI: 10.4018/979-8-3693-9556-1.ch009

Ling, P. (2023). "AI-Assisted Game Level Generation Based on Difficulty." *Aalto University*, Master's Thesis, pp. 1–75. DOI: URN:NBN:fi:aalto-202312187331.

Ma, Y. P. (2021). Extending 3D-GIS District Models and BIM-Based Building Models into Computer Gaming Environment for Better Workflow of Cultural Heritage Conservation. *Applied Sciences (Basel, Switzerland)*, *11*(5), 2101. Advance online publication. DOI: 10.3390/app11052101

Malenfant, S., Jaggi, P., Hayden, K. A., & Sinclair, S. (2022). Compassion in Healthcare: An Updated Scoping Review of the Literature. *BMC Palliative Care*, *21*(1), 80. Advance online publication. DOI: 10.1186/s12904-022-00942-3 PMID: 35585622

Nimo, J. R. A., & Ravishankar, K. (2024). *AI for Character Creation and Storytelling in Marketing*. Balancing Automation and Human Interaction in Modern Marketing., DOI: 10.4018/979-8-3693-2276-5.ch003

Rane, N., Choudhary, S., & Rane, J. (2024). "Machine Learning and Deep Learning: A Comprehensive Review on Methods, Techniques, Applications, Challenges, and Future Directions." Techniques, Applications & Future Research, pp. 1–20. DOI: DOI: 10.2139/ssrn.4850451

Ray, P. P. (2023). ChatGPT: A Comprehensive Review on Background, Applications, Key Challenges, Bias, Ethics, Limitations and Future Scope. *Internet of Things and Cyber-Physical Systems*, *3*, 121–154. DOI: 10.1016/j.iotcps.2023.04.003

Saboury, B., Morris, M., & Siegel, E. (2021). Future Directions in Artificial Intelligence. *Radiologia Clinica*, *59*(6), 1085–1095. DOI: 10.1016/j.rcl.2021.07.008 PMID: 34689876

Samal, A., & Misra, L. I. Mohit, Pougajendy, S, Chandel P S, Manjunath T C, & Selvakumar P. (2025). Musealization and Tourism Practices. In S. Oflazoğlu & M. Dora (Eds.), *Preserving Cultural Heritage in Post-Disaster Urban Renewal* (pp. 115-142). IGI Global Scientific Publishing. https://doi.org/DOI: 10.4018/979-8-3693-9097-9.ch006

She, R., Wong, K., Lin, J., Leung, K., & Zhang, Y. (2021). How COVID-19 Stress Related to Schooling and Online Learning Affects Adolescent Depression and Internet Gaming Disorder: Testing Conservation of Resources Theory. *Journal of Behavioral Addictions*, *10*(4), 953–966. DOI: 10.1556/2006.2021.00069 PMID: 34665762

Sreekanthaswamy, N., Anitha, S., Singh, A., Jayadeva, S. M., Gupta, S., Manjunath, T. C., & Selvakumar, P. (2025). Digital Tools and Methods. In Çela, E., Paliktzoglou, V., Sengar, S., Eappen, P., & Vajjhala, N. (Eds.), *Enhancing School Counseling With Technology and Case Studies* (pp. 25–48). IGI Global Scientific Publishing., DOI: 10.4018/979-8-3693-8392-6.ch002

Stahl, B. C., & Eke, D. (2024). The Ethics of ChatGPT–Exploring the Ethical Issues of an Emerging Technology. *International Journal of Information Management*, *74*, 102700. Advance online publication. DOI: 10.1016/j.ijinfomgt.2023.102700

Tamilarasi, C., Sowmiya, K., Vignesh, G. D., Jasmine, R. L., Nehru, P., & Selvakumar, P. (2025). AI in Renewable Energy Education: Teaching the Future of Sustainable Power Systems. In Chinedu, C., Mafarja, N., Hussein, M., & Saleem, A. (Eds.), *Rethinking the Pedagogy of Sustainable Development in the AI Era* (pp. 133–152). IGI Global Scientific Publishing., DOI: 10.4018/979-8-3693-9062-7.ch007

Usha, S. G. A., Maheswari, P. U., & Bharathi, K. (2025). *Next-Generation Image Enhancement and Restoration With Artificial Intelligence*. Modern Intelligent Techniques for Image Processing., DOI: 10.4018/979-8-3693-9045-0.ch010

Wang, Y. (2023). "Synthetic Realities in the Digital Age: Navigating the Opportunities and Challenges of AI-Generated Content." *TechRxiv*, pp. 1–20. DOI: DOI: 10.36227/techrxiv.23968311.v1

Zhang, K., & Aslan, A. B. (2021). AI Technologies for Education: Recent Research & Future Directions. *Computers and Education: Artificial Intelligence*, *2*, 100025. Advance online publication. DOI: 10.1016/j.caeai.2021.100025

Zhong, T., Yang, Z., Liu, Z., Zhang, R., Liu, Y., Sun, H., Pan, Y., Li, Y., Zhou, Y., Jiang, H., Chen, J., & Liu, T. (2024). "Opportunities and Challenges of Large Language Models for Low-Resource Languages in Humanities Research." arXiv preprint, arXiv:2412.04497. DOI: /arXiv.2412.04497DOI: 10.48550

Compilation of References

Aarseth, E. (2012). A Narrative Theory of Games. In *Proceedings of the International Conference on the Foundations of Digital Games* (pp. 129–133). ACM. DOI: 10.1145/2282338.2282365

Aarseth, E. J. (1997). *Cybertext: Perspectives on Ergodic Literature*. Johns Hopkins University Press. DOI: 10.56021/9780801855788

Abdelkhabir, S. G., Ezz-eldeen, S. S., Gabr, A. E., Eldakrory, A. M., Ali, A. M., Elkhameesy, O. K., . . . Ali, Z. H. (2025). Enhancing Antimicrobial Activity Predictors Based on Machine Learning Approaches. In Navigating Innovations and Challenges in Travel Medicine and Digital Health (pp. 257-276). IGI Global Scientific Publishing. DOI: 10.4018/979-8-3693-8774-0.ch013

Adams, T. (2019). Emergent narrative in dwarf fortress. In *Procedural storytelling in game design* (pp. 149–158). AK Peters/CRC Press. DOI: 10.1201/9780429488337-15

Aker, O. (2025). "AI-Assisted Music Mastering: An Exploration of Human and AI Practices in Contemporary Music Production." Understanding Generative AI in a Cultural Context, pp. 34. DOI: DOI: 10.4018/979-8-3693-7235-7.ch002

Akoury, N., Yang, Q., & Iyyer, M. (2023). A framework for exploring player perceptions of LLM-generated dialogue in commercial video games. *Findings of the Association for Computational Linguistics: EMNLP, 2023*, 2295–2311. DOI: 10.18653/v1/2023.findings-emnlp.151

Albaugh, L., McCann, J., Yao, L., & Hudson, S. E. (2021, May). Enabling personal computational handweaving with a low-cost jacquard loom. In *Proceedings of the 2021 CHI Conference on Human Factors in Computing Systems* (pp. 1-10). DOI: 10.1145/3411764.3445750

Almeida, P., Carvalho, V., & Simões, A. (2023). Reinforcement learning applied to AI bots in first-person shooters: A systematic review. *Algorithms*, *16*(7), 323. Advance online publication. DOI: 10.3390/a16070323

Alsharhan, A., Al-Emran, M., & Shaalan, K. (2023). Chatbot adoption: A multi-perspective systematic review and future research agenda. *IEEE Transactions on Engineering Management*, 1–13. DOI: 10.1109/TEM.2023.3298360

Anand, A., & Orkin, J. (2022). Toolkits for explainable AI in games [Paper presentation]. Proceedings of the IEEE Conference on Games (CoG), Virtual Event.

Andersson, F., Drachen, A., & Canossa, A. (2021). Player segmentation impact on engagement. *Journal of Gaming & Virtual Worlds*, *13*(2), 189–207.

Andrews, J. T., ... (2023). Ethical considerations for collecting human-centric image datasets. arXiv preprint arXiv:2302.03629. https://arxiv.org/abs/2302.03629

Angelov, D. (2020). Top2Vec: Distributed representations of topics. arXiv preprint arXiv:2008.09470. https://doi.org//arXiv.2008.09470DOI: 10.48550

Antony, V. N., & Huang, C. M. (2025). ID. 8: Co-Creating Visual Stories with Generative AI. *ACM Transactions on Interactive Intelligent Systems*. Advance online publication. arXiv2309.14228. DOI: 10.48550/arXiv.2309.14228

Antúnez-Medina, A., Garcías-Rubia, J., Sáez-Blázquez, F. J., Valle-Blanco, A., & García-Martín, A. (2013). Differences in Performance Indicator between Winning and Losing Team in Formative Stages According to Sex and Final Score Differences. *Rev. Cienc. Deporte*, *9*, 5–16.

Apple. (2020). *Logic Pro X user guide*. Apple Support. https://support.apple.com/de-de/guide/logicpro/welcome/mac

Araújo, D., Couceiro, M., Seifert, L., Sarmento, H., & Davids, K. (2002). Artificial Intelligence in Sport Performance Analysis; Routledge: New York, NY, USA, 2021; ISBN 9781003163589. Hughes, M.D.; Bartlett, R.M. The Use of Performance Indicators in Performance Analysis. *Journal of Sports Sciences*, *20*, 739–754.

Arbib, M. A. (2000). Warren McCulloch's search for the logic of the nervous system. *Perspectives in Biology and Medicine*, *43*(2), 193–216. DOI: 10.1353/pbm.2000.0001 PMID: 10804585

Arif, S., Arif, T., Haroon, M. S., Khan, A. J., Raza, A. A., & Athar, A. (2024). The Art of Storytelling: Multi-agent Generative AI for Dynamic Multimodal Narratives [Preprint]. *arXiv*. https://arxiv.org/abs/2409.11261

Art From The Machine. (2023, April 25). *ChatGPT in skyrim VR | mantella - lip sync & in-game awareness update*. YouTube. https://www.youtube.com/watch?v=Gz6mAX41fs0

Art from the Machine. (2024). *Mantella skyrim llama 3 8B GGUF*. Dataloop. https://dataloop.ai/library/model/art-from-the-machine_mantella-skyrim-llama-3-8b-gguf/

Art From The Machine. (2024a). *Mantella* [Computer software]. https://art-from-the-machine.github.io/Mantella/

Art From The Machine. (2024b). *Real-time NPCs*. Mantella. https://art-from-the-machine.github.io/Mantella/pages/real_time_npcs.html

Atzeni, D., Bacciu, D., Mazzei, D., & Prencipe, G. (2022). A systematic review of Wi-Fi and machine learning integration with topic modeling techniques. *Sensors (Basel), 22*(13), 4925. DOI: 10.3390/s22134925 PMID: 35808430

Ayyad, S. M., Badawy, M. A., Shehata, M., Alksas, A., Mahmoud, A., Abou El-Ghar, M., Ghazal, M., El-Melegy, M., Abdel-Hamid, N. B., Labib, L. M., Ali, H. A., & El-Baz, A. (2022). A new framework for precise identification of prostatic adenocarcinoma. *Sensors (Basel), 22*(5), 1848. DOI: 10.3390/s22051848 PMID: 35270995

Ayyad, S. M., Shehata, M., Shalaby, A., Abou El-Ghar, M., Ghazal, M., El-Melegy, M., Abdel-Hamid, N. B., Labib, L. M., Ali, H. A., & El-Baz, A. (2021). Role of AI and histopathological images in detecting prostate cancer: A survey. *Sensors (Basel), 21*(8), 2586. DOI: 10.3390/s21082586 PMID: 33917035

Aziz, S., & Dowling, M. (2019). Machine learning and AI for risk management. In Disrupting finance: FinTech and strategy in the 21st century (pp. 33–50). DOI: 10.1007/978-3-030-02330-0_3

Bahroun, Z., Anane, C., Ahmed, V., & Zacca, A. (2023). Transforming education: A comprehensive review of generative artificial intelligence in educational settings through bibliometric and content analysis. *Sustainability (Basel), 15*(17), 12983. Advance online publication. DOI: 10.3390/su151712983

Balaha, H. M., Ayyad, S. M., Alksas, A., Elsorougy, A., Badawy, M. A., Shehata, M., & El-Baz, A. (2023, October). Early diagnosis of prostate cancer using parametric estimation of ivim from dw-mri. In *2023 IEEE International Conference on Image Processing (ICIP)* (pp. 2910-2914). IEEE. DOI: 10.1109/ICIP49359.2023.10222716

Balaha, H. M., Ayyad, S. M., Alksas, A., Shehata, M., Elsorougy, A., Badawy, M. A., Abou El-Ghar, M., Mahmoud, A., Alghamdi, N. S., Ghazal, M., Contractor, S., & El-Baz, A. (2024). Precise Prostate Cancer Assessment Using IVIM-Based Parametric Estimation of Blood Diffusion from DW-MRI. *Bioengineering (Basel, Switzerland), 11*(6), 629. DOI: 10.3390/bioengineering11060629 PMID: 38927865

Barbosa, J., Silva, R., & Santos, A. (2024). Systematic review of DDA methods. *ACM Computing Surveys*, *56*(7), 178.

Barthes, R. (1977). The Death of the Author (S. Heath, Trans.). In *Image, Music, Text* (pp. 142–148). Fontana Press. (Original work published 1968)

Bartle, R. A. (1996). Hearts, clubs, diamonds, spades: Players who suit MUDs. *Journal of MUD Research*, *1*(1). http://www.mud.co.uk/richard/hcds.htm

Bateni, B., & Whitehead, J. (2024). Language-driven play: Large language models as game-playing agents in slay the spire. *Proceedings of the 19th International Conference on the Foundations of Digital Games*. https://doi.org/DOI: 10.1145/3649921.3650013

Bedini, S. A. (1964). The role of automata in the history of technology. *Technology and Culture*, *5*(1), 24–42. DOI: 10.2307/3101120

Beheshti, A., ... (2023). ProcessGPT: Transforming business process management with generative artificial intelligence. arXiv preprint arXiv:2306.01771. https://arxiv.org/abs/2306.01771 DOI: 10.1109/ICWS60048.2023.00099

Bellemans, M., Lammens, D., De Sloover, J., De Vleeschauwer, T., Schoofs, E., Jordens, W., Van Steenhuyse, B., Mangelschots, J., Selleri, S., Hamesse, C., ... Training Firefighters in Virtual Reality. In Proceedings of the 2020 International Conference on 3D Immersion (IC3D), Brussels, Belgium, 14–15 December 2020; IEEE: Piscataway, NJ, USA, 2020; pp. 1–8. DOI: 10.1109/IC3D51119.2020.9376336

Bender, E. M., Gebru, T., McMillan-Major, A., & Shmitchell, S. (2021). On the Dangers of Stochastic Parrots: Can Language Models Be Too Big? *Proceedings of the 2021 ACM Conference on Fairness, Accountability, and Transparency*, 610–623. DOI: 10.1145/3442188.3445922

Berthiaume, M., Kinateder, M., Emond, B., Cooper, N., Obeegadoo, I., & Lapointe, J.-F. (2023). Evaluation of a virtual reality training tool for firefighters responding to transportation incidents with dangerous goods. *Education and Information Technologies*, *28*, 2987–3012.

Bianchi, F., Terragni, S., & Hovy, D. (2021). Pre-training is a hot topic: Contextualized document embeddings improve topic coherence. In *Proceedings of the 59th Annual Meeting of the Association for Computational Linguistics and the 11th International Joint Conference on Natural Language Processing (ACL-IJCNLP 2021)* (pp. 759–766). Association for Computational Linguistics. DOI: 10.18653/v1/2021.acl-short.96

BioWare. (1998). *Baldur's gate*. Video game; Interplay Entertainment.

BioWare. (2007). *Mass effect.* Video game; Electronic Arts.

Bobel, M. C., Al Hinai, A., & Roslani, A. C. (2022). Cultural Sensitivity and Ethical Considerations. *Clinics in Colon and Rectal Surgery, 35*(5), 371–375. DOI: 10.1055/s-0042-1746186 PMID: 36111081

Boden, M. A. (2004). *The creative mind: Myths and mechanisms* (2nd ed.). Routledge. DOI: 10.4324/9780203508527

Bogost, I. (2007). *Persuasive Games: The Expressive Power of Videogames.* MIT Press. DOI: 10.7551/mitpress/5334.001.0001

Borderie, X. (2021). Soundtracking sur Amiga: Passion, explications et exemples. https://xavier.borderie.net/blog/2021/07/11/soundtracking-sur-amiga-passion-explications-et-exemples/

Bowey, J. T., Birk, M. V., & Mandryk, R. L. (2015, October). Manipulating leaderboards to induce player experience. In *Proceedings of the 2015 annual symposium on computer-human interaction in play* (pp. 115-120). DOI: 10.1145/2793107.2793138

Bozkurt, A. (2024). GenAI et al.: Cocreation, Authorship, Ownership, Academic Ethics and Integrity in a Time of Generative AI. *Open Praxis, 16*(1), 1–10. . DOI: 10.55982/openpraxis.16.1.654

Bracken, P. (1977). Unintended consequences of strategic gaming. *Simulation & Games, 8*(3), 283–318. DOI: 10.1177/003755007783001

Branch, B., Mirowski, P., & Mathewson, K. (2021). Collaborative Storytelling with Human Actors and Ai Narrators. In A. G. S. de Garza, T. Veale, W. Aguilar, & R. P. y Pérez (Eds.), *Proceedings of the 12th International Conference on Computational Creativity* (pp. 96–101). Association for Computational Creativity. https://computationalcreativity.net/iccc21/wp-content/uploads/2021/09/ICCC_2021_paper_118.pdf

Braun, V., & Clarke, V. (2006). Using thematic Analysis in Psychology. *Qualitative Research in Psychology, 3*(2), 77–101. DOI: 10.1191/1478088706qp063oa

Brisson, A., Pereira, G., Prada, R., Paiva, A., Louchart, S., Suttie, N., & Oliveira, M. (2012). Artificial intelligence and personalization opportunities for serious games. In *Proceedings of the AAAI Conference on Artificial Intelligence and Interactive Digital Entertainment* (Vol. 8, No. 5, pp. 51-57).

Brown, J. A. (2013). Evolved Weapons for RPG Drop Systems. In Proceedings of the 2013 IEEE Conference on Computational Inteligence in Games (CIG), Niagara Falls, ON, Canada, 11–13 August 2013; pp. 1–2.

Brown, L. (2024). Rethinking Remakes: Value and Culture in Video Game Temporalization. *Games and Culture*, *0*(0), 1–20. DOI: 10.1177/15554120231163655

Brown, T. B., Mann, B., Ryder, N., Subbiah, M., Kaplan, J., Dhariwal, P., Neelakantan, A., Shyam, P., Sastry, G., Askell, A., Agarwal, S., Herbert-Voss, A., Krueger, G., Henighan, T., Child, R., Ramesh, A., Ziegler, D. M., Wu, J., Winter, C., & Amodei, D. (2020). Language Models Are Few-Shot Learners. In Larochelle, H., Ranzato, M., Hadsell, R., Balcan, M. F., & Lin, H. (Eds.), Vol. 33, pp. 1877–1901). Advances in Neural Information Processing Systems. Curran Associates, Inc., https://papers.nips.cc/paper/2020/hash/1457c0d6bfcb4967418bfb8ac142f64a-Abstract.html

Brown, T., Mann, B., & Ryder, N.. (2020). Language Models are Few-Shot Learners. *Advances in Neural Information Processing Systems*, *33*, 1877–1901.

Brown, T., Mann, B., Ryder, N., Subbiah, M., Kaplan, J. D., Dhariwal, P., Neelakantan, A., Shyam, P., Sastry, G., & Askell, A.. (2020). Language models are few-shot learners. *Advances in Neural Information Processing Systems*, *33*, 1877–1901.

Bulger, S. M., & Housner, L. D. (2007). Modified Delphi Investigation of Exercise Science in Physical Education Teacher Education. *Journal of Teaching in Physical Education*, *26*(1), 57–80. DOI: 10.1123/jtpe.26.1.57

Buolamwini, J., & Gebru, T. (2018). Gender Shades: Intersectional Accuracy Disparities in Commercial Gender Classification. *Proceedings of the 1st Conference on Fairness, Accountability and Transparency - Proceedings of Machine Learning Research, 81*, 1-15. https://proceedings.mlr.press/v81/buolamwini18a/buolamwini18a.pdf

Buongiorno, S.. (2024). *PANGeA: Procedural artificial narrative using generative AI for turn-based video games*. https://arxiv.org/abs/2404.19721

Buongiorno, S., Klinkert, L. J., Chawla, T., Zhuang, Z., & Clark, C. (2024). PANGeA: Procedural Artificial Narrative using Generative AI for Turn-Based Video Games. https://doi.org/DOI: 10.48550/ARXIV.2404.19721

Burbach, J., Meyer, A., Plank, M., & Trautzsch, N. (2024a). AI-KI-DO: Künstliche Intelligenz in Design und Online-Medien – A research initiative on AI in creative practice. IU Internationale Hochschule. https://www.iu.de/forschung/projekte/ai-ki-do/

Burbach, J., Meyer, A., Plank, M., & Trautzsch, N. (2024b). Das Sanatorium [Video game]. IU Game Design. https://iu-gamedesign.itch.io/das-sanatorium

Calandra, D., Pratticò, F. G., Migliorini, M., Verda, V., & Lamberti, F. A. Multi-Role, Multi-User, Multi-Technology Virtual Reality-Based Road Tunnel Fire Simulator for Training Purposes. In Proceedings of the 16th International Joint Conference on Computer Vision, Imaging and Computer Graphics Theory and Applications (VISIGRAPP 2021)—GRAPP, Online, 8–10 February 2021; SciTePress: Setúbal, Portugal, 2021; pp. 96–105.

Caldas, O. I., Sanchez, N., Mauledoux, M., & Bourdot, P. (2022). Leading Presence-Based Strategies to Manipulate User Experience in Virtual Reality Environments. *Virtual Reality (Waltham Cross)*, *26*(4), 1507–1518. DOI: 10.1007/s10055-022-00645-3

Capcom. (2005). Resident Evil 4 developer interviews [Video interview transcript]. Capcom Co., Ltd. https://www.capcom.co.jp/ir/english/interview/2005/re4/

Castella-Martinez, S., & Saiz-Raimundo, M. (2024). Ramon Llull and the Communicating Vessels Between Catholicism and Occultism in Early Twentieth-Century France. *Romance Quarterly*, *71*(4), 277–291. DOI: 10.1080/08831157.2024.2399009

Cavazza, M., & Charles, F. (2005). Dialogue generation in character-based interactive storytelling. *Proceedings of the National Conference on Artificial Intelligence*.

Chamola, V., Bansal, G., Das, T. K., Hassija, V., Sai, S., Wang, J., Zeadally, S., Hussain, A., Yu, F. R., Guizani, M., & Niyato, D. (2024). Beyond Reality: The Pivotal Role of Generative AI in the Metaverse. *IEEE Internet of Things Magazine*, *7*(4), 126–135. DOI: 10.1109/IOTM.001.2300174

Chang, K. V., Wu, W. T., Chen, M. C., Chiu, Y. C., Han, D.-S., & Chen, C. C. (2019). Smartphone Application with Virtual Reality Goggles for the Reliable and Valid Measurement of Active Craniocervical Range of Motion. *Diagnostics (Basel)*, *9*(3), 71. DOI: 10.3390/diagnostics9030071 PMID: 31295869

Chen, M., Liu, W., Wang, T., Zhang, S., & Liu, A. (2022). A game-based deep reinforcement learning approach for energy-efficient computation in MEC systems. Knowl.-. *Knowledge-Based Systems*, *235*, 107660. DOI: 10.1016/j.knosys.2021.107660

Chen, X., & Koltun, V. (2017). Photographic Image Synthesis with Cascaded Refinement Networks. *Proceedings of the IEEE International Conference on Computer Vision*. DOI: 10.1109/ICCV.2017.168

Cheung, L. M. E., & Shi, H. (2024). Co-Creating Stories With Generative Ai: Reflections From Undergraduate Students of a Storytelling Service-Learning Subject in Hong Kong. *Australian Review of Applied Linguistics*, *47*(3), 259–283. DOI: 10.1075/aral.24101.che

Chib, S., Mehta, A. K., Selvakumar, P., Saravanan, A., Mishra, B. R., & Manjunath, T. C. (2025). Mental Health Challenges and Solutions in High-Pressure Work Environments. In Harriott, S. (Ed.), *Innovative Approaches to Managing Conflict and Change in Diverse Work Environments* (pp. 247–272). IGI Global Scientific Publishing., DOI: 10.4018/979-8-3693-9556-1.ch011

Cho, K., Jang, H., Park, L. W., Kim, S., & Park, S. Energy management system based on augmented reality for human-computer interaction in a Smart City. In *Proceedings of the 2019 IEEE International Conference on Consumer Electronics (ICCE)*, Las Vegas, NV, USA, 11–13 January 2019; pp. 1–3. DOI: 10.1109/ICCE.2019.8662045

Chowdhery, A., Narang, S., Devlin, J., Bosma, M., Mishra, G., Roberts, A., Barham, P., Chung, H. W., Sutton, C., & Gehrmann, S.. (2023). PaLM: Scaling language modeling with pathways. *Journal of Machine Learning Research, 24*(240), 1–113.

Chytas, D., Johnson, E. O., Piagkou, M., Mazarakis, A., Babis, G. C., Chronopoulos, E., Nikolaou, V. S., Lazaridis, N., & Natsis, K. (2020). The role of augmented reality in Anatomical education: An overview. *Annals of Anatomy*, *229*, 151463. DOI: 10.1016/j.aanat.2020.151463 PMID: 31978568

Colantonio, R. (2022, March). Live ops analytics in mobile games [Conference session]. Game Developers Conference (GDC), San Francisco, CA, United States. https://gdcvault.com/play/1027890/Live-Ops-Analytics-in-Mobile

Collins, K. (2008). *Game sound: An introduction to the history, theory, and practice of video game music and sound design. MIT Press.* https://mitpress.mit.edu/9780262033780

Compare Voice, A. I. (2025). *LLM pricing comparison 2025 | compare OpenAI, anthropic, google, meta*. Compare Voice AI. https://comparevoiceai.com/llm

Compton, K., & Mateas, M. (2006). Procedural Level Design for Platform Games. *Proceedings of the 2nd AIIDE Conference*.

Connor, A. (2025). In Real Life: Gaming Community Engagement in Museums. *Curator (New York, N.Y.)*, *00*(1), 1–14. DOI: 10.1111/cura.12622

Convai. (2024). *Pricing*. Convai Technologies Inc. https://convai.com/pricing

Cooren, F. (2015). *Speech acts theory*. Wiley Online Library., DOI: 10.1002/9781118611463.wbielsi055

Costa, G. D. C. T., Pedrosa, G. F., Souza, N. P. D., Gemente, F. R. F., Freire, A. B., & Castro, H. D. O. (2017). Type of Game Practiced in Handball According to the Positions of the Attackers: Analysis of the Women's World Handball Championship 2015. *International Journal of Performance Analysis in Sport, 17*(3), 360–373. DOI: 10.1080/24748668.2017.1345197

Cowley, B., Miettinen, M., & Ravaja, N. (2022). Ethical nudges in mobile games. *International Journal of Human-Computer Studies, 158*, 102735.

Crawford, C. (1984). *The art of computer game design*. McGraw-Hill/Osborne Media.

Crawford, C. (2004). *Chris Crawford on Interactive Storytelling*. New Riders.

Cuddy, L. (2008). *The Legend of Zelda and Philosophy: I link therefore I am* (Vol. 36). Open Court.

Dahiya, R., & Selvakumar, P. Vidyadhara & Manjunath T C. (2025). Design and Aerodynamics: Principles and Advances. In M. Mellal (Ed.), *Innovations and Developments in Unmanned Aerial Vehicles* (pp. 145-170). IGI Global Scientific Publishing. https://doi.org/DOI: 10.4018/979-8-3693-8462-6.ch007

Dartnall, T. (Ed.). (1994). *Artificial intelligence and creativity*: An interdisciplinary approach (Studied in Cognitive Systems, Vol. 17). Springer. https://link.springer.com/book/10.1007/978-94-017-0793-0

Davis, M., & Davis, V. (2005). Mistaken ancestry: The jacquard and the computer. *Textile (Oxford), 3*(1), 76–87. DOI: 10.2752/147597505778052594

de la Torre, J. C., Aragón-Jurado, J. M., Crespo-Álvarez, A., & Bárcena-González, G. (2024). GAGI: Game engine for Artificial General Intelligence experimentation. *SoftwareX, 26*, 101665. DOI: 10.1016/j.softx.2024.101665

Deconstructeam. (2021). *Interview with the whisperer*. https://deconstructeam.itch.io/interview-with-the-whisperer

DeepMind. (2019). AlphaStar: Mastering the real-time strategy game StarCraft II [Research article]. *Nature, 575*(7782), 350–354. PMID: 31666705

DeepSeek-AI. (2024). *DeepSeek-V3 technical report*. DeepSeek-AI. https://arxiv.org/abs/2412.19437

Denisova, A., Nordin, A. I., & Cairns, P. (2016, October). The convergence of player experience questionnaires. In *Proceedings of the 2016 Annual Symposium on Computer-Human Interaction in Play* (pp. 33-37).

Developer Blog, N. V. I. D. I. A. (2024). *Spotlight: Convai reinvents non-playable character interactions*. NVIDIA Corporation. https://developer.nvidia.com/blog/spotlight-convai-reinvents-non-playable-character-interactions/

Dixon, B. J., Daly, M. J., Chan, H. H. L. L., Vescan, A., Witterick, I. J., & Irish, J. C. (2014). In attentional blindness increased with augmented reality surgical navigation. *American Journal of Rhinology & Allergy*, *28*(5), 433–437. DOI: 10.2500/ajra.2014.28.4067 PMID: 25198032

Dodiya, K. R., Kumar, K., Thakar, A., & Pithiya, G. (2025). *Unleashing the Power of AI: Exploring the Transformative Landscape of Image Analysis*. Utilizing AI and Machine Learning in Financial Analysis., DOI: 10.4018/979-8-3693-8507-4.ch022

Drachen, A., Canossa, A., & Yannakakis, G. N. (2018). *Game analytics: Maximizing the value of player data*. Springer. DOI: 10.1093/oso/9780198794844.003.0019

Du Sautoy, M. (2019). *The creativity code*. The Science of Human Innovation.

Duggal, K., Gupta, L. R., & Singh, P. (2021). Gamification and Machine Learning Inspired Approach for Classroom Engagement and Learning. *Mathematical Problems in Engineering*, *2021*, 9922775. DOI: 10.1155/2021/9922775

Dwivedi, Y. K., Hughes, L., Baabdullah, A. M., Ribeiro-Navarrete, S., Giannakis, M., Al-Debei, M. M., Dennehy, D., Metri, B., Buhalis, D., Cheung, C. M., Conboy, K., Doyle, R., Dubey, R., Dutot, V., Felix, R., Goyal, D. P., Gustafsson, A., Hinsch, C., Jebabli, I., & Wamba, S. F. (2022). Metaverse beyond the hype: Multidisciplinary perspectives on emerging challenges, opportunities, and agenda for research, practice and policy. *International Journal of Information Management*, *66*, 102542. DOI: 10.1016/j.ijinfomgt.2022.102542

EA. (2021). The Sims Mobile churn-prediction live-ops AI [White paper]. Electronic Arts Inc. https://www.ea.com/games/the-sims/the-sims-mobile/ai-churn-prediction

Elgammal, A., Liu, B., Elhoseiny, M., & Mazzone, M. (2017). CAN: Creative adversarial networks, generating "creative" content [Preprint]. arXiv. https://arxiv.org/abs/1706.07068

Elsayed, M. Z., Hasoon, A., Zidan, M. K., & Ayyad, S. M. (2024, July). Role of AI for plant disease detection and pest detection. In *2024 International Telecommunications Conference (ITC-Egypt)* (pp. 824-829). IEEE. DOI: 10.1109/ITC-Egypt61547.2024.10620496

Eltahir, M. E., Alsalhi, N. R., Al-Qatawneh, S., AlQudah, H. A., & Jaradat, M. (2021). The impact of game-based learning (GBL) on students' motivation, engagement and academic performance on an Arabic language grammar course in higher education. *Education and Information Technologies*, *26*(3), 3251–3278. DOI: 10.1007/s10639-020-10396-w

Ensmenger, N. (2012). Is chess the drosophila of artificial intelligence? A social history of an algorithm. *Social Studies of Science*, *42*(1), 5–30. DOI: 10.1177/0306312711424596 PMID: 22530382

Essinger, J. (2014). *Ada's algorithm: How Lord Byron's daughter Ada Lovelace launched the digital age*. Melville House.

European Parliament. (2023). Loot box regulation & consumer protection (Report No. 2023/2020(INL)). European Union. https://www.europarl.europa.eu/doceo/document/TA-9-2023-0123_EN.html

Fanfarová, A., & Mariš, L. (2017). Simulation Tool for Fire and Rescue Services. *Procedia Engineering*, *192*, 160–165. DOI: 10.1016/j.proeng.2017.06.028

Feng, Z., González, V. A., Amor, R., Lovreglio, R., & Cabrera-Guerrero, G. (2018). Immersive Virtual Reality Serious Games for Evacuation Training and Research: A Systematic Literature Review. *Computers & Education*, *127*, 252–266. DOI: 10.1016/j.compedu.2018.09.002

Ferreira, L., Lelis, L., & Whitehead, J. (2020). Computer-Generated Music for Tabletop Role-Playing Games. In Proceedings of the AAAI Conference on Artificial Intelligence and Interactive Digital Entertainment, Worchester, MA, USA, 19–23 October 2020; pp. 59–65.

Ferreira, C., & Whitehead, J. (2019). Context-aware quest generation [Paper presentation]. *Proceedings of the 14th International Conference on the Foundations of Digital Games (FDG)*, San Luis Obispo, CA, United States.

Fetzer, J. H. (1990). What is artificial intelligence? In *Artificial intelligence: Its scope and limits* (pp. 3–27). Springer Netherlands. DOI: 10.1007/978-94-009-1900-6_1

Fidora, A. (2011). *Ramon Llull, from the Ars Magna to artificial intelligence* (Sierra, C., Ed.). Artificial Intelligence Research Institute.

Fillebrown, S. (1992). Faster computation of Bernoulli numbers. *Journal of Algorithms*, *13*(3), 431–445. DOI: 10.1016/0196-6774(92)90048-H

Flanagan, M. (2009). *Critical Play: Radical Game Design*. MIT Press. DOI: 10.7551/mitpress/7678.001.0001

Foong, N. W., On, C. K., Alfred, R., Teo, J., & Ibrahim, A. A. A. (2017). Interactive Procedural Generation for Items in Role-Playing Game. In Proceedings of the 2017 IEEE 2nd International Conference on Automatic Control and Intelligent Systems (I2CACIS), Kota Kinabalu, Malaysia, 21 October 2017; pp. 150–154. DOI: 10.1109/I2CACIS.2017.8239049

Foucault, M. (1979). What is an author? *Screen, 20*(1), 13–34. DOI: 10.1093/screen/20.1.13

Frasca, G. (2003). Ludologists Love Stories, too: Notes from a Debate that Never Took Place. In M. Copier & J. Raessens (Eds.), *Level Up: Digital Games Research Conference Proceedings* (pp. 92–99). Utrecht University. DOI: 10.26503/dl.v2003i1.64

Freiknecht, J., & Effelsberg, W. (2020). Procedural generation of interactive stories using language models. *Foundations of Digital Games.* https://doi.org/DOI: 10.1145/3402942.3409599

Friedman, B., Kahn, P. H., Borning, A., & Huldtgren, A. (2013). Value Sensitive Design and Information Systems. In N. Doorn, D. Schuurbiers, I. van de Poel, & M. Gorman (Eds.), *Early Engagement and New Technologies: Opening up the Laboratory* (Philosophy of Engineering and Technology, Vol. 16, pp. 55–95). Springer. DOI: 10.1007/978-94-007-7844-3_4

Fu, Y., Newman, M., Going, L., Feng, Q., & Lee, J. H. (2025). "Exploring the Collaborative Co-Creation Process with AI: A Case Study in Novice Music Production." arXiv preprint, arXiv:2501.15276. DOI: /arXiv.2501.15276DOI: 10.1145/3715336.3735829

Gallotta, R., Todd, G., Zammit, M., Earle, S., Liapis, A., Togelius, J., & Yannakakis, G. N. (2024). Large language models and games: A survey and roadmap. *IEEE Transactions on Games*, 1–18. DOI: 10.1109/TG.2024.3461510

Gemini Team. (2024). *Gemini 1.5: Unlocking multimodal understanding across millions of tokens of context.* Google DeepMind. https://arxiv.org/abs/2403.05530

Georgievski, I., & Aiello, M. (2014). *An overview of hierarchical task network planning.* https://arxiv.org/abs/1403.7426

Gerba, H. (2025). Universal Narrative Model: An Author-Centric Storytelling Framework for Generative AI. *arXiv.* https://arxiv.org/abs/2503.04844v3

Gerganov, G. (2023). *Llama.cpp: LLM inference in c/c++* [Computer software]. GitHub repository. https://github.com/ggml-org/llama.cpp

Ghaednia, H., Fourman, M. S., Lans, A., Detels, K., Dijkstra, H., Lloyd, S., Sweeney, A., Oosterhoff, J. H., & Schwab, J. H. (2021). Augmented and virtual reality in spine surgery, current applications and future potentials. *The Spine Journal*, *21*(10), 1617–1625. DOI: 10.1016/j.spinee.2021.03.018 PMID: 33774210

Gillespie, T. (2018). *Custodians of the Internet: Platforms, Content Moderation, and the Hidden Decisions That Shape Social Media*. Yale University Press.

Gill, S. S., Xu, M., Ottaviani, C., Patros, P., Bahsoon, R., Shaghaghi, A., Golec, M., Stankovski, V., Wu, H., Abraham, A., Singh, M., Mehta, H., Ghosh, S. K., Baker, T., Parlikad, A. K., Lutfiyya, H., Kanhere, S. S., Sakellariou, R., Dustdar, S., & Uhlig, S. (2022). AI for Next Generation Computing: Emerging Trends and Future Directions. *Internet of Things : Engineering Cyber Physical Human Systems*, *15*(3), 567–589. DOI: 10.1016/j.iot.2022.100514

Ginsburg, J. C., & Budiardjo, L. A. (2019). Authors and Machines. *Berkeley Technology Law Journal*, *34*(2), 343–388. DOI: 10.15779/Z38SF2MC24

Gisselbrecht, T., Bontrager, P., Togelius, J., & Hoover, A. K. (2019). Learning Level Design with Generative Adversarial Networks. *IEEE Conference on Games (CoG)*.

Glăveanu, V. P. (2014). *Distributed Creativity: Thinking Outside the Box of the Creative Individual*. Springer. DOI: 10.1007/978-3-319-05434-6

Gnatyuk, V., Koriukina, V., Levoshevich, I., Nurminskiy, P., & Wallner, G. (2025). In the Blink of an Eye: Instant Game Map Editing using a Generative-AI Smart Brush. DOI: 10.48550/ARXIV.2503.19793

Golab, M. R., Breedon, P. J., & Vloeberghs, M. (2016). A wearable headset for monitoring electromyography responses within spinal surgery. *European Spine Journal : Official Publication of the European Spine Society, the European Spinal Deformity Society, and the European Section of the Cervical Spine Research Society*, *25*(10), 3214–3219. DOI: 10.1007/s00586-016-4626-x PMID: 27282890

Gómez, M. Á., Lago-Peñas, C., Viaño, J., & González-Garcia, I. (2014). Effects of Game Location, Team Quality and Final Outcome on Game-Related Statistics in Professional Handball Close Games. *Kinesiology*, *46*, 249–257.

González Duque, C., Liapis, A., & Togelius, J. (2020). Intelligent trial-and-error for level difficulty. *IEEE Transactions on Games*, *12*(3), 267–278.

Goodfellow, I., Pouget-Abadie, J., Mirza, M., Xu, B., Warde-Farley, D., Ozair, S., & Bengio, Y. (2014). Generative Adversarial Nets. *Advances in Neural Information Processing Systems*, •••, 27.

Google. (2020). *The mystery of the three bots* [Computer software]. https://google.github.io/mysteryofthreebots/

Grabarczyk, P., & Walther, B. K. (2022). A Game of Twisted Shouting: Ludo-Narrative Dissonance Revisited. *Eludamos (Göttingen)*, *13*(1), 7–27. DOI: 10.7557/23.6506

Greenblatt, R. D., Eastlake, D. E., III, & Crocker, S. D. (1967, November). The Greenblatt chess program. In Proceedings of the November 14-16, 1967, fall joint computer conference (pp. 801-810).

Gulsoy, M., Kokach, V., Kocaçınar, B., & Akbulut, F. P. (2024, October). AI-Driven Contextual Story Creation with Integrated Text and Visual Generation. In 2024 Innovations in Intelligent Systems and Applications Conference (ASYU) (pp. 1-6). IEEE.

Gümüş, H., & Gençoğlu, C. (2020). The Effects of the Goalkeeper Substitution Rule as a New Strategy in Handball: Analysis of Men's European Handball Championship 2020. *Acta Gymnica*, *50*(3), 113–121. DOI: 10.5507/ag.2020.015

Guzdial, M., & Riedl, M. (2016). Game Engine Learning from Video. *Proceedings of the 2016 International Conference on the Foundations of Digital Games*.

Haddas, R., & Ju, K. L. (2019). Gait alteration in cervical spondylotic myelopathy elucidated by ground reaction forces. *Spine*, *44*(1), 25–31. DOI: 10.1097/BRS.0000000000002732 PMID: 29889798

Harikrishna, R., & Pandey, S. (2023). Game Level Design Automation Using Deep Reinforcement Learning. *Expert Systems with Applications*, *213*, 119157.

Harrell, D. F. (2013). *Phantasmal Media: An Approach to Imagination, Computation, and Expression*. MIT Press. DOI: 10.7551/mitpress/8834.001.0001

Harrell, D. F., & Zhu, J. (2009). Agency Play: Dimensions of Agency for Interactive Narrative Design. In *Proceedings of the AAAI Spring Symposium on Intelligent Narrative Technologies II* (pp. 44–52). AAAI Press.

Harris, A. (2014). *The Creative Turn: Toward a New Aesthetic Imaginary*. Sense Publishers., DOI: 10.1007/978-94-6209-551-9

Hassan, A., Pinkwart, N., & Shafi, M. (2021). Serious games to improve social and emotional intelligence in children with autism. *Entertainment Computing*, *38*, 100417. DOI: 10.1016/j.entcom.2021.100417

Hatzimanouil, D. (2020). Goalkeeper's Efficiency in Relation with Throws from Different Attacking Court Areas in Team Handball. *Journal of Physical Education and Sport Management*, *7*, 11–18.

Hayles, N. K. (2017). *Unthought: The Power of the Cognitive Nonconscious*. University of Chicago Press. DOI: 10.7208/chicago/9780226447919.001.0001

Hendrikx, M., Meijer, S., Van Der Velden, J., & Iosup, A. (2013). Procedural content generation for games: A survey. [TOMM]. *ACM Transactions on Multimedia Computing Communications and Applications*, *9*(1), 1–22. DOI: 10.1145/2422956.2422957

Higinbotham, W. (1958). *Tennis for two. Brookhaven National Laboratory*. Oscilloscope.

Hladky, A., Smith, A., & Brown, J. (2022). Reinforcement learning driven difficulty scaling [Paper presentation]. *Proceedings of the IEEE Conference on Games (CoG)*, Beijing, China.

Holmgård, C., Liapis, A., Togelius, J., & Yannakakis, G. N. (2014). Procedural personas for player type-based testing [Paper presentation]. *Proceedings of the 9th International Conference on the Foundations of Digital Games (FDG)*, Ft. Lauderdale, FL, United States.

Horsfall, D., Smith, A., & Liu, J. (2020). Recommender systems in MMOs. *Entertainment Computing*, *34*, 100356.

Hua, M., & Raley, R. (2020). Playing with Unicorns: *AI Dungeon* and Citizen NLP. *Digital Humanities Quarterly, 14*(4). https://www.digitalhumanities.org/dhq/vol/14/4/000533/000533.html

Hu, C., Zhao, Y., Wang, Z., Du, H., & Liu, J. (2024). Games for artificial intelligence research: A review and perspectives. *IEEE Transactions on Artificial Intelligence*, *5*(12), 5949–5968. DOI: 10.1109/TAI.2024.3410935

Hugging Face. (2025). *Quantization*. Hugging Face. https://huggingface.co/docs/optimum/en/concept_guides/quantization

Huynh, E., Nyhout, A., Ganea, P., & Chevalier, F. (2020). Designing Narrative-Focused Role-Playing Games for Visualization Literacy in Young Children. *IEEE Transactions on Visualization and Computer Graphics*, *27*(2), 924–934. DOI: 10.1109/TVCG.2020.3030464 PMID: 33048745

Hyman, A. (1985). *Charles Babbage: Pioneer of the computer*. Princeton University Press.

Ibáñez, M. B., & Delgado-Kloos, C. (2018). Augmented reality for STEM learning: A systematic review. *Computers & Education*, *123*, 109–123. DOI: 10.1016/j.compedu.2018.05.002

Image-Line. (2024). *FL Studio online manual.* Documentation of FL Studio features including the stem separation tool. https://www.image-line.com/fl-studio-learning/fl-studio-online-manual

Inie, N., Falk, J., & Tanimoto, S. L. (2023). Designing Participatory AI: Creative Professionals' Worries and Expectations about Generative AI. *arXiv (Cornell University).* https://doi.org//arXiv.2303.08931DOI: 10.1145/3544549.3585657

Inworld, A. I. (2024a). *Case studies.* Inworld AI Inc. https://inworld.ai/case-studies

Inworld, A. I. (2024b). *Inworld AI.* Inworld AI Inc. https://inworld.ai/

Inworld, A. I. (2024c). *Inworld's commitment to safety.* Inworld AI Inc. https://inworld.ai/blog/inworlds-commitment-to-safety

Inworld, A. I. (2024d). *Unreal playground: Goals & mutations demo.* Inworld AI Inc. https://inworld.ai/blog/unreal-playground-goals-mutations-demo

Inworld, A. I. Documentation. (2024). *Billing.* Inworld AI Inc. https://docs.inworld.ai/docs/resources/billing

Isaksen, A., Gopstein, D., Togelius, J., & Nealen, A. (2019). Constrained MAP-Elites for playable level design [Paper presentation]. *Proceedings of the Genetic and Evolutionary Computation Conference (GECCO),* Prague, Czech Republic.

Jacobides, M. G., Candelon, F., Krayer, L., Round, K., & Chen, W. S. (2023). Building synthetic worlds: Lessons from the excessive infatuation and oversold disillusionment with the metaverse. *Industry and Innovation, 31*(1), 105–129. DOI: 10.1080/13662716.2023.2279051

Jagatheesaperumal, S. K., Mishra, P., Moustafa, N., & Chauhan, R. (2022). A holistic survey on the use of emerging technologies to provision secure healthcare solutions. *Computers & Electrical Engineering, 99,* 107691. DOI: 10.1016/j.compeleceng.2022.107691

Jain, S., Liapis, A., & Togelius, J. (2021). VAE-GAN puzzle generation. *IEEE Transactions on Games, 13*(2), 145–156.

Jenkins, H. (2004). Game Design as Narrative Architecture. In Wardrip-Fruin, N., & Harrigan, P. (Eds.), *First Person: New Media as Story, Performance, and Game* (pp. 118–130). MIT Press.

Jessen, T. D., Ban, N. C., Claxton, N. X., & Darimont, C. T. (2022). Contributions of Indigenous Knowledge to Ecological and Evolutionary Understanding. *Frontiers in Ecology and the Environment, 20*(2), 93–101. DOI: 10.1002/fee.2435

Jo, D., & Kim, G. J. (2019). IoT+ AR: Pervasive and augmented environments for "Digi-log" shopping experience. Hum.-. *Centric Comput. Inf. Sci.*, *9*(1), 1–17. DOI: 10.1186/s13673-018-0162-5

Joda, T., Gallucci, G., Wismeijer, D., & Zitzmann, N. U. (2019). Augmented and virtual reality in dental medicine: A systematic review. *Computers in Biology and Medicine*, *108*, 93–100. DOI: 10.1016/j.compbiomed.2019.03.012 PMID: 31003184

Johnson, L., Yannakakis, G. N., & Togelius, J. (2010). Cellular Automata for Real-Time Generation of Infinite Cave Levels. *Proceedings of the 2010 Workshop on Procedural Content Generation in Games*. DOI: 10.1145/1814256.1814266

Johnson, M., Brown, T., & Lee, S. (2021). Multimodal AI in VR for emotion detection. *Presence (Cambridge, Mass.)*, *28*, 101–118.

Joyce, L. (2015). Creating Collaborative Criteria for Agency in Interactive Narrative Game Analysis. *Computer Games Journal*, *4*(1), 47–58. DOI: 10.1007/s40869-015-0004-x

Jung, T., Cho, J., Han, D. D., Ahn, S. J., Gupta, M., Das, G., Heo, C. Y., Loureiro, S. M. C., Σιγάλα, M., Trunfio, M., Taylor, A., & tom Dieck, M. C. (2023). Metaverse for service industries: Future applications, opportunities, challenges and research directions. *Computers in Human Behavior*, *151*, 108039. DOI: 10.1016/j.chb.2023.108039

Justesen, N., Bontrager, P., Togelius, J., & Risi, S. (2019). Deep learning for video game playing. *IEEE Transactions on Games*, *12*(1), 1–20. DOI: 10.1109/TG.2019.2896986

Juul, J. (2005). *Half-Real: Video Games between Real Rules and Fictional Worlds*. MIT Press.

Kanbach, D. K., Heiduk, L., Blueher, G., Schreiter, M., & Lahmann, A. (2023). The GenAI is out of the bottle: Generative artificial intelligence from a business model innovation perspective. *Review of Managerial Science*, *18*(4), 1189–1220. DOI: 10.1007/s11846-023-00696-z

Kanerva, S. K. (2024). "Utilising Artificial Intelligence in a 3D Video Game Environment Design and Creation Process." *Theseus.fi*, Bachelor's Thesis, pp. 1–58. DOI: URN:NBN:fi:amk-2024052817219.

Kao, L. C., & Liao, W. (2021). 5G Intelligent A+: A Pioneer Multi-Access Edge Computing Solution for 5G Private Networks. *IEEE Communications Standards Magazine*, *5*(1), 78–84. DOI: 10.1109/MCOMSTD.001.2000036

Karavidas, L., Apostolidis, H., & Tsiatsos, T. (2022). Usability Evaluation of an Adaptive Serious Game Prototype Based on Affective Feedback. *Information (Basel), 13*(9), 425. DOI: 10.3390/info13090425

Karth, I., & Compton, K. (2023). Conceptual art made real: Why procedural content generation is impossible. *Proceedings of the 18th International Conference on the Foundations of Digital Games*. https://doi.org/DOI: 10.1145/3582437.3587212

Karth, I., & Smith, A. M. (2017). Addressing the Fundamental Tension of PCGML with Discriminative Learning. *Proceedings of the 12th International Conference on the Foundations of Digital Games*.

Kates, J. (1950). *Bertie the brain*. Canadian National Exhibition.

Kaur, M., Selvakumar, P., & Dinesh, N. Mohit, Chandel P S, & Manjunath T C. (2025). Reconstruction and Preservation Strategies for Cultural Heritage. In S. Oflazoğlu & M. Dora (Eds.), *Preserving Cultural Heritage in Post-Disaster Urban Renewal* (pp. 385-412). IGI Global Scientific Publishing. https://doi.org/DOI: 10.4018/979-8-3693-9097-9.ch016

Kavitha, L. (2023). Copyright Challenges in the Artificial Intelligence Revolution: Transforming the Film Industry from Script to Screen. *Trinity Law Review*, *4*(1), 1–15. DOI: 10.48165/tlr.2024.4.1.1

Kaylor, J., Hooper, V., Wilson, A., Burkert, R., Lyda, M., Fletcher, K., & Bowers, E. (2019). Reliability Testing of Augmented Reality Glasses Technology: Establishing the Evidence Base for Telewound Care. *Journal of Wound, Ostomy, and Continence Nursing*, *46*(6), 485–490. DOI: 10.1097/WON.0000000000000585 PMID: 31633610

Kelly, J. W., Cherep, L. A., Lim, A. F., Doty, T., & Gilbert, S. B. Who are virtual reality headset owners? A survey and comparison of headset owners and non-owners. In Proceedings of the 2021 IEEE Virtual Reality and 3D User Interfaces (VR), Lisboa, Portugal, 27 March–1 April 2021; pp. 687–694.

Khan, A. A., Laghari, A. A., Li, P., Dootio, M. A., & Karim, S. (2023). The collaborative role of blockchain, artificial intelligence, and industrial internet of things in digitalization of small and medium-size enterprises. *Scientific Reports*, *13*(1), 1656. DOI: 10.1038/s41598-023-28707-9 PMID: 36717702

Khan, A. A., Shaikh, A. A., & Laghari, A. A. (2022). IoT with Multimedia Investigation: A Secure Process of Digital Forensics Chain-of-Custody using Blockchain Hyperledger Sawtooth. *Arabian Journal for Science and Engineering*, •••, 1–16.

Kim, S., Lee, J., & Park, H. (2022). Generalizable AI agents across game genres. *IEEE Transactions on Games, 14*(3), 334–345.

Kinateder, M., Müller, B., Jost, M., Mühlberger, A., & Pauli, P. (2014). Social influence in a virtual tunnel fire—Influence of conflicting information on evacuation behavior. *Applied Ergonomics, 45*(6), 1649–1659. DOI: 10.1016/j.apergo.2014.05.014 PMID: 24947002

King, D. L., & Delfabbro, P. H. (2019). Gambling-like features in digital games. *Current Addiction Reports, 6*(4), 439–446.

Kitano, H., Asada, M., Kuniyoshi, Y., Noda, I., & Osawa, E. (1997, February). Robocup: The robot world cup initiative. In *Proceedings of the first international conference on Autonomous agents* (pp. 340-347). DOI: 10.1145/267658.267738

Koenitz, H. (2015). Design Approaches for Interactive Digital Narrative. In H. Schoenau-Fog, L. E. Bruni, S. Louchart, & S. Baceviciute (Eds.), *Interactive storytelling: 8th International Conference on Interactive Digital Storytelling (ICIDS 2015)* (pp. 50–57). Springer. DOI: 10.1007/978-3-319-27036-4_5

Köknar, C. (2019). Who is at the Center?: Designing Playful Experiences by Using Player-Centered Approach. In Proceedings of the International Conference on Human-Computer Interaction, Orlando, FL, USA, 26–31 July 2019; pp. 11–21. DOI: 10.1007/978-3-030-22602-2_2

Kolve, E., Mottaghi, R., Gordon, D., Zhu, Y., Gupta, A., & Farhadi, A. (2017). AI2-THOR: An Interactive 3D Environment for Visual AI. arXiv preprint arXiv:1712.05474.

Kommineni, M., Chundru, S., Maroju, P. K., & Selvakumar, P. (2025). Ethical Implications of AI in Sustainable Development Pedagogy. In Chinedu, C., Mafarja, N., Hussein, M., & Saleem, A. (Eds.), *Rethinking the Pedagogy of Sustainable Development in the AI Era* (pp. 17–36). IGI Global Scientific Publishing., DOI: 10.4018/979-8-3693-9062-7.ch002

Kotlinski, J. (2009). *Amiga music programs* 1986–1995 – A historical overview of Amiga tracker software. https://goto80.com/chipflip/dox/kotlinski_(2009)_amiga_music_programs_89-95.pdf

Kraft, M. A., Marinell, W. H., & Yee, D. S. W. (2018). School organizational contexts, teacher turnover, and student achievement: Evidence from panel data. *American Educational Research Journal, 53*(5), 1411–1449. DOI: 10.3102/0002831216667478

Kraft, M. A., & Papay, J. P. (2014). Can professional environments in schools promote teacher development? Explaining heterogeneity in returns to teaching experience. *Educational Evaluation and Policy Analysis, 36*(4), 476–500. DOI: 10.3102/0162373713519496 PMID: 25866426

Kreminski, M., Dickinson, M., & Wardrip-Fruin, N. (2020). Why Are We Like This? The AI Architecture of a Storytelling Game about Intimacy. In Marino, M., Flores, A., & Pyne, J. (Eds.), *Proceedings of the Electronic Literature Organization 2020 Conference and Media Festival: (Un)Continuity* (pp. 1–10). University of Central Florida., https://stars.library.ucf.edu/elo2020/asynchronous/proceedingspapers/10/

Kroon, J. C. (2016). Nemesis Narratives: The relationship between embedded and emergent narrative in Middle Earth: Shadow of Mordor (Master's thesis).

Kuguoglu, B. K., van der Voort, H., & Janssen, M. (2021). The giant leap for smart cities: Scaling up smart city artificial intelligence of things (AIOT) initiatives. *Sustainability (Basel), 13*(21), 12295. DOI: 10.3390/su132112295

Kumar, A., Singh, R., & Bhardwaj, V. (2022). Sentiment analysis of student and teacher feedback using natural language processing. *Journal of Computer Assisted Learning, 38*(4), 517–529.

Kwon, H., & Kim, H. (2021). Predictive analytics in teacher retention: Leveraging AI for proactive HR management. *International Journal of Educational Technology in Higher Education, 18*(1), 112–130. PMID: 34977335

Kybartas, B., & Verbrugge, C. (2014). Analysis of ReGEN as a graph-rewriting system for quest generation. *IEEE Transactions on Computational Intelligence and AI in Games, 6*(2), 228–242. Advance online publication. DOI: 10.1109/TCIAIG.2013.2290088

Laghari, A. A., Khan, A. A., Alkanhel, R., Elmannai, H., & Bourouis, S. (2023). Lightweight-BIoV: Blockchain Distributed Ledger Technology (BDLT) for Internet of Vehicles (IoVs). *Electronics (Basel), 12*(3), 677. DOI: 10.3390/electronics12030677

Lago-Peñas, C., Gómez, A. M., Viaño, J., González-García, I., & Fernández-Villarino, M. (2013). de L. ángeles Home Advantage in Elite Handball: The Impact of the Quality of Opposition on Team Performance. *International Journal of Performance Analysis in Sport, 13*(3), 724–733. DOI: 10.1080/24748668.2013.11868684

Lamerichs, N. (2020, January 20). Is *AI Dungeon* the Future of Literature? *Nicolle Lamerichs.* https://nicollelamerichs.com/2020/01/20/writing-with-algorithms-in-ai-dungeon/

Latitude. (2024a, December 18). *Forge: A New Era of AI Models in AI Dungeon* [Blog post]. Retrieved from https://latitude.io/blog/forge-a-new-era-of-ai-models-in-ai-dungeon

Latitude. (2024b, May 23). *How the New Memory System Works* [Blog post]. Retrieved from https://latitude.io/blog/how-the-new-memory-system-works

Latitude. (2024c). *Getting Started with AI Dungeon.* https://help.aidungeon.com/getting-started

Latour, B. (2005). *Reassembling the Social: An Introduction to Actor-Network-Theory.* Oxford University Press. DOI: 10.1093/oso/9780199256044.001.0001

LeBlanc, M. (2000, March). *Formal Design Tools: Emergent Complexity, Emergent Narrative* [Conference presentation]. Game Developers Conference, San Jose, CA, United States. http://algorithmancy.8kindsoffun.com/gdc2000.ppt

Lee, M., Srivastava, M., Hardy, A., Thickstun, J., Durmus, E., Paranjape, A., . . . Liang, P. (2023). Evaluating Human–Language Model Interaction. *Transactions on Machine Learning Research.* https://openreview.net/forum?id=hjDYJUn9l1

Lewis, P., Perez, E., Piktus, A., Petroni, F., Karpukhin, V., Goyal, N., Küttler, H., Lewis, M., Yih, W., Rocktäschel, T., Riedel, S., & Kiela, D. (2020). Retrieval-augmented generation for knowledge-intensive NLP tasks. *Proceedings of the 34th International Conference on Neural Information Processing Systems*, 9459–9474. https://proceedings.neurips.cc/paper/2020/file/6b493230205f780e1bc26945df7481e5-Paper.pdf

Liao, K., Liu, L., & Smed, J. (2021). GAN-based Procedural Content Generation: A Survey. *Multimedia Tools and Applications, 80*, 24185–24221.

Liapis, A., Yannakakis, G. N., & Togelius, J. (2013). Sentient Sketchbook: Computer-Aided Game Level Authoring. *Proceedings of the 8th International Conference on the Foundations of Digital Games.*

Linares-Pellicer, J., Izquierdo-Domenech, J., Ferri-Molla, I., & Aliaga-Torro, C. (2025). *We Are All Creators: Generative AI, Collective Knowledge, and the Path Towards Human-AI Synergy.* https://doi.org/DOI: 10.48550/ARXIV.2504.07936

Ling, P. (2023). "AI-Assisted Game Level Generation Based on Difficulty." *Aalto University*, Master's Thesis, pp. 1–75. DOI: URN:NBN:fi:aalto-202312187331.

Liounakos, J. I., Urakov, T., & Wang, M. Y. (2020). Head-up display assisted endoscopic lumbar discectomy—A technical note. *International Journal of Medical Robotics and Computer Assisted Surgery*, *16*(3), e2089. DOI: 10.1002/rcs.2089 PMID: 32034967

Li, T., Liu, W., Xie, S., Dong, M., Ota, K., Xiong, N. N., & Li, Q. (2021). BPT: A Blockchain-Based Privacy Information Preserving System for Trust Data Collection Over Distributed Mobile-Edge Network. *IEEE Internet of Things Journal*, *9*(11), 8036–8052. DOI: 10.1109/JIOT.2021.3117971

Liu, M. (2021). Artificial intelligence in education: Challenges and opportunities. *Journal of Educational Technology Development and Exchange*, *14*(1), 47–60.

Lohre, R., Wang, J. C., Lewandrowski, K.-U., & Goel, D. P. (2020). Virtual reality in spinal endoscopy: A paradigm shift in education to support spine surgeons. *Journal of Spine Surgery*, *6*(S1, Suppl. 1), S208–S223. DOI: 10.21037/jss.2019.11.16 PMID: 32195429

Lucas, M., & Runge, J. (2022). Ethical Risks of AI-Generated Game Content: Bias, Appropriation, and Moderation. *Games and Culture*, *17*(5), 652–670.

Lucas, S. M., Liu, J., Kendall, G., & Togelius, J. (2021). *AI and Games: A Handbook for Practitioners*. Springer.

Lundberg, S. M., & Lee, S.-I. (2017). A unified approach to interpreting model predictions [Paper presentation]. *Proceedings of the 31st International Conference on Neural Information Processing Systems (NIPS'17)*, Long Beach, CA, United States.

Lytras, M. D., Al-Halabi, W., Zhang, J. X., Masud, M., & Haraty, R. A. (2015). Enabling Technologies and Business Infrastructures for Next Generation Social Media: Big Data, Cloud Computing, Internet of Things and Virtual Reality. *J. UCS*, *21*, 1379–1384.

Lyu, M., Madanapalli, S. C., Vishwanath, A., & Sivaraman, V. (2024, March). Network Anatomy and Real-Time Measurement of Nvidia GeForce NOW Cloud Gaming. In International Conference on Passive and Active Network Measurement (pp. 61-91). Cham: Springer Nature Switzerland. DOI: 10.1007/978-3-031-56249-5_3

Madduru, P. (2021). Artificial Intelligence as A Service in Distributed Multi Access Edge Computing On 5g Extracting Data Using IOT And Including AR/VR For Real-Time Reporting. *Inf. Technol. Ind.*, *9*(1), 912–931. DOI: 10.17762/itii.v9i1.220

Malenfant, S., Jaggi, P., Hayden, K. A., & Sinclair, S. (2022). Compassion in Healthcare: An Updated Scoping Review of the Literature. *BMC Palliative Care*, *21*(1), 80. Advance online publication. DOI: 10.1186/s12904-022-00942-3 PMID: 35585622

Manovich, L. (2013). *Software takes command*. Bloomsbury. DOI: 10.5040/9781472544988

Marshall, S. J. (2022). *The Story of the Robot: A Short History of Automation and Robotics*. Stephen J Marshall.

Mateas, M., & Stern, A. (2005a). Procedural Authorship: A Case-Study of the Interactive Drama Façade. In *Proceedings of the Digital Arts and Culture Conference* (pp. 1–16). Copenhagen, Denmark. https://users.soe.ucsc.edu/~michaelm/publications/mateas1-dac2005.pdf

Mateas, M., & Stern, A. (2005b). Build It To Understand It: Ludology Meets Narratology in Game Design Space. In *Proceedings of DiGRA 2005 Conference: Changing Views – Worlds in Play*. Digital Games Research Association. DOI: 10.26503/dl.v2005i1.172

Mavromoustakos, S., & Bakkes, S. (2019). Facial expression analysis in gameplay. *International Journal of Human-Computer Interaction*, *35*(12), 1098–1110.

Ma, Y. P. (2021). Extending 3D-GIS District Models and BIM-Based Building Models into Computer Gaming Environment for Better Workflow of Cultural Heritage Conservation. *Applied Sciences (Basel, Switzerland)*, *11*(5), 2101. Advance online publication. DOI: 10.3390/app11052101

McCarthy, J. (2017, March 15). The rise of game-as-a-service. GameIndustry.biz. https://www.gamesindustry.biz/the-rise-of-game-as-a-service

McCarthy, J., Minsky, M. L., Rochester, N., & Shannon, C. E. (2006). A proposal for the dartmouth summer research project on artificial intelligence, august 31, 1955. *AI Magazine*, *27*(4), 12–12.

McCormack, J., Gifford, T., & Hutchings, P. (2019). *Autonomy, Authenticity, Authorship and Intention in computer generated art*. /arXiv.1903.02166DOI: 10.1007/978-3-030-16667-0_3

McCosker, A., & Wilken, R. (2020). *Automating vision: The social impact of the new camera consciousness*. Routledge. DOI: 10.4324/9780429341175

McGill, K. M. (2022). The Digital Lineage of Narrative: Analyzing Interactive Fiction to Further Understand Game Narrative. In Bostan, B. (Ed.), *Games and Narrative: Theory and Practice* (pp. 70–97). Springer., DOI: 10.1007/978-3-030-81538-7_5

McGuire, J., De Cremer, D., & Van de Cruys, T. (2024). Establishing the Importance of Co-Creation and Self-Efficacy in Creative Collaboration with Artificial Intelligence. *Scientific Reports*, *14*(1), 18525. DOI: 10.1038/s41598-024-69423-2

McHenry, D. (2024, August 8). *Mapping AI music tools across a spectrum of co-creativity*. Medium. https://medium.com/@dsm98/mapping-ai-music-tools-across-a-spectrum-of-co-creativity-c2a076af579a

MDPI. (2024). Exploring DDA methods in FPS games [Special issue introduction]. *Applied Sciences (Basel, Switzerland)*, *14*(5), 1800.

Miller, C., Dighe, M., Martens, C., & Jhala, A. (2019). Stories of the town: Balancing character autonomy and coherent narrative in procedurally generated worlds. *Proceedings of the 14th International Conference on the Foundations of Digital Games*. https://doi.org/DOI: 10.1145/3337722.3341850

Mitchell, A. (2022, January 9). Repetition and Defamiliarization in *AI Dungeon* and *Project December. Electronic Book Review*. https://electronicbookreview.com/essay/repetition-and-defamiliarization-in-ai-dungeon-and-project-december/

Mohaghegh, S., Dehnavi, M. A. R., Abdollahinejad, G., & Hashemi, M. (2023). *PCGPT: Procedural content generation via transformers*. https://arxiv.org/abs/2310.02405

Monnens, D., & Goldberg, M. (2015). Space Odyssey: The long journey of Spacewar! from MIT to computer labs around the world. Kinephanos. Revue d'études des médias et de culture populaire, 124-147.

Mubert. (2023). *A remarkably in-depth study of AI music: Creators, composers, adopters*. https://mubert.com/blog/an-in-depth-study-into-ai-music-its-creators-composers-and-adopters

Murnane, E. (2018). *Emergent Narrative: Stories of Play, Playing with Stories* (Doctoral dissertation, University of Central Florida). https://stars.library.ucf.edu/etd/5799

Murray, J. H. (2017). *Hamlet on the Holodeck: The Future of Narrative in Cyberspace*. MIT Press.

Mustač, K., Bačić, K., Skorin-Kapov, L., & Sužnjević, M. (2022). Predicting Player Churn of a Free-to-Play Mobile Video Game Using Supervised Machine Learning. *Applied Sciences (Basel, Switzerland)*, *12*(6), 2795. DOI: 10.3390/app12062795

Mystakidis, S. M. (2022). Metaverse. *Metaverse. Encyclopedia*, *2*(1), 486–497. DOI: 10.3390/encyclopedia2010031

Mystakidis, S., Besharat, J., Papantzikos, G., Christopoulos, A., Stylios, C., Agorgianitis, S., & Tselentis, D. (2022). Design, Development, and Evaluation of a Virtual Reality Serious Game for School Fire Preparedness Training. *Education Sciences, 12*(4), 281. DOI: 10.3390/educsci12040281

Nacke, L., Drachen, A., Kuikkaniemi, K., Niesenhaus, J., Korhonen, H. J., Hoogen, W. M., Poels, K., IJsselsteijn, W. A., & De Kort, Y. A. (2009). Playability and Player Experience Research. In Proceedings of the 2009 DiGRA International Conference: Breaking New Ground: Innovation in Games, Play, Practice and Theory, London, UK, 1–4 September 2009.

Newborn, M. (2014). *Computer chess.* Academic Press.

Nimo, J. R. A., & Ravishankar, K. (2024). *AI for Character Creation and Storytelling in Marketing*. Balancing Automation and Human Interaction in Modern Marketing., DOI: 10.4018/979-8-3693-2276-5.ch003

Nintendo. (n.d.). Mario Kart rubber-banding mechanics [Developer documentation]. Nintendo Co., Ltd. (Original work published across multiple years, 1992–2023). Retrieved October 30, 2025, from https://www.nintendo.com/mariokart/technical/

Noble, S. U. (2018). *Algorithms of Oppression: How Search Engines Reinforce Racism.* New York University Press. DOI: 10.18574/nyu/9781479833641.001.0001

Nong, Y., Sun, J. Q., & Wang, K. (2025). AI-Driven Procedural Content Generation for VR/AR Environments. *Authorea Preprints.* DOI: 10.36227/techrxiv.173747345.50267117/v1

NVIDIA Corporation. (2024). *NVIDIA brings generative AI for digital humans, new RTX technologies and more DLSS 3.5 games to GDC.* NVIDIA Corporation. https://blogs.nvidia.com/blog/generative-ai-digital-humans-rtx-dlss-gdc/

NVIDIA Corporation. (2025). *CUDA toolkit.* NVIDIA. https://developer.nvidia.com/cuda-toolkit

Oberlander, J., & Salge, C. (2019). Evolutionary Algorithms for Procedural Story Generation. *IEEE Transactions on Games, 11*(2), 157–166.

Ohnjec, K., Vuleta, D., Milanović, D., & Gruić, I. (2008). Performance Indicators of Teams at the 2003 World Handball Championship for Women in Croatia. *Kinesiology, 40*, 69–79.

Oliveira, J., Aires Dias, J., Correia, R., Pinheiro, R., Reis, V., Sousa, D., Agostinho, D., Simões, M., & Castelo-Branco, M. (2024). Exploring Immersive Multimodal Virtual Reality Training, Affective States, and Ecological Validity in Healthy Firefighters: Quasi-Experimental Study. *JMIR Serious Games*, *12*, e53683. DOI: 10.2196/53683 PMID: 39446479

Open, A. I. (2019). OpenAI Five for Dota 2 technical report [Technical report]. OpenAI. https://openai.com/research/openai-five

Open, A. I. (2024). *GPT-4o system card*. OpenAI. https://cdn.openai.com/gpt-4o-system-card.pdf

Open, A. I. (2024). GPT-AI as creative collaborator in game writing [Technical report]. OpenAI. https://openai.com/research/gpt-game-writing

Ortiz, A., Santiago, R. R., Hernández, D. E., & Lopez-Montiel, M. (2025). Multi-class Evaluation of Vision Transformers for Industrial Welding Defect Detection. *Mathematical & Computational Applications*, *30*(2), 24. DOI: 10.3390/mca30020024

Parnas, D. L. (2017). The real risks of artificial intelligence. *Communications of the ACM*, *60*(10), 27–31. DOI: 10.1145/3132724

Pascual, A., Font, R., Pascual, X., & Lago-Peñas, C. (2024). Evolution of match performance parameters in elite men's handball 2012–2022. *International Journal of Sports Science & Coaching*, *19*(1), 301–305.

Patel, R., Smith, A., & Jones, M. (2022). Cross-platform player modeling techniques. *Entertainment Computing*, *41*, 100467.

Pathos14489. (2024). *Pantella* [Computer software]. GitHub repository. https://github.com/Pathos14489/Pantella

Peddie, J. (2023). The first era of GPUs. In *The history of the GPU-eras and environment* (pp. 105–150). Springer International Publishing.

Peng, Y., Ma, Y., & Zhang, J. (2022). A Review of Transformer-Based Models for Procedural Narrative Generation. *Artificial Intelligence Review*, *55*(6), 4937–4971. PMID: 35002010

Pezoa, F., Reutter, J. L., Suarez, F., Ugarte, M., & Vrgoč, D. (2016). Foundations of JSON schema. *Proceedings of the 25th International Conference on World Wide Web*, 263–273. DOI: 10.1145/2872427.2883029

Pfandler, M., Lazarovici, M., Stefan, P., Wucherer, P., & Weigl, M. (2017). Virtual reality-based simulators for spine surgery: A systematic review. *The Spine Journal*, *17*(9), 1352–1363. DOI: 10.1016/j.spinee.2017.05.016 PMID: 28571789

Pietrzak, B., Pucci, S., & Cohen, A. (2020). Semantic reactor: A tool for experimenting with NLU models. *Google Open Source Blog*. https://opensource.googleblog.com/2020/03/semantic-reactor-tool-for-experimenting.html

Ponce, B. A., Jennings, J. K., Clay, T. B., May, M. B., Huisingh, C., & Sheppard, E. D. (2014). Telementoring: Use of augmented reality in orthopaedic education: AAOS exhibit selection. *The Journal of Bone and Joint Surgery. American Volume*, *96*(10), e84. DOI: 10.2106/JBJS.M.00928 PMID: 24875036

Pontes e Silva, F., Silva, M. P., & Chaimowicz, L. (2021). Hybrid DDA in platform games. *IEEE Transactions on Games*, *13*(4), 378–389.

Preuss, M., & Risi, S. (2020). A Games Industry Perspective on Recent Game AI Developments. KI Künstl. *Intell.*, *34*, 81–83.

Prieto, J., Gómez, M.-Á., Volossovitch, A., & Sampaio, J. (2016). Effects of Team Timeouts on the Teams' Scoring Performance in Elite Handball Close Games. *Kinesiology*, *48*(1), 115–123. DOI: 10.26582/k.48.1.4

Primanita, A., Effendi, R., & Hidayat, W. (2017). Comparison of A* and Iterative Deepening A Algorithms for Non-Player Character in Role Playing Game. In Proceedings of the 2017 International Conference on Electrical Engineering and Computer Science (ICECOS), Palembang, Indonesia, 22–23 August 2017; pp. 202–205. DOI: 10.1109/ICECOS.2017.8167134

Promethean, A. I. (2023). The AI Assistant for 3D World Building. [Online]. Available: https://prometheanai.com

Qadir, H. M., Suleman, M. T., Khan, R. A., Sohaib, M., Hasan, M. J., & Hussain, S. A. (2025). Optimizing learning outcomes: A deep dive into hybrid AI models for adaptive educational feedback. *Journal of Big Data*, *12*(1), 1–26. DOI: 10.1186/s40537-025-01187-6

Qayyum, A., Butt, M. A., Ali, H., Usman, M., Halabi, O., Al-Fuqaha, A., Abbasi, Q. H., Imran, M. A., & Qadir, J. (2023). Secure and Trustworthy Artificial Intelligence-extended Reality (AI-XR) for Metaverses [Review of *Secure and Trustworthy Artificial Intelligence-extended Reality (AI-XR) for Metaverses*]. *ACM Computing Surveys, 56*(7), 1. Association for Computing Machinery. https://doi.org/DOI: 10.1145/3614426

Rabii, Y., & Cook, M. (2023). Why oatmeal is cheap: Kolmogorov complexity and procedural generation. *Proceedings of the 18th International Conference on the Foundations of Digital Games*. https://doi.org/DOI: 10.1145/3582437.3582484

Radford, A., Wu, J., Child, R., Luan, D., Amodei, D., & Sutskever, I. (2019). Language Models Are Unsupervised Multitask Learners. *OpenAI*. https://cdn.openai.com/better-language-models/language_models_are_unsupervised_multitask_learners.pdf

Radford, A., Wu, J., Child, R., Luan, D., Amodei, D., & Sutskever, I. (2019). Language Models are Unsupervised Multitask Learners. *OpenAI Blog*, *1*(8), 9.

Rahouti, M., Ayyash, M., Jagatheesaperumal, S. K., & Oliveira, D. (2021). Incremental learning implementations and vision for cyber risk detection in iot. *IEEE Internet of Things Magazine*, *4*(3), 114–119. DOI: 10.1109/IOTM.0011.2100019

Raji, I. D., Smart, A., White, R. N., Mitchell, M., Gebru, T., Hutchinson, B., Smith-Loud, J., Theron, D., & Barnes, P. (2020). Closing the AI Accountability Gap: Defining an End-to-End Framework for Internal Algorithmic Auditing. In *Proceedings of the 2020 Conference on Fairness, Accountability, and Transparency* (pp. 33–44). Association for Computing Machinery. DOI: 10.1145/3351095.3372873

Ram, A., Ontañón, S., & Mehta, M. (2007, May). Artificial Intelligence for Adaptive Computer Games. In *FLAIRS* (pp. 22-29).

Ramesh, R., Venkatesh, M., & Girish, G. P. (2024). The Symbiosis of Ai and Human Agency in Digital Authorship: Redefining The Landscape Of Contemporary Literature. In Vasant, P. (Eds.), *Intelligent Computing and Optimization (ICO 2023)* (Vol. 874, pp. 255–262). Springer., DOI: 10.1007/978-3-031-50887-5_26

Rane, N., Choudhary, S., & Rane, J. (2024). "Machine Learning and Deep Learning: A Comprehensive Review on Methods, Techniques, Applications, Challenges, and Future Directions." Techniques, Applications & Future Research, pp. 1–20. DOI: DOI: 10.2139/ssrn.4850451

Ranjitha, M., Nathan, K., & Joseph, L. (2020). Artificial intelligence algorithms and techniques in the computation of player-adaptive games. [). IOP Publishing.]. *Journal of Physics: Conference Series*, *1427*(1), 012006. DOI: 10.1088/1742-6596/1427/1/012006

Rao, S. S., Loeb, A. E., Amin, R. M., Golladay, G. J., Levin, A. S., & Thakkar, S. C. (2020). Establishing Telemedicine in an Academic Total Joint Arthroplasty Practice: Needs and Opportunities Highlighted by the COVID-19 Pandemic. *Arthroplasty Today*, *6*(3), 617–622. DOI: 10.1016/j.artd.2020.04.014 PMID: 32328510

Rathore, B. (2022). Digital Transformation 4.0: Integration of Artificial Intelligence & Metaverse in Marketing. Eduzone Int. Peer Rev. Multidiscip. J. 2023, 12, 42–48. Soto, I.B.R.; Leon, N.S.S. How artificial intelligence will shape the future of metaverse. A qualitative perspective. *Metaverse Basic Appl. Res.*, *1*, 12.

Ray, P. P. (2023). ChatGPT: A Comprehensive Review on Background, Applications, Key Challenges, Bias, Ethics, Limitations and Future Scope. *Internet of Things and Cyber-Physical Systems*, *3*, 121–154. DOI: 10.1016/j.iotcps.2023.04.003

Reddy, R. (2005). The Origins of the American Association for Artificial Intelligence (AAAI). AI Magazine, 26(4), 5-12.

Reis, V., & Neves, C. Application of Virtual Reality Simulation in Firefighter Training for the Development of Decision-Making Competences. In *Proceedings of the 2019 International Symposium on Computers in Education (SIIE)*, Tomar, Portugal, 13–15 November 2019; pp. 1–6. DOI: 10.1109/SIIE48397.2019.8970143

Ribeiro, M. T., Singh, S., & Guestrin, C. (2016). "Why should I trust you?": Explaining the predictions of any classifier [Paper presentation]. Proceedings of the 22nd ACM SIGKDD International Conference on Knowledge Discovery and Data Mining (KDD '16), San Francisco, CA, United States.

Riedl, M. O., & Bulitko, V. (2012). Interactive narrative: A novel application of artificial intelligence for computer games. *Proceedings of the Twenty-Sixth AAAI Conference on Artificial Intelligence*, 2160–2165.

Riedl, M. O., & Bulitko, V. (2013). Interactive Narrative: An Intelligent Systems Approach. *AI Magazine*, *34*(1), 67–77. DOI: 10.1609/aimag.v34i1.2449

Risi, S., & Togelius, J. (2020). Increasing Generality in Machine Learning through Procedural Content Generation. *Nature Machine Intelligence*, *2*(8), 428–436. DOI: 10.1038/s42256-020-0208-z

Rodríguez-Suárez, J., Torres-Jorge, J. M., & Piñeiro-Vera, J. D. (2025). *Usage of large language models in videogames* [Computer software]. GitHub repository. https://github.com/Universidad-de-La-Laguna/esit-aigames-llm-in-videogames

Roohi, N., & Bidarra, R. (2021). Explainable AI for Game Design: A Review. *Entertainment Computing*, *37*, 100414.

Runway, M. L. (2023). AI for Creatives: Tools and Use Cases. [Online]. Available: https://runwayml.com

Ryan, H., Abramov, D., Acker, S., & Elkins, S. (2025). Can AI Be a Co-Author?: How Generative AI Challenges the Boundaries of Authorship in a General Education Writing Class. *Thresholds, 48*(1), 40-56. https://files.eric.ed.gov/fulltext/EJ1468037.pdf

Ryan, M. L. (2006). *Avatars of story*. University of Minnesota Press.

Saboury, B., Morris, M., & Siegel, E. (2021). Future Directions in Artificial Intelligence. *Radiologia Clinica, 59*(6), 1085–1095. DOI: 10.1016/j.rcl.2021.07.008 PMID: 34689876

Sadek, M., Constantinides, M., Quercia, D., & Mougenot, C. (2024). Guidelines for integrating value sensitive design in responsible AI toolkits. In *Proceedings of the 2024 CHI Conference on Human Factors in Computing Systems* (Article 472, pp. 1–20). Association for Computing Machinery. DOI: 10.1145/3613904.3642810

Salen, K., & Zimmerman, E. (2004). *Rules of Play: Game Design Fundamentals.* MIT Press.

Samal, A., & Misra, L. I. Mohit, Pougajendy, S, Chandel P S, Manjunath T C, & Selvakumar P. (2025). Musealization and Tourism Practices. In S. Oflazoğlu & M. Dora (Eds.), *Preserving Cultural Heritage in Post-Disaster Urban Renewal* (pp. 115-142). IGI Global Scientific Publishing. https://doi.org/DOI: 10.4018/979-8-3693-9097-9.ch006

Santiago, V. (2023). How to Use *AI Dungeon* to Create Interactive Stories. In MacDowell, P., Moskalyk, K., & Korchinski, K. (Eds.), *Teaching and Creating with Generative AI.* University of Saskatchewan., https://www.saskoer.ca/etad402teachingandcreatingwithgenai/chapter/vincent-santiago/

Sarkar, A., Momennejad, I., & Lake, B. M. (2023). Generative Agents: Interactive Simulacra of Human Behavior. arXiv preprint arXiv:2304.03442.

Sarkar, A., Guzdial, M., Snodgrass, S., Summerville, A., Machado, T., & Smith, G. (2023). Procedural content generation via knowledge transformation (PCG-KT). *IEEE Transactions on Games, 16*(1), 36–50. DOI: 10.1109/TG.2023.3270422

Sasse, L., Nicolaisen-Sobesky, E., Dukart, J., Eickhoff, S. B., Götz, M., Hamdan, S., Komeyer, V., Kulkarni, A., Lahnakoski, J. M., Love, B. C., Raimondo, F., & Patil, K. R. (2025). Overview of leakage scenarios in supervised machine learning. *Journal of Big Data, 12*(1), 1–23. DOI: 10.1186/s40537-025-01193-8

Sawyer, R. K. (2012). *Explaining Creativity: The Science of Human Innovation* (2nd ed.). Oxford University Press.

Scenario.gg. (2024). Interactive AI design assistant [Product documentation]. Scenario.gg. https://www.scenario.gg/ai-design-assistant

Schmidt, T., Bakkes, S., & Spronck, P. (2021). Ethical frameworks for digital game design. *Ethics and Information Technology, 23*(4), 567–579.

Seboek, T., Bakkes, S., & Roijers, D. (2020). Fairness in skill-based matchmaking. *IEEE Transactions on Games, 12*(4), 412–423.

Sepulveda, G. K., Besoain, F., & Barriga, N. A. (2019). Exploring Dynamic Difficulty Adjustment in Videogames. In Proceedings of the 2019 IEEE CHILEAN Conference on Electrical, Electronics Engineering, Information and Communication Technologies (CHILECON), Valparaiso, Chile, 13–27 November 2019; pp. 1–6.

Serbanescu, A. (2024). Human-AI System Co-creativity to Build Interactive Digital Narratives. In Zanella, F., Bosoni, G., Di Stefano, E., Iannilli, G. L., Matteucci, G., Messori, R., & Trocchianesi, R. (Eds.), *Multidisciplinary Aspects of Design. Design! OPEN 2022* (pp. 388–398). Springer., DOI: 10.1007/978-3-031-49811-4_37

Shafi, K., Lovecchio, F., Forston, K., Wyss, J., Casey, E., Press, J., Creighton, A., Sandhu, H., & Iyer, S. (2020). The Efficacy of Telehealth for the Treatment of Spinal Disorders: Patient-Reported Experiences during the COVID-19 Pandemic. *HSS Journal : the Musculoskeletal Journal of Hospital for Special Surgery, 16*(1_suppl), 17–23. DOI: 10.1007/s11420-020-09808-x PMID: 33169072

Shaker, N., Togelius, J., & Yannakakis, G. N. (2016). Procedural content generation in games. Springer. Andrade, G., Santana, H., & de Souza, J. (2019). Effects of adaptive difficulty on player engagement. *Entertainment Computing, 30*, 100294.

She, R., Wong, K., Lin, J., Leung, K., & Zhang, Y. (2021). How COVID-19 Stress Related to Schooling and Online Learning Affects Adolescent Depression and Internet Gaming Disorder: Testing Conservation of Resources Theory. *Journal of Behavioral Addictions, 10*(4), 953–966. DOI: 10.1556/2006.2021.00069 PMID: 34665762

Sheth, S., Baker, H. P., Prescher, H., & Strelzow, J. (2024). Ethical Considerations of Artificial Intelligence in Health Care: Examining the Role of Generative Pretrained Transformer-4. *The Journal of the American Academy of Orthopaedic Surgeons, 32*(5), 205–210. DOI: 10.5435/JAAOS-D-23-00787 PMID: 38175996

Short, E., Cook, M., & Smith, A. M. (2020). Procedural Generation of Video Game Levels Using Evolutionary Algorithms. *ACM Transactions on Multimedia Computing Communications and Applications, 16*(1s), 1–20.

Short, T. X., & Adams, T. (Eds.). (2019). *Procedural Storytelling in Game Design*. CRC Press. DOI: 10.1201/9780429488337

Shoulson, A. (2013). *Producing immersive interactive narratives in complex 3D open worlds*. AIIDE., DOI: 10.1609/aiide.v9i6.12604

Shrager, J. (2024). ELIZA Reinterpreted: The world's first chatbot was not intended as a chatbot at all. arXiv preprint arXiv:2406.17650.

Sicart, M. (2009). *The Ethics of Computer Games*. MIT Press. DOI: 10.7551/mitpress/9780262012652.001.0001

Sicart, M. (2013). *Beyond Choices: The Design of Ethical Gameplay*. MIT Press. DOI: 10.7551/mitpress/9052.001.0001

Silva, M., Silva, F., & Gomes, T. (2017). DDA in MOBA games. *Journal of Interactive Media, 16*(1), 45–60.

Silver, D., Schrittwieser, J., Simonyan, K., Antonoglou, I., Huang, A., Guez, A., Hubert, T., Baker, L., Lai, M., Bolton, A., Chen, Y., Lillicrap, T., Hui, F., Sifre, L., van den Driessche, G., Graepel, T., & Hassabis, D. (2017). Mastering the Game of Go without Human Knowledge. *Nature, 550*(7676), 354–359. DOI: 10.1038/nature24270 PMID: 29052630

Singh, R., Sharma, S., & Kumar, V. (2021). Green Communication Technology, IOT, VR, AR in Smart Environment. In *Cognitive Computing Using Green Technologies: Modeling Techniques and Applications* (p. 1). CRC Press. DOI: 10.1201/9781003121619-1-2

Smith, D. L., & Barr, D. A. (2017). Functional and psychological responses of firefighters to live-fire training. *Fire Technology, 53*, 1447–1465.

Smith, D. L., Horn, G. P., Petruzzello, S. J., Fahey, G., Woods, J., & Fernhall, B. (2014). Clotting and Fibrinolytic Changes after Firefighting Activities. *Medicine and Science in Sports and Exercise, 46*(3), 448–454. DOI: 10.1249/MSS.0b013e3182a76dd2 PMID: 23924919

Smith, G., & Mateas, M. (2011). Answer set programming for level design [Paper presentation]. *Proceedings of the 7th AAAI Conference on Artificial Intelligence and Interactive Digital Entertainment (AIIDE)*, Stanford, CA, United States.

Souchleris, K., Sidiropoulos, G. K., & Papakostas, G. A. (2023). Reinforcement learning in game industry—Review, prospects and challenges. *Applied Sciences (Basel, Switzerland), 13*(4), 2443. Advance online publication. DOI: 10.3390/app13042443

Soundful. (2024). *The role of AI music generation for content creators*. Blog post. https://soundful.com/ai-music-generation-content-creators/

Speicher, M., Hall, B. D., & Nebeling, M. What is mixed reality? In *Proceedings of the 2019 CHI Conference on Human Factors in Computing Systems*, Glasgow, Scotland, UK, 4–9 May 2019; pp. 1–15.

Sreekanthaswamy, N., Anitha, S., Singh, A., Jayadeva, S. M., Gupta, S., Manjunath, T. C., & Selvakumar, P. (2025). Digital Tools and Methods. In Çela, E., Paliktzoglou, V., Sengar, S., Eappen, P., & Vajjhala, N. (Eds.), *Enhancing School Counseling With Technology and Case Studies* (pp. 25–48). IGI Global Scientific Publishing., DOI: 10.4018/979-8-3693-8392-6.ch002

Stahl, B. C., & Eke, D. (2024). The Ethics of ChatGPT–Exploring the Ethical Issues of an Emerging Technology. *International Journal of Information Management*, *74*, 102700. Advance online publication. DOI: 10.1016/j.ijinfomgt.2023.102700

Stefan, H., Mortimer, M., & Horan, B. (2023). Evaluating the effectiveness of virtual reality for safety-relevant training: A systematic review. *Virtual Reality (Waltham Cross)*, *27*(4), 2839–2869. DOI: 10.1007/s10055-023-00843-7

Stephenson, E., & Renz, J. (2019). Adaptive level generation in Angry Birds [Paper presentation]. *Proceedings of the AAAI Conference on Artificial Intelligence and Interactive Digital Entertainment (AIIDE)*, Atlanta, GA, United States.

Strong, C. R., & Mateas, M. (2008). Talking with NPCs: Towards dynamic generation of discourse structures. *Proceedings of the National Conference on Artificial Intelligence*. https://doi.org/DOI: 10.1609/aiide.v4i1.18682

Summerville, A., Snodgrass, S., Guzdial, M., Holmgård, C., Hoover, A. K., Isaksen, A., Nealen, A., & Togelius, J. (2018). Procedural content generation via machine learning (PCGML). *IEEE Transactions on Games*, *10*(3), 257–270. DOI: 10.1109/TG.2018.2846639

Sumner, J. (2014). Defiance to compliance: Visions of the computer in postwar Britain. *History and Technology*, *30*(4), 309–333. DOI: 10.1080/07341512.2015.1008962

Sun, Y., Ni, X., Feng, H., Lc, R., Lee, C. H., & Asadipour, A. (2022). *Bringing stories to life in 1001 nights: A co-creative text adventure game using a story generation model*. 651–672. https://doi.org/DOI: 10.1007/978-3-031-22298-6_42

Tang, K.-Y., Chang, C.-Y., & Hwang, G.-J. (2021). Trends in artificial intelligence-supported e-learning: A systematic review and co-citation network analysis (1998–2019). *Interactive Learning Environments*, •••, 1–19.

Tatar, S., & Ali, A. (2018). Evaluating Procedural Generation Systems for Game Design. *Entertainment Computing*, *26*, 56–64.

Taylor-Giles, L. (2020). Player-centred design in role-playing game branching dialogue systems. In *Game developers and narrative design*. https://doi.org/DOI: 10.1007/978-3-030-37643-7_13

Þorgeirsson, S., Pic, M., Lozano, D., Sigurgeirsson, O., Sekulic, D., & Saavedra, J. M. (2022). Gender-Based Differences in Game-Related Statistics between Winning and Losing Teams in an Amateur Handball League. *Acta Gymnica, 52*, e2022. DOI: 10.5507/ag.2022.001

Þorgeirsson, S., Pic, M., Lozano, D., Sigurgeirsson, O., Sekulic, D., & Saavedra, J. M. (2022). The Difference Between Winners and Losers in Balanced Handball Games in the Final 10 Minutes. *Montenegrin Journal of Sports Science and Medicine, 11*(2), 37–43. DOI: 10.26773/mjssm.220905

Thorne, S. (2020). Hey Siri, Tell Me a story: Digital Storytelling and AI Authorship. *Convergence (London), 26*(4), 808–823. DOI: 10.1177/1354856520913866

Tiedemann, J., Aulamo, M., Bakshandaeva, D., Boggia, M., Grönroos, S.-A., Nieminen, T., Raganato, A., Scherrer, Y., Vazquez, R., & Virpioja, S. (2023). Democratizing neural machine translation with OPUS-MT. *Language Resources and Evaluation, 58*(2), 713–755. DOI: 10.1007/s10579-023-09704-w

Touvron, H., Lavril, T., Izacard, G., ... (2023). LLaMA: Open and Efficient Foundation Language Models. arXiv preprint arXiv:2302.13971.

Touvron, H., Lavril, T., Izacard, G., Martinet, X., Lachaux, M.-A., Lacroix, T., Rozière, B., Goyal, N., Hambro, E., Azhar, F., ... (2023). LLaMA: Open and efficient foundation language models. *arXiv Preprint arXiv:2302.13971.*

Treanor, M., & Mateas, M. (2013). An Account of Proceduralist Meaning. In *Proceedings of DiGRA 2013: DeFragging Game Studies*. Digital Games Research Association. https://scispace.com/pdf/an-account-of-proceduralist-meaning-49zpv2i2n8.pdf

Turing, A. M. (1980). Computing machinery and intelligence. Creative Computing, 6(1), 44-53.

Ubisoft. (2020). Rainbow Six Siege toxicity detection system [Technical blog post]. Ubisoft Entertainment. https://www.ubisoft.com/en-us/game/rainbow-six/siege/news-updates/toxicity-detection

Unity Technologies. (2018). Unity ML-Agents Toolkit white paper [White paper]. Unity Technologies. https://github.com/Unity-Technologies/ml-agents/blob/master/docs/ML-Agents-Overview.pdf

Unity Technologies. (2022). ML-Agents Toolkit: Using Reinforcement Learning in Unity Games. [Online]. Available: https://github.com/Unity-Technologies/ml-agents

Unity Technologies. (2023). AI-assisted co-design in Unity Editor [White paper]. Unity Technologies. https://unity.com/resources/ai-assisted-codesign

Usha, S. G. A., Maheswari, P. U., & Bharathi, K. (2025). *Next-Generation Image Enhancement and Restoration With Artificial Intelligence*. Modern Intelligent Techniques for Image Processing., DOI: 10.4018/979-8-3693-9045-0.ch010

Valve. (2008). Left 4 Dead AI Director technical documentation [Technical report]. Valve Corporation. https://developer.valvesoftware.com/wiki/AI_Director

Valve. (2022). For Honor live balancing via reinforcement learning [Developer update]. Valve Corporation. https://news.ubisoft.com/en-us/article/for-honor-ai-balancing-2022

van Assen, M., Muscogiuri, E., Tessarin, G., & De Cecco, C. N. (2022). Artificial intelligence: A century-old story. In *Artificial Intelligence in Cardiothoracic Imaging* (pp. 3–13). Springer International Publishing. DOI: 10.1007/978-3-030-92087-6_1

Van Der Linden, R., Lopes, R., & Bidarra, R. (2013). Procedural generation of dungeons. *IEEE Transactions on Computational Intelligence and AI in Games*, *6*(1), 78–89. DOI: 10.1109/TCIAIG.2013.2290371

Vaswani, A., Shazeer, N., Parmar, N., Uszkoreit, J., Jones, L., Gomez, A. N., Kaiser, Ł., & Polosukhin, I. (2017). Attention Is All You Need. In *Proceedings of the 31st International Conference on Neural Information Processing Systems (NIPS'17)* (pp. 6000–6010). Curran Associates Inc. https://proceedings.neurips.cc/paper_files/paper/2017/file/3f5ee243547dee91fbd053c1c4a845aa-Paper.pdf

Vaswani, A., Shazeer, N., Parmar, N., Uszkoreit, J., Jones, L., Gomez, A. N., Kaiser, Ł., & Polosukhin, I. (2017). Attention is all you need. *Advances in Neural Information Processing Systems*, *30*, 5998–6008.

Vaz, V., Ferrari, W., Sarmento, H., Couceiro, M., Sousa, T., & Dias, G. (2023). Handball Offensive Analysis: Comparative Evolution of Linear Tendency Lines between Finalist Teams in the EHF CL. *Applied Sciences (Basel, Switzerland)*, *13*(3), 1366. DOI: 10.3390/app13031366

Veloso, C., & Prada, R. (2021). *Validating the plot of interactive narrative games*. IEEE Cognitive Systems., DOI: 10.1109/CoG52621.2021.9618897

Verma, A., Sankhyayan, S., Jawanda, K., & Tandon, S. N. (2025). Generative Artificial Intelligence and Cybersecurity Risks: Issues and Challenges. In *Lecture notes in networks and systems* (p. 321). Springer International Publishing. https://doi.org/DOI: 10.1007/978-981-97-8602-2_29

Volz, V., Schrum, J., Liu, J., Lucas, S. M., & Smith, A. M. (2018). MarioGAN: Playable level generation with GANs [Paper presentation]. *Proceedings of the IEEE Conference on Computational Intelligence and Games (CIG)*, Maastricht, Netherlands.

Wagner, H., Hinz, M., Melcher, K., Radic, V., & Uhrmeister, J. (2023). The PlayerScore: A Systematic Game Observation Tool to Determine Individual Player Performance in Team Handball Competition. *Applied Sciences (Basel, Switzerland), 13*(4), 2327. DOI: 10.3390/app13042327

Wang, G. (2019). *Humans in the Loop: The Design of Interactive AI Systems*. Blog Post. https://hai.stanford.edu/news/humans-loop-design-interactive-ai-systems

Wang, J. Y. (2015). A Variety Weapons and Armors Design Algorithm for Role-Playing Games. In Proceedings of the 2015 IEEE/ACIS 16th International Conference on Software Engineering, Artificial Intelligence, Networking and Parallel/Distributed Computing (SNPD), Takamatsu, Japan, 1–3 June 2015; pp. 1–5.

Wang, Y. (2023). "Synthetic Realities in the Digital Age: Navigating the Opportunities and Challenges of AI-Generated Content." *TechRxiv*, pp. 1–20. DOI: DOI: 10.36227/techrxiv.23968311.v1

Weidinger, J. (2022). What Is Known and What Remains Unexplored: A Review of the Firefighter Information Technologies Literature. *International Journal of Disaster Risk Reduction, 78*, 103115. DOI: 10.1016/j.ijdrr.2022.103115

Will, A. I. (2012). The Manifest Destiny of Artificial Intelligence.

Williams-Bell, F. M., Kapralos, B., Hogue, A., Murphy, B., & Weckman, E. (2015). Using serious games and virtual simulation for training in the fire service: A review. *Fire Technology, 51*(3), 553–584. DOI: 10.1007/s10694-014-0398-1

Williams, J. P., Hendricks, S. Q., & Winkler, W. K. (2014). *Gaming as Culture: Essays on Reality, Identity and Experience in Fantasy Games*. McFarland.

Wu, J., Chen, X., & Zhang, Y. (2020). Dynamic offer optimization via contextual bandits. *IEEE Transactions on Games, 12*(1), 89–98.

Wu, Z., Ji, D., Yu, K., Zeng, X., Wu, D., & Shidujaman, M. (2021). AI Creativity and the Human-AI Co-creation Model. In Kurosu, M. (Ed.), *Human-Computer Interaction. Theory, Methods and Tools - HCII 2021* (pp. 171–190). Springer., DOI: 10.1007/978-3-030-78462-1_13

Xiao, C., & Yang, B. Z. (2024). *LLMs may not be human-level players, but they can be testers: Measuring game difficulty with LLM agents*. https://arxiv.org/abs/2410.02829

Xu, Y., Feng, D., Zhao, M., Sun, Y., & Xia, X. (2023). Edge Intelligence Empowered Metaverse: Architecture, Technologies, and Open Issues. *IEEE Network, 37*(6), 92–100. DOI: 10.1109/MNET.2023.3317477

Yan, C., Wu, T., Huang, K., He, J., Liu, H., Hong, Y., & Wang, B. (2021). The Application of Virtual Reality in Cervical Spinal Surgery: A Review. *World Neurosurgery*, *145*, 108–113. DOI: 10.1016/j.wneu.2020.09.040 PMID: 32931993

Yang, G., Wang, J., Zhang, Y., Tang, Y., & Cui, S. (2023). A Survey of Diffusion Models in Generative AI. arXiv preprint arXiv:2307.09004.

Yannakakis, G. N., & Togelius, J. (2018). Artificial intelligence and games. Springer. Bakkes, S., Tan, C. T., & Pisan, Y. (2012). Player modeling for adaptive difficulty adjustment [Paper presentation]. Proceedings of the 8th AAAI Conference on Artificial Intelligence and Interactive Digital Entertainment (AIIDE), Stanford, CA, United States. Canossa, A., & Drachen, A. (2011). Player behavior analysis using telemetry [Paper presentation]. Game Developers Conference (GDC), San Francisco, CA, United States.

Yannakakis, G. N., & Togelius, J. (2011). Experience-Driven Procedural Content Generation. *IEEE Transactions on Affective Computing*, *2*(3), 147–161. DOI: 10.1109/T-AFFC.2011.6

Yannakakis, G. N., & Togelius, J. (2025). *Artificial Intelligence and Games* (2nd ed.). Springer. DOI: 10.1007/978-3-031-83347-2

Yi, Q., He, Y., Wang, J., Song, X., Qian, S., Yuan, X., Sun, L., Xin, Y., Tang, J., Li, K., Lu, K., Huo, M., Chen, J., & Shi, T. (2025). SCORE: Story Coherence and Retrieval Enhancement for AI Narratives. *arXiv*. /arXiv.2503.23512DOI: 10.2139/ssrn.5243040

Yin, K., He, Z., Xiong, J., Zou, J., Li, K., & Wu, S. T. (2021). Virtual reality and augmented reality displays: Advances and future perspectives. *JPhys Photonics*, *3*(2), 022010. DOI: 10.1088/2515-7647/abf02e

Yoo, J. S., Patel, D. S., Hrynewycz, N. M., Brundage, T. S., & Singh, K. (2019). The utility of virtual reality and augmented reality in spine surgery. *Annals of Translational Medicine*, *7*(S5, Suppl. 5), S171. DOI: 10.21037/atm.2019.06.38 PMID: 31624737

Zhai, X., Chu, X., Chai, C. S., Jong, M. S. Y., Istenic, A., Spector, M., Liu, J.-B., Yuan, J., & Li, Y. (2021). A Review of Artificial Intelligence (AI) in Education from 2010 to 2020. *Complexity*, *2021*(1), 8812542. DOI: 10.1155/2021/8812542

Zhang, K., & Aslan, A. B. (2021). AI Technologies for Education: Recent Research & Future Directions. *Computers and Education: Artificial Intelligence*, *2*, 100025. Advance online publication. DOI: 10.1016/j.caeai.2021.100025

Zhang, Y., Liu, H., & Wang, L. (2023). Real-time inference optimization for games. *ACM Transactions on Graphics*, *42*(4), 123.

Zhan, T., Zou, J., Xiong, J., Liu, X., Chen, H., Yang, J., Liu, S., Dong, Y., & Wu, S. T. (2020). Practical Chromatic Aberration Correction in Virtual Reality Displays Enabled by Cost-Effective Ultra-Broadband Liquid Crystal Polymer Lenses. *Advanced Optical Materials*, *8*(2), 1901360. DOI: 10.1002/adom.201901360

Zhao, Y., Jiang, J., Chen, Y., Liu, R., Yang, Y., Xue, X., & Chen, S. (2022). Metaverse: Perspectives from graphics, interactions and visualization. *Visual Informatics*, *6*(1), 56–67. DOI: 10.1016/j.visinf.2022.03.002

Zhu, X. (2019). Behavior tree design of intelligent behavior of non-player character (NPC) based on Unity3D. *Journal of Intelligent & Fuzzy Systems*, *37*(5), 6071–6079. DOI: 10.3233/JIFS-179190

Zohaib, M. (2018). Dynamic Difficulty Adjustment (DDA) in Computer Games: A Review. *Advances in Human-Computer Interaction*, *2018*, 5681652. DOI: 10.1155/2018/5681652

Zou, D., Huang, Y., & Xie, H. (2021). Digital game-based vocabulary learning: Where are we and where are we going? *Computer Assisted Language Learning*, *34*(5-6), 751–777. DOI: 10.1080/09588221.2019.1640745

About the Contributors

João Paulo Sousa is graduated in Electrical and Computer Engineering from UTAD University. After three years, he gets a Master's degree in Engineering Technology. He received his Ph.D. degree in Computer Science at UTAD University. He published dozen of publications in international journals and conferences. He served as Chair of Videojogos2020 - 12th International Conference on Videogame Sciences and Arts and is on several scientific committees of international journals and conferences. His research activities concern video games, serious games, gamification, and artificial intelligence. He was the director of the Computer and Communications bachelor's and Games Design bachelor's degree at Polytechnic Institute of Bragança (IPB), and director of ESACT's IT Resource Center. Currently is an Adjunct Professor at Polytechnic Institute of Bragança (IPB) and an internal member of the Research Centre in Digitalization and Intelligent Robotics (CeDRI), Instituto Politécnico de Bragança. He was recently elected director of the Master in Design and Development of Digital Games.

Rogério Junior Correia Tavares is adjunct professor at IPB - Instituto Politécnico de Bragança. Holds 112 participations in boards and judging committees, 77 short courses taught, 74 participations in events, 32 published works, 30 event organizations and 22 paper presentations. Works in the Humanities area with an emphasis on Arts. Technology and Design. He lived in Brazil so his Lattes Curriculum is more complete, but he is gradually updating the Portuguese curriculum Ciência Vitae.

Syed Ibad Ali is an Innovative Professor holding Doctor of Philosophy in electronics & communication engineering with Fourteen years of experience and bringing proven success in implementing technology-based curriculum delivery & assessment tools.

Kush Bhushanwar is an Assistant Professor in Department of CSE-Artificial Intelligence and Machine Learning at Parul Institute of Engineering and Technology, Parul University, Vadodara. They have 15 years of Teaching experience. They had a PhD awarded in 2024. They have completed M.Tech in 2013 in Computer Science and Engineering. They have published 2 books, 3 book chapters and over 20 research paper. They have reviewed over 50 research paper for various national and international conferences.

Aparajita Biswal is currently serving as an Assistant Professor in the Department of Computer Science and Engineering at Parul University, Vadodara. She holds a postgraduate degree from Atmiya Institute of Technology & Science, specializing in Computer Networking and the Internet of Things (IoT). With a strong academic background and a passion for innovative teaching, she has contributed significantly to research in areas such as intelligent systems and data-driven forecasting. Aparajita is the lead author of the research paper titled "Intelligent Stock Price Prediction: A Data-Driven Forecasting System." Her current research interests focus on effective teaching methodologies, IoT applications, and the integration of emerging technologies in education. She is actively involved in mentoring students and developing curriculum strategies that bridge the gap between theoretical knowledge and practical application. Aparajita's dedication to academic excellence and interdisciplinary research continues to impact both her students and the broader academic community.

Jörg Burbach is a Professor of Game Design at IU International University of Applied Sciences, specializing in development and game history. He studied at the Cologne Game Lab (TH Köln), where his master's thesis, The Future Perspectives of Point & Click Adventures, predicted a resurgence of the genre. His lectures often explore the enduring value of retro games and what contemporary developers can learn from them. Since 2015, he has led his own studio, Ducks on the Water, which focuses on games, apps, and digital concepts. On his website, he blogs about technology, AI, and game culture. His publications include Das Kreative Volumen (with Nadine Trautzsch) and the forthcoming Das ultimative Buch zu Point & Click-Adventures, both published by Springer in 2025.

Satheesh Kumar D is working as Associate Professor in Department of Artificial Intelligence and Machine Learning, at Hindusthan College of Engineering and Technology, Coimbatore. He has completed Ph.D at Anna University, Chennai, M.E. Software Engineering at Anna University Coimbatore, and B.E Computer science and Engineering at Anna University. He has 19 years of experience in teaching and published 45 papers in reputed international journals. He also published 7 books and 12 patterns.

Cátia Ferreira holds a PhD in Communication Studies from Universidade Católica Portuguesa. Currently, she is Assistant Professor at the Faculty of Human Sciences, at Universidade Católica Portuguesa. She is a main researcher at CECC (Research Centre for Communication and Culture) and collaborating researcher at CETAPS (Centre for English, Translation, and Anglo-Portuguese Studies). Her research and teaching areas focus on media studies, in particular digital media: digital games, audiovisual and multimedia communication, and emerging strategies for content production, such as transmedia and cross-media.

Pallavi Jaggi is an Assistant Professor in the Department of Management at Chandigarh School of Business, Chandigarh Group of Colleges, Jhanjeri. She holds a Ph.D. in Marketing Management from University Business School, Panjab University, Chandigarh (2023) and has qualified UGC NET in Commerce three times. She completed her Master's and Bachelor's degrees in Commerce with a specialization in Management. With over 4.5 years of teaching and four years of research experience, she has previously worked at SRM University and Chandigarh University, where she also served as Programme Coordinator. Dr. Jaggi has published nine research papers in Scopus-indexed, UGC CARE-listed, and peer-reviewed journals and presented more than 15 papers at national and international conferences. Her teaching interests include marketing, management, research, entrepreneurship, and economics. She is known for her student-centric approach and was awarded "Best Team Player" in an administrative role.

T.C. Manjunath was born on 6th February 1967. He did his BE from RV College of Engg. in 1989, ME in Robotics & Automation from LD College of Engg. in 1992 with First Rank and PhD in Systems & Control Engg. from IIT Bombay in the year 2007. He is currently working as the Dean Research R D and as Professor in the Dept. of Computer Science & Engineering with specialization in IoT, Cyber Security & Blockchain Technology in Rajarajeswari College of Engineering, Bengaluru, Karnataka. He has completed B.E. Degree from R.V. College of Engg., M.E. Govt.'s LD College of Engg., Gujarat Univ., Ahmedabad in First Rank and Ph.D. in Systems and Control Engineering from the Indian Institute of Technology Bombay IIT Bombay He has got a teaching academic, research and administrative experience of more than 35+ years 10 years as Principal, 8 years as HoD rest as faculty and has published more than 1200+ research papers in various national & international journals and conferences, with 175+ patents, 25 book-chapters, 25 awards and also published 25 text books in various field of science, engineering and technology, completed projects worth Rs. 9 Crores till date apart from guiding 10 PhD scholars. He is a member of 30 Professional Society Chapters and is a fellow of IE, IETE, AMIEE and a chartered engineer. He got the best research scholar award in 2006 in IIT Bombay amongst all the research scholars of the institute. He has got 10 awards in academics and research activities.

P. Selvakumar is currently an Associate Professor in the Department of Science and Humanities at Nehru Institute of Technology, Coimbatore, Tamil Nadu, India. Prior to joining Nehru Institute of Technology, he held positions as an Assistant Professor in the Department of Science and Humanities various engineering colleges in Coimbatore, Tamil Nadu, India, spanning from 2011 to 2023. Dr.P. Selvakumar's academic and research interests lie primarily in the field of phytochemistry. He has made significant contributions to his field, with an impressive record that includes 30 journal publications, 12 patents, and 20 conference papers. Additionally, he has organized 5 seminars and conferences, further demonstrating his commitment to academic and scientific exchange. Throughout his career, Dr. P.Selvakumar has been recognized for his dedication and excellence in teaching, having been honored with several awards, including the Best Teacher Awards. He holds a prominent position in the academic community, contributing actively to research.

Parag Paija is currently working as an Assistant Professor at B.H. Gardi College of Engineering and Technology, Rajkot, with over a decade of experience in teaching and research in Mechanical Engineering. They have completed their B.E. in Mechatronics from G.H. Patel College, Vidhyanagar, and earned their M.Tech in CAD/CAM (Mechanical) from Nirma University, where they were awarded a Gold Medal for academic excellence. They have guided numerous undergraduate and postgraduate projects, focusing on practical, industry-oriented solutions. They have published several research papers in reputed journals and conferences and have been awarded for their research contributions at the institutional level. Their expertise lies in CAD/CAM, machine design, product development, and innovative mechanical systems. They are passionate about integrating modern technologies such as 3D printing, sustainable mobility solutions, and design automation into both teaching and research. They strongly believe in a student-centric teaching approach and strive to mentor students in building problem-solving and innovation-driven mindsets.

Damodharan Palaniappan works as an Associate Professor & Head in the Department of Information Technology, Marwadi University, Rajkot, Gujarat. He completed his Ph.D. at Anna University, Chennai, M.E. in Computer Science and Engineering at C.I.E.T, Coimbatore and B.E. in Computer Science and Engineering at CSI College of Engineering, Ketty, Nilgiri. He has 19 years' experience of teaching and research. Currently, he guides 6 Ph.D. research scholars. He has authored 8 book chapters, and he has published research papers in reputed journals. His interested areas of research are Data Mining, Image Processing, Software, Machine Learning and Deep Learning.

José D. Piñeiro is an Associate Professor at the University of La Laguna, where he currently teaches courses related to computer architecture and video games. His research interests focus on applications of Artificial Intelligence and Machine Learning, with a particular emphasis on artificial neural networks applied to areas such as medical diagnosis, computer vision, robotics and video games.

Prangya Parimita Pradhan an Assistant Professor in the Department of Electrical and Electronics Engineering at Centurion University of Technology and Management (CUTM). She holds an M.Tech and Ph.D. in Electrical Engineering from the prestigious National Institute of Technology (NIT) Rourkela. Her research interests lie in the areas of Renewable Energy Systems and Smart Grid Technologies, where she continues to contribute through teaching, research, and academic mentorship.

Juan Rodríguez-Suárez graduated in Computer Engineering from the University of La Laguna (2021–2025) with multiple honors and the Excellence Award. His final degree project focused on developing a video game prototype that integrated language models—both locally and in the cloud—to interpret character dialogues based on assigned "character profiles." The research explored how dialogue generation and model capabilities evolve over time, with the goal of enhancing various aspects of player accessibility and interaction.

S. Poorani is currently working as an Assistant Professor in the Department of Computer Technology - UG, Kongu Engineering College, Tamilnadu, India. She has 19 years of teaching experience. She published 22 articles in International journals and conferences. Her area of interest includes data mining, machine learning and deep learning.

Mohit Sharma is a research scholar at the Institute of Management Studies and Research, Maharshi Dayanand University, Rohtak, Haryana, India. His research focuses on the dynamic relationship between brand image and purchase intentions, particularly in the context of brand extensions within the FMCG sector. He has co-authored several scholarly works and continues to contribute to the academic community. Mohit can be reached at mohitattri.rs.imsar@mdurohtak.ac.in

Ayush Shekhar, a Computer Science graduate with a focus on Artificial Intelligence from Marwadi University, Rajkot (CPI: 8.91, 2025). They are passionate about building smart systems, exploring machine learning, and solving real-world problems with data. Their journey includes hands-on work in AI, IoT, and intelligent automation, along with published book chapters in the field of AI and IoT.

Premavathi T is an Assistant Professor in the Department of Computer Engineering – Artificial Intelligence at Marwadi University, Rajkot, Gujarat. A distinguished academic, she earned her M.E. in Software Engineering with Distinction from Anna University and is currently pursuing her Ph.D. at Marwadi University. With over 15 years of academic experience, she is a leading expert in Machine Learning, Deep Learning, and various core computer engineering subjects. She is a dedicated mentor who actively guides students, supervises academic projects, and spearheads research and innovation. Her impressive academic profile includes 31 book chapters, 5 patents, and 5 research articles, 2 of which was published in a prestigious SCI-indexed journal. Her recent conference paper also received a Best Paper Award. She has presented and published her work at five national and international conferences. Additionally, she is a proud member of both the IEEE and ISTE, further solidifying her commitment to the academic and technical communities.

Kaushalya Thopate is an Assistant Professor in the Computer Engineering Department at Vishwakarma Institute of Technology. With a strong academic background and research focus on AI, they have contributed to several innovative studies in their field. Dr. Kaushalya Thopate has published multiple papers and actively collaborates with both industry and academic researchers. Their work emphasizes the practical applications of technology to address real-world challenges in relevant sectors like education, health, or engineering. They are dedicated to fostering academic growth and mentoring students in their journey toward research and innovation.

Jesús Miguel Torres Jorge is an associate professor at University of La Laguna and the Academic Director of the Master's degree in Game Development. He mainly teaches subjects about operating systems, game development and virtual reality. Also, he is a researcher focused on the applications of machine learning and deep learning to prediction, classification and data analysis, mainly in areas like energy, health, games and tourism.

Vinod Waiker is a full time Researcher and an Academician having a vast experience of more than 20 years. He has authored some of book titled ERP Implementation-Issues and Challenges, Data Science and Logistics-The Road

Ahead. He is also author of many peer-reviewd, scopus indexed reserch paper as a contribution in a research domain.

Khyati Zalawadia Associate Professor, Parul Institute of Engineering and Technology (PIET) Dr. Khyati Zalawadia is an accomplished academician and Associate Professor at Parul Institute of Engineering and Technology, Parul University. With over two decades of experience in teaching, curriculum development, and academic leadership, she specializes in Electronics and Communication Engineering with a strong focus on emerging technologies. She plays a key role in implementing Outcome-Based Education (OBE), integrating NPTEL MOOCs into core curricula, and fostering innovation through hands-on and project-based learning. Under her academic coordination, PIET's NPTEL Local Chapter earned an AAA rating and ranked among the top 20 chapters in India. Dr. Zalawadia has organized and led multiple Faculty Development Programs (FDPs) and workshops on Industry 5.0, Blockchain, IoT, AI-based applications, and REST API Development. She teaches a wide range of subjects including Internet of Things (IoT), Image Processing, Digital Electronics, and Business Analytics. She has guided numerous student projects on AI, embedded systems, and smart applications and also contributes to foundational education by designing worksheets for school-level learners. Publications Dr. Khyati Zalawadia has published more than 20 research papers in reputed international journals and conferences, covering areas such as: • Internet of Things (IoT) and Smart Systems • Blockchain Applications in Engineering • Artificial Intelligence and Education • Digital Signal & Image Processing

Index

Symbols

3D Reconstruction 7, 8, 9, 314

A

Adaptive Difficulty 37, 47, 50, 60, 61, 66, 67, 72, 247
Adaptive Game Systems 26
Adaptive Level Design 212, 217
AI 1, 2, 3, 4, 6, 7, 9, 15, 16, 17, 25, 27, 28, 29, 34, 35, 36, 40, 41, 42, 43, 44, 47, 48, 49, 50, 51, 52, 53, 54, 55, 56, 57, 58, 59, 60, 61, 63, 64, 65, 66, 67, 68, 69, 71, 72, 73, 75, 76, 77, 78, 79, 80, 84, 85, 87, 88, 89, 90, 91, 92, 93, 94, 96, 97, 98, 99, 100, 101, 102, 103, 104, 105, 106, 107, 108, 109, 110, 111, 112, 113, 114, 115, 116, 117, 118, 119, 120, 121, 122, 123, 124, 125, 126, 128, 129, 130, 131, 132, 134, 135, 136, 137, 138, 139, 140, 141, 142, 152, 158, 159, 166, 168, 169, 170, 171, 172, 173, 174, 177, 179, 180, 182, 183, 184, 185, 186, 187, 188, 189, 190, 191, 192, 193, 194, 195, 196, 197, 198, 199, 200, 201, 202, 203, 205, 206, 207, 208, 210, 211, 213, 214, 215, 216, 217, 218, 220, 221, 222, 223, 224, 225, 226, 227, 228, 229, 230, 231, 232, 233, 235, 236, 237, 238, 239, 240, 241, 242, 243, 244, 245, 246, 247, 248, 249, 254, 255, 256, 257, 259, 260, 261, 262, 263, 264, 265, 266, 267, 268, 269, 270, 271, 272, 273, 274, 275, 276, 277, 278, 279, 281, 282, 283, 284, 285, 286, 287, 288, 289, 290, 291, 292, 293, 294, 295, 296, 297, 298, 299, 300, 301, 302, 303, 304, 305, 306, 307, 308, 311, 312, 313, 314, 315, 316, 317, 318, 319, 320, 321, 322, 323, 324, 325, 329, 330, 331, 332, 333, 334, 335, 336, 337, 338, 339, 340, 341, 342, 343, 344, 345, 346, 347, 348, 349, 350
AI Dungeon 87, 88, 90, 93, 98, 99, 100, 101, 103, 104, 105, 110, 111, 112, 114, 115, 118, 119, 120, 121, 210, 211, 216, 220, 226, 227, 297
Artificial Intelligence 1, 3, 9, 20, 21, 22, 25, 51, 52, 60, 61, 63, 64, 69, 72, 81, 82, 83, 84, 85, 87, 119, 121, 124, 126, 129, 172, 173, 175, 180, 202, 205, 206, 224, 231, 233, 234, 235, 236, 237, 238, 239, 240, 241, 245, 246, 247, 248, 249, 253, 254, 255, 256, 257, 259, 260, 261, 268, 269, 270, 271, 277, 278, 279, 280, 282, 283, 284, 293, 304, 306, 307, 308, 309, 312, 314, 317, 322, 323, 329, 331, 337, 339, 341, 343, 345, 347, 348, 349, 350
Augmented Reality 1, 2, 6, 9, 18, 19, 20, 21, 23, 239, 249, 254, 294, 343, 346

B

Bi-stacked GRU 1, 6, 7, 9, 15, 16, 17
Bi-Stacked LSTM 69, 70, 72, 73, 75, 80

C

Co-Authorship 87, 88, 90, 91, 92, 96, 98, 100, 103, 104, 105, 107, 108, 109, 110, 111, 113, 115, 122, 198
co-creativity 90, 121, 180, 182, 186, 197, 203
Cognitive Assemblage 96, 99, 122

D

DAW 188, 189
Dialogue Systems 123, 124, 125, 126, 127, 129, 131, 132, 133, 136, 137, 140, 142, 143, 147, 151, 157, 160, 167, 168, 169, 170, 171, 176, 177, 178, 217, 338
Diffusion Models 56, 205, 207, 211, 212, 215, 222, 224, 232, 311, 315
Dynamic Game Balancing 25, 28, 29, 63,

69, 70, 71, 72, 73

E

Editorial Intervention 87, 95, 103, 107, 111, 115, 122
Ergodic Literature 90, 94, 110, 116
Extended Reality 1, 2, 6, 9, 253, 254, 321, 323

F

Feature Selection 6, 7, 8, 9, 17, 69, 70, 71, 72, 80

G

Game AI 49, 84, 124, 132, 270, 285, 286, 288, 291, 303
game audio 179, 180, 181, 183, 190, 193, 199, 201, 335, 336, 337
game design 26, 27, 28, 32, 41, 47, 48, 49, 60, 66, 67, 87, 97, 101, 105, 110, 111, 115, 117, 118, 119, 121, 124, 126, 135, 136, 159, 173, 179, 186, 196, 200, 201, 202, 205, 206, 208, 214, 215, 221, 224, 226, 229, 231, 232, 233, 235, 236, 238, 241, 245, 260, 279, 293, 297, 302, 303, 304, 305, 315
Game Narratives 242, 246
Game Optimization 34, 71
Gaming 25, 38, 43, 46, 50, 52, 57, 58, 64, 65, 73, 85, 131, 136, 141, 151, 161, 165, 170, 206, 221, 222, 233, 234, 235, 236, 237, 238, 239, 240, 244, 245, 246, 247, 248, 249, 250, 251, 252, 253, 254, 255, 259, 261, 270, 274, 276, 277, 278, 279, 287, 288, 292, 293, 294, 296, 298, 299, 300, 301, 302, 303, 304, 306, 308, 311, 312, 314, 315, 317, 326, 328, 329, 330, 331, 333, 334, 335, 342, 343, 344, 345, 347, 348, 349
Generative AI 87, 88, 90, 92, 94, 96, 98, 99, 100, 112, 114, 116, 117, 120, 121, 122, 129, 136, 138, 141, 172, 174, 180, 182, 183, 191, 193, 196, 205, 207, 208, 210, 214, 215, 216, 217, 218, 222, 227, 228, 229, 232, 233, 236, 239, 240, 242, 243, 244, 245, 261, 266, 276, 279, 289, 290, 291, 292, 293, 296, 297, 298, 299, 302, 303, 311, 312, 314, 315, 316, 317, 318, 319, 321, 322, 323, 324, 337, 347
Generative AI in Game Design 297, 302
Generative music 179, 180, 182, 184, 186, 187, 189, 192, 196, 201

I

Immersive Gaming 239
Interactive Narrative 87, 88, 91, 98, 112, 115, 118, 120, 124, 125, 132, 134, 171, 175, 176

L

Large Language Models 93, 96, 97, 98, 112, 124, 168, 172, 175, 234, 242, 282, 290, 297, 307, 311, 315, 320, 340, 350
Ludonarrative Agency 87, 91, 94, 95, 96, 100, 114, 115, 122

M

Machine Learning 25, 28, 29, 30, 34, 42, 44, 48, 49, 50, 51, 52, 57, 65, 68, 71, 81, 83, 117, 119, 133, 172, 175, 196, 214, 217, 228, 231, 234, 238, 244, 245, 247, 256, 267, 269, 270, 272, 274, 275, 277, 282, 289, 299, 305, 309, 313, 320, 331, 332, 338, 341, 342, 347, 349
Metaverse 6, 19, 21, 22, 23, 248, 252, 311, 312, 313, 314, 315, 317, 318, 319, 320, 321, 322, 323, 324
Mixed Reality 1, 2, 6, 9, 22, 313

N

Narrative Drift 87, 90, 102, 103, 105, 106, 113, 115, 122, 130, 131
Natural Language Processing 47, 124, 132, 136, 169, 211, 215, 237, 238, 256, 257,

275, 278, 330, 338

P

Particle Swarm Optimization 6, 7, 8, 9
Player Agency 87, 89, 90, 91, 94, 97, 98, 103, 115, 124, 125, 126, 133, 134, 135, 168, 216, 220, 291, 304
Player Behavior Modeling 25
Player Engagement 25, 52, 60, 77, 115, 131, 133, 136, 141, 167, 168, 170, 206, 247, 285, 294, 301, 333, 338
Procedural Authorship 94, 96, 97, 100, 119, 122
Procedural Content Generation 25, 39, 42, 44, 50, 60, 64, 66, 70, 123, 131, 174, 175, 177, 205, 206, 208, 216, 221, 229, 230, 231, 232, 234, 239, 240, 245, 246, 247, 249, 282, 289, 290, 297, 307, 308, 309, 314, 339
Procedural Dialogue Generation 129, 133
Prompt Engineering 97, 143, 144, 167, 168, 169, 177, 200, 243

R

Real-Time Gameplay 125, 142, 165, 169
Reinforcement Learning 25, 28, 34, 36, 37, 39, 42, 44, 50, 53, 56, 57, 59, 61, 68, 81, 172, 175, 205, 212, 214, 218, 220, 223, 228, 230, 232, 243, 245, 272, 275, 276, 297, 338, 343
Remora Optimization 63, 69, 70, 71, 72, 73, 80

S

sound design 183, 186, 188, 200, 202, 219

T

Telemedicine 5, 7, 8, 10, 12, 17, 21
The Role of AI in Preserving and Remastering Classic Games 325
tracker software 179, 181, 202
Transformers 16, 53, 129, 174, 205, 207, 211, 215, 217, 222, 229, 304, 323, 338

V

Video Game Development 337
Video Games 3, 28, 46, 64, 118, 123, 125, 126, 136, 142, 160, 168, 172, 176, 246, 273, 294, 311, 322, 325, 326, 327, 328, 329, 331, 333, 335, 337, 339, 343, 344, 345
Virtual Reality 1, 4, 6, 9, 10, 18, 19, 20, 21, 22, 23, 55, 239, 294, 313, 317, 343, 346
Virtual Worlds 2, 3, 11, 58, 126, 311, 312, 313, 314, 318, 320, 321

www.ingramcontent.com/pod-product-compliance
Lightning Source LLC
LaVergne TN
LVHW080907300926
849162LV00003B/594